COMMONSENSE
HORSEMANSHIP

OTHER BOOKS BY THE AUTHOR

Bert Clark Thayer

The author with *Barnaby Bright*

COMMONSENSE
HORSEMANSHIP

Vladimir S. Littauer

ARCO PUBLISHING, INC.
NEW YORK

Published by Arco Publishing, Inc.
215 Park Avenue South, New York, N. Y. 10003

NEW REVISED EDITION

Third Arco Printing, 1983

Library of Congress Catalog Card Number 73-79483

ISBN 0-668-02602-2 (Cloth Edition)
ISBN 0-668-05791-2 (Paper Edition)

Edited and designed by Eugene V. Connett

Manufactured in the United States of America

TO MY WIFE
AS A MATTER OF EQUESTRIAN TACT

Preface to the 1974 Edition

This book was written very informally and the popular horsemen's expressions always had preference over precise scientific terms. For the reasons stated at the end of this note, I believe that *today* I should explain three cliches: "bending the horse in the side" (as when making a circle) and the "curving up" and "caving in" of the horse's *back* in jumping.

In informal usage the term "back" is apt to be taken to mean the whole length of the top line of the horse. Anatomically, however, the back proper is only a part of the top line (between the withers and the loins). This part of the horse's body has little flexibility. Its 18 vertebrae are connected with the 18 pairs of ribs and the whole forms a sort of a box (thorax) which contains and protects such important organs as the heart, lungs, and stomach. One of the proofs of its solidity is the fact that it can support a man. In front of it, however, the seven cervical vertebrae (those of the neck) form the most flexible part of the vertebral column. At the other end, immediately behind the back, the six lumbar vertebrae (the loins) are also relatively flexible. Beyond these are five sacral vertebrae which are fused together, and then comes the tail. So, when we say that in making a circle the horse's body should take the shape of the path along which it moves, we really mean that the head alone or together with the neck, bending at one end, and the hindquarters, bending in the loins at the other end, give the horse's body the required curve. While the superficial impression is that the whole back (the top line) of the horse is curved, actually the back proper remains straight.

Observing the horse's jump, we often say that the horse "arcs" well, meaning that his back curves up (see Pic. 9, opposite page 32). In reality this is an illusion created by the fact that the neck makes a gesture down at one end, while the hind legs hang at the other. Picture 7 explains the expression "caved-in back." Actually, the "back" is straight, while the hindquarters have been thrown up; this was possible because of the flexibility in the loins, which also helps the "arcing."

There is nothing new in our appreciation of the fact that the anatomical "back" has little flexibility, but we horsemen have been rather reluctant to admit the full extent of its rigidity. Thus, for instance, one can read in the text book of the U.S. Cavalry School at Fort Riley *(Horsemanship and Horsemastership,* 1945 edition, Part III, page 7) that the movement in the back proper is "somewhat limited." In 1967 an English veterinary surgeon, R. H. Smythe, emphasized this point very forcefully, saying in his book *The Horse, Structure and Movement* (1967) that ". . . the horse has an *almost rigid* spine incapable of any useful degree of flexion . . ." and again, "The surprising thing about the horse is that handicapped as it is by an almost *complete absence of spinal flexibility* . . . it is still able . . . to hoist a bulky, heavy and unhelpful body over obstacles as formidable as the Aintree jumps"; and more of the same. My own recent book *How a Horse Jumps* (1972) has also furnished arguments on this subject. Thus, today more and more horsemen talk about this matter and I expect this theme to become even more popular with time.

This change in understanding of what happens in the horse's body may influence the details of a schooling method but will not change the techniques of ordinary jumping. As to riding on the flat, it might affect some methods of executing certain movements where "bending the horse in the side" is required.

Preface to the First Edition

This book is a summing up of what I have learned while teaching riding. Twenty-four very active years of it, thousands of pupils and an astronomical number of hours spent watching riders and horses perform have taught me a great deal. Without this experience I could be a rider or an armchair theoretician, but I could not have conceived a practical method of riding. Every pupil, by his successful or futile efforts, by his wise or stupid questions, by his resistance to or acceptance of my teaching, has contributed to the writing of this book.

But besides these anonymous thousands, my particular thanks go to numerous friends and pupils who kindly read the first drafts of some chapters and offered their criticism and suggestions. I wish to express my especial appreciation to Miss Harriet H. Rogers who devoted so much time and patience to my manuscript and gave me much valuable advice. I am also grateful to Mr. and Mrs. David H. Munroe, Miss Evelyn Droge and Mr. Clayton E. Bailey.

For permission to quote the author's thanks are due to:—

The author	The book	The publisher
Captain Piero Santini	"The Forward Impulse" "The Rider and Driver" (a magazine)	Huntington Press
Roy Chapman Andrews	"Meet Your Ancestors"	The Viking Press
Colonel Paul Rodzianko	"Italian Cavalry School" "L'Eperon" (a magazine)	
Col. Harry D. Chamberlin	"Training Hunters, Jumpers, and Hacks"	The Derrydale Press (in England—Hurst & Blackett)
Com. Benoist-Gironière	"Concours Hippique"	Librarie des Champs-Elysees
Dr. Gustav Rau	"Die Reiferkampfe bei den Olympischen Spielen"	Schickhardt & Ebner
E. Schmit-Jensen	"Equestrian Olympic Games"	Welbecson Press
Major General Sir F. Smith	"A Manual of Veterinary Physiology"	Bailliere, Tindall and Cox
	"Official Individual Sports Guide"	National Section on Women's Athletics
James Fillis	"Breaking and Riding"	Hurst and Blackett

For permission to reproduce photographs the author's thanks are due to: Mrs. Elizabeth Correll, Mr. Chester A. Braman, Dr. Walter T. Kees, Mr. George Hoblin, Mr. Fritz Stecken, American Museum of Natural History, and Mr. J. Hamilton Coulter (who took photographs of the author).

All these names from many countries point toward the fact that while any knowledge is international, riding is not an exception. But, recognizing this, I still feel that the bulk of this book is definitely "Made in U.S.A." The following pages are the result of thinking amidst typical American experiences which required typical American methods of solving constantly arising problems. The fact that my equestrian education began in Russia doesn't make this book the less American; as a matter of fact it disassociates itself completely from the riding principles on which I was brought up. And the even more important factor that a great deal of my teaching is based on ideas first evolved by Federico Caprilli still leaves this book a product of the U.S.A., for the Italian beliefs of the beginning of our century are considerably altered here as a result of the progress of the times and on the basis of the needs of American amateur riders.

Contents

CHAPTER I

What This Book Is About
and How to Use It

A perfect book on riding could be written only by a horse. Only he could easily answer all the questions endlessly argued by us riders. Only a horse could say positively how the rider should sit in order to abuse him less; how his rider should control him so that the aids are easily understood, and how the trainer should school him so that the training proceeds in a comprehensible manner. As long as little pertaining to horses, and hence to riding, can be stated with mathematical precision, riders are bound to disagree.

In my unoriginal opinion any technical book is worthwhile only if it has something constructive to say and, therefore, provides valid arguments against generally accepted theories and practices. Only such a book stimulates thinking and may contribute to progress. The above statement obviously indicates the trend of this book; its pages present some new ideas and many new arrangements of old principles, comparing the old with the new. Consequently this book is a two-fold argument—against old-fashioned riding, on one hand, and against certain adaptions of modern ideas on the other. I am particularly averse to an incongruous mixing of the old and the new.

I do not like the word "argument"; to some it may easily suggest a noisy squabble. I use the word because I don't know of a better one to designate a logical reason for substituting certain ideas for others. If I personally were still blindly adhering to what I was taught in my youth, my present thinking about riding would be on a par with the model T Ford. Progress depends on independent reasoning and dispute. In this respect the term "modern riding" may mislead some into thinking that it represents the *final* achievement. I use this term throughout the book merely to indicate the contemporary point of view; unquestionably it will be considered old-fashioned in a few generations; as a matter of fact it is changing all the time.

The first problem which I faced when beginning to plan this book was whether to conceal the argument as much as possible by merely describing my present point of view without explaining how I had arrived at it, and without comparing it with other methods or, just the opposite, to emphasize the evolution of my thinking. I chose the latter course; first, because the story of my riding life is typical of innumerable others, and,

1

second, its motto—"anything can be done better," may influence those riders who tenaciously adhere to the old just because they never took time to think, or are ashamed to change. My riding life began by knowing nothing; it flourished for many years with little knowledge; then it went through a long period of following the teaching of recognized authorities, and finally it reached independent thought. Without the latter anything in life is stagnant and riding is no exception. But somehow it happens that theoretical thinking among riders is not often to be found. The reluctance to think has always been the greatest obstacle that I encountered as a teacher, and my lessons were always constructed so as to stimulate thought. I purpose to do the same in this book. In order to do this I have had to describe how I personally began to doubt those who had been my gods. The technical arguments which you will find in this book will not help you to keep the heels down but they may enable you to understand *Riding*.

Since riding in the course of centuries has been affected by geography, wars, social conditions, current tastes and so forth, it has taken different forms in different periods and countries and has been governed by different principles. For instance, in the 17th and 18th centuries European courtiers of the major continental kingdoms, living most of the time at court and adding prestige to the throne by all sorts of lavish spectacles, would naturally develop High School, particularly because its baroque movements were in the taste of the epoch. On the other hand, the average English aristocrat, spending most of his life on his estate and amusing himself with country pleasures, would use his saddle horses for hacking and hunting and would develop an informal type of riding. The Napoleonic wars, which required constant replacements for the huge French cavalry, replacements which had to be produced over-night, led to discarding the sophisticated teaching of the Versailles school and the invention of a very simple method of riding on loose reins. Le comte d'Aure in his TRAITÉ D'EQUITATION (3rd ed. published in 1847) says: "it is with this, so unscientific riding that our armies made the tour of Europe." The widespread antiquarianism of the second half of the 19th century, so pronounced in the arts, was also dominant in riding. On the continent there was a return to the pre-Napoleonic times and to the manège type of riding, sometimes for even cross-country. Today, in our part of the world, riding has ceased to be a necessity; it has remained only as a sport, and if you consider the general tempo of our times it becomes evident that only a fast and hazardous type of riding could attract youth. Streamlined trains, jet planes, even the speed of the ordinary automobile are bound to change our tastes in this direction. And so a sort of revolution in theories of riding was bound to take place, affecting primarily hunting and jumping—the two most admired forms of riding today. Add to this the modern search for efficiency in all our activities, combined with no time for details, and you will have the direction which these new ideas would be bound to take.

This revolution began fifty years ago, had a very slow start for twenty-five years and is in full bloom today. In any transition period, misconceptions and confusion of ideas are natural. It will probably take another generation before all the new principles are assembled into a perfectly logical system. Until then there will be, and *should be*, arguments. Consequently this book does not pretend to be the last word; it merely makes an attempt to give a better arrangement of modern principles.

In the course of this book I often talk about "my method." It sounds too grand for what it actually is, for I am not the man who invented houses but merely an architect who plans them for modern living. Not the fundamental ideas of horsemanship, but their practical adjustment to the popular types of contemporary riding constitutes the original part of this book. The assembly of a multitude of details into a logical system of riding, schooling horses, and teaching riding gives me, I feel, the right to call it my method.

My method of riding, schooling horses and teaching was born out of actual experiences such as the following: recently I was invited to teach for a few days in a hunt club; in this case all my pupils had enjoyed hunting for many years, some for over twenty, two for almost fifty. Obviously anyone with a system of riding which was a sort of "short-cut to horsemanship" or "fun in the saddle" would be out of place there, for everyone in this particular group already knew much more than that. On the other hand an *abstract* representation of the *art* of riding as professed and described by many great horsemen would be as out of place. It would have been of no interest to this particular group—they merely wished to hunt better; after all when in the field they had neither time nor use for the little technicalities which fascinate an equestrian artist. Obviously I was expected to give suggestions which would better the *actual performance* of their horses and would add to the riders' safety and pleasure, but would not require months of tedious work; no one had time for that. This work on technical details may help one win an international competition, under the rules which govern it, but only in exceptional cases can it help one to hunt or jump better.

I by no means expect everyone to agree with my method. On the contrary I anticipate some adverse criticisms which will differ with different types of riders. Among these will unquestionably be some valid ones, for no method is ever perfect in its first edition. These sound points of disagreement are ones that I could not foresee; otherwise I would have further corrected the details of my method. But there will be many others based on tradition, habit, ignorance, fear of the new, lack of logic, and on exceptional individual cases. With some of these arguments I am already familiar and I shall mention them in describing, point by point,

TABLE I

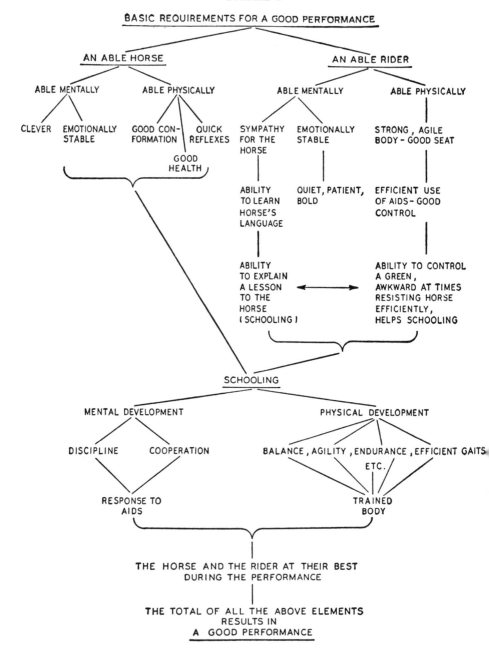

the principal ideas of this book. The main elements of my method are as follows:

1) A simple and nonchalantly dropped statement, "this was a good performance," if analyzed reveals that the good performance is a complicated combination of many items, as Table I shows. This book is really nothing more than a detailed description of this chart. Some types of riding may require the presence of all the elements specified in the chart in large doses, while others, such as hacking, for instance, will call for these elements in very small quantities. But no matter whether a certain type of riding calls for a simple or for a sophisticated performance, it can be good only if all the elements mentioned in this chart are happily combined.

This chart merely tells facts, and there cannot be any real argument against its content aside from personal disagreements with insignificant details of it.

2) In the chapter BRINGING CONTROL DOWN TO EARTH AND FORWARD one will find knowledge of riding divided into three grades, with an explanation of the amount of knowledge required in order to hack, or to hunt, or to show or to school horses. In other words, this book approaches riding from an expedient angle. Hence, instead of making such positive statements as "the horse *must* be on the bit," or "the rider *must* sit during the last two strides during the approach to an obstacle," this book asks the reader to analyze himself and his horse, to decide how well he wishes to ride and how hard he is willing to work while learning, and then to choose the suitable technique. This technique may or may not require the horse being on the bit (which by the way is hard to do well) but it must fit the selected game.

Far from all of us, or all of our horses, possess the essentials to become great, and futile attempts to imitate outstanding riders, and to school average horses the way the best are trained, only succeed in making frustrated riders and unhappy animals. On the other hand, everyone who knows his own and his horse's limitations and chooses a suitable form of riding and suitable manner of participating in it, may derive much pleasure from it.

Some will say that a full knowledge of riding is necessary in order to participate well in any mounted game. I do not share this theoretical point of view which is constantly refuted by daily practice. After all, many hunt well or win ribbons with only a rather elementary knowledge of riding.

3) All those who have read my previous books, or who have taken lessons from me, know that I teach Forward Riding. In this respect my method, like any rational system of riding, is based on the understanding that the principles of the seat, of control and of schooling must present a harmonious whole. The unity of these three elements of Forward Riding is the keynote of this book. I am particularly opposed to the often-

encountered cases where a modern seat is awkwardly combined with the old-fashioned conceptions of how the horse should perform; some people talk in one breath about the Forward Seat and collected gaits. I believe that a hunter or a jumper performs at his best when kept keen but *relaxed,* both mentally and physically, and when allowed to move in a way which is natural to a quiet horse (extended attitude, long, flat strides). This belief is the cornerstone of this book.

Here I expect a great deal of talk and shouting, both about the Forward Seat and about the principles of Forward Riding.

The situation with the Forward Seat is a very peculiar one. Almost everyone in jumping competitions employs it—well or badly—and it even has penetrated quite far into hunting circles; but many who practice it argue against it. I explain the purely psychological reasons for this in the book.

There will be violent arguments as to the principles of a "free-going" horse (of which the Forward Seat is a part) as opposed to a stiff, gathered horse, constantly dominated by the rider's legs and hands, from all those who have read many 19th century books and who, consciously or unconsciously, ride on the principles of simplified High School. These, to be persuaded, have not only to read this book but to study it, and to practice its principles for half a year or so. This is a big argument, this is the argument of the 20th century, and it cannot be solved in an armchair; unfortunately some will try to.

As to the unity of seat, control and schooling, I doubt if anyone will say a word against it, and I am afraid that the majority won't pay much attention to it unless the attitude of riders has been changing while I am writing these lines. A lack of appreciation of this unity is most unfortunate, for in it are concealed most of the secrets of a good performance.

4) Forward Control, as it is described in these pages, has for its principal aim the obtaining of an efficient performance from the horse without any gingerbread of unnecessary details. Its second aim is to obtain this in the simplest possible way.

Only outstanding riders can *forcibly* put the horse into a certain attitude and *better* his performance by doing so. Ninety-nine per cent of amateur riders, for whom this book is written, cannot do it, and if they were to attempt to do it they would merely upset and stiffen the horse, thus ruining all chances of a good performance. The less one asks of the horse, the less resistance one encounters, and the gradual raising of requirements must parallel the progress of the rider. Therefore, for instance, my method suggests that all beginners, if properly mounted, should ride *mostly* on loose reins; intermediate riders on soft, *mostly* passive contact and that only advanced riders be permitted the luxury of having the horse on the bit.

Since I personally have witnessed lessons during which the instructor was talking about having the horse on the bit while still working on the position of his pupil, I know that my method will find opposition, at least among those who lack the logic of gradual progress. As a matter of fact, several times in the course of years riders have argued against my method, demonstrating their reasons on their own horses which were so upset and stiff that even a decent performance was out of the question. The fact that some of these riders didn't even realize this, naturally made the discussion very difficult. This may sound like a catty remark but it happens to be true.

5) Any rational method of schooling consists primarily in the physical development of the horse; a part of any method of schooling is teaching the horse the meaning of the aids. They are taught by a combination of human ingenuity, reward and punishment. Some methods emphasize discipline and the forceful dexterity of the rider's legs and hands; other systems aim at establishing cooperation on the part of the horse and try to turn strong aids into mild signals. I believe that schooling and riding on the principle of signals and cooperation are much more within the abilities of the average rider than are any forcible means. As a matter of fact the other extreme, the highly finished Olympic Dressage performance, largely depends on cooperation, and is possible only if the horse consciously responds to mere signals of the rider's legs and hands.

I expect that riders with an old-fashioned education, which was based on constant leading the horse between the legs and hands, and who themselves have never reached a high degree of perfection, will argue against my method, saying that by such mild means one cannot teach a horse to perform well. The riders who belong to the German school will particularly object. I fully sympathize with these critics, for they preach what I was taught in my youth and what I believed for many years of my riding life; about this in more detail later.

6) Green horses react surprisingly alike to schooling; hence it is possible to systematize schooling and present it in the form of a program which will fit 75% of horses; it will have to be altered variously to suit the remaining 25% of individual cases. There is nothing new about this; all great masters used definite methods in schooling, and it is how schooling is described in many books. In this book I am merely presenting a logical method of schooling which will make efficient hacks, hunters and jumpers, and which is so simple that almost any rider can learn to use it successfully. There are people who derive pleasure from complicating any subject they tackle; others like to simplify life. This book, in general, is an expression of the latter tendency.

Since schooling, as educated riding understands it, is seldom encountered in this country, I don't very well see how people who have no experience in this art can criticize my schooling program; but they will and their argument will be a sweeping one: "This is all unnecessary; look at us; we don't practice any of this sort of business but our horses hunt and jump well." Self-satisfaction, of course, has stopped progress many times before in many fields of human endeavor.

There is also a small group of serious riders, scattered from coast to coast, who school their horses, but they learned long ago and hence practice it in an old-fashioned manner. These riders will be naturally upset that I relegate collection to a secondary place; that I suggest that a good part of riding be done on loose reins, etc. Seldom, if ever, do they consider in their learned discussions the practical situation in which American riding finds itself. To this group should be added today (in 1962) a number of riders who make use of dressage in their schooling because of the vogue for it.

7) The riding and schooling which I teach make a strong point out of the happiness of the horse. I personally don't derive any pleasure out of riding if I know that my horse is not cheerful. A frequently recurring subject of this book is the horse's character and mentality, and how to approach it. On the purely practical side of the question I believe that learning the horse's language, and trying to obtain his cooperation, is a much shorter road to success than mere dependence on a strong seat and dexterity of the hands and legs by which "the brute is conquered." I really dislike the term "breaking."

I doubt very much if anyone would argue against humane handling of the horse, but I know from experience that there is tremendous confusion of minds on such subjects as cruelty, abuse and punishment. Hence many pages of this book are devoted to a discussion of these things.

8) Our present standards of civilian riding, although improved during the last twenty-five years, are still rather low. Years ago I was invited to participate in judging a group of candidates for our civilian Olympic team for the 1952 Games. When one looked at these candidates, our best young men and girls, not from the point of view of the American horse show but from that of an international competition, it was discouraging to realize that probably only four out of thirty odd candidates were already started on the road they would continue in their training for the Olympics; all the others would have to begin from scratch. This book, in its aim to raise existing standards, strongly stresses the necessity of an ideal. It seems to me that a modified form of the Three-Day-Event of the Games could represent such a practical goal; it could be attained by anyone who would study riding sensibly and work conscientiously.

I doubt whether this ideal itself will arouse many objections, especially now when the riding world seems to be intensely interested in the next Games. But my suggestions to modernize the ideal by taking out of the program most of the collected gaits and replacing them with the ordinary ones will, of course, be condemned by old-fashioned riders.

9) In order to stimulate thinking, many parts of this book are devoted to what can be called the philosophy of horsemanship, without which I do not believe riding can be really good. On the other hand, no text book on riding is complete without such common-place explanations as why

the heels should be kept down or how to halt a horse. This book contains all this elementary knowledge, but it is partially presented from the point of view of a student. A pupil of mine, Alexis P. Wrangel, has written chapters on position and intermediate control; in these he puts in this type what I tell him to do, and in Italic type his own account of the difficulties he encountered while learning some point, and how it felt when he had achieved it. I hope that such a type of presentation may be of help to the majority.

I doubt whether many will object to this form and I also believe that any thinking person, who is accustomed to reading in general, will welcome the simple *philosophical* paragraphs in this book which will help him to understand the essence of Riding.

10) Quite a few pages of this book are devoted to a description of the background of American riding life in the second quarter of the 20th century. I have done this because my surroundings have greatly influenced my work, my thinking and the creation of my method. Furthermore, without being familiarized with it, many points of this book would be incomprehensible to the reader. For instance, if one were not made aware of the widespread, often unconscious, abuse of horses, then my constant talk about sympathetic treatment of them might seem unnecessary.

All the lines on the subject of the background of my teaching life are written without any personal feelings; they were not meant to hurt anyone and I have done my very best to be absolutely impartial, and to present things as they actually are.

11) Average young human beings react to learning as uniformly as horses react to schooling; hence teaching and learning riding can proceed along the lines of a rather definite program which takes pupils from lesson to lesson. I don't know of any book which has offered such a complete program. I myself and several of my pupils, also riding teachers, started this pioneering work several years ago. We published a few articles on the subject and the last four chapters of this book represent the continuation of this work. These chapters are meant not only for professional teachers but also for the innumerable private individuals who attempt to teach members of their family or friends. A person who is endeavoring to learn riding by himself will find part of the material in these chapters a helpful guide.

Here I expect a great many arguments. Many professionals will be reluctant to admit that my method is good, merely because such an admission would mean that theirs is not. Personal feelings, or simply business considerations, will prevent many from acclaiming anything that is not their own. But I know from experience that young riding teachers who are not yet set in their ways, and particularly those who are not in business but in physical education, accept my method of teaching most enthusiastically and apply it with success.

Besides these two categories of teachers there will be a third one which will resent my method merely because its procedure is new and unfamiliar to them. I would like to suggest to them to give it a try before criticizing it. Teaching position, for instance, doesn't take long and in a couple of weeks they could see for themselves how well my method works.

The above eleven points represent the general plan of the book, while its main subject, as I have already pointed out, is Forward Riding. I know that while all my pupils easily grasp the idea of the Forward Seat, the theory of Forward Control and Forward Schooling, and the unity of these three parts of Forward Riding, require much repetition before they sink in. Hence, before I close this chapter I would like to speak about it once more in different words.

A cross-country horse and a jumper perform at their best if schooled and ridden in such a way that they go up and down hill and over obstacles in the same manner in which they would move if free (unmounted) and *quiet*. If free and quiet, horses move with long, flat strides (at all gaits), holding themselves in an extended attitude. Consequently, their constantly fluid balance is on the average a "forward balance," because the centre of gravity of the horse is (on the average) not over the centre of his body but over the area immediately behind the withers.

If the horse has been schooled to move under the rider in this natural way, and is controlled in such a way that the results of schooling are preserved, then in order to be united with the horse the rider must use the Forward Seat which puts his centre of gravity over the area immediately behind the horse's withers. Good performance in cross-country riding and jumping depends on this unity of the Forward Seat, Forward Control and Forward Schooling.

The better the horse is schooled, the less forceful control is necessary. The aids become mere signals, and discipline is replaced with cooperation. It is not difficult to arrive at this level, providing that the method of schooling is stripped of movements which are not essential and which easily upset the horse and hence provoke resistance, for instance—collection on a full bridle.

Schooling is primarily a physical education of the horse. This education must have a practical aim, as an example—to make a hunter. Once the aim is clearly established, then only those exercises which may contribute something toward achieving it should be practiced. All schooling exercises are merely gymnastics and it is absolutely unnecessary to aim at obtaining perfection in every individual movement. Approached from this expedient point of view the art of riding and schooling horses is much simpler than all sorts of simplifications and adaptations of the old principles of "manège riding;" the latter can never be perfectly united with galloping and jumping. On the other hand, Forward Riding has been created for fast riding over varied terrain dotted with obstacles.

The amount of information in this book can hardly be digested all at once; it would therefore be a mistake to attempt to read it in one gulp from cover to cover. However, skimming through it may be a good way to get a feeling of the spirit of my method. After this preliminary introduction to it I would suggest the following use of the book:

If you are a beginner, read and study chapters:

IMAGINE YOU ARE A HORSE
LEARNING THE FORWARD SEAT
ELEMENTARY CONTROL
HOW TO TEACH THE FORWARD SEAT AND ELEMENTARY
CONTROL

and if you intend to be more than a superficial student read chapters:

THE SEARCH FOR BALANCE
TROUBLES WITH THE FORWARD SEAT

If you are a rider with considerable experience and your seat requires no correction, and you wish to begin to hunt and show, then you will find particularly useful chapters:

IMAGINE YOU ARE A HORSE
THE SEARCH FOR BALANCE
CRYSTALLIZING A METHOD
BRINGING CONTROL DOWN TO EARTH AND FORWARD
LEARNING CONTROL ON THE INTERMEDIATE LEVEL
MODERNIZING THE IDEAL
HOW TO TEACH INTERMEDIATE AND ADVANCED
CONTROL

and if your horse needs bettering in his performance you will be interested in some parts of chapters:

WHAT IS A GOOD PERFORMANCE OF THE HORSE?
ALMOST ANYONE CAN LEARN FORWARD SCHOOLING
THE PROGRAM OF FORWARD SCHOOLING

If you wish to learn to school hunters and jumpers, give particular attention to chapters:

IMAGINE YOU ARE A HORSE
THE SEARCH FOR BALANCE
BRINGING CONTROL DOWN TO EARTH AND FORWARD

WHY COLLECTED GAITS HAVE NO PLACE IN FORWARD
   SCHOOLING
LEARNING CONTROL ON THE INTERMEDIATE LEVEL
MODERNIZING THE IDEAL
WHAT IS A GOOD PERFORMANCE OF THE HORSE?
ADVANCED CONTROL
ALMOST ANYONE CAN LEARN FORWARD SCHOOLING
THE PROGRAM OF FORWARD SCHOOLING
HOW TO TEACH SCHOOLING

But if you belong to this category of riders, it would be better if you
would read the whole book.

If you are a riding teacher you will have to study this book from cover
to cover, and

if you are a riding enthusiast, beginner or advanced, you probably will
do so without my suggesting it.

CHAPTER II

Imagine You Are a Horse

The experience of my thirty odd years of teaching brought me to the conclusion that the major difficulties in making *horsemen* (not merely riders) lie not in physical but in mental obstacles. It is rather easy to teach someone to hold his legs in this or that position, or to remain with the horse on the jump; but, at this same time, it is hard to make him think about riding in an honest, profound way which would assemble the disconnected pieces of acquired knowledge into a rounded whole. This reluctance to think in riding is often combined with all sorts of traditional notions which one has accepted emotionally. So many of us believe grandmother's statement that *Beauty* adored her—a kind of wishful thinking which has been conveniently turned into—"my horse *loves* to jump in horse shows." Our grandparents were sentimental, so they bestowed sentimental feelings upon their animals; we are highly competitive, so we bestow competitive ones. This sort of wishful thinking, which usually is based on an unconscious desire to justify one's behavior, knows no limit. I once met a man who maintained that a fox loves to be chased. Rationalizing our behavior is a natural thing for all of us to do.

Further confusion is often added by the natural human nostalgia for the good times one has had; and those which occurred in the saddle one does not forget easily, no matter how bad the actual riding was or how much the horse suffered. As a matter of fact, very few of my old friends, former Russian cavalrymen, share my relief that horse cavalry has been replaced by a motorized one. Yet with so many of them I went through the whole of the first World War and at least a part of the Russian Civil War, and we saw the same sufferings and agonies of animals involved in the human struggle which was not theirs at all. The great number of arguments in this country in favor of preserving a mounted cavalry would seem to indicate that nostalgic feelings are to be found everywhere. It seems to me that any real lover of animals should welcome the fact that the machine has reached a stage of perfection where it can replace the horse in battle, thus eliminating one form of great cruelty to animals. For our romanticizing of ourselves on his back the horse has continuously suffered.

Like practically everyone who has begun to ride in childhood, I had a great love of horses, liked to feed them carrots, to talk baby-talk to them, and I invented all sorts of pretexts to spend hours in the stable. At the same time, I was never bothered by the question of how the horse felt about being ridden, or, when not ridden, being locked up in a prison

13

cell. It took years before I became conscious of the fact that the horse could not possibly share the pleasures of the rider. But once I had arrived at this conclusion I could enjoy riding only when I was certain that I was not abusing my mount beyond the unavoidable minimum. I shall probably use the word *abuse* quite often in this book, so I think I should explain what I mean by it. I shall not discuss the obvious cruelties which are within the scope of the S.P.C.A., such as underfeeding the horse, overworking him for commercial purposes, stabling him in unsanitary conditions, depriving him of veterinary care when he needs it, beating him causelessly, etc. A child can see that these are cruelties. But there are other less conspicuous abuses which take place in well-built and well-kept stables where feed is plentiful, where the doctor is on call, and the hooves are well-oiled. Really to appreciate this second category of abuses you have to imagine for a moment that you are a horse.

If you possess the imaginative power for such a metamorphosis then, becoming a horse, you will suddenly feel yourself very large, shy, stupid by comparison with your former human mentality, easily upset when bewildered, endowed with an excellent memory, almost completely inarticulate and with a much stronger herd instinct than you possessed in your human form. In the course of the thousands of years that your ancestors have served man, a spirit of cooperation has been bred in you. Some of your forebears revolted but they were rarely given a chance to multiply; thus through selective breeding you were turned into a rather consistently docile animal. And today, with your limited mentality, you would never be able to explain why you, so big and strong, don't kill the man who tries to mount you. And, of course, you never can understand why the man mounts you, trots you for a couple of miles, then suddenly orders you to gallop for another mile and then makes you go over half a dozen obstacles, or forces you to execute all sorts of movements in strange combinations.

Your natural pleasures are all associated with being free, in company with other horses, in fields where grass is green, where one can find cool water, shady trees and plenty of room to play if one desires. If you should not be given these, being of a docile character you quietly suffer imprisonment in your cell while munching oats and hay. After being locked up for the greater part of twenty-four hours, you are ready to enjoy going out, even carrying a burden; if you feel fresh, then a stimulating gallop under the rider may be better than no gallop at all. But why the rider makes you gallop and jump when he does, sometimes when you feel sleepy or lazy, is incomprehensible to you, and it is also hard to understand why, at other times, he holds you back when you wish to go on. When you gallop and jump in the hunting field, with other horses galloping and jumping to right and left, the excitement of the herd carries you on, but when, from your point of view, for no reason at all, you are made to jump alone in an enclosure surrounded by automobiles and people, then it is just forced labor. However, having in you a long established tradition of submissiveness and cooperation, you normally obey your rider's orders, and because of your good memory you even learn to know what he means by a certain application of his legs and hands. As long as to obey is in your nature you feel pleased when your good behavior is rewarded by a lump of sugar or something else as tasty. But, naturally, plain loafing is to you the ideal.

Some riders sit on you in such a way that it is easy for you to carry them, while others feel heavy on your back, although perhaps light themselves and, in a couple of hours, if not sooner, you feel a pain in your back and sometimes an aching in the kidneys. It is particularly hard to jump under such riders, for just at the moment when you are making your supreme effort to negotiate the obstacle your master suddenly plumps down on your back and gives you a jab in the mouth. To avoid this jab you try to jump with your head up, but this would cave in your back and bring your whole body into a stiff, unnatural position and the landing then would be painful to your feet. You begin to refuse, while some of your friends, having a different nature, upset by the sight of a fence which their memory connects with inevitable pain, begin rushing. But even when jumping under good riders who feel easy on your back and give you freedom to jump as it is natural for you to jump, you never learn to like jumping; jumping just isn't in your blood. Your ancestors lived and developed your present body on prairies where there was nothing to jump but an occasional stream which could always be more easily forded. This is why you, who can easily jump a four-foot fence under the rider, can be confined in a pasture inclosed by fences no higher; only a few of your friends jump willingly of their own accord.

It is easy for you to understand the signals of some riders and difficult to understand those of others. The latter are never clear enough, neither with their legs nor their hands. The succession of their orders is too quick; the succession of changes of movements they require from you too erratic. It is upsetting to you and, becoming nervous, you start to jog and fret and pull without any sense or reason; you become very apprehensive about being mounted by such people.

I hope I have started you thinking about riding from the horse's point of view. So let us end the transformation and talk again like human beings. There are several points that you, as a rider, should consider and they are:

1) An understanding of the horse's character and his mentality helps to keep the horse calm. A calm horse is a relaxed horse, and a horse can perform at his best only when his body is alert but not tense.

2) The quality of the horse's performance can be considerably bettered by the rider distributing his weight in the saddle in such a way that it in-

terferes as little as possible with the efforts of the horse's body. I hope to persuade you, in the course of this book, that the Forward Seat is the seat best qualified to do this.

3) Control, although definite and efficient, should not upset the horse either mentally or physically. Later in this book you will find many arguments for Forward Control which, in my opinion, since it abuses the horse less than many other forms of control, is able to raise his standard of performance.

4) A green horse has neither balance, strength nor agility to perform well under the rider. If left to his own devices he will eventually get the knack of how to carry the rider; but the performance of such a self-made horse can satisfy only a very elementary taste. On the other hand, riding a horse unprepared, both mentally and physically, for the work asked of him, can easily turn him into a bad actor or cripple him forever. The only way not to be cruel to your colt is to school him; in other words put him through a course in physical education, before requiring him to work for you. Forward Schooling does not call for a highly specialized rider; anyone with a good equestrian education and something like a year and a half's experience in the saddle can do it, or at least can begin to learn how to do it.

I would like to elaborate a little more on these points. The first association of man and horse was that of flesh-eater and his prey. Roy Chapman Andrews in his book MEET YOUR ANCESTORS (page 178), The Viking Press, says: "The Solutreans, cousins of typical Cro-Magnons, had a vast plains camp at Solutre, Lyons, France, which they probably occupied during the summer. They were great lovers of horse meat, and the remains of one hundred thousand horses together with thirty-five thousand flint implements were discovered at this place alone. There is no evidence, however, to show that they had domesticated the horse. That discovery probably was made later in the Far East and not in Europe." This was about 20,000 years ago. I have read somewhere, I unfortunately cannot now remember where, that later man domesticated the horse to the point where it could be herded like cattle but was still used exclusively for food. In many countries the horse is still eaten and in my youth, in Russia, in its southeastern prairies there were semi-nomadic Mongolian tribes living off the milk and flesh of the horse; I was brought up on the idea that mare's milk (kumis) is the best cure for T.B. The burden-bearing period of the horse's association with man is much briefer than the meat-eating period, and I suppose this is one of the reasons that we still need the S.P.C.A.

I have a book by Cesare Fiaschi, who, in the first quarter of the 16th century, founded the riding school in Ferrara, Italy. Forty pages of it are devoted to illustrations of different bits, each one of which could easily be an instrument of torture. By comparison the sharpest curb bit of today is a child's toy. Obviously those of us who ride on a snaffle, and comfortably retire horses when they are through with their services instead of eating them, have gone a long way in the course of the last 20,-000 years.

Probably the first steps in domesticating, and particularly in mounting the horse, were not easy. The man who first tried to vault onto the back of a half-wild animal took his life in his hands; and for many generations it must have continued to require strong muscles and strong nerves. It was a conquest of the beast. But those days belong to prehistory; the character of the horse has changed and men have learned how to break him without struggle. A quiet, humane training of colts has been practiced by civilized riders for scores of years but, in spite of all the knowledge accumulated on the subject, in some corners of the globe the horse is still being subdued by cave-man methods. The distressing part of it is that many of us still derive sincere pleasure out of a brutal mastery of the horse. Many times I have completely failed to eradicate this instinct in the hearts of my pupils. I can remember several instances when my pupils of many months standing, who were trying to learn how to get the best, artistic performance out of a horse, would derive their greatest pleasure not from the latter but out of the emergency subduing of a bucking or rearing horse.

While it is easy to abuse your horse mentally without noticing the little inconsiderate things which one may do without meaning harm, it is also as easy to acquire a habit of thinking about your mount as a living being. It is encouraging to realize that the horse by his nature normally tries to cooperate and be good, and it is disturbing to know how often he is not given a chance to do so. Great satisfaction can be derived by any civilized human being out of the consciousness that he is kind to his animals, particularly those he uses for his pleasure. There are thousands upon thousands of riders in this country who have a great accumulation of delightful experiences derived from companionship with their horses. If you don't happen to be one of them I would like to suggest your trying it; it will increase greatly your pleasure in being in the saddle. I am particularly addressing these words to a young woman who, while sitting on the horse's kidneys and pulling with all her might on the curb, was overheard to say: "Oh boy, ain't riding fun!"

And what about punishment? If your schooling is based on the ancient law of reward and punishment, and you are very faithful in observing it, then the horse quickly learns to understand the meaning of both. He learns to understand the meaning of punishment especially fast if the rider is careful never to ask more than the horse can easily do at that particular stage. In such cases, and when the punishment is in proportion to the disobedience, the punishment is not a cruelty but merely an unpleasant though just necessity. Omitting rewards while exaggerating pun-

ishments is an abuse. As a general and not always accurate rule one can say
that the better the trainer the less punishment he needs to apply to his
horses. Most disobedience takes place when a rider, lacking in equestrian
tact, asks from his horse more than he can do that day without straining
himself.

And here is another fundamental point to consider. Nature did not
form the horse for riding. It just so happened that his size, his swiftness
and his comparative docility made him attractive to man as a mount.
For instance, as approximate alternatives, the average deer or antelope
would have been too small, the ox too slow and the zebra wholly intrac-
table.

If you were to look at the skeleton of the horse, at the distribution of
the heavy bones, you would agree that pulling is easier for the horse than
carrying weight on his back, which is strong only in the area immediately
behind the withers. But if the horse wasn't made for riding he was made
still less for jumping. Dr. S. H. Chubb, curator of comparative anatomy at
the Museum of Natural History in New York, in one of his articles says:
". . . the earliest ancestral horse . . . was a small animal hardly
larger than a fox. In order to escape from his carnivorous enemies which,
in his early day, were beginning to develop to a menacing degree, and
also to cover the ever widening distance between his gradually drying
pasture land and his drinking resorts, he and his descendants were obliged
to increase their speed, if the species was to be perpetuated. To this end
size must be developed within practical limits. . . ." The horse as a grass-
feeding animal originated and developed on the flat plains where there
was no necessity for adapting his body to high jumping. The histories of
all the better jumping animals are quite different. In searching for the
horse's inability, rather than ability, to jump high we have to examine his
body and compare it with those of other animals which jump better, particularly of the feline and canine families. To be thorough we should
really compare many items, such as muscles, reflexes, etc., but for our purpose a comparison of the skeletons will suffice. Pictures 1, 2 and 3 show,
respectively, skeletons of a horse, a Russian Wolfhound (both at a run)
and of a cat. Comparing these skeletons we will easily notice the following
differences:

1) The horse has eighteen pairs of ribs; the dog and the cat have only
thirteen. Consequently, the last two animals have more room to draw
their hindquarters under their bodies than has the horse. The greater the
ability to engage the hindquarters (combined with greater flexibility of
the spinal column), the mightier the spring of the take-off.

2) In the case of all three animals that we discuss the hind legs are
longer than the front ones. But they are especially long in the case of the
cat and the dog. This length added to the ability to close the angles to a
greater degree, increases the power of the spring.

3) The paws of the dog and of the cat have many joints and soft paddings. These give added impetus to the spring at the take-off and are excellent shock-absorbers when landing. In comparison with the paw, the hoof is a very unsatisfactory arrangement for jumping.

Everything that I have just said doesn't mean that you should never jump the horse or gallop him, or that you should ride him always at a walk. Not at all. It merely means that there should be limits to your requirements, limits which vary with different horses and, therefore, that you should consider the limitations of your particular horse. It also means that you should, by schooling, gradually prepare your horse for work and should sit and control him rationally. Under these conditions a great deal can be asked of the horse without mental or physical abuse.

Inadequately as the horse's body is constructed for jumping, he still can jump rather high and broad and in doing so instinctively tries to use his body as efficiently as he is able to. Pictures 4 and 5 show what different efforts a free horse makes during the take-off and the landing. In between these two extremities of the jump there is a period of flight with its own quite different efforts. These pictures demonstrate conspicuously that the rider, in order not to abuse the horse, must learn to avoid interfering with the horse's natural efforts and particularly with those of the back and neck. In the chapter WHAT IS A GOOD PERFORMANCE OF THE HORSE you will find a detailed description of the horse's efforts in jumping; here I merely wish to make you conscious of the fact that a rider can be a considerable hindrance to the horse in jumping. I am extremely sorry that I am unable to reproduce here pictures of the latest world record high jump made in Chile in 1949. The rider was Captain Larraguibel, the name of the horse is *Huaso,* and the height of the jump 2m 47cm. (a little better than 8'1"). A glance at these pictures would show you that the rider was not interfering with the efforts of either the back or the forehand of the horse with his weight, while his hands gave full freedom to the neck and head. So evidently at the moment of the jump this rider was not disturbing his horse. But, of course, this is not sufficient reason in itself for clearing such an obstacle. There must have been at least two more factors: a naturally talented horse and gradual preparation for the day of the record. Here is a short account of the development of *Huaso:*

Huaso was foaled in 1933.
In 1945 his record was 2m 12cm.
In 1947 his record was 2m 20cm.   (1 meter: 3'3")
In 1949 his record was 2m 47cm.

The previous world record was made by a horse *Osopo,* ridden by an Italian officer, Captain A. Guttierez, 2m 44cm., in 1938.

And here is the description of *Huaso's* final conditioning during the four months which preceded the record jump. The above and following data are taken from the French magazine *L'Eperon,* for February, 1950:

Feed: 13 lb. of oats, 9 lb. of hay, 4½ lb. of Luzerne, 2 lb. of carrots.
    During the last weeks: 33 lb. of oats, 9 lb. of hay, 6½ lb. of Luzerne, 4 lb. of carrots.
Water: One spoonful of bicarbonate of soda added to water given after work.
Tonics: Aracil, Tomopofan, vitamin B during the last fifteen days.
The Work: Twice daily. General work in the morning; in the afternoon a walk in hand.
    The periods of trot and gallop were gradually increased. Finally a gallop of fifteen minutes on each lead was asked from *Huaso.* Also the increase and the decrease of gaits, halts, backing, flexions, circles, semi-circles, half-turns on the forehand and on the haunches, changes of leads, etc. Jumping was practiced once a week without a rider; never higher than 2m. Once every two weeks he was jumped mounted never higher than 2m 20cm.

After such a careful conditioning the already outstanding jumper *Huaso* could establish a world record without being harmed either mentally or physically. There is not an ounce of cruelty in this case. On the other hand, a horse may be abused by the seat and control of his rider or through lack of training on a comparatively small jump; twenty such jumps daily, and in a couple of months the horse will begin to show signs of mental and physical wear and tear.

From my experience in making horsemen I know what a tremendous satisfaction the majority of people derive from jumping horses which have been prepared for this work by gradual schooling and which hence jump naturally and athletically. If you were the owner of such a horse (and I hope you are), and knew how to sit and control him (and I hope you know), then you would never be satisfied with the awkward jump of a half-trained horse. The pleasure of jumping a schooled horse is two-fold: it consists in the wonderful physical sensation of a really good jump, as well as in the emotional satisfaction that the horse is not hurt while giving pleasure.

There is at least one more abuse of the horse, which unfortunately is frequently encountered; that is working the colt too early in life. The horse, particularly the thoroughbred, grows till he is six or seven years old. At the age of three years he is just a baby and neither his bones, tendons nor his mentality can stand vigorous work under the weight of the rider. His size, and the energy which he displays when playing free in the fields, deceive the inexperienced human eye by overemphasizing his strength and hiding his weaknesses. By working the horse hard, and particularly by jumping him, at the age of three, you are taking the chance of crippling him and by the time he is five years old he may be through with his serviceable life. It is just a matter of luck whether he will be crippled merely to the point where he can be allowed to exist as an un-important hack or will have to be destroyed. Of course, even in the latter case the human tendency to justify one's actions may unconsciously invent other reasons for the horse's injuries. I have heard people blaming he-redity, the horse's bucking when playing free, his misbehavior in the stall, slippery ground, a particular incident, bad luck with capital letters, etc. Very few people will have the courage to say honestly—"I have murdered my horse." Many of those who work and jump their horses too early have read, and probably several times, the advice of experienced, intelligent horsemen that work with the horse should not begin before he is four years old and that nothing really strenuous should be asked of him before he is fully mature, that is six years old. Now, if they have read it, why don't they practice it? For many reasons: some cannot afford to keep a horse idle for so long; others don't have the patience; many are ready to take a chance, hoping that their horses will prove exceptions (there *are* excep-tions); but often riders cripple and kill their horses just because they don't think. Here we are back to where I started this chapter: the major difficulties in making horsemen (not merely riders) revolve around people's reluctance to think *honestly* about their horses, themselves and their riding.

The character and mentality of many animals which can be easily kept in laboratories, have been analyzed scientifically; it hasn't been done with the horse. "Why, in order to do it we would have to move to a farm," a specialist in animal behavior once said to me. So, it looks as if until some scientist consents to rusticate, all our knowledge of the matter will con-tinue to consist of the accumulation of practical experiences. All out-standing horsemen agree that:

1) The horse's intelligence and reasoning powers are low in comparison with those of some other animals such as the monkey, elephant, dog, cat, etc. This is an important fact to remember, for the usual mistake of an inexperienced trainer is to over-estimate the intelligence of the horse and hence to present the lesson to his pupil in a manner way over his head. Due to this misunderstanding many horses are turned into nervous wrecks.

2) The horse has an excellent memory and clearly remembers not only roads but lessons which he has learned, and pleasant as well as unpleas-ant experiences. This memory is the great ally of a good trainer and the first enemy of a bad one. Bewildering use of the aids by the rider, a jerk on the jump, senseless punishment, etc., will be as vividly remem-bered by the horse as the comparatively pleasant sensation of non-abuse when well-ridden.

3) The horse learns by association of ideas. For instance, as a rule the horse understands a new movement more quickly if it is started every time at the same place in the ring. For the same reason, when teaching a

new movement the aids must be always exactly the same and punishment or reward come close on the heels of the action. It is usually agreed in this respect that about three seconds is the time limit of the horse's ability to associate cause with effect. Since in actual work these three seconds may be much too short to check the horse to give him a piece of carrot, or even to pat him, the horse must learn to know two special intonations of the voice, one meaning "bad" and the other meaning "good."

4) Disappointing as it may be to some, it must be admitted that the horse has no real love for us human beings. He recognizes us; he is relaxed when mounted by a rider with whom he has had pleasant experience; he becomes nervous when a bad rider, whom he recognizes, puts his foot into the stirrup, and is pleased to see a man who feeds him, particularly if the latter appears during feeding hour, but that is about all.

5) He is very gregarious, shy even to the point of being panicky at times, and now, after centuries of domestication, cooperates with man, on whom he depends. Trainers and riders must do everything to encourage this cooperation. Many bad riders kill it at the outset and only provoke resistance which eventually becomes a habit.

The above-listed characteristics, which are perhaps the most important for a rider to remember, don't cover, of course, the whole character of the horse. Just to stimulate further your thinking on the subject, I would like to quote from MANUAL OF VETERINARY PHYSIOLOGY, by Major General Sir F. Smith, first published in 1892 by Balliere, Tindall & Cox, London. I think it contains many thought provoking ideas.

". . . In the horse the moral sense is very small; we do not think he knows he is doing anything wrong when he periodically kicks his stable into matchwood, or runs away, but he understands that he should not refuse a jump, and a horse careless in his walk or trot knows exactly what every stumble will be followed by, and anticipates matters accordingly. The use of the term, 'moral sense,' is open to objection in the case of animals, but it appears to the writer that something equivalent to the moral sense does exist in them. The expression on a dog's face when he has done something he knows to be wrong, or at any rate, which he knows is against the rules laid down for his life, conveys a conception of the existence of moral sense. Strength of will most animals lose as the result of domestication: . . . but there are notable exceptions—for instance, the ass, mule and occasionally the horse. The so-called stupidity of the ass and provoking obstinacy of the mule are not indications of want of intelligence. The majority of horses, on the other hand, have no great strength of will; they can be rendered docile and tractable, they will gallop until they drop, work at a high pressure when low would suffice, can never apparently learn the obvious lesson that it is the 'willing horse' which suffers, and that the harder they work the more they get to do. All this is due to defective intelligence and a want of the higher faculties; they cannot reason like the dog or elephant, and are more flexible than the ass or mule. Some horses show signs of reasoning and are capable of grasping a position. A load so heavy as to be beyond the limit of his power, or some other cause, has taught him to refuse to work; to use the familiar expression he 'jibs,' he has learned to disobey, he has learned his own strength, and the comparative powerlessness of his master, and this through an exercise of reason. In other words, the horse which refuses to wear himself out in the service of man is one possessing too much intelligence and strength of will for a slave; a 'jibber' is an intelligent and not a stupid horse. . . . If the horse possesses but little affection, this defect is compensated for by his cherishing no ill will; to all his hard life and the abominable cruelties of domestication he shows no sign of resentment; water and feed him, and give him a place to lie in, and he forgets the past in his anxiety for the present. He is a peculiar mixture of courage and cowardice; physical suffering he can endure, no animal bears pain better; when his blood is up nothing is too big or too wide for him in the hunting-field, . . . but the same horse is frightened out of his life by a piece of paper blowing across the road, or by his own shadow . . . no animal is more readily seized with panic, and this spreads amongst a body of horses like an electric shock. Yet panic must not be held to indicate an absence of reason, though the rapidity of its spread in the case of a stampede may suggest it. . . . The dog, with all his intelligence, is acutely affected by a pot tied to his tail, but it does not cause all the dogs he meets to stampede. . . . Distinct acts of reason are rare; of the lack of these we daily see examples in our hospitals—namely, horses injured in the most severe manner through their own struggles when placed in a little difficulty, such as a head rope around the leg, or an inability to rise when down, owing to being too close to the wall, or some trifling circumstance of this kind. In these difficulties, if he employed any reasoning powers he would remain quiet until released, instead of which he behaves like a lunatic, inflicting on himself in a short time injuries which may lay him up for months. . . . Every horse knows a truss of hay or straw by sight. The point need not be laboured, yet no horse will pass a truss of either lying in the road. He appears unable to reason that what he is familiar with in the stable may be no more dangerous when met with in an unusual situation. . . . The horse is very conservative; he does not like anything new or any departure from his ordinary mode of life. . . . His gregarious instincts are proverbial; he frets at the absence of his companions and if used to work amongst a body of horses, as in cavalry, he will take any degree of punishment rather than leave them for a few minutes. During the absence of his companions he neighs, sweats, paws with the fore-legs, and almost screams with delight on rejoining them . . . his predominant feature, and the feature of all animals below adult man, is the childishness present throughout life; probably the absence of care, worry and anxiety may account for this. The horse will play all day with a piece of rope, or nibble his neighbour persistently; even the oldest horses, when fresh, will perform the antics of a foal, and imitation amongst them is so universal that, if one of a string of horses being led along happens to kick out, this repeats itself all along the line as if by preconceived arrangement. . . . Lord Avebury remarked that he had always felt a great longing to know how the world appeared to animals. It seems impossible to believe that their minds are a blank. A dog in search of his master has had his mind occupied, and as during sleep he dreams, it is evident that the thoughts which have passed through it have left an impression. Even with the horse it is impossible to believe that daylight and darkness, food and water, work and rest, form the only subjects of thought as they present themselves. The whole question bristles with difficulties and as Avebury says, we have tried to obtain information of the senses and intelligence of animals by teaching them our ideas, rather than devising a language or code of signals by means of which they might communicate theirs to us."

When a person realizes that his love for the horse will have to be one-sided it may discourage him to the point where he will lose all feeling for the animal. However, in addition to the fact that a beautiful animal attracts normal human beings, there may be also a strong sense of responsibility toward a dumb creature who gives us pleasure and is exclusively dependent on us. These and other feelings, uniting in some sort of manner combine in many of us into a true love of horses. When this love goes beyond the superficial admiration of the horse as a physical organism then a very humane and civilized attitude toward horses takes place. As an example of such an attitude and as (I hope) an inspiration for the novice, I would like to quote here from a letter. This letter was written in the late thirties by a gentleman breeder in Northern Ireland when about to ship my horse *Barnaby Bright* to America. It was written after all the papers were signed and the money paid:

". . . Poor *Barnaby's* neck was very sore and stiff after the second inoculation . . . he was rather snappy for a couple of days when it was sore, but is as amiable and friendly as ever now. He sometimes puts his ears back and looks quite cross when you first go into the stable, but once you get up to him no horse could be more gentle, and he will lick your hands and clothes for ages without ever nipping with his teeth. He hates being spoken crossly to, and gets quite nervous and frightened if anyone does so, although he has never been treated with anything but kindness, and he is so good that one never has to speak crossly to him. He is very fond of his food, and we had more difficulty in keeping him from getting too fat than in getting condition on him. He is very quick for a big horse and inclines to be playful, but I have never known him either to buck or kick. He is very sensible and careful of himself; for instance if it is slippery he will shorten his stride. . . . I hope he will get a nice calm voyage; it has been rather stormy here lately, but the wind has dropped

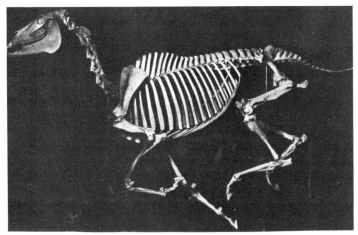

Pic. 1. The horse (18 pair of ribs).

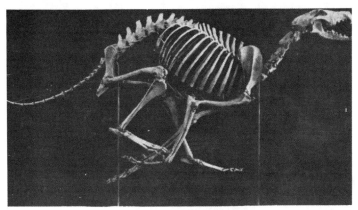

Pic. 2. The dog (13 pair of ribs).

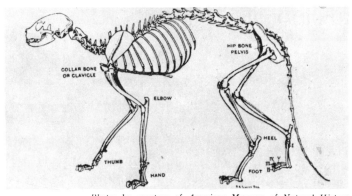

Photos by courtesy of American Museum of Natural History

Pic. 3. The cat (13 pairs of ribs and a longer back)

A comparison of the three skeletons shows how a lesser number of ribs and a longer back result in greater flexibility of the back and therefore in greater ability to engage the hindquarters. The comparative stiffness of the horse's back is one of the reasons for his inferior jumping ability; for other reasons also depending upon the skeleton see text, pages 18 and 19.

Pic. 4. This picture, taken at the moment of the release of the spring which was previously accumulated in the hindquarters, shows how the impulse which originated in the muscles and joints of the hindquarters goes through the whole body, stretching the back and neck. Now the neck and head begin their gestures downward to facilitate the clearing of the obstacle by the forehand. Notice excellent folding of the forelegs.

From "Jumping the Horse" by V. S. Littauer

Pic. 5. This picture was taken a fraction of a second before the first foot to land touched the ground. In preparation for the landing the forelegs are stretched forward; the neck and head are making upward gestures which will free the shoulders for extension and also will help to absorb some of the shock of impact. A fraction of a second earlier, when the hindlegs were still over the obstacle, the back was caved in still more, thus helping to raise them.

altogether today. He is due to sail from Belfast on Saturday 17th and it will be very sad parting from him, but it is some comfort to know that he is going to someone who will appreciate him and be fond of him, as I am sure you will be when you get to know him, as he is a most likeable horse. I hope you will never regret the day you bought him, and that he will be a tremendous success with you; but even if he is not, I hope you will still be kind to him, and will never let him go down the hill."

Every chapter in this book while still in the rough has been read and criticized by several friends and pupils. The following part of this chapter is being added on the strength of their suggestions. All my readers expressed the opinion that, so far, I have not made my point clear enough, at least to those who are already in the habit of unconsciously abusing the animal or to those novices who don't know anything about horses, are very much impressed by the outward show of riding, and may as easily fall under bad influence as under good. All my readers advised me to discuss three terms at greater length—*Cruelty, abuse and punishment.*

Cruelty is wanton, abuse is unconscious and punishment is justifiable; although there are moments when, to all outward appearances, these three may resemble each other very closely. Let me illustrate this.

Several years ago at Madison Square Garden one of the horses of a visiting military team refused two or three times in the course of the first evening. He did the same thing the following day under a different rider. The horse had been a very willing and good jumper (or he would not have been brought here across the sea) and naturally the officers' first suspicion was that the horse was in pain in some way. Two veterinaries inspected the horse very carefully and pronounced him completely sound. No reason could be found for it to hurt the horse to jump. It was obviously a case of sheer stubbornness. So the captain of the team mounted the horse himself, wearing sharp spurs, and pushed the horse through the course without getting a single refusal. But somewhere along the way he used one of his spurs too severely, broke the skin and the horse's side showed a little blood. This was noticed by another rider who was standing at the gate when the horse was led away and he reported it to the judges. This rider, by the way, whom I knew personally very well, did not do this through maliciousness; he really loved horses and merely wished to protect an animal. But being an elderly man he had neither a correct nor a sufficiently firm seat, was usually left behind, banging the horse's back and jerking his mouth. After the first rider had had an unpleasant conversation with the officials of the show he approached the rider who had complained about him and said in his broken English—"when you jerk your horse on every jump, I don't tell it to the judges."

This story presents the complicated situation in which a person who constantly but unconsciously inflicts pain on the horse was sincerely aroused when he saw the visible result of one moment of pain. In his case it was abuse, which has only the excuse of ignorance, while the use of sharp spurs in the other case was a justifiable punishment. The only argument may be whether it was too severe or not.

Now, if the horse in question were to refuse the jumps, not due to an attack of stubbornness but because the fences were too big or too complicated for him (perhaps because he was not schooled and had not the physique to negotiate such obstacles) and the rider knowing it, with spurs and whip attempted to force him to jump the course, that would be cruelty.

I would like to give you a few more examples of the difference between abuse and cruelty.

Abuse: 1) When the rider has a poor seat which is disturbing to the horse.
2) When the rider hangs on the horse's mouth and jerks him because he does not know how to use his arms and hands properly.
3) When for the sake of staying with hounds for his own pleasure a rider, unknowingly exhausts his horse who is not fit for such strenuous work.
4) When one jumps very high fences on a three-year-old, believing that it will not hurt the horse.
5) When one jumps too much, not realizing that the horse cannot take it, etc.

All the above listed are cases of abuse when done unthinkingly. But cases like jumping too high or too much (for a certain horse), or making him work too hard in general, if practiced by people who know exactly what they are doing and still do it, are examples of cruelty. Words like *abuse* and *cruelty* are rather strong and I would never venture to say what I just have were it only my personal opinion.

No matter how good a rider and trainer one is, and how cooperative one's horse, punishment can never be completely avoided in riding. Of course, if the resistance which has necessitated punishment was brought about by bad, inconsiderate riding, then the punishment itself is either abuse or cruelty. For instance if I know that my horse's jumping limit is 4' and I am whipping him into a 4'6" obstacle, this is cruelty. But if one omits all the cases of unnecessarily inflicted punishment, justifiable punishment will still remain in the picture. After all, no matter how good the horse is, he is no better than us human beings and we all need occasionally to be put in our places.

Superficial thinking on these matters results in the peculiar situation where people who abuse horses, may at the same time be reluctant to punish a horse. In this respect a "jerk" is held in particular horror.

The rider can punish the horse with spurs, whip or reins. Practically every book on riding recommends the first two means and disapproves of punishing with a jerked rein, implying that is is too severe. To me this point of view doesn't make sense—for two reasons:

1) The horse may disobey the rider's legs or he may disobey the rider's hands. The spurs and the whip are the obvious means with which to punish the disobedience to the legs, but it would take a genius among horses to understand that the whip is a punishment for pulling or trying to run away.

2) A jerk does not have to be severe. As a matter of fact it can be very mild, so mild that it will inflict no pain at all; it will be merely a restraint. This is particularly so if one rides on a plain hunting snaffle and this whole book is about riding on the snaffle. On the other hand, we all know that a lash with the whip can be very painful.

People say that even soft jabs will ruin the sensibility of the horse's mouth. I don't see how they can do it if used only as a punishment, for, after all, how many times will you use the jerk as such? If you are a sensible rider obviously very rarely. On the other hand, I have two films of Dressage riders, both internationally known, one of them among the world's best, and on the screen it is very conspicuous that they jerk their horses about once every couple of strides at the extended trot—and this is while riding with a full bridle. And still the mouths of their horses are obviously not ruined (for, if they were, it would be impossible for them to execute the remainder of the Dressage program with the finesse with which it is done). What really ruins a horse's mouth is constant hanging on the reins.

Two days ago I was at a horse show and saw how a number of riders were diminishing the speed of their horses during the approach to obstacles by a series of "half-halts." Now, a "half-halt" is a very hard thing to execute *softly* as the theory of it calls for, and consequently all but one of the riders in this particular show were merely jerking their horses back. But it is very possible that at least some of them held jerking in horror. There is some sort of mental black-out concerning this word. It has reached such an absurd point that I have heard some riders, when recommending a mild jerk, call it "a bump on the mouth from the bit."

Obviously avoiding use of the word "jerk," or even avoiding the actual use of the jerk itself as a punishment does not make the horse happier if the rider hangs on his mouth or jerks him without realizing it and for no reason whatever but the defects of his own riding.

The gist of all this is that any kind of deserved punishment administered as lightly as practical and as rarely as possible is unavoidable in riding, while senseless infliction of pain should have no part in it.

A teacher must always do everything possible to make his pupils *conscious* of unjustifiable jerking of the horse. This, by the way, is why I rarely teach "half-halts," and why I insist that the ordinary rider should put his hands on the horse's neck with the reins looping during a jump, and why I require that a jerk as punishment (always with the snaffle) should be inflicted judiciously and only if there is no other way to stop the horse's disobedience to rider's hands. If the horse is never jerked in riding except when he misbehaves, then he quickly learns to understand what it means and punishment becomes less and less necessary. Punishment does not have to spell cruelty if the rider thinks straight. Knowing what one is doing is usually less cruel than preaching one thing and practicing another.

The subject of humane riding is inexhaustible and I have not intended to cover it fully in this chapter. I merely wanted to point out how easy it is for a novice to become confused in his emotional treatment of the horse and how carefully he should think about the seemingly simple points of his relationship with his mount.

Obviously any humane approach to the horse would recognize the necessity of schooling, in other words, of developing the horse physically, and preparing him mentally, before he is required to do strenuous work in the hunting field or show ring. In this respect I would like to quote from a booklet of The Canadian Equestrian Society, and organization to develop horses and riders for a Canadian Equestrian Team in the Olympic Games of 1952. Paragraph 25 of this booklet reads as follows:

"Proper training methods develop sound, humane techniques as apposed to practices which cannot be considered humane. Therefore, all horse-lovers should encourage the efforts of the Society in raising the standards and knowledge of the proper techniques in training horses for equestrian competition."

CHAPTER III

The Search for Balance

The term "rider" is very indefinite. Anyone who mounts and masters his horse for one purpose or another is a rider; even a gentleman who rides twice weekly at the prescription of his doctor can be called so. Under this definition the primitive tribesman of Asia and the polished exhibitor of High School horses rub elbows.

The term a "good rider" is equally unspecific, its interpretation depending on local aims and standards. Some nomads will unquestionably be considered good riders by their fellow tribesmen, while many High School riders, not so accomplished as others at the same art, will be classified by us as poor. If you were to visualize these two riders side by side you would appreciate the fact that the term good rider doesn't mean much outside the local situation.

There is another term which is somewhat more definite—a "horseman." The very word implies the cooperation of two beings and it always sounds to me as if it designated some sort of partnership between them, instead of the mere mastery of the one by the other. To me a horseman is not necessarily a man who uses his aids artistically, but rather a human being who practices his riding on the basis of complete consideration of his mount's abilities and limitations. If one accepts the term horseman in this sense then a High School rider may be a horseman and may not be; the same applies to the primitive tribesman and the latter, despite the simplicity of his aims, may happen to be a better horseman than an educated rider of the Western world. For instance, a man who cripples his horse in a supreme effort to win in a competition may be considered a sportsman (at least by some), may be a good rider, but his lack of consideration of the horse deprives him of the right to be called a horseman.

Many years ago I heard somewhere a definition of horsemanship which I have repeated ever since. It runs: "Horsemanship consists of obtaining from the horse the best possible performance, using the least of his nervous and physical energies." This definition should be accompanied by the notation that this ideal performance can be obtained only through a happy combination of schooling, control and seat. Hence every rational method of riding consists of a harmonious use of these three elements.

This definition seems to imply that, for instance, clearing a 4'6" course while making the horse nervous and over-jumping every fence is not good riding. But, judging by the applause which normally follows such a winning round, the spirit of this definition obviously is not shared by all. A horseman's appreciation of riding is not general, while a competitor's point of view is common and although we refer, in prose and verse, to the horse as a "noble animal" our feelings toward him often go no deeper than beautiful phrases. In actuality the horse is frequently an abused animal. In the majority of cases he is unwittingly abused, merely through ignorance, often by the very same people who are so sentimental about him. Life in our mechanized age, with its nervous tempo and ever-present spirit of competition, is not conducive to an instinctive appreciation of horsemanship, in the sense I have described. Therefore education is necessary and to this end this book is dedicated.

My own riding life began without benefit of such sophisticated considerations. On my twelfth birthday I was given a horse; a groom escorted me several times, giving me a few most elementary pointers, after which I was turned loose in the steppes of southern Russia. The horse was a single-footer, of a type probably similar to the old-fashioned plantation horse. Three years later, in preparation for the cavalry, which began to loom as my future career, I took lessons from a sergeant of the regiment stationed near-by. He taught me to sit smartly erect, with long stirrups, feet parallel to the horse, hands held high, and to keep the horse's chin in. Such things I learned to do well; what it was all about I had no idea, but everyone said that I was "a natural," and it seemed to me that I was.

It was said in the old Russian army that a cavalry officer is born with spurs on, a phrase which jokingly expressed an emotional belief that once you belonged to this caste you were a perfect horseman. Unquestionably today to most of my readers the pictures which illustrate the riding of fifty years ago will be uninspiring, to say the least, but many friends of my youth still like to talk of the splendid riding of the good old days; the map of this country is covered with similar "mutual admiration societies."

I graduated from the cavalry school in 1913. You probably have seen many pictures of the riding and jumping of the time, the riders sitting erect or leaning back, while the horses jump in a stiff, unnatural way, backs caved-in and heads jerked upward; as a rule, to make the point stronger, modern books reproduce really bad examples of the riding of the period. These are easy to pick out, for then as always, more people rode badly than well and, then as today, horses were often abused.

This writing does not intend to concern itself with various local equestrian fads but rather with an analysis of the evolution of educated riding, hence I reproduce a picture which illustrates the ideal of the period. It is from one of the text books which we studied in school; as a matter of fact, it is taken from an internationally known book, BREAKING AND RIDING by James Fillis (Pic. 6). The best riders, of course, knew how to put these ideas into effect and the French officer (Pic. 7) must have been greatly admired. In every country educated riding was the same, the method was universal, and today we usually call it "Dressage." It was primarily ring riding and it did not develop artistic jumping as we know it now.

The Dressage method of riding, as any real horseman's method, considered that a knowledge of the balance of the horse, the mechanics of his motion and peculiarities of his character should be the basis in conceiving the rider's position, the system of control and the routine of schooling. At this point I can see some of my readers beginning to skip lines and turn pages, looking for what is commonly termed "practical advice." So, to arrest your attention on these very lines, here is some which is one hundred per cent practical. Believe me, you will never become a horseman if the only type of suggestions you are going to look for are such as these: "keep your heels down and hold your stirrups under the balls of your feet;" "to start the canter on the right lead keep your right leg at the girth, while with the left leg etc., etc." These are secondary and elementary considerations. In riding, as in everything else, an understanding of fundamental ideas is all important, while details like heels down don't make horsemen. Appreciation of the importance of the horse's balance is basic and hence the whole of this chapter is devoted to it. There are no other ways, there are no short-cuts, and to make your efforts in the saddle worthwhile you just have to learn the basic theory. To cheer you up—it is very simple.

Although formed on generally sound principles, the theory of Dressage riding had many erroneous ideas and one of them was, that the horse under the rider is in a state of perfect equilibrium only if his weight is evenly distributed on his four feet. The stability of a squarely-standing, four-legged table was brought up as a parallel example by every teacher that I had. Perhaps you know that such a distribution of weight can be obtained only through collection; hence collection was the foundation of this method of riding (for the definition of collection see Chapter IX). And although freedom was given to horses at the full gallop and on the jump itself, this freedom could not live happily with the basic principle of collection; a hodge-podge resulted the moment a horse was taken into the open. In riding halls, in the hands of good riders, the collected (Dressage) horses performed with great precision and style while some able jumpers leaped six feet and better in spite of the abuse they suffered under their riders. Of course there were not enough of "natural jumpers" to go around, and attempts at collection in the hands of the majority, then as today, disintegrated into mere pulling on the curb. Most horses under troopers hung on the rider's hands and moved forward with short, ugly steps. But somehow for years everyone was pleased, and members of various groups admired each other as members of such groups do today.

It was a static period in riding which, with minor changes and excitements, lasted for about seventy-five years. Then suddenly these happy, peaceful, self-satisfied times came to an abrupt end around the year 1900, when an Italian officer, Federico Caprilli, came forth with entirely new principles of how to school, control and sit a cross-country horse and a jumper. Naturally, when I say that the pleasant slumber was over, I mean that it was over for the upper level of horsemen, the majority of riders remaining in a state of mental inertia; some of them still today see the dreams of the 'nineties. While the majority was not interested in the new method, some began actively to oppose it primarily because it was new. To so many of us the first version of a story remains the only true one for the rest of our lives.

I insert here the portrait of Federico Caprilli (Pic. 8) for you may like to see the kind, clever face of the father of modern riding. Caprilli died in 1907. Pictures 9 and 10 are of Italian officers jumping prior to 1910. Looking at these free, natural, quietly-jumping horses, the riders following their movements with their bodies and arms, I feel rather sick when I remember that three years later I was still learning an archaic method of riding.

As early as 1906 one of the foremost sportsmen of the Russian army, Lt. P. P. Rodzianko, was studying in the Italian cavalry school and, if I am not mistaken, the first Americans to go there were Major H. D. Chamberlin and Major W. W. West, Jr., both in 1923. By the time I was a lieutenant a dozen or so of the outstanding riders of the Russian army were "Italians" and many young officers like myself were enthusiastically welcoming the new ideas. As an organization, the old army, while it existed, never accepted the new method and hence never gave courses in it. Prior to the revolution only one book and one pamphlet (both inadequate) were published in Russia and individual efforts like mine were generally governed by hearsay, reading and attempts to do the impossible, that is, to imitate what one saw in horse shows and photographs. The normal result was, in my case anyway, a mixture of the old, of the new and of my own; a rather absurd hash, which unhappily combined some points of the new seat with mostly old principles of schooling and control. The old predominated, particularly in difficult moments, such as during the approach to an obstacle, when we placed our horses and drove them forward with "the small of the back"—a typical idea of old-fashioned Classical riding.

As I am writing this chapter, the book which was one of the main inspirations of my youth—THE ITALIAN CAVALRY SCHOOL AND THE NEW METHOD OF CROSS-COUNTRY RIDING AND THE TEACHING OF IT, written by P. P. Rodzianko upon his return from Italy and published in 1911, is before me. Now, that I know this method so well, it is obvious to me why I myself and a couple of my friends in the regiment, who were trying to change our riding primarily by reading, could not be successful; the new method was too radical. For instance on page X one reads (translation is mine):

"Depending on the gaits, the character of the ground and the size of obstacles, the equilibrium of the horse undergoes different, and often considerable changes. The main aim of the rider is to feel these and to follow them with the movements of the body so as not to interfere with the natural balance of the horse . . . the flexibility of the rider's torso

Pic. 6. The Taste of 1900. Shows the popular ideal of the rider's position on a fence as depicted in an illustration from the most influential book of the period. The best riders of fifty years ago could faultlessly put into practice the unfortunately erroneous ideas of their generation (Pic. 7). The method was universal and this picture of a French officer could be replaced by one of a rider of any nation except the Italians, who had already begun to work on new ideas under the leadership of Captain Federico Caprilli.

Pic. 8. Captain Federico Caprilli, as he looked at the turn of the century. The majority of schools of today despite their differences and their vestiges of the old are fundamentally based on Caprilli's teaching. He can truly be called the father of 20th century jumping and cross-country riding.

Pics. 8, 9 and 10 are from a book on the Italian Cavalry School, by Captain P. Rodzianko, published in Russia, in 1911.

Pic. 9 and 10. Italian officers jumping about 1905. These are some of the first pictures of the practical and very successful application of Captain Caprilli's ideas.

Pic. 11. Shows the Piaffe, a fully collected trot in place with the preponderance of weight on the hindquarters. This is a case of no forward movement at all. (The rider—Mr. Fritz Stecken).

and the softness of his arms are particularly important . . . while collection with the curb disturbs the natural balance of the horse, forcing him to transfer his center of gravity to the quarters and confines the freedom of movements of his head and neck, making it difficult for the horse both to restore and to change his equilibrium in motion."

And here are some quotations, from the same book, concerning jumping (pages 61, 74, 75 and 145):

". . . it is insisted that a cavalryman approaching an obstacle should in no case disturb his horse by too severe tightening of the reins or by useless urging him with the legs . . . as a general rule no means should be used to urge the horse on the jump for it is too difficult to catch the right moment . . . urging is permissible only if a horse, after starting for a jump quietly and rhythmically, begins to slow down approaching the obstacle. The greater the obstacle the greater the passiveness of the rider should be, for in such cases one should avoid interfering with the horse and instead give him an opportunity to figure out his jump . . . in general the horse must acquire the habit of jumping willingly . . . the horse should approach the obstacle quietly, without fear, and attentively; hence the rider should by all means avoid actions and movements which might be painful or disturbing to the horse . . . the cavalryman should urge the horse only in cases when it is absolutely necessary for sustaining the gait."

Now, after years of experience in schooling, I know how easy it is to apply these principles and what pleasant jumpers can be made if worked according to this method. But it was not so, in my case anyway, thirty-seven years ago. Then, just out of cavalry school, where I was taught riding based on the principle of Dressage that the horse must be led between the legs and hands, I, lacking instruction by a master of the new method, was bound to make a pretty sorry mess of it. I am a little ashamed of this period of my riding life and it was rather consoling the other day to meet a group of riders who now, almost half a century later, and with all the instruction available are still making a mess out of jumping, both physically and mentally.

Finding excuses for my obvious inability to think straight in 1913, I would like to say that P. P. Rodzianko's book was primarily a military report, describing the method of teaching troopers in the Italian cavalry. A great deal of it was devoted to the discussion of normal cavalry activities and comparatively little was said about the new method as applied to a sportsman. The description of the seat, for instance, was very sketchy and mechanics of it were not presented; I learned them much later, in New York.

I began teaching in the United States in 1927 and late in 1929 I wrote my first book (in collaboration with my associate, the late Captain S. Kournakoff)—TEN TALKS ON HORSEMANSHIP, really a series of lectures, which later were delivered over the N.B.C. network. I have just glanced through it again and I don't know of anything which is as good a presentation of my riding beliefs at that time as its one hundred and fifty pages. Obviously the key to its philosophy is the chapter entitled—"The Balance of the Horse in Motion." In it, after describing, more or less accurately, how the peculiarities of the structure of the horse's body result in a forward distribution of weight at a free stand-still and why a green horse under the rider will have a tendency to become over-balanced to the front, and how this should be overcome by at least an elementary collection (which is wrong) I say:

". . . the balance on the hindquarters, as described above, is just a part of the balance in a wider sense. By this we mean that the horse must be able to raise his head and bring his weight back for all slow movements and bring his weight forward by extending his neck for all fast movements . . . the horse having been taught to balance himself on the hindquarters through work on slow gaits in the ring, will easily acquire the balance on the front when worked in the field on extended gaits; we might even say that the horse will *find that balance by himself* . . . *the horse's balance, in a wider sense, is his ability to shift his center of gravity according to circumstances."*

The part of this quotation which refers to the fact that the horse in nature, depending on circumstances, will move holding his body collected or extended is, of course correct. What is disconcerting is that I was still thinking of the horse's balance as a certain static distribution of weight preserved permanently while the horse is in motion. This statement sounds as if the horse would distribute his weight forward or back, would hold it and then would be moved on a conveyer.

Not only the movement of the horse, but that of all animals, including the human being, is based on the losing and recapturing of equilibrium. In walking, for instance, a man shifts his balance forward, taking it off the foot which is left on the ground and catching it again on the one which is being put down ahead of the body, aiding himself with balancing gestures of his arms. If he were to carry on his shoulders a monkey who, with some arrangements of ropes, were to try to keep his torso back and confine his arms it would certainly make the man nervous, awkward and impede his progress forward.

The repeated loss of and retrieving of balance is more pronounced at fast, free gaits than at slow, collected ones. The horse's ability to maintain balance during fast movements and the jump depends on his strength and agility and knack of using those two factors. Exercises which call for rapid changes from slow collected to fast extended gaits unquestionably develop this important agility; but the mere fact that the horse is well-balanced at collected gaits does not mean that he will automatically have as good balance when moving free. This is the glaring mistake in the passage which I have quoted from my first book which, as a matter of fact, only repeated the then popular conceptions.

The correct, intelligent understanding of the horse's balance in motion is very well expressed in the Fort Riley Cavalry School's manual HORSE-MANSHIP AND HORSEMASTERSHIP, 1945 edition; in essence it says: "Theoretically, movement is determined by the various positions of the center of gravity with respect to the base of support. In the state of rest the center of gravity is sustained by that base. *Movement is but disturbance of that equilibrium, the members intervening to steady the mass and prevent a fall.*" (Page 207, italics are mine.)

On page 208 we find the following axioms:

1) "With rare exceptions, as soon as the horse is mounted, the natural equilibrium is disturbed by the rider's weight."

2) ". . . the voluntary or involuntary actions of the aids provoke numerous contractions so that a part of the horse's muscular power is employed in resisting the rider . . . the less the horse resists his rider, the better he can balance himself."

3) ". . . at the beginning of his training the horse must be allowed *great liberty* for if his movements are restricted he will be unable to recover his balance." (Italics are mine.)

Whenever in this book you come across the terms "Forward Balance" or "Central Balance" they will merely refer to the average tendency. Picture 11 shows a collected horse in motion while Picture 12 is of a free moving horse.

Along with all this, the fact should be underlined that the horse in motion uses his neck and head as a balancer in a similar manner to the way we humans use our arms. These balancing gestures of the neck can be effective only if the rider allows his horse to keep the neck and head extended and follows their motion with his arms. If the neck is raised and is kept up, while the chin is brought in, as in collection, then the horse, deprived of his balancer, finds himself in the situation of a man who runs with his hands in his pockets. Picture 13 illustrates the use of the neck and head on the jump. The extreme use of the neck on this jump is the result of the take-off being too close to the fence.

Clear as all this is, the fact that the horse's balance is fluid, that his motion is really based on a repeatedly lost equilibrium which is constantly recaptured by legs acting as supports, assisted by the balancing gestures of the neck and head, I didn't grasp fully until about 1930. Up to then my method of riding and teaching was as indefinite as my understanding of what balance is.

When today you hear an intelligent trainer say that the balance of a certain horse needs to be improved, it doesn't mean that he intends to force the horse, with his legs and hands, into a certain attitude and make him keep it while moving. It means something very different. To better the horse's balance the trainer has to develop his strength, agility and freedom in the use of the neck and head (through schooling exercises) to the point where, under the rider, the horse will be able to repeatedly restore that equilibrium which is constantly disturbed in producing movement. I wish you would read this paragraph once more.

On a correct understanding of the horse's balance in motion is largely based the contemporary method of schooling, controlling and sitting hacks, hunters and jumpers. We shall revert to this matter many times in the course of this book but if you would like to have an example immediately, here it is: if you should decide that, let's say, your hunter should be allowed to move balancing himself in a natural way (average forward balance) then, to be united with your horse, you will have to accept a forward seat. This, of course, is obvious, but perhaps this one example is not enough, so here is another one: a horse approaching an obstacle quietly and freely makes an extra extension of the neck and head about one stride before the jump. One of the reasons for this gesture seems to be the preparation for several balancing gestures during the jump, and the rider should allow him the freedom to make it. But if your horse approaches the jump excitedly, probably due to bad schooling and bad previous riding, and you have to hold him back, then, by doing so you will interfere with his natural balance on the jump. In such a case if you wish to insist upon "good riding" you have to reschool the horse. While schooling green, unspoiled horses is easy, reclaiming incorrectly-going ones is a long and tedious job which is rarely one hundred per cent successful. In view of this fact I should really recommend your getting rid of the horse, and I don't do it merely because I can see how many of my readers have open jumpers which, rushing and pulling, win regularly, while others have hunters, which hanging on their hands and galloping and jumping stiffly, have carried them safely for years after hounds. Hence the question should arise in the minds of these readers—"why should we change our horses and method of riding when we get such pleasure from what we own and practice today?" I think that all those who are satisfied with their achievements should, of course, not even think of changing; but the others for whom a ribbon does not mean much may want to ride better. I belong to the latter category and as long as part of this book is about myself, I think I should state my beliefs. Here they are:

1) It pleases me to have a happy horse under me. An upset, tense animal never gives me pleasure, no matter how high he jumps or how fast he gallops.

2) In the course of years of observing and riding horses I have arrived at an appreciation of the beauty of *natural, relaxed* movements. A horse which has lost these, due to some quack method of schooling or riding, is disturbing to my eye and feelings.

3) I appreciate the fact that good schooling, being the physical education of a horse, develops athletes, and the plastic qualities of an athletic performance are to me a source of great pleasure. I am sincerely bored to watch a horse clearing, let us say, a 5′ obstacle on the strength of his natural abilities, but with the efforts of a country bumpkin.

I am fond of beauty in this life in general and to me a graceful, athletic performance means much more than a merely winning one. When these two qualities are combined, as in the case of Colonel F. F. Wing (U.S.A.) riding *Democrat,* as well as other horses of his, then I really have the time of my life watching them.

4) My years of experience in making horses and riders have persuaded me that the majority of both perform at their best on the principles to which this book is dedicated (a free, forward movement). But I also know that there are innumerable exceptions.

5) Long ago it became obvious to me that all lovers of horses should promote sound riding-education in the United States. This, today mechanically-minded country, furnishes many young riders who, with little appreciation of the horse as a living creature and with a strong competitive spirit, will try to be first in any field of riding and at any cost to the horse; a sportsman is not necessarily a horseman. By riding education I do not mean merely learning how to keep the heels down or how to start a canter on the right lead. I am primarily referring to a certain horseman's philosophy of riding and a horseman's understanding and appreciation of the horse, that is, both of the mechanics of his body and the nature of his character.

To finish with the story of natural balance, a few paragraphs should be added on collected gaits in today's cross-country riding.

Observing free horses in the field one notices that when quiet the horse maintains an extended attitude and hence moves with long, flat, *efficient* strides, but when excited he changes this "forward balance" to a "central" one by shifting some weight to the hindquarters. As a result of this collected attitude the action becomes high, inefficient (from the point of the relationship of energy consumed to progress *forward*), but poised and graceful. If a horse's ordinary movements can be compared with the human walk and run, then the collected gaits resemble the dance. It is rather common to observe a free excited horse doing Passage and even a few steps of Piaffe. Obviously both ordinary and collected movements and corresponding "forward balance" and "central balance" are natural to the horse, each of them expressive of a certain emotional state. Dressage, as a special game, primarily concerns itself with emotionally stimulated movements of the horse, while any sensible trainer of a cross-country horse hopes that eventually his pupil will carry him across the fields and over fences in exactly the way he would do it by himself when free and quiet.

Of course a free horse, when tired or lazy or half-asleep from boredom, will hold the neck forward and down and move with awkward, unfirm steps. The same horse when alert will move holding the neck and head extended forward and somewhat raised, 45 degrees or less, depending on his conformation. This last attitude is the one which we wish to duplicate in cross-country riding and jumping.

This understanding of two kinds of natural balance in the horse I included in my little book for beginners, RIDING FORWARD, published in 1934. On the basis of this understanding is built the METHOD of riding hacks, hunters and jumpers which I teach and which aims to reproduce under the saddle the horse's natural way of going. The fundamental points of my method are:

1) SCHOOLING must restore in the mounted horse his natural balance and way of going, those which he would instinctively use when *free, quiet* and *alert*.

2) CONTROL should be complimentary to the results of schooling, and promote efficient movement. Which means that, at least most of the time, the rider must allow the horse to move freely (on light contact) with neck and head extended, not interfering with his natural balancing efforts of the body and gestures of the neck.

3) THE SEAT must unite the rider and the horse, interfering as little as possible with the horse's efforts to balance himself. It should not abuse the horse and must give the horse an opportunity to move almost as if free.

This method, as any other method, will work at its best only if its three parts—schooling, control and seat—are harmoniously combined.

My life as a professional in New York City didn't start in a well-defined manner. At first my own riding occupied as much time as my teaching and I even tried hitting the polo ball, which was obviously not in my line. But soon it became clear that it was humanly impossible to be good in any one thing while trying to do everything.

I myself was taught in the army with a great deal of shouting, by being locked up for a few hours if I rode badly, and by an extra-long driving whip which, if it landed on my back, would always be accompanied by the gentle remark of my teacher—"I beg your pardon—I meant the horse." The virtue of these lessons was that I didn't have to pay for them.

The problem of teaching Americans without a whip and without locking them up was very intriguing, and the fact that people were willing to pay five dollars an hour for being shouted at was too good to be true. And so I became a teacher and for the last twenty years all my efforts have been concentrated in this direction.

CHAPTER IV

Crystallizing a Method

At a superficial glance the United States in the twenties would seem to offer unlimited opportunities for a riding teacher with a decent equestrian education; in this era of prosperity the popularity of riding was mounting by leaps and bounds. At the same time merely a dozen or so of Russian cavalry officers, who had come here after the revolution, and another dozen or perhaps two of intelligent riding teachers of different nationalities were all that were good on the market; the average "riding master's" knowledge was very elementary. A common sight in Central Park was such a "master" riding next to his pupil, trying to teach him to post by lifting him up by the elbow. Unfortunately for us, the public was so used to such methods that when I, with my friends, opened a riding school in New York, we often had to persuade our pupils that beginners learn faster and better in a ring.

On the whole it seemed that there should be practically no competition. But it came, fast enough, and from an absolutely unexpected source; we soon realized that success in the riding business depended almost exclusively on the personality of the teacher, while his knowledge and abilities were less important factors. All over the country in "riding academies" sat little gods, blessed with forceful and winning characters, whose pupils would swear by their varied and fanciful riding ideas. This ignorance on the part of the public, of course, could be explained as natural, due to the lack of a tradition of educated riding like that which for generations had existed in Europe; but understanding this didn't make things easier for us.

Being a teacher didn't consist merely in teaching a rational method well; it was also a struggle to persuade your potential and even actual pupils that the quite standard method which you taught would enable them to hunt or to win ribbons in the horse shows. How would they know it? And their arguments would run along the simplest and hence most discouraging lines; something like this: "In my town there is a fellow who teaches one to hold the legs forward and not back as you do, but he certainly makes fine riders. The other day his pupils won most of the ribbons in our show." And it was of no use to point out the possibility that it might have been the case of the soldier who received a medal for being the last to run away from the battlefield. "They won; didn't they?" Practical Americans were satisfied with practical results.

Horse shows, by the way, were rarely any help from a teaching point

39

of view. Since they were a combination of sport, social activity and popular entertainment, and their existence largely depended on their financial success, they could hardly assume the role of leaders in the promotion of new riding ideas; obviously they had to cater to the majority. It would be unreasonable to expect that horse shows would be in the forefront of education, but the fact that every show includes classes for junior riders, the majority of whom were prepared for these competitions by riding teachers, gives the impression that the Horse Show is a supreme court. At all events, this is how many parents and children feel about it.

On the other hand, the horse show was quite a help from the business point of view. Every horse show increased the activity in all the local riding schools; people who otherwise wouldn't have taken lessons at all would take them in anticipation of the competition, and a winning pupil was good publicity for the teacher. I remember how the school which I helped found advertised one autumn that in the course of the past summer our pupils had won several hundred ribbons; and this, naturally, brought us quite a bit of new business.

On rereading the last two paragraph in 1962 I find that much of their content already belongs to history, and only as such am I leaving them in the text; they may serve as a reminder of the progress riding has recently made. Man's memory is short and we are apt to forget the past.

In the course of the thirteen years since the original edition of this book was written the standards of horse shows have steadily risen. Today the level of riding in horsemanship classes is really high—at least in big shows. And judging has improved at the same time. True enough, one still finds judges with old-fashioned points of view who favor the dressage position on the flat and like to see horses move with necks high and chins in, even in Hunting Seat Equitation classes, but many others have a more educated approach to riding. In any case, in the *Rule Book* of the *American Horse Show Association* the position required in such classes is now described—even if incompletely, which is, just the same, a great advance.

So, in the course of thirty-five years, the American horse show has made substantial progress. On the one hand, this has been due to the improvement in the standards of teaching riding and the consequent generally raised level of riding, and corresponding requirements of the participants. On the other hand it has been due to new rules (in open jumping, for instance) passed by the American Horse Show Association under the beneficial influence of the International Equestrian Federation. Judging by the fact that in some cases these new rules were objected to by regular exhibitors, it seems that here and there the American Horse Show Association was even making an attempt to take the lead.

One of the important factors in raising standards of the horse show was the appearance of international army teams in Madison Square Garden, as well as in some other shows. In fact, it probably was one of the greatest contributions to the bettering of civilian riding.

There is one thing that has always intrigued me about the horse show; that is that, in a country where jokes are made at the drop of a hat, I have never heard a single one about riders and horses in the arena. Someone tried to explain this phenomenon to me by the fact that to many of the people involved it is a serious business; but it is about business that many American jokes are made. And when you think that anecdotes of the hunting field abound, then their absence concerning the show is baffling. And perhaps this lack of a sense of humor is in part responsible for some of the less attractive human aspects of the horse show.

It was difficult enough to teach an internationally-accepted method. To change, incorporating new ideas into your teaching, was a Herculean task; even one's own pupils resented it. I can think of several cases when my best pupils, and personal friends to boot, refused to go ahead with me and insisted on adhering to what I had taught them originally. Only those of us who were idealistic, ambitious, and had nerve, dared to be among the first in following the new theories. The majority of instructors just couldn't make head or tail of what was happening in the intelligent riding world; some understood, but were afraid that to change would hurt their business. So progress was bound to proceed at a snail's pace. What was done during a quarter of a century in riding would have been accomplished in three years in the automobile industry. This comparison is not completely fair, but it illustrates the fact that the slogan "Bigger and Better" does not apply to riding.

Occasionally during the course of the last thirty-five years a letter to the editor or a short article would appear in equestrian magazines suggesting the necessity of an organization which would certify riding teachers. I lost count of my own efforts to promote such a move and hence it gave me great pleasure to learn, in 1947, that the National Section on Women's Athletics of the American Association for Health, Physical Education and Recreation had begun to work in this direction by establishing standards for teaching riding in colleges and girls' schools, and by giving courses to riding teachers who are on physical education staffs, and rating them on the basis of an examination in riding and an examination in theory. I think this is one of the most significant events which has occurred during my teaching life, and the fact that a good many in the group which initiated the movement are my former pupils, of course, delights me.

Since this movement originated I have been working with this outstandingly intelligent and progressive group of teachers, mostly graduates of women's colleges. I have conducted some of their week-long courses for riding teachers and helped with their meets which they call "clinics." Each one of these clinics, which lasts one or two days, has a dominant theme such as, for instance, position in jumping. Every teacher brings a couple of pupils who ride for a few minutes and their good and bad points are discussed by the teachers; then remedies to correct defects are suggested and the efficiency of the proposed cure is immediately tried out. The last such clinic that I took part in had an attendance of approximately 80 people, all dressed to mount and practically all of them knew what they were doing. The consistency of knowledge, theoretical and practical, was most impressive and I never before met a group with such high standards. I believe this movement deserves the enthusiastic support of every idealistic horseman.

A big obstacle on the road to progress was, and still is, the fact that riding is a touchy subject; somehow it takes a special effort to admit that one's riding is bad. It is particularly so in the case of one born in a family of long riding standing. It seems that in such instances to admit one's deficiencies in the saddle is almost equal to a confession that one is not a gentleman. Perhaps this is the reason for a peculiar phenomenon: as an inaccurate generalization, one may say that the richer the family and the longer its association with horses, the less the chances of finding open minds among its members. In general, riding circles are full of inhibitions: I have actually known people whose sincere riding ambition was to look in the saddle like an English fox-hunter in a colored print of 1820. There are many riding groups, scattered all over the country, which have decided a priori that no one can teach them anything. I could never figure out whether it is a sincere belief or a protective screen behind which they can bolster up their egos.

Probably the greatest difficulty that the riding teacher faced in my active days was that general reluctance to study and work which created the term—"natural rider." When using this expression people didn't mean to imply that they were speaking of a person with special abilities to which only knowledge needed to be added to make him a great horseman. Not at all. This term indicates a person who, without ever taking lessons, or reading a book, but merely through years in the saddle and with the help of providence, has become a "superb rider." All over the country you hear about these "natural riders" and it takes nothing short of an attempt to organize a civilian Olympic Games team to realize how really few riders we have on an international level. Those who maintain that experience is everything in life forget somehow that someone who ate all his life is not necessarily a connoisseur of food.

Nearly all my pupils took lessons in the hope that very soon they would reach a point where they could at last participate in one mounted game or another; whether they were really good or not didn't matter. Once a pupil told me that instead of paying me five dollars a lesson he would much rather give me five thousand dollars cash if I could make a magic which would cause him to wake up the next morning a good rider. It was obvious that the slow, thorough army method to which I was accustomed had to be abolished and a new one, both rapid and practically efficient, had to be created. Everything was pointing toward the necessity of simplifying the principles of artistic riding, and streamlining the method of teaching. The problems were: 1) how to do it while preserving the essentials of good riding, and 2) what the essence of the approach to the education of the pupil should be. Unexpectedly I was given a clue.

In 1931 my second book, JUMPING THE HORSE, was published; and among the reviews there was one uncomplimentary one which appeared in *Polo*. In part it read: ". . . in brief, it presents this thesis; don't try to play tennis the way Tilden does it, because you cannot; don't pay any attention to Bobby Jones because you couldn't possibly hit a ball the way he does. Or, to come right down to it, don't bother to try to go over obstacles the way Major Harry Chamberlin does, because you never will be able to anyway; just leave the reins loose enough so that the horse will do the work, without interference from you. . . ."

There was the answer to my problem. Less than one per cent of my pupils may have the riding genius of Major Harry Chamberlin,* and very few of them will ever devote as many hours a day, and as many years of such days, to riding and thinking about riding as he did; a few of them may be professionals but the majority will be bankers and lawyers and business men, and their wives and daughters who, in their turn, will marry doctors and lawyers. Of course it is foolish to try to teach them to ride the way men who devote their lives to riding do. For most of my pupils riding is merely a relaxation and I just have to make them ride *efficiently and without abusing their horses* on the trails, in the hunting field, in the horse shows, etc. What was said in Jumping The HORSE was perhaps too simple for *Polo*, but was too complicated for hundreds of my pupils, young and old, fat and lean, brave and frightened. This is how my work lost its abstract aspects and acquired the tendency to adjust sound riding ideas to contemporary life.

Frankly, I am a riding enthusiast and perfectionist by nature; hence my instincts were, for a long time anyway, in opposition to the practicalities of life. Little by little I have trained myself to look upon teaching riding from the point of view of popular requirements. Eventually I found out that the work toward raising the standards of riding within practical limits and creating a new, efficient method of teaching it are tremendous fields for the application of one's enthusiasm for horses and riding. In conceiving my method, my train of thought was something like this:

1) A certain number of my pupils merely wanted to learn to hack. These people usually were not interested in the art of riding; they loved horses, enjoyed being outdoors in the saddle and that was about all. Any

* At the time of his death Harry D. Chamberlin was a Brigadier General. His various ranks in this book coincide with his rank at the time when mentioned. This is true of other officers mentioned.

technique of fine riding was of no interest to them and of no practical value—particularly if they had quiet horses. Obviously, torturing these people by trying to teach them such things as the flexing of the horse's mouth would be absurd. What they needed was merely a *decent seat* and a knowledge of *elementary* but effective control.

Perhaps some of these people, particularly those who hack regularly and own fine horses, could be persuaded to learn more about riding and would enjoy it. So for these a method could be devised, more refined than the elementary one, but still without the finesses of artistic riding, and it could legitimately be called—*intermediate control.*

2) The majority of my pupils wanted to hunt and to show. For hunting well and for showing hunters and jumpers successfully a knowledge of control at least on the *intermediate* level is imperative. Furthermore, for these two games the rider's seat must be really strong and easy on the horse.

It is true that a great deal of hunting is actually done on the basis of elementary control with some individual refinements added. If this is done by people who have a strong physique, lots of nerve and a knack of controlling the horse quickly and if necessary forcibly, they may hunt in this primitive manner for years without any mishap. But even if they are satisfied, their horses rarely are and so here, I think, an attempt should be made to raise the standards of riding without bringing in the artistic side of it. The *intermediate level of control* must fit better hunting and better showing; it also must enable a rider to school, in a simple way, a hack, hunter or jumper.

Thus the intermediate control as an efficient way of riding and schooling hacks, hunters and jumpers should be the main part of my method.

3) A certain, comparatively small, number of my pupils were real horsemen at heart. Whether hacking, hunting or jumping, they were always interested in the quality of the horse's performance; good movement was a real joy to them. So, for these people I should add to intermediate control the knowledge which is necessary to obtain movement of a high quality from a schooled horse, or to develop it in a green one. Riding and schooling horses on this level could be called *advanced* riding.

In developing the method of advanced riding I should still have in mind hunters and jumpers and keep the method free from all the curlicues of manège riding.

In Chapter VII there is a table which compares the elementary, intermediate and advanced controls as I later conceived them. For the time being the big question was what I could change immediately in the *general principles* of my actual method of riding and teaching in order to increase the efficiency of my lessons and to satisfy the practical aspirations of the majority of my pupils.

This is how I solved this question:

1) *The balance of the horse.* Most horses perform at their best when allowed to go freely. They also are easiest to control when moving forward naturally, because then they offer less resistance. Therefore my method should be based on the principle of free movement. Collection should be reserved only for sparing and judicial use as an exercise, only by those who are very able and are interested in schooling horses on advanced level. Only a method which is based on a freely moving horse can be practical for the multitude. Collection used indiscriminately results in abuse of horses; soft collection is really difficult to achieve.

What I have just said about collection would be anathema to any 19th century rider, but today I am far from being alone in my estimate of it. To illustrate this, let me quote from TRAINING HUNTERS, JUMPERS AND HACKS by Lt. Col. Harry D. Chamberlin (English edt., 1946, page 59):

"As has been indicated, high collection should be undertaken only by finished horsemen. The periods of collection should be very brief and it should be thoroughly realized that all preceding work, done for the purpose of producing calmness through developing a natural head carriage, may be quickly nullified by an inexperienced rider in his efforts to obtain a higher head carriage, more flexion and collection. As a matter of fact many experienced riders, in their efforts to proceed too far in collection and high-schooling succeed in inculcating nothing more than irritability, nervousness, and inability to jump or gallop fast across country."

In nature the horse collects himself only when excited and only for short periods of time. He is not made for moving at collected gaits fast or for a great length of time and this is the main reason why a hunter or a jumper performs better and remains calmer if allowed to move the way he was made to move at speed and for great distances; that is, holding himself in an extended attitude.

2) *The Seat.* The Forward Seat unites the rider with a forward moving horse. It is fortunate that the most rational seat—the Forward Seat—is the easiest to learn. So I must stop teaching the Dressage Seat, even for slow movements. And if I am to discontinue the Dressage Seat then I can probably cut down on its fundamental exercise—the sitting trot with and, particularly, without stirrups. Later I learned that a good Forward Seat could be taught with a negligible use of the sitting trot.

Some of the finer points of the Forward Seat could be simplified. For instance: following the horse's neck and head on the jump, moving the arms forward through the air, is only for the able riders who jump almost daily. It is silly to try to teach such fine points to those who ride three hours a week and are not in perfect physical shape. For them, horses must be taught to jump on loose reins (which is easy) and the riders must move their hands forward, placing them on the horse's neck, thus giving yet more room to the horse's neck to stretch, and getting additional balancing support for themselves. Using this method I can considerably accelerate the preparation of my pupils for the hunting field and for the horse show.

3) *Control.** The use of the aids and all the movements of Intermediate and Advanced control can be simplified. Such simplification may diminish the finesse of the movement but must preserve its essential values. This wasn't hard to do. Here is an example (the first quotation is taken from a well-known contemporary manual):

". . . if it is desired to turn the haunches from left to right, the weight of the mass must first be placed on the shoulders by closing the legs and relaxing the fingers until the movement forward becomes imminent. The center of gravity is then prevented from further forward displacement and the weight is carried on the left shoulder by closing the fingers on the right indirect rein of opposition in front of withers and on the left direct rein, care being exercised to hold the head and neck in the direction of the axis of the horse. While this is taking place, the left leg is moved a little in rear of the girth to displace the haunches to the right. The right leg is closed on the girth to maintain the forward displacement of the center of gravity, to prevent the horse from backing and to stop the displacement of the haunches to the right when desired. The seat is carried to the right to facilitate displacement of the haunches."

A corresponding part of the description of the same turn, only to the left instead of to the right, in my last book BE A BETTER HORSEMAN, published in 1941, reads as follows (page 161):

"To rotate the quarters to the left the rider takes his right leg back and with it pushes the quarters to the left while his hands are merely watching that the horse does not step forward from the urging of the leg.

"It might happen that sometimes from the action of the right leg the horse, while rotating the quarters to the left, will make a step to the left with the whole body; very often this is nothing but a sign of poor balance. It should be avoided, for only if done in place is the exercise beneficial. In order to prevent this movement the rider should close in his left leg before the right one begins to act. The action of this leg (the left one in this case) regulates and, if necessary, stops the rotation."

I am inclined to believe that the artistic aims embodied in the first quotation are more apt to discourage than encourage the majority of civilian riders.

Furthermore, I believe that certain points of artistic riding, like always riding "on the bit," the "half-halts," "full collection" and some others should be preserved only for unusually good riders schooling ex-

* The definitions of Elementary, Intermediate and Advanced control are given in Chapter VII.

ceptionally able horses and taking time at it. In the hands of the majority, attempts to attain the above result in abuse of the horse and, instead of contributing anything for hunting and jumping, are detrimental to both of these games. For efficient riding by the majority a merely "soft contact" most of the time, loose reins part of the time, and always a freely going horse (if calm and obedient) is much more sensible.

4) *Schooling.* The schooling of hunters and jumpers can also be considerably simplified by comparison with the highly artistic methods described in some books while still producing better horses than the average.

5) *The ideal.* Adjusting one's teaching to contemporary possibilities made it, of course, necessary to establish at the same time an ideal which would be attainable at least within the course of a generation. Choosing this ideal was simple; the Three-Day-Event competition of the Olympic Games embodied it all. It contains schooling for hacks, hunters and jumpers, riding cross-country with negotiation of varied, trappy obstacles and arena jumping. Furthermore, it could always be simplified to adjust it to local needs; the training test should be also modernized (I shall devote a chapter to this). Since the original edition of this book was written I have further modernized the formula of the Three Day Event so as to make it yet more practical for the American amateur of today. In this revised edition it is described under the title of *The Complete Test for Hunters.* It seems to me that it is more realistically constructed than the so-called *Horse Trials* of the *Combined Training Test,* which are much closer to the original Three Day Event, with the latter's Dressage type of test.

6) *Teaching.* Teaching should be systematized. The last minute snap decisions on what a particular lesson should be about must be replaced by a logically constructed course. Naturally such a course should be flexible enough to consider the individual characteristics of the riders and horses involved. The course of teaching must have three main parts: teaching position, teaching control and teaching schooling.

7) *Theory.* Theory must be presented in such a way that the pupil is forced into thinking; it should not merely consist in memorizing facts. A humane attitude toward the horse must be stressed.

When, in the ensuing years, I succeeded in putting the above plan into practice I possessed a method all my own. The component parts of this system were not new; it was the arrangement and the manner of using them which distinguished this method from others. Its efficiency has been proven to me by long practice.

Looking over my plan, you will see that it was not a popular "shortcut"; it was, rather, an adjustment of the technique of artistic riding to practical conditions. There was nothing vulgar in it. But what was the use of discussing how a perfect turn on the haunches should be made when the real problem was to persuade the riding public to make such a turn at all? The love of working for hours on details is not an American characteristic, but it seemed that attempts to convince the public that schooling movements, such as a *decent* turn on the haunches, were valuable exercises for both riders and horses could be successful. And in the spirit of a sincerely impartial observer, I would like to say that my best pupils, both human and equine, could easily have competed with the performances in the Three-Day-Event training test of the Olympic Games which I witnessed in England in 1948. This merely means that putting into practice little finesses of riding is not such an easy task even for the Olympic riders.

But, simple as was the course charted by my ideal, it was a struggle to make the majority accept it. For instance, a number of types of resistance were expressed by one word—"impractical." Naturally, for those who ride once or twice a week anything above very simple aims is impractical; so in conceiving the final ideal, I had primarily in view those who rode regularly and had their own horses. Of these, many hunting circles in particular, resented schooling and seemed to glory in the excitement of hunting green horses. It was of no use to try to point out that the performance hardly could be good or the sensation pleasant; it seemed that the satisfaction of such an experience lay in the feeling it gave one of being real he-man. And probably this sensation is responsible for the attitude of many young men who consider anything short of steeplechasing a "sissy game;" this is one of the reasons why the majority of our riders and many of the best of them are women. But it is the result of other reasons as well; on the whole women have more feeling for animals, are gentler, have less of the spirit of brutal conquest and, instead, possess more ingenuity to solve a problem by indirect means; and, speaking of amateurs, they have in general more time to devote to riding.

There cannot be any argument that the results of schooling are practical for both the hunting field and the horse show ring. A schooled horse is safer and performs better so that the impractical part may consist only in the time required for schooling. Some people may really be short of it, but many of those whom I know among the hunting and horse show groups have the time. And if they don't school their horses the actual reasons are different. I think it all goes back to an unhorsemanlike attitude, and to the fact that Americans are not much interested in theory; under these conditions a horse cannot be schooled. As a matter of fact, some of the methods of riding which are popularly taught today in this country are so devoid of any theory that they are really completely impractical. They may be considered practical only if one doesn't mind making a fool of himself, breaking his neck or crippling his horse.

The word "practical" was sometimes used so unthinkingly that I have heard people say that preoccupation with Dressage is impractical, while

Photo by Bert Clark Thayer

Pic. 12.   Shows an energetic ordinary trot which is efficient because all the energy is used to cover ground; there is a minimum of upward action. (The rider— Mr. George Hoblin).

Pic. 13.   The above picture shows a balancing gesture too great for this height of fence; it was necessitated by too close a take-off. The completely relaxed hands and arms of the rider maintain soft contact with the horse's mouth, and follow the gesture of the neck and head.

From "More About Riding Forward" by V. S. Littauer. Photo by Bert Clark Thayer

PIC. 14. Depending on the relative conformation of the rider and the horse the stirrups may be a little shorter (particularly for show jumping) or even a little longer (particularly for ring schooling) and different members of the rider's body be in slightly different attitudes; this picture represents the average. This picture of a pupil of mine was taken in the thirties.

hunting is a practical type of riding. It would seem that the simple, realistic idea that in our day and in our country the cowboy is one of the few riders who uses a horse for practical purposes, while the rest of us, whether practicing Dressage or hunting, do it just for pleasure, never occurs to some people. Dressage or the horse show or hunting are merely different games. Certainly there is one practical aspect to hunting, polo, and horse shows today in the United States, just as there used to be to musical rides, but it's of a purely social character. They are group games; they may even be part of a certain kind of community life, that of the "set;" while advanced, classical Dressage is essentially a solitary art. As such, it carries the taint of "impracticality" with which many solitary arts or hobbies are regarded in contemporary America. Ordinarily people ride to chase a ball or a fox, to see western scenery; some do it to flirt; all do it to get together and a teacher of pure riding, riding for riding's sake, often finds its discouraging. There are individuals who appreciate the pleasure of riding a well-schooled horse, do the schooling themselves, and then show or hunt, whatever the occasion may be, deriving great satisfaction out of the horse's performance under varied and often difficult conditions. These are the people who make a teacher's life worth while. I have been lucky enough to know many such, both in the horse show and in the hunting field.

There was another expression commonly used and which was troublesome: "I want to ride for pleasure only." Of course I understood that this was just a form of expressing one's humble aims, of saying that one wants merely to hack, perhaps occasionally to hunt. But somehow, it also implied, in many cases, that the fellow who schools horses doesn't derive any pleasure from it; he is just working. And sometimes it was hard to explain that tastes differ, that some people prefer bridge to pinochle and that many loving, let us say, Dressage or horse show jumping, are bored with hacking or hunting. This "riding for pleasure" was one of many protective screens, all of which were genteel substitutes for a really rather unpleasant admission—"I am not interested in riding well."

Negligible as was the harm done by any single one of these misused terms, the quantity of them was such that altogether they added up to a great deal. For instance, the way in which another two words were regularly employed expressed the confused state of mind of the riding world; these were "equitation" and "dressage." Webster's dictionary defines "equitation" as "the act or art of riding; horsemanship." Which means that jumping, for instance, is equitation. However, here and now under equitation is usually understood a competition in which juniors only participate and during which the rider, besides showing his riding ability at gaits, is required to perform simple movements, such as a figure of eight, change of leads and backing. Instead of calling this elementary or intermediate riding or elementary schooling we call it *equitation* and by doing so separate it from the rest of riding. Some sort of psychological process sets up and results in the conclusion that changes of leads or really good turning have nothing to do with cross-country riding or jumping; they are something special—"equitation."

The confusion over Dressage, today in 1962, when I am inserting the following, is much more than a question of terminology—it is also one of practice. While in this chapter I have described how I began to abandon Dressage (on which I was brought up) as unnecessary to the schooling of hunters and jumpers, other people today, some of whom never practiced it previously, have taken it up for this very purpose. Because of this I feel it essential to discuss the subject at length.

It is not for the first time that the French word, *Dressage*, is used in the English-speaking world. The few 17th century English horsemen, like the Duke of Newcastle, who were influenced by Continental riding, employed the term in the form of "dressing horses." It is also to be met with even in early 19th century literature. It later went out of vogue and has recently slipped back into the English language again, when some horsemen of the English-speaking nations have once more come under the sway of the European continent in matters of equitation.

Accepting this term in a superficial manner, both the English and the Americans have missed the fact that the French themselves, advancing with the times, have come to distinguish between *Dressage de Manège* (ring schooling), which eventually may lead to High School (*Dressage Académique*), and *Dressage Sportif* (for sport), which is schooling for horses destined for cross-country riding or for jumping. The latter dressage is conceived under the Italian influence but, its method still being in process of formulation, it more often than not preserves some practices from the past.

Today one often hears that the French word *Dressage* merely means schooling. This is correct. But do those people who prefer the French word *dressage* to the English word *schooling* use the first in referring to a cowboy's schooling of a cutting horse, or to schooling a gaited horse, or to the early-morning, last-minute schooling over the outside course on the show grounds? Why not be consistent? A Frenchman would use the word *dressage* in all the cases cited; as a matter of fact, *dressage d'obstacles*—that is schooling over fences—is a standard French expression. Those English-speaking people who insist that the French word *dressage* is equivalent to the English word schooling do not seem to practice what they preach.

But another factor has influenced our use of the word: in the days before Caprilli, when there was only one basic system of schooling (manège schooling), the word dressage signified this and nothing else. At that time, variations were limited to individual interpretations of what was fundamentally the same method. But today, with two systems existing side by side, the logical French, who like to express themselves very accurately, define which kind of dressage they mean by adding either the term *de manège* or the word *sportif* to it. Today in France the word dressage is used without a modifying adjective only in reference to manège dressage, and this is why both competitions of the Olympic Games, the Dressage phase of the Three-Day-Event and the Grand Prix de Dressage—are so termed. Both of these competitions represent fundamentally the same type of riding, but they are on two very different levels. What is it that relates them? Collection, of course. All educated riding in the past was based on collection (more or less of it), while the first thing Caprilli's revolution did was to abolish it. Today, in English, the word dressage really refers to a specific type of schooling on the flat, based on collection. If one insists on using the same word *dressage* to designate schooling of Caprilli's type, the adjective "sporting" should be added. Whether it is called this, or *Forward Schooling* or *Natural Schooling*, or by some entirely new name, does not matter; but the user of the term should know what he is talking about and make it clear to his listeners.

Elementary Dressage, of which we hear so much today—that is the elementary level of ring dressage—is considered by some people to be practical basic training for hunters and jumpers. This is an inheritance from the days of the military horse, and if one's hunter or jumper was expected to be as versatile as the old-fashioned military horse, some schooling of this type might be necessary. In an age of little time on the one hand, and on the other of that narrow specialization which leads to high standards in competitions, the only really practical training is that directed toward the special end one has in view for a horse.

Even the elementary level of ring dressage is based on collection, on *giving the horse a central balance.* This means *moving* with central balance, neck high and chin in. It is not only of little use to the hunter or jumper, but it will delay, if not actually impede, his acquisition of a good *forward balance* with stretched neck and long flat strides—the balance at which he will ultimately be required to function. Efficient elementary schooling for any type of horse must be based on the *type of balance at which he will be expected to perform* (see text on balance).

Some people who watch me teach movements like the half-turn on the haunches say with surprise, "So you teach Dressage!" Actually, the superficial similarity between Dressage and Forward Schooling is even greater than that—both schools, for instance, make their horses walk, trot and canter! The difference between Dressage and Forward Schooling is not so much in the movements the horse is required to execute as in the manner and balance in which he executes them.

Then why, despite this being simple enough to be common knowledge, do many American horsemen today use the real Dressage method of schooling inappropriately, for instance, for jumping, while others call any type of schooling by this name.

It all started with the abolition of mounted cavalry and the resultant substitution of civilian international teams for the military ones. Thus the door was apparently opened for everyone to take part in the Olympic games. This promoted unprecedented interest in the latter, and in anything that might lead up to or be connected with them. Although practically no one aimed at competing in the big Dressage event, a lower level of Dressage still played a part in the Three-Day-Event; the U.S. Equestrian Team used some Dressage methods in training for the Prix des Nations, and the Pony Club introduced certain disconnected Dressage terms and practices.

That was how it started. At present, however, the picture is much more complicated, and different people use the term Dressage for different reasons. Disregarding the pretentious use of this term by ignoramuses who wish to appear knowledgeable, we should first of all take into consideration those who sincerely believe that the old-fashioned type of ring schooling is helpful in making hunters and jumpers. Then there are others who wish to school their hunters and jumpers, but have neither experience nor reason to prefer one type of schooling to another. To these the word *Dressage,* as a foreign term still used in international competitions, carries a prestige which the plain English word *Schooling* does not. So it often happens that it is not the principles of Dressage but its associations and historical prestige that have encouraged the number of people who are working in different organizations to promote it. Many of these people will readily admit in private that they do not know the first thing about Dressage. Once the term Dressage became fashionable, all those professionals who have no particular convictions and are in business just to make money, began either to teach Dressage or to pretend that they were teaching it.

Still another element plays a role: in Forward Schooling the cooperation of the horse—that is, a certain partnership between the horse and the rider—plays an important role. Dressage, on the other hand, is based on the domination of the horse by the rider. The latter idea is more appealing to some people and they plunge into Dressage without realization either of the fine techniques such a method demands or the time consumed in developing these.

If you look back on the American riding scene of, let us say, fifty years ago you will find that there was precious little educated schooling as we know it today. When Forward Riding appeared on this continent, a few years before the revival of Dressage, it had little trouble in selling the *Forward Seat,* which was a simple mechanical conception; any mounted pedestrian could understand its advantages for galloping and jumping. *Forward Schooling,* however, because it was more complicated, and because it involved thinking like a horseman, did not fare so well. As a matter of fact, Dressage has not yet taken hold either, in spite of the organized effort of several years to promote it. People are apt to find the routine of any type of schooling too tedious.

The simpler the schooling, the better chance it has of becoming popular. This, of course, is why *Forward Schooling* has advantages over Dressage for helping to raise the standards of general riding. The collected gaits of Dressage have always been the stumbling block of most of those who mounted a horse.

In order to keep Dressage competitions going they are continually being simplified; and in some of them even the corner stone of Dressage, collected gaits, have been abolished. The programs of such Dressage competitions resemble those of the Program Rides of the elementary level of Forward Schooling. If so, then it might be said that no harm is done and that we all pursue the principles of Forward Riding under different names. But, harm is actually done, to both the physical and the theoretical sides of riding.

Take, for instance, the matter of the rider's position. In many instances, even where collected gaits are abolished, the riders are still required to use a Dressage Seat. In such cases, the horses thus move in *Forward Balance,* while the riders maintain a position which originally aimed to unite them with horses moving at collected gaits and in *Central Balance;* consequently these riders are behind their horses. This particular anomaly has even penetrated our regular horsemanship classes on the flat and has encouraged the unfortunate practice of sitting behind the horse in order to win. I know many good Forward Seat riders who have won their blue ribbons in this manner, feeling that they cleverly outwitted the judges. Such loss of judges' prestige is, of course, undesirable.

In the second place, we should consider the mental confusion that has resulted from the promotion of an unfamiliar type of riding. I have before me one of the questionnaires of the United States Pony Club (published in 1959). In it I find, for instance, the following questions and answers:—
1) "What is meant by 'collection'?
   To have the horse in a state of proper balance. . . ."
Obviously in this case the central balance of collected gaits is taken as the *only* state of satisfactory balance which, of course, is completely inaccurate. (See the text on "The Balance of the Horse in Motion.") After all, race horses usually remain upright without the help of collection.
2) "When is a horse said to be 'up to the bit'?
   When his head and neck are in correct position (Direct flexion) . . ."
And what about having the horse on the bit with extended neck and head, as winning working hunters approach fences?

Such a questionnaire can hardly be considered helpful in educating our youth.

But not all of the factors were on the debit side. For instance, practically all young people were showing the results of the modern emphasis on health and physical development and were strong, agile and bold. Enthu-

siasm for the horse and riding which some of the girls possessed led them
to choose riding as a profession after majoring in physical education.
Without thinking twice, I could make a list of fifty such girls who teach
riding and are in correspondence with me; while, looking through my
files, I could easily give another fifty names of both women and men who
are good teachers. If you were to consider that each such teacher influences
on the average fifty pupils a year, the figure of five thousand pupils all
told means quite a broad dissemination of sound ideas. And there must be
quite a few good teachers of whom I have never heard. Negligible as these
figures are, in comparison with the total number of riders and teachers
in the United States, yet this result couldn't be achieved without the
enthusiasm of some. Looking at this aspect of the scene in 1962 I find I
must remark on the tremendously increased general popularity of riding
and showing today.

The equestrian magazines and book publishers were of tremendous help
in the spreading of intelligent riding ideas, despite the fact that the periodicals, trying to stimulate interest through controversy, published as
much worthless material as good, and that some of the book publishers
quite naturally were looking for good business first. Just the same, a number of sound books and articles, by different authors, have been published
in the course of the last twenty-five years; so, all told, the printed word
was one of the great allies of better riding. In this respect the Derrydale
Press is particularly to be congratulated; Mr. Eugene V. Connett having
a special flair for selecting books on riding, has soundly enriched many
equestrian libraries. Some of his publications later appeared in popular
editions, which is a sign of the growing demand.

Some years ago my little book, RIDING FORWARD, was published by
William Morrow & Co. and sold five thousand odd copies. Then much
later it was reprinted in a $1.00 edition and in eight months I received
royalties for twenty thousand copies.

One could, of course, argue that the books could be better, for although
the majority of them create the impression that they are written for the
general public, in reality it is not so. Many of them fall in one of
the following two categeries. The first group was written by great
enthusiasts who, after devoting all their lives to riding and reaching
very high levels of technical thinking, have described in great detail the
finesse of riding. To the second group belong the books written by amateurs who, the moment they learn how to back a horse, have an irresistible
urge to share this wonderful knowledge with the rest of the world.

But nothing being perfect on this globe, one has to admit that many
of the books published recently truly belong to the 20th century for, in
one way or another, well or badly, competently or amateurishly, they
discuss riding from the point of view of modern ideas. Comparatively few
recent authors consistently think in the spirit of the past century but, on

the other hand, most of the modern books still contain vestiges of the old and, the longer ago they were published, naturally the more of them they have. A shelf of such books is an historical document on the progress of thinking in riding. Aiming to provoke thinking in my pupils I discuss opinions of other riders whenever the occasion presents itself during my lessons. The many quotations from different authors which I give in this book are merely an extension of this practice.

Books, better teaching, the great increase in competitive riding and many other factors, large and small, working independently totaled up to the existing progress.

CHAPTER V

Troubles with the Forward Seat

In the middle thirties an English team came to the National Show in Madison Square Garden. The positions in which the officers rode were not only most awkward and peculiar, but even grotesque, and the first evening Major X of one of the other army teams and myself were very amused watching them. But they made one clean round after another and Major X, who is, by the way, a very fine horseman, lost that evening. The same score more or less persisted night after night and finally he, who was laughing no longer, said to me that he was going to ask one of the English officers "why they sit so badly?" I remember the answer, word for word, as Major X passed it on to me. The English officer said: "We know that we do not sit very well but we are all very light and all our horses are very powerful; there is no need to change." I am telling this story to point out to you, before we begin to discuss the seat, that I personally don't put too much stress on it. I believe that the average rider sits more firmly, rides better, abuses his horse less and hence obtains a better performance from an average mount if he uses the Forward Seat *correctly*. But no truly great performance was ever achieved on a perfect seat alone. A good Forward Seat enables one to school the horse better, to control him better and the horse, being less abused, will probably perform better; but the possibility of a good performance will also depend on the natural abilities of the horse, on the equestrian tact of the rider, on the physical and emotional condition in which they both are at the time of the performance and last, but not least, on the ability of the rider to think logically and quickly from the first day of schooling to the day of the performance in question. (See the table of Chapter I.)

However, everyone must begin by learning the seat by the book; it is only much later, on the basis of experience in controlling the horse, that one may find out that the standard seat should be modified in various small ways to suit one's particular physique.

In the inseparable trio, *schooling, control* and *seat,* the latter is the junior partner; the new development in cross-country riding didn't start by inventing a seat and then adjusting schooling and control to fit it. All these parts were conceived by Caprilli as one; he created a fully rounded method of riding and this is why he exerted such an influence on the riding thinking of the 20th century. The simple idea of the Forward Seat by itself occurred to several riders before Caprilli. In MORE ABOUT RIDING FORWARD I say:

"On my shelves I have a three-volume work by John Adams (a riding teacher) entitled AN ANALYSIS OF HORSEMANSHIP, published in London in 1805 . . . He discusses positions for High School, for hacking, for military purposes and for hunting. Out of about twenty pages on the hunting seat I will select certain phrases and will put them together in such a way that you will immediately recognize the modern Forward Seat. He does not have these points as well connected nor has he any good scientific explanation of them. Furthermore, he has other points which contradict the good ones, but he unquestionably had the idea of the Forward Seat. John Adams writes: '. . . the hunting seat is that of riding in the stirrups . . . the Intention of this style of riding is . . . to relieve yourself from that friction and heat which the bottom would receive from such strong and continued gallop, if seated close on the saddle . . . the first thing to be considered is the length of the stirrup, which must not be too short, though somewhat shorter than what was recommended for military or road riding . . . when the horseman is raised in the stirrups he must have a forward inclination from about twenty to forty-five degrees short of a perpendicular, as the rider shall find most pleasant and convenient for himself; for from twenty to twenty-five degrees of inclination might be most pleasant and to stoop to forty-five degrees would look ridiculous as being unnecessary . . . But whether the body has a great or small inclination the position otherwise must be the same as when upright; that is the breast open, the shoulders down, the back hollow, the head firm . . . If you find it necessary you may turn your toes out a little to strengthen your hold . . . and when the thighs are not sufficient then the legs are applied, which is a deeper and stronger hold . . . the hands must be kept low.' " This seat he intends for the gallop only. He did not go so far as to work it out for the jump.

I was told that it was for purely military reasons that Caprilli *began* his work of modernizing riding; his problem was to increase the mobility and tenacity of cavalry in order to adjust it to the changing conditions of warfare. I wasn't there and so I don't know the sequence of Caprilli's thoughts, but it seems to me that their normal logic should have proceeded along the following lines: to increase the endurance and the average speed of the cavalry, horses must be schooled in such a way that their natural, long, flat strides are preserved and developed, while the control should not interfere with this natural, free way of going. Allowed to move in this natural way, horses will cover more ground per minute and will use less energy per mile, while a Forward position which will unite the rider and his forward-moving horse will ease the horse's efforts still more. An appreciation of the natural balance of the horse and of the mechanics of his movements would be the foundation stones in my reasoning. I imagine that I am not far from the truth in thinking that such were the mental processes of Caprilli; at any rate the Italians are proud primarily of their method, "*Il Sistema*," and not merely of a part of it—the Forward Seat. I can see that, to a beginner, whose mental and physical capacities are completely absorbed in learning how to sit properly, such things as schooling, or the horse's performance are so remote that they don't really mean much. But somehow even people who like to think of themselves as horsemen often miss this point also. The average experienced American rider talks primarily seat. It is usual for people, when arguing about the causes of someone's winning a ribbon, to try always to boil them down to some point of the seat. One will say that Mr. A won because he sat down in the saddle the last two strides before the jump or because he was out of the saddle throughout the approach, whatever the case may be. Of course, either of the above cases may often be responsible for a good jump; but it is not the basic point. You may look, if you have the opportunity, through a book by Gustave Rau (REITKUNST AN DEN OLYMPISCHEN SPIELEN, 1936) on the Olympic Games in Berlin in 1936. You will see in its pages more bad positions than you have ever seen in beginners' classes, and the jumps in Berlin were enormous, so that is where a perfect position should have really counted; but, just the same, many of the officers who were caught by the camera in most peculiar attitudes made very creditable performances. So these men and horses possessed something else on the strength of which they were clearing fences; these factors, besides luck, could only be the talents of the riders and horses, and the results of schooling and artistic control. But the results of schooling and fineness of control are not to be seen easily by an inexperienced eye, while the seat seems to be obvious.

Quite repeatedly, when I lecture I am introduced as an authority on the Forward Seat. To be frank, it always rather hurts me; I like to think of myself as a specialist on a certain method of Forward Riding and to leave me with a mere detail of it I don't think does me justice. And even two of my books RIDING FORWARD and MORE ABOUT RIDING FORWARD were reprinted in England under the changed titles—THE FORWARD SEAT and MORE ABOUT THE FORWARD SEAT! Both books actually devote a comparatively small number of pages to the discussion of the position. And hence I am very grateful to the English reviewer for *The Field* who wrote: "It is a pity . . . that Captain Littauer has selected this particular title for his book, especially as when one reads it one realizes that '*Less* About the Forward *Seat*' would have described the work quite accurately."

In all my lessons I endlessly discuss this point; most discouragingly it seldom sinks in. Many years ago I had a pupil, a man who began to ride at the age of fifty-one and, in about a year, less if I am not mistaken, he was able to participate in a horse show, in easy jumping classes, which I thought was extremely creditable. Soon afterwards his interests changed, he stopped riding and when, several years later, we met and I complimented him on his former success in riding he said: "No, no; I never really rode well; my heels were never quite enough down."

Little as the preoccupation with the perfection of the Forward Seat and its details interested me as a rider, it filled years of my life as a teacher. Normally, sixty per cent of my new pupils were beginners, and the majority of those with riding experience had such poor positions that they had to be corrected before any constructive work could be done. The quality which I aimed at in a seat was that it should be non-disturbing to the horse, secure, and should enable the rider to work the horse well. The belief that the seat which I should teach must be the forward one was clear by 1930, but its mechanics could vary somewhat as, for instance, the mechanics of the Italian Seat differ from those of the Fort Riley Seat. From the different possible mechanics I had to select the ones which would suit the aspirations of my average rider, besides satisfying myself; then a method of efficient teaching of such a seat had to be invented. All in all, the question of position rarely left my mind. And after long mental and practical groping I arrived at the following simple formula of what a good seat should be. It must (in motion):

1) Unite the horse and the rider
2) Offer security to the rider
3) Not abuse the horse
4) Place the rider's legs and hands in a position from which he will be able to control the horse quickly, and firmly and, if desired, with finesse.

Here are a few explanatory words about these four points. It is obvious that the unity of the rider and the horse largely depends on such a distribution of the rider's weight in the saddle that his line of center of gravity and that of the horse nearly coincide (this means the forward seat in the case of a horse which moves ahead with forward balance).

This unity of the horse and the rider abuses the horse the least, enables him to move freely without the interference of the rider's weight, and, at the same time, gives to the rider a great deal of possible security. Naturally the rider's security is very much diminished if his efforts are not in harmony with the movements of the horse. The basic security derived from being one with the horse must be increased by the execution of mechanical details of the Forward Seat. In some of these *details,* and only in these, I was forced to disagree with both the Italian and the Fort Riley schools— but about this later.

Once the rider has taken his weight from the horse's loins and placed it forward, on a stronger part of the horse's back, he already has decreased the abuse of the horse and, if after this, he proceeds to follow the movements of the horse with his torso and arms, the remaining unavoidable abuse becomes minimum.

As to the best position for the legs and hands for efficient control, just a few changes had to be made, varying only slightly from the classical version; they primarily consisted of lowering the hands and of holding them farther apart.

A correct execution of the details of the Forward Seat increases the firmness of the rider in the saddle as well as his unity with the horse and thus enables the rider to approach the ideal described in the four fundamental points of a good Forward Seat. In my method these details are as follows: 1) Balance, 2) Rhythm, 3) Spring, and 4) Grip.

I have put them in the order of their importance as I see it, and their description follows:

1) A state of balance in the saddle is the result of unconscious muscular efforts of the rider's body, primarily of his torso, which aim to keep the rider's center of gravity over his base of support, while being disturbed by the shocks of locomotion.

2) Rhythm consists of instinctive movements of the rider's torso and arms which adjust his self-balancing efforts to the movements of the horse (balanced not only in the saddle but also with the horse).

3) Spring is the ability of the rider to absorb a part of the effects of the shocks of locomotion by a) keeping his body in an angular position (angles in the hips, knees and ankles) and b) instinctive, timely opening and closing of these angles, while receiving the impetus from the stirrups —for instance, posting from the stirrups and not from the knees.

4) Grip may be of two kinds: frictional, which depends merely on the correct placing of the legs in the saddle, without any additional effort on the part of the rider, and the muscular grip, which results from a muscular effort by the same parts of the legs which are already in frictional contact. These parts are the lower thighs, inner surfaces of the knees and the upper calves.

Experience has taught me that it is wise first to develop a correct position by the use of balance, rhythm, spring and frictional grip, adding muscular grip later. In the case of the average beginner, attempts to grip hard stiffen him and, once stiff, he loses the sense of balance, rhythm and spring. I have encountered many riders with a strong, picture-seat but so hopelessly stiff that any work with the horse was precluded. A seat which is not a "workman's seat" is, in my estimation, worthless. A "workman's seat" is the seat which gives the horse ease of action and the rider ease of control. Picture 14 illustrates such a seat at a standstill, with the stirrups adjusted for cross-country riding.

As I have said previously, it is in the matter of the, so to speak, "insides" of the Forward Seat and not in its external appearance that I unfortunately had to disagree with so many other schools of forward riding. A clear comprehension of the inner workings of the Forward Seat, being the basis of the method of teaching, was, of course, of utmost importance to me. The silhouettes of well-executed Forward Seats, whether Italian, or Fort Riley or the one which I teach, at the gaits as well as over the

Pic. 15.

Pic. 16.   *From "More About Riding Forward" V. S. Littauer*

Pics. 15 and 16.   (Mr. Chester A. Braman and Dr. Walter Kees) illustrate the
fundamental points of good jumping:— 1) the complete ease of the rider in
handling his body and, 2) the complete freedom enjoyed by the horse as a result
of the former.

As to the martingale in picture 15—fifteen years ago I was not yet as definitely
against it as I am today (these pictures of two pupils of mine were taken in the
middle thirties).

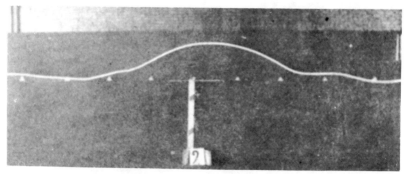

Pic. 17. Shows the trajectory of the withers of the horse.

Pic. 18. Shows two trajectories—one of the withers and the other of the croupe. The fact that the two lines merge for a good half of the jump indicates that the efforts of the horse's body were well synchronized. In this case the rider used the forward seat.

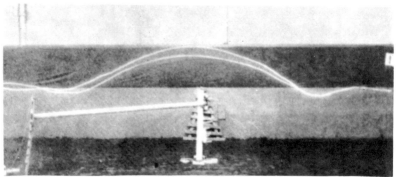

From "The Defense of the Forward Seat" by
V. S. Littauer and S. N. Kournakoff

Pic. 19. Illustrates the jump of the same horse ridden by the same rider using the backward seat. The trajectory of the croupe remained consistently on a lower plane than the trajectory of the withers.

The near merging of the two trajectories is typical for a good jump of a free horse and therefore these pictures give additional proof that the natural efforts of the horse in jumping are disturbed less by the forward seat than by any other position.

These photographs were taken by the following means:—a flashlight was attached either to the withers or to the croupe and the pictures were taken at night in a subdued light in the riding ring. See text page 67.

jump, may be practically alike, differing only as the riders' conformations differ. (Pics. 15 and 16 show my pupils taken in the thirties.)

The mechanics of human bodily actions can be analyzed quite precisely. To choose a ludicrous example: I once knew a riding teacher who, being over-apprehensive of broken arms and legs, conceived a way of falling which would prevent fractures of the limbs and who taught it to his pupils. It must have been well-reasoned for they all fell alike; but there was one flaw in it—they all fell on their faces!

But in spite of this general knowledge of human mechanics and considerable acquaintance with those of the horse, the Forward Seat as we know it today was not conceived at once. The early Forward Seats had many defects and mine was not an exception. For instance, in three of my books, all written from twelve to sixteen years ago, I omitted at least one important point, and twice I explained details badly:

1) I never mentioned that the fleshy part of the buttocks should be forced rearward, toward the cantle, but that owing to the torso's forward inclination there is no weight in them.

2) While insisting upon pulling the heels down, I should have added that all the weight going into the stirrups should go into the heels, which of course is a physical impossibility but is very descriptive of the feeling that the rider should have.

3) Instead of saying that the lower legs should be held back so that the toes and knees are on approximately the same vertical line I should have said "so that the stirrup leathers hang vertically," or are held slightly behind the vertical.

Work on bettering the details of the Forward Seat and the development of the application of modern principles to control and schooling still goes on. The French in particular have done very interesting work along these lines since World War II. In the way of forgetting Caprilli they went a step ahead of us and called the Forward Seat "position Danloux."

I am not giving here a full description of all the points of the Forward Seat, for my collaborator, Alexis Wrangel will do that in his part of the book.

Speaking of the understanding of how the Forward Seat functions and what efforts the rider should make to maintain it, my disagreement with the Italian school revolved around really one point: that of having the knees as a pivot for the whole position, as it was described in an excellent book by Captain P. Santini, RIDING REFLECTIONS. It seemed to me in 1933, when this book appeared (and I haven't changed my mind since), that if the rider's position depended primarily on firmly fixed knees then he was greatly hampered in the use of his legs. For, as long as a strong use of the legs releases the wedging of the knees, it would seem that the rider's position would be weakened every time he had to control the horse forcibly. Of course, on perfectly schooled horses, such moments may occur very rarely and don't have to be considered seriously; but a perfectly schooled horse is far from being a general case in this world, at least today.

I am also against gripping strongly with knees alone because as a result of abrupt movements of the horse which the rider has not been able to follow rhythmically he often loses his position by pivoting on the knees, usually landing on the horse's neck or beyond. All of us have seen this happen to such riders during unexpected refusals or irregular take-offs for the jump. Obviously, gripping with the lower thighs, knees and upper calves is stronger than with the knees alone.

Furthermore, a strongly fixed knee interferes with the flow of the weight into the stirrups and stiffens the knee joints, thus greatly diminishing the amount of spring in the rider's body. This spring, which is rarely mentioned by other schools of forward riding is to me a very important element in a good, effortless forward seat. And last, but not least, I am quite certain that a hard grip stiffens a beginner and, once in the habit of being stiff, some never relax in their lives. So how am I to produce relaxed *riders* (not merely sitters) if my teaching from the outset is to be based on a fixed knee? Thus, with great regret, I had to reject for my work this part of the Italian method, of many principles of which I personally am so fond.

Lately one hears more and more often about the evil of fixed knees. For instance in CONCOURS HIPPIQUE by Y. Benoist-Gironière one reads:

". . . the knee ought to remain in contact with the saddle but only in an elastic contact so that it can open and close . . . So don't grip with the knee, it will lose all its elasticity and the lower leg will oscillate around it as a wooden leg . . . The rider's legs must adhere to the horse principally at two areas—the calves and parts of the legs slightly above the knee . . ." (translation is mine).

Along these lines a French officer, Colonel Danloux, designed a jumping saddle on which the so-called knee rolls end before reaching the knee, giving support only to the lower thigh and leaving the knees free for action. On this saddle there are also rolls at the bottom and rear of the skirts, to prevent the lower legs from slipping back.

Speaking of the description of the mechanical details of riding and especially of the seat, I found that in civilian life one had to be very careful to be logical and exact when teaching men, many of whom were either professional engineers or 20th century mechanics at heart. For example, at a certain period of my teaching life, I used to recommend widely the United States Cavalry manual—HORSEMANSHIP AND HORSE MASTERSHIP, which I still consider contains a good description of position at the gaits and in jumping. As long as this description was very similar to what I was teaching, the authority of the book in my estimation should have backed up my teaching. It worked in many cases, but not in all, and it was occasionally pointed out to me that some statements in it were mechanically illogical and, although they were of a general nature and unimportant to beginners, they created doubt in those parts of the book recommended by me. Of these I remember two:

1) "The Military seat . . . is dependent upon balance augmented by suppleness, muscular control of the body and the use of the legs." (Page 21, edit. 1945).

It was pointed out to me several times after I had recommended the book that this definition mechanically doesn't hold water. How can the balance be augmented by suppleness and muscular control when the state of balance itself is the result of muscular control executed (primarily) by a semi-supple (alert) torso?

2) On the same page, paragraph #4 states: "the principal elements in the discussion (of the seat) are the rider's upper body, his base of support and his equilibrium or balance."

Obviously, mechanically speaking, neither does this phrase make any sense, for one cannot put in the same category concrete things such as body and legs and abstract qualities such as balance.

The fact that there were and still are disagreements between different schools of forward riding is, of course, a healthy sign; it merely means that there are riders who think and experiment. But in one sense it has been unfortunate—there has been no common front, while common enemies have been numerous. Not only in private conversations but even in print the Forward Seat riders were called "monkey on the stick," "frog on a rock," etc., while the air in tack-rooms was heavy with a specific use of the English vocabulary. Well-mannered people, of course, didn't resort to bad language but often the essence of their criticisms were of a primitive order. Even such a civilized and intelligent riding teacher as the late Barretto de Souza wrote in *The Rider and Driver,* as recently as 1933, about a picture of a jump in which the rider was sitting on the cantle of the saddle with legs stuck forward, as follows:

"*The Rider and Driver* could not have selected a better example to demonstrate the beauty and effectiveness of the Old Time Jumping Seat . . . even a person knowing nothing about riding cannot help admiring the grace and form . . . a horseman, of course, would realize that the lady's sitting close to the saddle did not prevent her mount's hindquarters from rising high above the obstacle." The jump in question was very much like the jumps in Pictures 6 **and** 7 of this book.

The absence of intelligent criticism, by the way, was a great hindrance in my work. Remarks like: "When using the Forward Seat the rider will fall off if the horse refuses or pecks on the jump" could not be taken seriously, while no really constructive ideas came from the enemy's camp. I often had to think of arguments myself, arguments against the method on which I was sold, and this was rarely a help. And I personally needed wise advice very badly. I have said already that not until 1930 did I have a clear-cut idea of the Forward Seat, and it took me another year or two before I learned how to produce pupils who sat well. For instance, my book JUMPING THE HORSE (published in 1931) has many illustrations of riders jumping with faulty positions which are accepted by the text as good ones. Excusing myself, I wish to point out the long road that all of us who were changing from the old to the new had to travel. For instance, in an old Fort Riley MANUAL OF EQUITATION (edit. 1929) the description of the seat begins with the following paragraph:

"The buttocks should be pushed well forward underneath the body and bear equally upon the middle of the saddle " (page 17).

While in the same manual rewritten a few years later, one reads:

"The fleshy parts of the buttocks are forced to the rear and in no case form part of the seat " (page 21).

The changes were coming fast.

"The steam that blows the whistle, doesn't turn the wheels," and so the activities of most of our critics were purely negative ones. With the growth of the popularity of Forward Riding, some of its many enemies felt that the time had come to change, associating themselves with something new but not yet completely with the Forward Seat; it probably seemed to them that the market wasn't quite ready for it. These people often advertised that they taught the "modified" or the "balanced" seat. There is nothing wrong with either of these terms. I, myself, teach a seat which is nothing else but a certain modification of the *original* Italian Forward Seat, while any good seat gives the rider a chance to be balanced with the horse in motion. The old classical seat also balanced the rider with the collected movements of his horse. So, of course, the seat which I teach is a balanced one also. Lt. Col. H. Chamberlin sometimes referred to the Forward Seat as the "balanced seat;" many graduates of the United States Cavalry School use the latter term. Many good riding teachers prefer it. All this is quite right, but many professionals use these terms as a smoke screen. So often the teaching camouflaged by these terms "modified" and "balanced" merely means a Classical seat, with shortened stirrups, for the gaits, combined with a sort of Forward Seat on the jump; the latter, naturally, mechanically poor. In other words, they today teach something like that with which I started twenty-four years ago, in 1927.

And today, when at least in jumping-classes one rarely sees anything but the Forward Seat (well or badly executed is another matter), many riders who use it prefer not to admit that their seat is the forward one. This peculiar situation is owing to their reluctance to admit that they actually are practicing something which they and the tradition of their riding group have long been against in theory. Occasionally well-wishing people suggest to me that I should, while continuing to teach what I do teach, disguise it all under another name.

In one of this summer's shows I pointed out a rider to a friend and asked: "Who is this girl? Her forward seat is as perfect as they come." My friend laughed and said: "Don't tell her; she will get really angry. She wants to believe that she doesn't ride forward."

This girl is not alone in her sentiments and, as I have said above, represents a group which is reluctant to admit that anyone can teach them anything and which likes to think that they have always instinctively known the best way to ride. Hence they cannot associate themselves with any theories promoted by someone who doesn't belong to their little circle.

There are several good technical reasons for using the name "Forward Seat." It goes well together with the other two terms of Forward Riding— "Forward Control" and "Forward Schooling," thus underlining the fact that the seat is just a part of a method. Have you ever heard anybody saying "Balanced Control" or "Balanced Schooling"? Of course not; these expressions do not make sense. Thus the term "Balanced Seat" tends to imply that the seat is something by itself, that riding begins and ends with it, or that modern cross-country riding is a combination of a new seat and old-fashioned methods of controlling and schooling. Besides this, the term "Forward Seat" also synchronizes well with the terms—"forward-balanced horse" and "forward-moving horse;" both terms being the foundation for the "Forward Seat."

There is another, purely ethical, reason for my using the term Forward Seat. This is the original term; all the early writers—McTaggart, Santini, Chamberlin, etc., used it. By now it is an historical term and I do not see why we should change it, thus making it harder to remember the work of the pioneers. The issue has already been obscured to the point where many forward riders of today don't even know who Caprilli was.

Looking back at my early days of teaching the seat to civilians, I can see a period of two childish phases, neither of which, luckily, lasted long. The first one consisted in using the methods for teaching troopers in the old Russian army. It was a sort of a drill, with a great deal of shouting, very short rest periods and little explanation. At the end of the hour the horses were steaming, the riders red in the face and perspiring; nobody learned much but all got a lot of exercise and were made happy. The second phase was the result of my preoccupation with the theoretical research which eventually resulted in my creating a method of riding and teaching. During this phase my poor pupils had to listen to lengthy discussions on the theory of riding, most of which were to them both incomprehensible and impractical. I don't see why so many of them took it so patiently.

By about 1931 my teaching was based on a sensible, practical method and from then on it was merely the matter of keeping on improving its efficiency. Throughout my teaching life I never stopped working in this direction, and even now, semi-retired from active teaching, I still work with riding teachers, some of whom, in their turn, cooperate with me by experimenting with my new teaching ideas. Just as an illustration: some years ago I came to the conclusion that a good position could be more quickly taught if the sitting trot, as one of the fundamental exercises, were to be entirely replaced by "a galloping position at a walk and slow trot." Miss Harriet H. Rogers and Mr. Clayton Bailey of Sweet Briar College, Va., Miss Elise White of Mexico, N. Y., as well as other teachers in women's colleges, all of them my former pupils, experimented with this change in exercises. After a couple of years of working with this new detail of the method they have come to the conclusion that they can now teach a correct position (secure enough for hacking at all gaits and jumping over obstacles 2½' high) in fifteen lessons. These riding teachers consider that this figure represents a gain of five hours in comparison with my older method which they previously used. I couldn't dream of anything like this in 1927 and I know many stables today where learning position is a never-ending process.

THE SEAT IN JUMPING

In 1932 Captain S. Kournakoff and I began our detailed study of the efforts of the horse in negotiating an obstacle. The idea behind this work was that a horse naturally jumps better free than under the rider (when the horse wants to), that no matter how good the rider is he is always a burden disturbing the horse by his weight and by his efforts to control him. This point of view, of course, can hardly be disputed and hence we thought that if we were to obtain a very clear picture of the natural efforts of a free horse jumping we would know how the rider should sit and behave in order to be the least possible hindrance to his mount. Deciding to make a very thorough study of the subject, we came to the conclusion that the question must be analyzed by at least three entirely different methods and the result of the analysis accepted as proven only if all three methods pointed to the same answer. I, for my part, did research by means of movie and instantaneous photography; Captain Kournakoff made a mathematical study of the jump under the laws of ballistics and we together worked on a rather ingenious method, suggested by Kournakoff, which consisted in the following experiments:

In the course of our study we were often referring to the shape of the horse's flight over the jump; to its length, to its height and to its curvature; in other words to the trajectory of the horse's flight. These trajectories differed with the horses; some took off very early and covered the obstacle with long and flat trajectories; others came near to the jump and went over it with short and sharply climbing trajectories. This word—trajectory—was always present in our conversation, but we actually had never seen the trajectory itself, in its purety, without being obscured by the mass of the horse's body. The word "trajectory" is defined in ballistics as follows: "An imaginary line described by a fixed point on a projectile in flight." The problem was to transform this imaginary line into a visible one, and this is how we did it:

A small, but very bright, electric bulb was attached to a part of the horse's body. The current was fed by a dry battery attached to the saddle. A camera was placed exactly on the line of the jump, which was installed in an artificially lighted ring. Shortly before the horse started for the jump the shutter of the camera was opened and was left open until the jump was completed, the result being that the fast moving body of the horse would hardly leave a blur (due to poor lighting conditions), while the light of the bulb would trace a clear-cut line on the plate. Thus the trajectory ceased to be "imaginary" (Pic. 17). Many most enlightening experiments were possible with this method. For instance, Picture 18 shows two trajectories—one of the shoulder and the other of the hip, made by two electric bulbs, attached accordingly to the horse's body. In this particular case both lines nearly merge, proving that the horse jumped in a state of almost perfect ballistic equilibrium. In many cases such perfect jumps of free horses could be duplicated under riders who used the Forward Seat well. On the other hand, as a rule, in the cases of riders in backward positions the trajectory of the hip would remain below the trajectory of the shoulder during the entire jump (Pic. 19). This was one of the proofs that the old-fashioned seat interfered with the natural jump of the horse.

We had approximately twenty horses of different types at our disposal and all through 1933 the progress of our research appeared in the form of articles in the magazine *The Rider and Driver*. In 1934 we published them as a book, the 142 pages of which are exclusively devoted to this one second and a half which is approximately the duration of an average jump. The name of the book, THE DEFENSE OF THE FORWARD SEAT, implies the results which we obtained in our study. It was published in a limited edition of three hundred odd copies, and is by now a bibliographical rarity which may be, in some ways, unfortunate, although it tickles my ego as a book-collector. The mathematical formulae which cover so many of its pages make it look rather frightening and for the average rider it is not the formulae but the conclusions which are of interest. On page 122, we read:

"The study of the horse's movements while leaping has shown us that not a single part of the horse's body remains passive during the jump; that all the major parts are active throughout the entire jump. These parts are: the hindquarters, the back, the forehand and the neck and head—practically the entire horse. Consequently, there is no place where the rider can be carried without interfering with the horse's natural and necessary movements. Evidently, all that the rider can do is to find the position which will be the least disturbing; this position must have the following elements:

"1) The rider's buttocks during the entire jump should not be in contact with the horse's back. The horse's back must be free to extend, contract, curve upward and cave in, following and uniting the actions of his hindquarters and forehand. A horse's back, abused by the constant banging of the rider's seat, loses its activity and this diminishes the activity of the rest of the body, especially of the hindquarters.

"2) The rider should not abuse the horse's forehand with his weight. The forehand must be free to produce thrusts and to rise when it is necessary.

"3) The rider should not keep the horse's neck and head held tightly. The 'balancer' must be free to take part in inner-motions in accordance with the rest of the movements of the body.

"In summing up what has been said: the rider, from the horse's viewpoint, must give complete freedom to the neck and head and keep his body away from the horse's back as well as from the forehand. Then only one point of the horse's body is left for the rider to use for the application of his weight. This is the area immediately behind the withers. This particular part of the horse, during the jump, is a kind of a pivot. Everything ahead of it is active, as well as everything behind it. This *center of oscillation* is the most passive part of the horse during the entire jump.

"The position of the rider, once assumed, must be preserved throughout the jump. Any change means a change of distribution of the rider's weight and is disturbing to the horse. Moreover, the position must be assumed long before the jump, so that, long before the take-off, the horse can balance his body according to the distribution of his rider's weight. No sudden changes should take place. A simple comparison to this is, that if any one of us had to take a jump while carrying a certain weight, we should be very careful to attach this weight to a part of our body which will be the least active (near the shoulder-blades) and to attach it so firmly that it will not disturb us during the leap."

Of course, one could arrive at the same conclusions without ballistics, movies and attaching electric bulbs to the horse's withers, but it gives one a comfortable feeling to know that all that was said above is substantiated by serious study and doesn't rest merely on a flight of the imagination.

I don't wish to imply that the technique of maintaining the Forward Seat on the jump which we recommended in this book is the best, but our research proved beyond a doubt that two things are to be striven for: 1) the Forward Seat, 2) passiveness of the rider during the jump and, if possible, during the approach. The latter can be only the result of a certain type of schooling. Perfect behavior, even on the part of a well-schooled horse, exists in books only and hence practical riding is based on compromises between the ideal passiveness and the often present necessity of controlling the horse during the approach. This is where the arguments can take place.

There are two points which seem to be generally argued. They are: 1) Should the rider sit or be out of the saddle during the approach to an obstacle? 2) Should the rider actively control his horse or should he be passive during the approach to an obstacle?

These points are so important that I feel that instead of merely giving my opinion on the subject it will be worth while to take your time to quote you from a few outstanding and somewhat differing authorities on the matter.

Here is how different schools of forward riding solve the problems of the rider's position and of the use of the aids during the approach to the jump:

1) The manual of the United States Cavalry School (ed. 1945) follows, almost word by word, the description of how to approach the obstacle which one finds in Lt. Col. H. Chamberlin's book—RIDING AND SCHOOLING HORSES (published in 1934). In part it reads:

". . . A horseman should always *sit down* in his saddle during the last fifteen or twenty yards of the approach . . . When seated for the approach, the buttocks should be well to the rear, the loins hollowed-out, the heels driven far down, and the calves and knees glued to the saddle and horse. The body should retain the same marked forward inclination that it has when standing in the stirrups. The tendency to sit up a little straighter should be avoided, since, from the moment of take-off until landing is completed, the rider should be standing in the stirrups. . . ." (page 150, the italics are mine).

"Normally, at about fifteen yards from the obstacle, after the horse has been rated and the rider is seated in balance, the legs should administer a strong squeeze with the calves, or, in dealing with a timid or unreliable hunter or jumper, a hard pinch with the spurs. The purpose of this leg action is to push the horse momentarily into his bit more firmly . . ." (page 151).

"During the last few yards of the approach, the rider must give the greatest attention to following the movements of the horse's head and neck with semi-relaxed shoulders, elbows, and hands. . . . Upon arriving at the point of take-off the tension (on the reins) should never be heavier than the normal feel, and with a trustworthy horse, it is preferable to have the lightest contact possible" (pages 149 and 150).

2) Lt. Col. H. Chamberlin in his second book TRAINING HUNTERS, JUMPERS AND HACKS (first published in 1938) on pages 130 and 131 (English edition of 1946—the italics are mine) says:

". . . Too often riders believe that they are assisting their horses over obstacles by using their hands and legs in various ways other than those to be described. The idea that one can 'place' his horse for each jump over a course of big and imposing obstacles is erroneous. Many really brilliant riders have tried it, but without complete success. The horse must do the jumping, and the less he is bothered, except to encourage and rate him, the better he will do.

". . . Do not stand in the stirrups during the immediate approach, but *allow your weight to settle on your thighs* by relaxing the knee joints . . . keep the reins very slightly stretched and be certain that the hands with relaxed fingers, accentuate the following of every oscillation of the horse's head and neck . . . his 'balancer' must have the absolute freedom that results from complete relaxation of fingers, elbows, and shoulder joints. . . .

"While approaching, your legs are continuously active with the intensity of action varying according to the sensibility of the horse, but always sufficient to sustain the speed required by the height and breadth of the obstacle. The best jumper in the world some day will refuse if the rider's legs are passive or weak . . . determined squeezing is usually sufficient encouragement."

3) The Italian Cavalry school, in Caprilli's lifetime, taught the following (my translation from Captain P. Rodzianko's book, published in Russia, in 1911):

"As a general rule the horse should not be urged approaching the jump, for it is too difficult to catch the moment . . . urging is permissible only when the horse, after starting to move toward the obstacle quietly and rhythmically, begins to slow down approaching it. The bigger the obstacle the greater should be the passiveness of the rider, for in such cases interference with the horse must be minimal and the horse must be given an opportunity to figure out the jump . . . some squeezing of the horse's sides should take place just before the jump so as to preserve the momentum. In general the horse must learn to jump willingly. It is considered that the horse is well schooled only when he doesn't require urging before the jump" (page 140).

4) In my book BE A BETTER HORSEMAN (published in 1941), which is written in conversational form, the following conversation takes place at the very end of page 67:

"ANNE: I heard somewhere that the rider should sit during the last two or three strides before the jump. But I see that you don't, and that when nearing the fence all of you are out of the saddle in a normal galloping position."

"MR. STRONG: This is because our horses are well-schooled. They go at the jump boldly and we don't have to push them. If I were to ride a poorly-schooled horse, in the habit of refusing, I would sit also in order to be able to use my legs better. As a result I would probably have difficulty in getting out of the saddle in time, and going forward sufficiently. I might even be left behind, and unquestionably would disturb my horse by the shifting of my weight; but it is often better to take the jump somehow than not to take it at all."

In short, I believe that there is little black or white in riding and that there may be cases when *sitting in the saddle* for the last 15 yards of approach, or merely *allowing the weight to settle in the thighs* (for one or two strides) by relaxing the knee joints may be reasonable and should be used. But I also think that minimizing the shifting of weight and minimizing control during the approach is very helpful for a boldly-going horse. My average teaching is based on the following considerations:

1) It is easy to accept a galloping position and to maintain it without any voluntary changes throughout the approach and the jump. Attempts to change this position even slightly, just before the take-off, too often result in the rider being left behind.

2) It is easier to school a horse to do the jumping himself than to teach a rider to control the horse *softly* during the approach. The latter is almost impossible with pupils who ride only three times a week.

3) Only a well-schooled horse will react correctly to the advanced rider's attempts to put him "on the bit" when starting for the jump. Seldom do I have an opportunity to work with such horses. Hence normally I teach only the continuous "soft contact."

I must be very wary in suggesting as a rigid rule urging the horse forward when approaching an obstacle, for I know that many of my readers have horses which go to the jump with too much impulse and ambition, and they should be "rated" rather with the hands than with the legs.

In the case of a well-schooled horse which knows the meaning of the aids and which approaches the jump boldly and quietly, the legs should be used to maintain the speed and impulse.

4) Attempts to follow with the arms through the air the balancing gestures of the horse's neck and head, in the case of the majority of riders result in banging the horse's back and jerking the reins or hanging on them. On the other hand, it is easy to teach riders to release the tension on the reins by moving the hands forward and putting them on the horse's neck, without transferring too much of the weight onto the forehand (without abusing the forehand).

Considering the above points, in my *normal teaching of the average pupil,* I have adhered to the following formula for riding during the approach (more artistic riding I reserve for some individuals only):

1) Approach the fence in the galloping position and maintain it during the jump itself.

2) The nearer the jump you are, the softer should become your contact with the horse's mouth (arms following the gestures of the horse's neck).

3) About two or three strides before the jump move your hands forward, so that the reins *gradually* become loose, and place your hands on the horse's neck, firmly enough so that they will not jerk upward or backward. (Loose reins must give plenty of room for the balancing gestures by the neck.) Beware of abusing the horse's front with the weight of your body. If, *later on,* you can learn to follow with your arms the extension of the horse's neck through the air, so much the better.

4) About four or five strides before the jump close in your calves as strongly as you feel necessary to maintain the desired speed and impulse.

5) If, on some jumps, you feel that the squeeze which you can give from standing in the stirrups is insufficient then *sink down on your thighs or simply sit down in the saddle* so as to be able to use the legs with more force. However, consider such cases undesirable emergencies.

6) If your horse habitually slows down before the jump, refuses, runs out, pulls, rushes etc., he should be schooled or reschooled (as the case may be), which is the only sound way to cope with such situations. Attempts to correct faulty jumping merely through dexterity in riding never bring permanent and fully satisfying results.

Riders who lead their horses to the jump between their legs and hands, place them and indicate the moment of take-off, doing it all rather softly and winning consistently, appear periodically in the horse shows. To me, a teacher of amateur riders, such a technique is unacceptabe as a method. The best of such performances are based on intensive schooling, the riding talent of these horsemen and their extremely cool nerve; all this can hardly be applied to an average rider. But many people diagnose such cases differently and boil down the winning technique of such performances to a few simple and incorrect assumptions. They naively say: "To ride as well we must sit down approaching the jump, body erect; collect the horse; place the horse by checking him strongly a couple of times; during the last stride suddenly release the reins and give a strong leg-signal to jump. That is all." All this done on half-schooled horses, by half-educated riders leads to plastically ugly jumps made by horses with their mouths wide open from the hard pull of the reins and, such performances, whether winning or not, are unnatural, ugly and one may say cruel. But just the same, such performances are often the winning ones. The statement that bad riding may sometimes have a better chance of winning than good riding may seem senseless, but let me give you an illustration of such a possibility. Once I had a mare in schooling who, being bold but unambitious and having excellent balance and good agility, eventually developed into a sound but not brilliant jumper. It was rather pleasant to watch her go over courses not higher than 4'; a good, even gallop at the approach, well-figured take-off, closely-figured jumping efforts, the obstacle negotiated plastically. But, if ridden well by a nondisturbing rider who allowed her the full liberty of going and of figuring the obstacle herself, she would get careless and one or two knocked, or at least touched, fences would be the rule. But the rider could considerably increase the chances of a clean performance by up-setting her a stride or two before the jump by a strong pull on the reins or a sudden kick with the legs or by quickly switching the weight backward in the saddle. Then, feeling her balance upset, she would become fright-ened and would leap the fence in some ugly, awkward manner but with a strong effort which would leave a good foot to spare.

The ever-present desire of so many riders, novices among them, to imitate winners is often disturbing to the riding teacher. Every new star, no matter how unorthodox his method, may start a small mutiny among certain pupils. It is very hard to combat at the time, for to many people winning is the best argument, and it is only with the years that those who have gained some perspective and remember the rise and fall of idols may realize what a false scent they were following. In the course of my own life, I can think of half a dozen teams, besides many more individ-ual riders, who successively rose to supremacy and fell into obscurity. In all these cases of teams but one (the details of which I don't happen to know), I can trace their success to an unusually able head of the team, rather than to the method. And when I refer to the talent of the captain of the team, I don't merely mean that in every case he was an outstanding horseman; I primarily mean a *very clever*, energetic and ambitious person.

I am a horseman rather than a sportsman and hence never could really get excited by the fact that a certain horse, after running for a mile, finished one length ahead of the rest of the field. Nor am I taken off my feet by the fact that a horse has won a class after taking, let us say, twenty or thirty obstacles without a fault, while half a dozen other horses lost just because they cleared only nineteen or twenty-nine obstacles. Naturally from the point of view of a collection of trophies the difference is enor-mous, but from the point of view of riding there may be none. The impres-siveness of such winning begins when it can be repeated day in and day out, and to explain it I believe one has to search for human ingenuity rather than for the points of a certain method. No method can aim at making great riders or great horses; they are made in heaven. But any sound method raises the performances of a multitude of average riders and average horses. And this is precisely what Forward Riding has ac-complished.

Since first writing this book I have come to realize that a term which I frequently employ, "average rider," is apt to be taken in rather a different way from that in which I meant it. "Average," as I use it here, has no belitting connotation; it simply means any good rider outside the excep-tional ones; it applies to people who have no intention of participating in international competitions or of making a life career of riding, who have only the average amount of time to devote to riding—it means the usual (actually or potentially) good rider, not the usual poor rider.

CHAPTER VI

Learning the Forward Seat

BY ALEXIS WRANGEL

When I had my first opportunity to do much riding two courses of action lay open to me. One was to study, starting from scratch under a competent teacher; the other to get on the horse and have fun across hill and dale, trusting that time, and falls, and other experiences would eventually teach me to ride—as so many of my hunting acquaintances who had ridden "all their lives" had assured me they would.

What prompted me to choose the first alternative was the mental comparison between the magnificently smooth and masterful riding of young graduates from military cavalry schools, Riley, Tor di Quinto, Hanover, etc., and the painful performances of so many self-made horsemen with long experience in the hunting field, shows and elsewhere. The loose, sloppy seat, arms and legs flopping, did not seduce me, nor was I enthralled by the immediate and brusque transition from a long, floating rein to a sharp pull and inevitable jerk when something unforeseen happened and the rider rectified his position by hanging on to the reins. So I decided to study riding seriously.

My first study was under the instruction of a very forward-seat-minded teacher; but it was of a distinctly exaggerated character.

The main features of this type of seat were: a fixed knee—the pivot of the rider's position—a very short stirrup with the lower leg drawn well back—depressed heel with slightly turned-out sole—a very hollow loin—the rider's torso leaning *always* forward. The shoulder, knee and toe of the rider always formed a straight line (Pic. 20).

The disadvantages of this seat were: at the gallop my crotch was completely out of the saddle, consequently I only felt my horse through the knee; because of the short stirrup I could only use my heel and spur when requesting additional forward motion—progressive squeezing with the calf was almost impossible due to the immobile position of the lower leg wedged between the stirrup iron and the fixed knee. The short stirrup length also made a marked forward inclination of the body imperative at the walk and trot in order not to sit on the cantle of the saddle. In the event of an unsuccessful jump I did not have sufficient grip area to maintain my position and, pivoting on the knees, wound up occasionally on the horse's head (Pic. 21).

The advantages of such a seat were markedly pronounced at the gallop

Pic. 20.   An exaggerated, mechanically incorrect, forward seat. Too short stirrups
are the beginning of the trouble.

Pic. 21.   Pivoting on the knees creates insecurity, particularly on a difficult jump.

and over jumps on a free-going and willing horse when no struggle or special efforts were required to control him or to make him jump.

My second teacher, a very talented rider himself, rode the old classical seat adapted to modern methods of riding and jumping. He made me lengthen my stirrups, ride much more erect, and sit deeply in the saddle when galloping and approaching jumps. The lower leg was not drawn back from the knee, and the back was relaxed, the loins being slack. My teacher's explanations were that my horse could at all times be held between hands and legs and I could thus have complete control while, with a soft, flexible spine, I followed the horse's movement by sitting deeply in the saddle and feeling the horse with my seat   (Pic. 22).

The greatest disadvantage of this seat was that I was always slightly behind my horse, and compensating movements of my body were constantly required to catch up with the horse's movements. In jumping this was most apparent and often caused overriding—i.e. strenuous efforts of legs, hands, and body. This created interference with the horse's strides in approaching the jump, while the violent lurch forward of my body upset him at the take-off.

This seat did teach me to follow through with my arms during the jump, because, however behind I might be with my body, my arms had to give in order not to jab the horse in the mouth. Also, with a sticky horse, I could use my legs with great force as I sat deeply in the saddle and drove the horse forward.

With a forward-going horse the disadvantages of this seat were very strongly felt—the exaggerated forward seat was much easier, particularly at the gallop and over jumps.

With sticky, reluctant, behind-the-bit horses the deep seat was more satisfactory, but required skill from the rider, split-second timing and much rhythm and suppleness. When my timing was the slightest bit off disaster was inevitable—I was left behind   (Pic. 23).

In reviewing in my mind these two methods of riding it struck me that each stressed a certain principle, and the two points formed a sharp contrast.

The exaggerated forward seat demanded the absolute freedom of the horse, whereas the other method put all its emphasis on control by the rider. When I gave the horse complete liberty, assuming for that purpose an attitude devoid of security and power to control, I sacrificed everything for the betterment of the horse's freedom of action. Were the horse a mere automaton controlled by pushbuttons this would be the only natural way to ride. Unfortunately—or fortunately, whichever way you like to look at it—this is not so; efficient control is necessary when riding and most essential when schooling. This lack of control was the main defect of the exaggerated forward seat to which I was first exposed. However, when in the second method of riding which I subsequently studied control became predominant, and my seat subjugated entirely to it, I found

Pic. 22.   This is one of many versions of an old-fashioned seat. Many riders still use it at gaits and then shift to some sort of forward seat for jumping.

Pic. 23.   It takes an acrobatic rider to change quickly from an old-fashioned seat on the approach to the forward seat over the jump. The majority of riders are left behind.

that forward free movement (the sine qua non of modern riding) suffered distinctly.

When I first started my studies with Captain Littauer the lines to be drawn between these two influences were not clear in my mind—I tended to jump from one extreme to the other. Gradually, as Captain Littauer corrected my seat and worked on my control, the two opposites came into balance. It is my personal opinion that the system which draws the most from both these schools without subtracting from either is the best one for all normal purposes; and my intention is to describe in this chapter Captain Littauer's method of teaching the correct seat—which, in my estimation, blends into unity the two conflicting factors.

All through my equestrian studies it has been my impression that lots of words in lengthy, loose sentences—even when coming from the lips of an expert—seem only to confuse the pupil.

When a novice is told to put the horse on the bit and approach the jump riding in balance, it means as much to him as Einstein's theories to the African bushman. However, if the advice is offered thus: "Weight in stirrups, squeeze with legs, hollow loin, light feel on reins" things begin to look clearer.

In the course of my studies with Captain Littauer I have found that his indications as to the execution of any particular movement on horseback (i.e. position of the rider) were boiled down to sentences where each word meant something quite precise. Therefore I have decided to reproduce these sentences, in order to show as concisely as possible what one must try to achieve when walking, trotting, galloping and jumping. It *can* be done differently; after all, many experts win shows rounding their backs with heels in the air. If you can ride and jump better standing on your head—go ahead and do so, more credit to you! But if you are a novice, with an average amount of equestrian ability, I think the following method is the simplest.

Capt. Littauer's instructions are printed in Roman, my own reactions are in italic:

1) Place yourself in the saddle so that the crotch of the breeches touches the pommel.

2) Sit with pelvis tipped forward, not on the buttocks; push knees forward and down (Pic. 24).

Executing the above commands I felt strongly wedged into the saddle.

Draw the lower leg back so that the stirrup leathers are vertical (Pic. 25) or slightly behind the vertical.

4) Then the stirrups will come directly under the body and the rider can at will stand in them as he would on the floor.

When doing this I felt that were the horse to be suddenly withdrawn from under me and my body lowered in that same position to the ground I would find myself standing on the ground, squarely on both my heels.

5) Put part of your weight in the stirrup and, pulling your heels down, feel as if the weight in the stirrups actually went into the heels (Pic. 26).

When this happened the muscles in my calf stretched while those in the thigh were contracted—this made my leg hard and I was able to grip the saddle more strongly.

6) Tilt your torso forward from the hips—until your body gets balanced in the stirrups (Pic. 27).

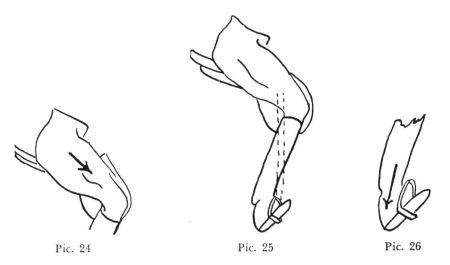

Pic. 24   Pic. 25   Pic. 26

Then I realized that with only a small inclination forward of my body I was united with my horse moving at a walk.

7) When leaning forward keep your torso in a normal, alert position with chest open and head up. Push your buttocks back toward the cantle (no weight on them).

When my head was up and my chest open my hollowed loins started pressing the pelvis forward wedging it further into the saddle. With an alert position of the torso I found it easy to balance myself and to remain united with the horse in motion. After I was able to execute the above points I found myself about half standing in the stirrups with a very springy body which hinged on three main springs (in the hips, knees and ankles). When rounding my back the whole structure of my body collapsed into the saddle. I found myself sitting on the buttocks, and, although per-

haps in balance in the saddle, *I was not any more in balance* with the horse (Pic. 28).

8) Rider's weight should be distributed through three springs A, B, C (hip, knee and ankle). Tension in these springs should increase with increase of the shocks of locomotion, and reach a maximum in jumping (Pic. 29, I, II, III).

I felt that the benefits of these springs could be lost by: a) greatly decreasing the weight in the stirrups. Without using the stirrups the tension in those springs was completely gone. b) If I pinched the saddle strongly with my knees the flow of weight into the stirrups was partially cut off.

9) At the walk, trot and canter, when the horse behaves, use the grip

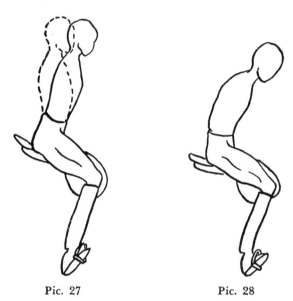

Pic. 27   Pic. 28

which merely consists of a permanent, effortless contact between the saddle and the lower thighs, inner surfaces of the knees, and upper calves (Pic. 30).

10) During the gallop or jumping, or when the horse misbehaves, increase the frictional grip with a muscular effort of these three parts of the leg.

Having ridden in the past that type of seat in which the fixed knee was the basic part of the rider's position, I find that I retain to this present day a certain stiffness due to a harder grip of the knee than is warranted under normal circumstances.

When starting a gallop and approaching a jump—hence changing from a contact grip to a strong one—I found that unless I had my weight well into the stirrups the action of gripping strongly squeezed me up and out of the saddle. A constant strong grip for a lengthy period made me stiffen up. Little by little I learned to use the strong grip only in those instants when it was really necessary.

11) For better gripping and in order to bring the upper calf in contact with the saddle:—a) keep your toes open about 30 degrees; b) hold your stirrup so that the foot touches the inside bar—and press more on the

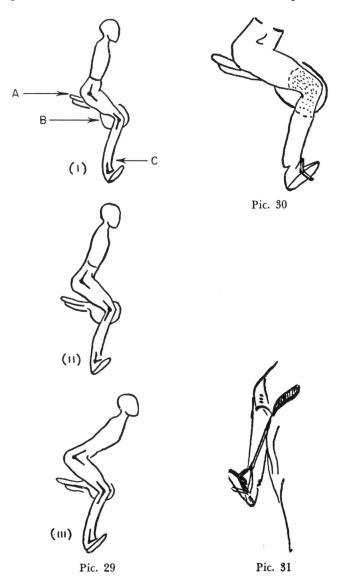

Pic. 30

Pic. 29   Pic. 31

inside of the stirrup than the outside. This may turn your sole slightly outward (Pic. 31).

With point a) I had no trouble whatsoever from the outset, the turned out toes came naturally; as regards point b) the stirrup remained in the correct position only when I had learned to subordinate gripping to balancing with my weight in the stirrups. With insufficient weight in the stirrups the stirrups moved along the sole of the foot.

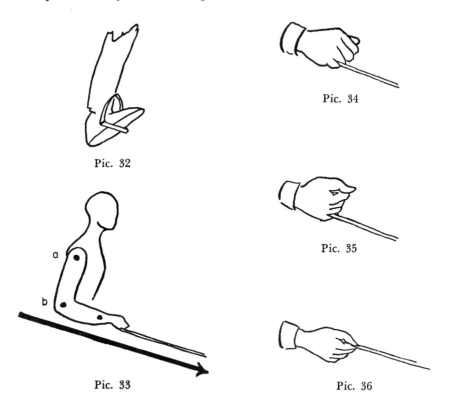

Pic. 34

Pic. 32

Pic. 35

Pic. 33   Pic. 36

12) Hold your stirrup under the ball of your foot or home, whichever gives you a better position of the lower leg. The stirrup leathers then lie flat-pressed against the side of your boot just inside the shinbone; this binding effect of the stirrup leathers adds to the stability of the rider's lower leg wedged against them. Never hold it under the toe—it's too easy to lose, and with this hold it is hard to use the stirrup as a base of support (Pic. 32).

Personally I found it more comfortable to ride with the stirrups home; I found it easier thus to press on the inner tread of the stirrup, as well as to keep the stirrups in the correct position under my body in order to put my weight into them.

13) Relax your arms in the shoulder, elbow and wrist joints. Bend your arms at the elbows, keeping the latter slightly ahead of the torso.

Maintain a straight line of action from elbow to horse's mouth (Pic. 33), at least when special efforts of control don't require for a moment a different attitude of the arms. In order to hold the reins on both sides of the horse's neck without touching it, the rider's hands will have to be approximately 10″ apart. The hands should be approximately parallel to the horse's shoulders (Pic. 34), not thumbs upward as shown in Pic. 35 . This attitude permits a natural, unconstrained position of the wrist.

I was well along in my riding studies before I learned to ride on contact with my arms following the horse's mouth at all times, and before I realized the importance of keeping the hands well apart and away from the horse's neck.

The snaffle rein should enter the rider's hand between the ring and little fingers (or under the little finger, whichever you like better), and emerge between thumb and forefinger. There is another way of holding the reins known as the driving rein in which the snaffle rein enters the rider's hand between forefinger and thumb, and emerges from under the little finger. This attitude permits very soft contact, and can be profitably used when no forceful action of the hand is necessary (Pic. 36).

As we are dealing solely with riding in a snaffle bridle we need only point out how to hold four reins without going further into this most delicate subject. The snaffle reins are on the outside entering under the rider's little finger, whereas the curb reins enter between the ring and little fingers. Both snaffle and curb reins emerge between the index finger and the thumb.

Action of the hand will be discussed in Chapter X.

14) A saddle constructed for an old-fashioned seat will require a struggle by the rider to maintain a forward position.

The following two principal points of a properly constructed modern saddle enable the rider to maintain the forward seat easily (Pic. 37):

1—The dip of the saddle near the front combined with a low pommel and raised cantle.

2—The skirts well advanced to permit a forward position of the knee.

I happen to be tall and furthermore equipped with a long torso, consequently it is of great importance for me, personally, to distribute my weight correctly so as to be in balance over the stirrups. Unless I have a correctly fitted saddle permitting my knee to go well forward with my crotch in the throat of the saddle I find that the efforts I have to make to maintain my balance are such that they interfere with that relaxed freedom conducive to good control. The more I advanced in riding, and details of control became important, the more irked I became when constrained to allot part of my efforts to maintaining my position in a badly built saddle. Riding forward in an old-fashioned saddle Pic. 38 seems to me as efficient as playing billiards with a baseball bat.

Three different lengths of stirrup leathers may be used in the course of riding and jumping (Pic. 39, I, II, III).

a) Fairly long stirrup leathers for schooling work in the ring, where a deeper seat and greater leg mobility may be necessary.

b) 1 to 2 holes shorter for hunting and field riding, permitting greater spring while keeping sufficient depth of seat for better control and to avoid fatigue during long stretches of riding.

c) 1 to 2 holes shorter for jumping in the ring over large obstacles on a well-schooled jumper—both security and control being sacrificed for

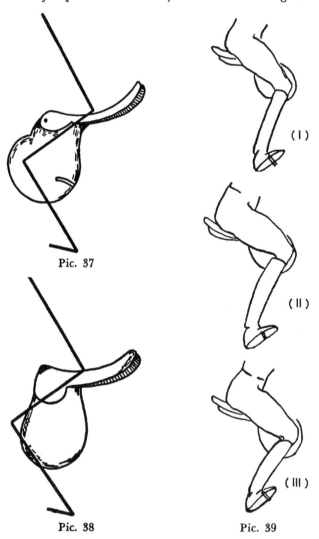

Pic. 37

Pic. 38

(I)

(II)

(III)

Pic. 39

greater spring and a more forward position of the rider. However, too short stirrups are a fallacy; for though they give stability to the rider's lower legs they do not give stability to his overall position.

I learned that length of stirrup leather is a most flexible question. Not only did I find that I needed to alter the length of my leathers for different types of riding (schooling, jumping, etc.), but also that the conformation and gaits of different horses made riding easier on longer or shorter stirrups depending on the particular horse.

Throughout this book you will often read that the forward seat unites the rider with the horse moving ahead in a forward balance. If you read Chapter III, you will know that the above phrase is much more intricate than it sounds—for the horse's balance is fluid, and correspondingly fluid must perforce be the rider's seat. The illustrations depicting the mechanics of the forward seat should be accepted with the understanding that they all represent really a moment—an ideal moment—but *not* a movement. In actuality neither the horse nor the rider are static; a slow-motion picture camera shows the split seconds during which both rider and horse are caught in such a position as would not seem true to the naked eye. All the above is said here to caution you not to be a wooden soldier and freeze in position as a rider in your favorite picture. After all, a good seat is primarily important as one of the means of *riding* well. At first when learning how to ride you must think about your position all the time, and in this period of your learning your picture matters a great deal. But later, when the contour of your position is correct—when your spring, grip, balance, etc. are working effectively—then there are only two criteria of your position; a) are you in fluid balance and rhythm with your horse or not? b) does your seat enable you to control your horse efficiently?

Soon after you have begun the study of position you will learn how to stay with the horse at an even trot or even canter, or over a low obstacle. It will take you considerably longer to remain with the horse during sharp increases or decreases of speed—abrupt stops, sharp turns, violent lateral movements, particularly when produced unexpectedly for you. In this respect you have to train yourself by practicing these movements at will.

Having explained in the previous pages the mechanics of the rider's seat let us examine the ways of applying them to the walk, trot, canter, gallop and jump.

The Walk (from the halt) (Pic. 40): Sitting in the correct position previously depicted the rider leans slightly forward from the hips in anticipation of the horse's forward movement, so that when this movement occurs he may not be left behind. His whole attitude may be described as one of "Alert Relaxation." Apart from the slight tightening of the muscles in his back helping to maintain a hollow loin, and the muscles in his ankle, all the other muscles are relaxed—the frictional grip of the knees and calves is very light, merely in contact with the saddle skirts. The greatest freedom in all the structure of the rider's position is claimed by the shoulders, arms, wrists and fingers. The arms follow the balancing gestures of the horse's head and neck in piston-like motion. The three hinges of Pic. 33 are completely free in their motions, just as free as ball bearings in some highly sensitive and well-greased machine. (This point will be taken up in the chapter on INTERMEDIATE CONTROL.) If anything sudden were to happen, the rider in a split second would have a very strong position by stiffening from the waist down—thighs, knees, calves will then grip strongly—but while just walking quietly the rider

Pic. 40. A walk. (*See text*)

relies mostly on his balance. To see whether he is really in balance with the horse, the rider should try the following experiment; without perceptible increase of inclination in his torso and without any lurching up or forward he rises slightly in his stirrups and stays up while the horse walks, without toppling forward or collapsing backwards. The rider's weight is then supported by the stirrups, and this attitude is given stability by the tension in the three springs of Pic. 29, I, II, III. This, incidentally, is also the rider's position during the upward beat of the posting trot and at the gallop (with added grip)—but more about this later.

Having started my riding on forward seat principles I became quickly accustomed to this attitude, and had really no trouble preserving it during long stretches of riding. However, many of my friends who had "gone forward" after many years in the saddle along classical lines have complained to me that they get stiff backs from keeping the loin caved in, and stiff ankles from having their weight in the stirrups. It is true that complete relaxation of all the rider's muscles and joints can be had when walking with the leg hanging down and the back slack, but this practice makes the horseman "ride heavy" (a dead weight on the horse's back). So, while indulging occasionally in the slothful luxury of riding like a sack to rest one's weary bones, I think that all should give a thought to the poor animal for whom this way of riding is just that much more work. (Especially at fast gaits, or during really long walking periods, particularly if the rider is heavy.)

Pic. 41. The trot. (*See text*)

The Trot (‖Pic. 41): There are two ways for the rider to behave at the trot —to sit or to post. It will be easier to understand the difference when the mechanics of the gaits are examined. The trot is a movement of two beats—each beat is constituted by the movement of a diagonal pair of legs. This movement throws the rider up, and if, when getting thrown up, the rider makes no effort of his own his weight will sink almost immediately back into the saddle and will again be bumped upwards by the advance of the next diagonal. If, on the other hand, after being thrown up by one diagonal the rider himself *slightly* prolongs the forward and upward movement of his torso, then he will still be in the air as the next diagonal moves forward and he will return to the saddle in time to be caught by the diagonal that gave him the initial thrust. Thus, when posting, the bumps are cut in half, which makes it easier for both horse and rider. The posting trot is used exclusively when hacking or hunting. The

sitting trot, however, is sometimes of great advantage when schooling a horse, at which time it permits a constant and consequently greater
use of the leg; for when posting the horse can be urged forward only at
the moment when the rider has returned to the saddle, as at the rising
beat the rider's legs are active in maintaining his position. Therefore,
when posting, the rider can squeeze the horse's sides once in every stride.
During the sitting trot, however, with a certain dexterity of the legs the
horseman can urge the horse (if necessary) half-a-dozen times in one stride.

Obviously during the posting trot the work is not evenly distributed on
both diagonals; in order to equalize this work the rider must change the
diagonal once in a while, while trotting for any length of time. To do this
he should sit out two beats instead of a normal one. Due to the fact that
the horse's body is not equilaterally developed one diagonal may be the
easier to post on, and it will, therefore, be easy for the rider to recognize
on which diagonal he may be posting.

Now, having explained the actual working of the trot, let us see how
the rider will apply his seat to it. Again—just as when moving from the
halt into the walk—he will lean forward from his hip joints in anticipation of the increase in forward motion; if he desires to sit the trot his
seat will not deviate much from that of the walk. Again only spring C
(the ankle) will be tightened; the other two springs (hip and knee) will
merely act as well-oiled hinges—the tension in them will be minimal. The
calf and thigh muscles will be relaxed almost as much as during the walk.
This will not be the case during the posting trot, for there springs A and
B will work in conjunction, opening on the rider's upward movement,
and closing as the rider sinks back into the saddle. The tension in these
two springs will have the effect of tightening slightly the calf and thigh
muscles. The rider's loin must be hollowed, and his toe must never be
ahead of the knee. (This has been pointed out in previous pages dealing
with the mechanics of the Forward Seat.) During the posting trot the application of these two principles is most essential, as deviation from either
one of these two rules means posting on the cantle of the saddle—behind
the motion of the horse. This results in banging the horse's back each
time the rider returns to the saddle. The forward inclination of the rider's
torso, the fact that his loin is hollow and his knee ahead of his toe will
make the rider post *forward* and up, instead of just up and down.

The experienced rider when posting will let the horse's movement carry
him up with little effort on his part, just sufficient to skip a beat. He will
post close to the saddle! The beginner on the other hand will have to
propel himself upward, consciously rising in his stirrups to the rhythm of
the trot. There is one exception to this rule; when riding with short
stirrups for ring jumping or fast cross country work even a good rider
will not be able to post close to the saddle, but will have to rise somewhat
higher in the stirrups when posting.

Having had my early riding on short stirrups with a very forward inclination of the body I used to post as just described, and it took me quite a while to master a workmanlike trot close to the saddle. I subsequently found the latter essential when schooling horses.

The Canter (Pic. 42): The rider's position at the canter is similar to that of the sitting phase at the trot. Consequently when starting from the trot into the canter the rider will usually stop posting during the transition. This also will enable him to apply his aids more effectively. (See chapter on INTERMEDIATE CONTROL.) He will have a forward inclination of his body just as when doing the sitting trot, and will maintain his loin under muscular control well hollowed out; his buttocks

Pic. 42.   The canter.   *(See text)*

therefore will be pushed out. The ankle spring will be cocked, but the knee and hip springs will have little tension; in other words they will be again (as in the sitting trot) functioning more as smooth working hinges. The horse's head and neck sway considerably at the canter, and the rider's arms will follow with piston-like motions centered on the two free-playing hinges (a and b, Pic. 33).

My main difficulty when cantering lay in getting the knee and hip spring to cease functioning as such and become free moving hinges—for otherwise with tension in knees and hips the position, though very springy and strong and well suited to galloping and jumping, is devoid of that relaxation which I subsequently found most necessary when schooling in the ring.

The Gallop (Pic. 43): The gallop is a fast gait, the shocks of locomotion increase considerably—therefore the rider's position must be such as to give the horse plenty of freedom, and yet give the rider a firm and secure position on board the horse. At the gallop the horse uses his forelegs as a pole vaulter would use his stick—the hindquarters propel the horse forward by a series of strong pushes against the ground. The rider must be completely out of the saddle although low above it, well forward, and in no way interfere with the horse's "motor"—his hindquarters. The rider's position is, as mentioned above, similar to the suspension period of the posting trot, except for a stiffer torso and stronger grip through thighs, knees and upper calves. When starting a gallop the rider will get

Pic. 43.   The gallop. (*See text*)

out of the saddle and lean forward from his hips keeping as always his loin hollowed. He will shorten his reins in order to maintain the straight line from elbow to bit conducive to efficient control. Tension in the three springs, hip, knee and ankle (Pic. 29) will increase considerably, and his whole position will become more springy and tense. When increasing the grip at the gallop the rider should first rise in the stirrups and markedly pull his heels down, then grip; otherwise, if he were to grip first, he would merely be squeezing himself upward and backward due to not having the proper weight in his stirrups.

The nearest way I can describe my feeling of this tightening in my whole body is to compare it with the movement when taking a dive from a spring-board. The diver is then tense as a coiled spring. This I found much resembled the situation when galloping. The difference is in the fact that in riding the shoulders, arms, wrists and fingers will continue to relax—except when deliberately stiffening to control the horse. It became clear to me what Captain Littauer meant in saying that the Forward Seat in galloping and jumping is not a seat at all—it is a dynamic attitude.

Up and Down Hill (Pic. 44): The forward seat in approximately its galloping manifestation should be maintained when moving up or down hill, although the reasons in each instance are different, and the position of the rider differs in details when going up or down. When going up hill the rider must be off the saddle to free the horse's back and thus give free play to the hindquarters which propel the horse upwards. The reins must be completely loose (looping) so as not to interfere with the balancing

Pic. 44. Going downhill. (*See text*)

gestures of the horse's head and neck. If the hill is very steep the rider must hold the mane to prevent himself sinking back into the saddle.

When going down a sharp incline the horse is pulled down by its weight and prevents itself from falling by using its forelegs as props. The horse's hindquarters are of no assistance whatsoever, for the croup being close to the ground the hindlegs are cramped under the belly and cannot be of any value as supports. Due to the fact that the cannon bones of the hindlegs are at times parallel to the incline (on very steep inclines) the horse's hoofs cannot grip the ground to steady the hindquarters, which may easily sway to the left or right, even overturning the horse. This is the reason why it is very important to go straight down sharp inclines. All this means that the hindquarters and back of the horse are in no position to support the rider's weight—they have trouble enough fending for themselves. Hence the rider must stay off the saddle. On the other hand, the loading of the forehand if anything helps the forelegs to be efficient props, for the greater the pressure exerted by them against the ground, the steadier will be the descent. The reins must be loose and to help the steadiness of the seat the rider should put his hands on the crest of the horse's neck. Due to the angle of the rider's body in relation to the ground and the hands pressed against the horse's neck, the rider's back will be slightly rounded.

All the above statements about rider and horse pertain, in milder form, to movement up or down smaller gradients.

Increase and Decrease of Speed: You will see from Picture 29, I, II, & III that with the increase of velocity the rider will increase the amount of weight in the stirrups, and his body will lean further forward in order to unite with the motion of the horse. In decreasing the velocity the reverse will be true—the rider will gradually straighten his torso—however, he should be careful not to get back of the vertical, where he will be out of balance and consequently behind the horse (Pic. 45, I and II). There will, however, be cases when he might find himself back of the vertical, such as when the horse bucks or when some sort of fright occurs. But these are exceptions, and the golden rule is: BE ALWAYS SLIGHTLY AHEAD OF THE PERPENDICULAR. This applies to the horse moving in forward balance and the rider being correspondingly in a forward position. However, when the horse shifts to a central balance, such as when moving at collected gaits, the rider must make his center of gravity concur with that of the horse. He will therefore sit erect, and there may be times when his torso will even be behind the vertical. If he remains forward he will be just as much off balance in regard to the horse as the rider who sits deep and erect on a horse moving in forward balance (Pic. 46, I & II). The ability of the rider to change from forward to central position in perfect accord with the horse is that fluid balance about which we spoke before in this chapter.

But there are cases when the horse switches his weight so quickly and so unexpectedly that the rider can hardly be asked to remain united with him from the very beginning. Take, for instance, a last minute refusal before a jump; if it is completely unforeseen by the rider, then at the precise moment when the horse stops the rider is all set to go forward and in most cases will be caught in the forward position. What then will keep him from toppling forward? Weight in the heels, grip, and a hollow, tense loin may be the three steadying factors. The rider's head should be up and his chest out. The rider's head plays its part in his equilibrium; if his head is down then his shoulders are rounded and as a result his loin will become slack and he may crumple forward, collapsing on the horse's neck. Last minute placing of his hands on the horse's neck will also help.

When writing these lines on sharp decrease of gaits, I reminisce about refusals I have had in the normal course of jumping. The times I came off were not the ones when I remained forward, loin hollow, head up and weight in the stirrups. However strong the forward inclination of my body, refusals then had no further consequence. But when, through some mishap or other, the refusals occurred when my head was down and my back round, or when the heels were higher than the toes; then whether

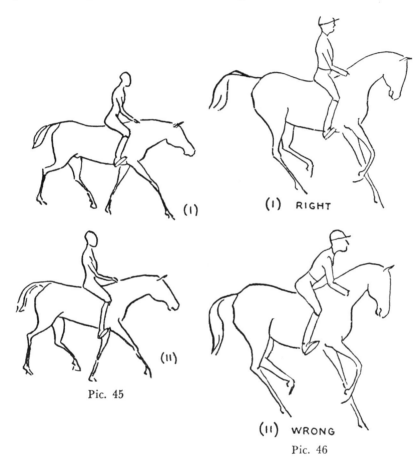

(1)

(1) RIGHT

(II)

Pic. 45

(II) WRONG

Pic. 46

sitting forward or back, I still paid the penalty—and if I did not find myself on the ground, I usually ended up tenderly embracing the horse's neck with my face buried in a not too tender mane.

Backing: The rider's position does not change from that at the walk when backing the horse. There is absolutely no sound reason for the rider to lean backwards—by so doing he merely will press on the horse's back, thereby reacting adversely on the movement of the horse's hindquarters.

Turning, Circling: When moving fast along a curved line (the rider will

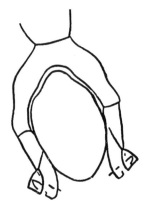

Pic. 47

lean inward toward the turn; he should do so by merely putting his
weight predominantly on the inside stirrup, not by twisting the hips. This
allows the rider to synchronize his weight with that of the horse, as the
horse itself leans inward when turning at speed   (Pic. 47).

Jumping(Pics. 48, 49 and 50): A jumping position is fundamentally the same
as the position for galloping, but with more abrupt and more conspicuous
momentary changes in the rider's attitude. This fluidity in the rider's position is the result of constant shifting of balance on the part of the horse
and of changes of speed during the jump. The galloping position may be
preserved almost intact only over a low jump taken at a high speed.

Pic. 48.   The approach to the jump.   (*See text*)

Primary objects of correct position:

1) To remain in balance and rhythm with the horse.
2) Not to interfere with the jumping efforts of the horse's back, and hence with the efforts of his hindquarters.
3) Not to interfere with the jumping efforts of the forehand.
4) Not to interfere with balancing gestures of the horse's head and neck. (They are, by the way, synchronized with the efforts of the back.)
5) To maintain a firm position conducive to control if necessary.

Pic. 49.   The apex of the jump. (*See text*)

In early jumping, while the seat lacks balance over the obstacle, assist yourself by placing your hands on the crest of the middle part of the horse's neck (reins loose). If this is not sufficient and you are still unable to stay forward hold onto the mane   (Pic. 51). With the horse galloping toward the jump quietly yet boldly, place hands on the neck three to four strides before the jump and execute the following four points:

1) Weight in the stirrups (galloping position). Feel your weight going into the heels.

When putting my weight strongly into the stirrups I think it most imperative not to shove my lower leg forward, but to concentrate on having the point of the knee ahead of the toe. Pressure against the stirrups with a lower leg stuck out means only that the rider's weight is back on the cantle instead of well forward. I think that the feeling of complete independence of the rear portion of the saddle before, during and after the jump is a good gauge of one's correct position at the approach.

Pic. 50.   The landing. (*See text*)

2) Make certain that the buttocks are pushed back, and the body is sufficiently inclined forward to be in balance in the stirrups.

As in the previous point I found that while pushing my seat back it was most important to keep my stirrups under me supporting all my weight; this meant not allowing my lower leg to jut forward or swing too far back—the ankle being in the correct place and a recipient spring of my weight. Another way of putting it is: Feel that your weight is right over the stirrups.

Pic. 51

3) Grip (particularly with upper calves, but also with knees and lower thighs).

4) Head up. This will help you to keep the loin caved in.

Focusing my eyes on some object beyond and above the obstacle and not looking at the fence made this much easier.

Later on, upon acquiring an easy and firm seat over obstacles, try to follow the gestures of the horse's neck by extending the *relaxed* arms forward through the air (instead of putting the hands down on the neck). A good way to learn "following" is first to keep the hands pressed against the sides of the horse's neck with the reins loose; then gradually to learn moving the hands forward during the flight. When you can do this without disturbing your seat, only then take up the slack in the reins and

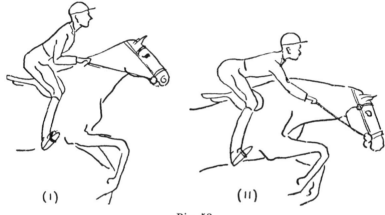

(I)   (II)

Pic. 52

start following. Before you do this first be sure that your seat has become quite firm before, during and after the jump.

When following, the arms move back and forth in piston-like motions as shown in Pic. 52, I & II. The reins are merely lightly stretched, but not pulled. This latter point pertaining to control will be discussed fully in Chapter XI.

While "following," all above points of position must be preserved.

When jumping at speed the horse's trajectory through the air is low and long, consequently the rider's position is but little disturbed during the whole jump. He approaches, jumps and gallops away without any major change in the position of the galloping approach—save for the piston-like forward thrust of his arms as they follow the balancing gestures of the horse's head and neck during the actual jump. However, high obstacles taken at slow speed necessitate short and high trajectories of the horse's body. The rider must adapt himself to this by going up and forward in rhythm with the horse. He should not do this by only bending forward from the waist, which would mean that his weight would still remain behind centered in his buttocks; nor should he spring forward, as the chances are then that he would merely jump ahead of his horse with the direst of consequences for himself. The correct way is to increase the angle between thigh and lower leg while preserving the forward inclination of the body. With the rider's weight in the stirrups this will mean that he will be thrust up and forward during the jump (Pic. 53, I and II).

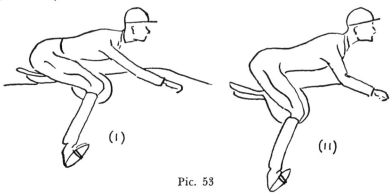

(I)

(II)

Pic. 53

When jumping at the trot it will be necessary for the rider to stop posting and assume the galloping position during the approach in order to prepare himself for the jump with strong tension in the springs a, b and, c (Pic. 29).

There are no mechanical reasons whatsoever for changing the rider's attitude during a drop jump or when jumping down or uphill. The animal instinct of self-preservation may make us lean back as the horse jumps down from a bank, but it will certainly not help the horse. Instead it will reward the poor animal for its efforts with a painful thump on the loins.

A good seat is the result of a certain set of well established habits, and it is difficult to alter these at a moment's notice. The Dressage Seat and the Forward Seat do not mix well, because the balance of the first is based in the saddle but that of the second primarily in the stirrups. Most attempts to switch in short order from a dressage seat to a forward seat and back again, or vice versa, are usually unsuccessful,—although there are a few riders capable of doing so.

Any attempt to teach the Forward Seat for only jumping, and consequently only while jumping, can rarely be successful, because the duration of the jump is too short and the number of jumps that can be taken at one session without abusing the horse too few. Thirty jumps during a lesson are enough for any horse, and because each jump lasts only a couple of seconds the pupil would have no more than a total of one minute's practice in the Forward Seat per lesson. On the other hand, consistent use of the Forward Seat in its different variations for different gaits and movements prepare the rider's muscles and balance for the Forward Seat on the jump.

CHAPTER VII

Bringing Control Down to Earth and Forward

Teaching civilians was a very different matter from teaching troopers in the army. My American pupils asked questions, sometimes refused to obey orders, didn't take kindly to hard work and wanted quick practical results effortlessly achieved. The questions could range from "why do I have to learn this? I don't see what good it will do me," to a technical and often intelligent pulling apart of paragraphs in the text books on riding. Disobedience could range from the case of a lady who refused to kick a stubbornly immobile horse, saying—"I'm afraid he will turn his head and bite me," to "I can't jump today; I was up late last night and I'm tired." And even if a teacher didn't pay much attention either to arguments or to disobediences, the general desire to learn effortlessly and quickly, and only practical things, was so strong that simply in order to remain in business one had to look for means of bettering existing teaching methods. The progressive development of my method depended as much on these practical considerations as on my idealistic ambitions.

Answering pupils' questions, by the way, required a knack. While replying to the query of one pupil I had always to watch the faces of the rest of my class, because, the mentalities varying, a perfectly reasonable conversation on one level between one pupil and myself could sound quite absurd to somone else in the group. I could easily find myself in the situation described in the story of two country bumpkins dining in a fashionable New York restaurant. When the finger bowls were served, one of them, against the strong opposition of the other, called the waiter and asked him "What do you do with these things?" "You dip your fingers in them sir, and wipe them off with the napkins," replied the waiter. "You see," said the other man, "if you ask foolish questions you get foolish answers."

The matter of changing the control from the Classical to the one which better fits cross-country riding and jumping was a yet more complicated task than to change the seat. The fact that control is in general a far more complicated subject than position, probably accounts for forward control being still relatively little understood, while the Forward Seat is universally recognized. Therefore, quite naturally, the transitional period even among superior, thoughtful riders is bound to be quite a long-drawn-out process.

When around 1930, I reached the stage of dissatisfaction with old "classical" ideas it was not easy to find books on modern control or teachers who taught it. Even such an enlightened institution as the United States

Cavalry School had not yet completely switched to the new. While the army team under the leadership of Lt. Colonel H. D. Chamberlin was illustrating modern riding brilliantly at Madison Square Garden, the Fort Riley manual, vintage of 1929 was a quarter of a century behind. As in any transitional period, consistency was not to be found.

To any horseman who likes to know what makes the wheels go around an illustration of how ideas changed is, of course, of interest and for such of my readers I have included the next couple of pages which will give them a sample of how the new ideas replaced the old ones. But if you are not interested in this historical information you may skip it and your riding be none the worse.

Barretto de Souza once said that "any fool can make the horse go; it takes a rider to stop him." So let me give you, as an illustration of the transition from classical to forward riding, a description of the change which took place in the understanding of how the horse should be halted. Fort Riley manual (edition 1929, page 51) says:

"TO HALT. . . . Being at a walk, at the command *Squad* the rider gathers the horse. At the command HALT, he uses the direct reins and the weight in combination and with quickly repeated applications, until the horse halts. The rider's legs remain in normal position.

"In using the weight, the rider should keep the buttocks in the saddle, the legs in their proper position, and should carry the upper part of the body backward repeatedly by bending hinge-like, at the waist . . ."

There is no use of quoting this description any further, the gathering of the horse to halt him, and the hinge-like repeated bending of the body backward (as a rule) just wouldn't mix with the principles of the forward seat.

But this manual was on its last legs and it was soon to be replaced by a new one which explained the halt in the following manner:

". . . halting . . . the rider must not lean back. If necessary, the forward inclination of the body decreases just sufficiently to enable the rider to remain in balance."

The above quotations mean that if the horse stops gradually, preserving forward balance, then the rider decreases his inclination forward just enough to correspond to the diminished speed of the movement. But if the horse stops abruptly, switching the preponderance of his weight to the engaged hindquarters then, in order to remain united with the horse, the rider may decrease his inclination forward to the point where his torso will be vertical to the ground. This by the way is the presently accepted technique.

Unfortunately, from my point of view, the above description of the halt included a finesse which was absolutely impractical for my work. The old pulling back on the reins assisted by the weight of the body, was, in this text, replaced by no pull at all—only fixed hands.

"To execute the halt, from the walk, the action of the hands must be

changed from lightness to fixity and resistance of the fingers. If the horse
halts, the desired result is obtained. If however, he is but slightly trained, he
generally raises his neck in slowing up. The rider then draws his hands to
the rear or shortens his reins in order to maintain contact with his mouth,
and again fixes his hands until the horse halts. *Care should be taken that
the rearward action of the hands does not at any time precede the retro-
grade movement of the mouth,* as in such a case there would be traction
on the reins, which, as has been shown, must never be the case. . . ."

While I personally appreciated the above method of using hands in
halting, my daily life in the riding ring convinced me that it was on too
high a plane for my average pupils. A soft halting by merely fixing the
hands just wouldn't work on half-schooled, strong, ambitious horses,
especially when ridden in company and by light-weight girls whose fixed
hand didn't amount to much.

In sharp contrast to the above quoted refinements was my own method
of the period which, catering to the average amateur rider, was overemphasizing simplifications and often leaving a good, ambitious rider without any advice. In BE A BETTER HORSEMAN (published 1941), on page 23,
the following conversation takes place about halting the horse:

"INSTRUCTOR: . . . Look, Miss Randall, how differently you and I have
stopped our horses. Your horse has raised his neck and head, pulled it to
the side, and opened his mouth, while my horse kept his mouth shut, did
not change the natural position of his neck and head, and came to a stop
softly.

"ANNE: I know why; your horse obeyed you and mine resisted and
wanted to go ahead in spite of my pulling on the reins; and then I had
to pull very hard.

"INSTRUCTOR: That might have been so, but it is also possible that you
pulled very heavily. When pulling on the reins to slow down, turn, back
or stop you should never pull consistently for any length of time; you
should increase and decrease the tension on the reins so that the bit moves
in the horse's mouth . . . The increase and decrease of tension which I
have described is known as 'give and take'; its reactions in the horse's
mouth are as follows: when the reins take, then the bit presses in the corners of the mouth, and when they give, then the bit slides down a little.
This keeps the mouth sensitive. And another thing—the fact that your
horse's neck and head not only went up, but to the side as well, makes me
suspect that you have pulled on one rein more than on the other. Unless
the horse himself tries to bring his head into a crooked position, the rider's
pull should be even on both reins."

Even if we were to consider that a halt which includes "give and take"
is a tremendous improvement on the standards of the average riding of
today, this description is inadequate, for it leaves a more ambitious rider
without any information.

What happened to the halt was typical of what happened to principles of control in general in this transition period. It was simply impossible for anyone to strike the perfect note at the first attempt.

It was only approximately six years ago that I was able really to crystallize the subject of control by dividing it in three categories:—elementary, intermediate and advanced, with their respective applications for different types of riding. Here is how I did it.

Elementary control is necessary for:

1) guidance of horses while learning position.

2) in many cases it may be sufficient for hacking quiet, obedient horses.

Intermediate control:

1) will make hacking more pleasant;

2) is necessary in the hunting field for an average rider who wishes to avoid making a fool of himself.

3) is necessary for horse shows; it will give a rider a better chance to win.

4) is sufficient for simple schooling of hacks, hunters and jumpers.

Advanced control:

1) is necessary to obtain from a schooled horse the highest quality of performance that he is capable of.

2) is necessary in making superior hunters and jumpers.

The following table (No. II) gives detailed definitions of these three grades of control as I use them in my teaching. I believe that this table adjusts this elusive subject to the practical aims of different groups of civilian riders. It also greatly increases the efficiency of lessons.

Efficient as tables are for presenting a complicated subject in a concise form, usually some additional text is necessary to explain their practical application. So here are a few pages about what this table should mean to the three groups of riders which are the subject of this book: those who hack, those who hunt and show in jumping classes, and those who, besides hunting and showing, school hunters and jumpers, aiming to obtain truly good gaits, great agility and athletic jumping.

1) ELEMENTARY CONTROL

You will notice that the table implies that elementary control should consist of controlling the horse *quietly*, effectively, perhaps roughly at times, and going on loose reins between the periods when control is necessary to change gaits, speeds, etc. I know that these "loose reins" will raise many objections; I know that to riders brought up in riding academies where the horses could hardly be held in check by strong bits and often strenuous means, I may seem to be someone who only yesterday got acquainted with horses. In actuality I know very many riding schools where a class of half a dozen or even a dozen will walk, trot, canter and jump low obstacles following each other on loose reins, a good half of

TABLE II

	ELEMENTARY CONTROL	INTERMEDIATE CONTROL	ADVANCED CONTROL
GENERAL AIMS.	*Authority* over the horse through *definite* and *quick* control in primitively executed gaits, transitions, halts, turns, backing and in simple low jumping. *Roughness* is permissible when elementary rider is unable to obtain results by gentle means.	*Soft* and *precise* control over gaits, transitions, all recognized movements and in jumping whether in a ring, outside, hunting or showing. Primary aim: a *soft* but *definite* cooperation of rider's hands and legs with horse's efforts and reactions.	Primary aim: a *high quality* of horse's performance in schooling, hunting or showing.
RIDER'S LEGS.	*Tapping* or *kicking* to urge the horse forward.	Mostly merely *squeezing* with calves; varying the pressures depending on circumstances.	Same as intermediate but at times in *full cooperation with hands.*
ARMS AND HANDS.	Riding on *loose* or *semi-loose* reins outside the moments when giving orders.	A *soft* contact with horse's mouth; *arms following* the balancing gestures. *Give and take.*	Same as intermediate plus at times *on the bit* and using *flexions.*
VOICE COMMANDS.	Liberal use of voice to give orders and to talk to the horse.	If necessary on occasion. Also when teaching a horse.	Liberal use of voice in schooling; on occasion in riding.
GAITS. (GENERAL CONSIDERATIONS)	*Even speed on loose reins,* most of the time. The horse relaxed to the point of almost being lazy.	*Relaxed, alert, soft* at all speeds. On *contact* most of the time, with the neck and head stretched forward.	Same as intermediate plus: *Movement of high quality* maintained throughout the performance. Occasionally *on the bit.* *Flexions* in slowing down. *Semi-collection.*
WALK.	*Steady, ordinary* walk on the line. Loose reins whenever possible.	*Free, fast, relaxed* walk with head and neck extended, on *soft contact* with *following arms* and *give* and *take.*	Same as intermediate plus: continuous *good movement* and a few steps of *semi-collected* walk with *flexions.*
TROT.	*Ordinary* trot, *even speed,* on the line. *Loose reins* whenever possible.	*Three speeds* at trot:— slow, ordinary, fast. *Soft contact* with neck and head extended. *Give and take.*	Same as intermediate plus: the *best possible movement;* slowing down with *flexions;* occasionally *on the bit;* few steps of *semi-collected* trot; a few steps of *semi-extended* trot.

TABLE II (Continued)

	ELEMENTARY CONTROL	INTERMEDIATE CONTROL	ADVANCED CONTROL
GALLOP.	*Ordinary* canter only. *Even speed; loose reins* whenever possible. On the *line.* Canter departure executed *promptly* even if roughly, but keeping the horse's neck and head straight. No specific lead is required.	*Three speeds* at gallop: slow, ordinary, fast. On *soft contact,* neck and head extended; *following arms. Give* and *take. Soft* canter departure on a desired lead. Change of leads with interruption.	Same as intermediate plus: consistently *good movement;* slowing down with *flexions;* few steps of *semi-collected* gallop; occasionally *on the bit.* A flying change of leads.
TRANSITIONS.	*Quick* and *precise* (at a designated point). Rough if necessary to obtain the above results. Return to loose reins as quickly as possible.	*Soft, gradual* but *precise.* Neck and head extended at all times.	*Good movement* maintained to last stride of first gait and restored almost on *first* stride of new one. *On the bit* when increasing the speed; slowing down with *flexions.*
HALTS.	*Quick* and *definite,* at a desired point, even if rough. Horse relaxed at a halt; reins loose.	*Gradual, soft* and *precise.* Neck and head extended. *Give* and *take.* The horse stands still on loose reins.	*Soft, precise* through *flexions.* Some abrupt.
TURNS WITH MOVEMENT FORWARD.	*Wide* turns, wide circles, entirely by *means of reins.*	Turns of *normal size,* the horse properly led by rider's *legs* and *hands.* Larger turns at speed.	Same as intermediate. Good movement preserved throughout the turn.
HALF-TURN ON THE FOREHAND.	*On loose reins,* except for the short moments of checking.	On *contact* with neck and head extended and straight. From a halt; later from a walk.	On soft contact. Neck extended. From a halt, later from a walk.

Pic. 54. A trot on "loose reins" (stabilization).

Pic. 55. A trot on "soft contact."

Pic. 56. A trot "on the bit."

Pics. 54, 55 and 56. The same horse in three different manifestations of the ordinary trot show:

1) How the mental alertness of the horse increases (you can see it by his face) with the increased efforts of the rider's aids;

2) How the physical alertness of the horse increases;

3) How a sloppy movement when on loose reins becomes not only alert but "well-connected" when the horse is ridden on the bit.

The movement on the bit is the best for almost any individual performance but in many cases it will be much too stimulated for the hunting field where riding on contact will be more practical for the majority.

TABLE II (Continued)

	ELEMENTARY CONTROL	INTERMEDIATE CONTROL	ADVANCED CONTROL
HALF-TURN ON THE HAUNCHES.	Omit.	On *contact* with neck and head extended and straight. From a halt, and while walking.	In about *four united steps* with *one fore leg crossing* in front of the other and *animated hindquarters.* From a halt, while walking and after a short stop during trot or canter. On soft contact; the head straight or slightly turned toward the direction of the movement.
BACKING.	Only four steps, straight if possible.	*Soft* backing a few steps by means of *give and take* with *head and neck extended, mouth closed, body straight.* From a walk resuming the walk.	Backing a *definite number of steps,* in some cases, by means of *flexions.* From all gaits; always resuming the interrupted gait.
COUNTER-GALLOP.	Omit.	Large circles, Serpentine and Zig-zag on *soft contact.* Relaxed horse.	Same as intermediate.
SHORT TURN AT GALLOP.	Omit.	On contact, with straight neck and head.	Same as intermediate.
TWO TRACKS.	Omit.	A *few steps* on *soft contact* with *neck* and head *extended.* At a walk and trot.	At a *walk* and *trot* with a good *movement* forward and to the *side.* On *soft* contact, sometimes on *the bit.*
JUMPING.	Fences 2½'-3'. Mostly *single* obstacles. *Loose reins* during the approach and during the jump. Holding mane.	Fences 3'-4'. Different combinations of obstacles and courses. *Soft contact* during the approach; *loose reins* on the jump. Hands on horse's neck.	Any height that horse can take. *Any course.* On *loose reins, soft contact* or on *the bit,* whichever may be the best in the particular case. With following arms.
FIELD RIDING.	Hacking.	Hacking, hunting, showing, cross-country competitions. Also a somewhat simplified schooling of hacks, hunters and jumpers.	Hacking, hunting, showing, cross country competitions. Also superior schooling of hacks, hunters and jumpers.

the class keeping their proper distances. In my personal experience at least 80% of the horses which were in my hands, school horses, hunters and open jumpers, hacked on loose reins. This is very easy to achieve with an average horse, particularly with half-breds, but only under one condition, that the horses are not in the habit of being abused physically or mentally; that is, that no rider ever pulls on their mouths consistently, jerks them most of the ride, kicks them with the heels when a squeeze with the calves would be sufficient, asks them to gallop full tilt one second, then walk a few steps only to make a mad rush again, and in general behaves in the saddle like a wild Indian.

Hence it follows that a riding school can supply for its pupils quiet hacks only providing the education of these pupils has been sensible from the very start, and that riding on loose reins was a rule while learning how to sit. Obviously it is the only efficient way to behave while learning position, for it teaches one to establish balance in the saddle without abusing the horse by hanging on his mouth. The beginner may, and often should, help himself by holding the mane, but the sensitive bars of the mouth should be left alone. Using this method the teacher kills two birds with one stone—pupils learn to sit correctly very quickly and horses acquire the habit of going quietly, evenly and obediently on loose reins. Riders and horses brought up this way can hack together on loose reins most of the time, to the mutual satisfaction of both parties. To ride on soft contact requires the ability to follow with the arms the balancing gestures of the horse's neck and head and the knowledge of how to give and take; these points are outside the scope of a possible beginner's knowledge. More will be said about this riding on loose reins in the chapter on how to teach position, while here, once more and very emphatically, I want to state that it is very easy to achieve. Any riding instructor who has a head on his shoulders can get his horses and pupils organized along these lines, and those who can't have no right to be in business.

Although the ability of the rider to ride on loose reins, and the calmness and responsiveness of the horse which makes this possible, are the foundation of any type of riding, no matter how high its aims, loose reins when used exclusively and as an ultimate spell primitiveness. Hence for a more discriminating rider who, although no longer a beginner, still limits his riding to hacking, I would suggest learning intermediate control. Of course to enjoy the effects of this finer control, a better schooled horse will be necessary; the fine points of the rider's control will be wasted on a horse which for years has been guided in a primitive manner. In the great majority of cases a better-schooled horse means a privately owned one. As a pretty general rule the hacks from livery stables, being ridden by all sorts and kinds cannot be decently schooled horses and the knowledge of intermediate control will be wasted on them. While a few such horses, being old and tired, will go on loose reins, others will be young, nervously upset, and will have to be held back all the time. Some ignorant people consider these poor, nervous wrecks better horses and get a great kick out of the excitement of riding them. This attitude of a mounted pedestrian is rather common among young, bold people who ride occasionally without ever having taken riding and horses to their heart. If you should be unfortunate enough to find yourself riding one of these spoiled horses (very few horses are nervous by nature) the best that you could do would be to feel the moments when the reins might be loosened, hoping that this comfort would have a soothing effect, that gradually the horse would become calmer, and rather consistent riding on loose reins possible. In handling such cases the knowledge of intermediate control is very helpful, for in studying it, through different exercises, the rider's feeling of the horse and the cooperation of his legs and hands with the efforts of the horse are developed.

Although a knowledge of intermediate control is not absolutely essential for hacking (just as a Cadillac is not essential for getting there) if you have your own horse then applying the rules of intermediate control will make your horse perform better and gradually, even without any benefit of special schooling, it will become a better balanced, a softer, a more responsive, a more pleasant horse to ride. In other words, a consistent use of a finer type of control is in itself a form of schooling minus the gymnastics of a regular schooling program.

All over the country, in small communities, there are people, both adults and children, who own their hacks, often take care of them themselves, and ride them pleasantly without any technical knowledge of how to control a horse. In their quiet riding, which is unabusive to the horse, the efficiency of control is based on well-established mutual confidence; here a pat, there a word or two, are more effective in such cases than a pull on the reins. This love of the animal and the understanding of his mentality and emotions is always pleasant to observe and one could only wish that the knowledge of control on an intermediate level could be added to this ideal type of association between the mount and his rider.

An understanding of the horse's mentality is extremely important in schooling. As a rule its consideration distinguishes a good trainer from a bad one, but such simple things as that the horse is easily upset by a rapid succession of orders, by sudden and frequent changes of speeds and, once upset by a certain behavior of the rider will remember it for a long time, should be appreciated even by riders who ride on the elementary level. Through a considerate behavior in the saddle, which a horse will remember as well as a disturbing one, one can build up the horse's confidence to the point where minimum and truly elementary control with hands and legs will be all that will be necessary to go through woods and across fields.

I have discussed the psychology of the horse in Chapter II, and more will be said about it in the chapter on schooling. I wish there were enough information on the subject to fill a special chapter—but there isn't. About five years ago I read somewhere that experiments had been made on the mentality of cockroaches. This intrigued me and I decided to find out if any such thing had been done scientifically with horses. And so I went to the Museum of Natural History in New York City, to consult one of its curators. To him, in 1930, I had addressed the question why horses jump so badly by comparison with many other animals, particularly of the cat family. He had answered all my questions very thoroughly and interestingly from the point of view of archaeological background. I remember how impressed I was by his ability to pick a little bone out of a huge heap of such that he had on a table and immediately identify it as such-and-such a vertebra of a horse which had lived so many million years ago. The curator was an old man then and, older by fifteen years when I saw him again, was still occupied with assembling skeletons. When I posed my question—whether the mentality of the horse had ever been analyzed scientifically—he was discouragingly honest, answering: "I don't know and, frankly, I don't care; I'm interested in dead horses only." During the course of that afternoon in the museum I˙found that no one thus far had been interested. So all that we know on the subject is what some of us have observed through years of association with horses. It boils down to something like ten points (such as strong herd instinct, tenacious memory, limited mentality, etc.) on which the majority seem to agree and I doubt that it represents anything like all that could be known.

2) Intermediate Control

The difference between intermediate and elementary control is immense and boils down to an additional knowledge of how to ride the horse on soft contact with give and take and following arms, keeping the neck and head extended, plus the ability to make all the movements and transitions precisely and *softly*. All this obviously involves the cooperation of the rider's legs and hands with the efforts of the horse's body. This cooperation has to be developed and don't deceive yourself that you can attain it by merely riding. As actuality shows, one can hack or hunt for years without ever reaching this harmonious activity of the rider's legs and hands and the horse's muscles. This cooperation can be developed in the rider efficiently only by doing exercises such as the increase and decrease of speeds at the gaits, making varied turns, changing leads, two-tracking, etc. All these exercises, if aiming at precision and softness, develop the rider's control, and at the same time constitute a schooling gymnastic for horses. This always seems very fortunate to me, as the rider is formed through true horseman's exercises.

One can begin to learn intermediate control only after he has learned: a) from the point of view of position: how to sit correctly and firmly enough so that neither holding the mane nor hanging on the horse's mouth is necessary; b) from the point of view of control: how to hack a quiet, cooperative horse effectively on loose reins most of the time.

The first point to learn when switching from elementary to intermediate control is to ride on soft contact with following arms; at a walk and gallop, these two items are inseparable, and this is why: do you remember the third chapter?—the chapter on the balance of the horse in motion, the understanding of which I then presented as the foundation stone of the whole method of Forward Riding? Well, here we have a good illustration of this statement. As you probably know, during the walk and gallop, as well as on the jump, the horse makes balancing gestures with the neck and head; it is only during the trot, the most stable gait, that the neck and head remain practically immobile. If one rides on completely loose reins then the hands don't interfere with these balancing gestures. But once contact is established between the rider's hands and the horse's mouth, then the rider's arms must follow through the air these gestures of the horse's neck and head. The final touch to this soft contact with following is given by the occasional opening and closing of the fingers which results in the displacement of the bit in the horse's mouth and is called "give and take." By means of this give and take really soft slowing downs, halts and backing, as well as the regulation of gaits, can be achieved.

While riding on soft contact, it is important to keep the horse's neck and head extended; only when extended is the neck in a position to deliver powerful balancing gestures. However, when slowing down and halting, particularly when it is done abruptly, the neck may go up and back a little while the head may come in somewhat; the latter as a result of the flexion of the poll.

A horse that has been schooled on the principles of intermediate control will not become a great athlete but will unquestionably be a horse with better gaits, more flexibility, softness and obedience than is exhibited by the actual hunters, horse show hunters and open jumpers of today. A rider who possesses such a horse and who himself knows how to ride well along the principles of intermediate control should be able to make better performances than the average rider of today who merely hunts and shows. The question is: Is it difficult? Does it take too much time to learn? Here are the answers and I shall begin at the beginning.

If one is young (but not a child) with normal physique and average boldness, and has a good instructor with a well-organized school, one can learn in fifteen lessons how to sit decently and how to hack school horses on loose reins. I have already stated that some riding schools are able to accomplish it in as few hours. To be on the safe side let us add another five lessons, so that if one rides three times a week, in about seven weeks one *may be ready to begin* to learn intermediate control. In the majority of cases, however, an interim period of two or three months of plain hacking may be necessary to acquire the so important habits and feelings as distinct from the technique alone. After this I am unable to give you very exact figures. For the success of learning finer control depends tremendously on the ability of the rider to feel the horse, and on the speed and accuracy of his reflexes to these feelings. This may vary greatly from individual to individual, but I would say that in a great many cases it can be accomplished in thirty to forty hours of lessons and homework (in the saddle). Upon achieving it a person would be doing superior hacking, but would he be ready to begin hunting? Yes, in some cases. In cases where the physique of the rider is such that his seat, besides being correct and easy to work from, is a secure one. Those riders whose conformation unfortunately doesn't give them this advantage will have to hack and jump for three or four months more (without taking lessons) before beginning to hunt. Will this person, who was a rank beginner eight or nine months ago, ride better in the hunting field during his first months at it than those who have done it for years, although without any equestrian education? In the majority of cases the answer is no; new surroundings, a probably changed behavior of the horse in the excitement of the chase, inexperience in judging terrain, etc. will require time to make adjustments and only after one is acclimated will one really begin to benefit by his training.

I would like to say once more that many hunt without any knowledge of intermediate control, but merely on the principle of the elementary one to which a bold character, years of experience, etc. are added. This is done all over the world and from the point of view of undiscriminating riders is done successfully. If one were to place one's self on such an undiscriminating, primitive level, then one would feel that hunting a green horse is about the apex of human achievement. Hence it is generally practiced and the abomination of such performances is not noticed, while the human daring is greatly admired. Technically such performances don't depend on knowledge; many fine riders would not be able to do it; it depends on a great deal of experience which develops a certain knack.

3) Advanced Control

The principal difference between intermediate and advanced control lies in the aims. While the former aims primarily at softness of control without considering the *quality of the movements and gaits* of the horse, the latter aims at producing good movement at the gaits and in jumping. In order to obtain a good movement advanced control calls for riding at times on the bit with flexions, as well as obtaining, in schooling, a few steps of semi-collected gaits. It seems to be little, but it is in reality a great deal.

"On the bit" means increasing the merely soft contact of intermediate control to the point where the action of the hindquarters becomes connected in motion with the action of the forehand. If the action of the rider's legs produces energy in the horse's hindquarters in such a way that this energy going forward through the horse's body reaches the head which extends and takes the bit, then it results in a perfect connection (in movement) of the horse's quarters and forehand. This connected movement (not collected) on the bit, with the horse's neck and head extended is the basis of *good* movement. Riding this way one can develop the horse's movement to its very best. Teaching the horse to go on the bit when moving ahead should be developed together with flexions of the mouth (flexions are taught after the horse has taken the bit) when slowing down or stopping; if not, moving on the bit may degenerate into pulling.

In general the purpose of advanced control in the abstract is to make the horse perform at its best. "At its best" is, of course, a big term, and to achieve such results one has to be an artist in the saddle and spend a great deal of time on schooling. Since this is outside the scope of all but a few riders, the aims of advanced control, as they are brought down to earth in this book, are merely to concentrate the attention of the rider on improving the typically clumsy, stiff movement of a horse which has only been broken and ridden but never really schooled.

A good performance chiefly consists in efficient movement which is the result of long, flat, relaxed strides. Besides this the characteristics of a good performance are general agility and athletic jumping. The horse's agility largely depends on his ability to gather or extend himself, depending on the circumstances, and this is why a few steps of partially-collected gaits, practically always followed by extensions, are an important part of advanced control. Athletic jumping depends on good balance, good movement, general agility plus a special knowledge of how to utilize the above items when negotiating an obstacle.

Much more about this advanced riding will be said in the chapters on advanced riding and on schooling. Here I merely want to say that it is not necessary for hacking, nor hunting, nor the average showing of jumpers, but there is nothing pleasanter than to have a really well-schooled hack or hunter, and it may be at times of advantage even in normal American jumping competitions.

In actual teaching or schooling there is often an overlap between the *Intermediate* and the *Advanced* levels of riding. For instance, a horse who is naturally an excellent mover may show a high quality at gaits while being an intermediate horse in every other respect. Or a horse with a certain conformation may be able to make abrupt halts efficiently even before he is fully on the bit and has learned to respond to aids on the advanced level.

The same is true of the riders—some will be able to use "following arms" over fences while otherwise still riding on the intermediate level.

All such instances of progress due to specific natural abilities should, of course be encouraged and this is where the teacher or the trainer must exhibit the flexibility of his thinking and of his method.

A horse schooled on an advanced level and ridden by an advanced rider will make a truly good performance whether in the hunting field or in a horse show ring. The same horse given to an intermediate rider will drop back to an intermediate level probably within from three to five months. But the same horse ridden by a harsh, abusive, unintelligent rider may become upset and lose all the good qualities of his former performance within a couple of weeks.

The feeling of the horse, and quick and correct muscular reflexes in response to these feelings, plus consideration of the horse's mentality and his physique, constitute what we call *equestrian tact*. Some people are born with the seeds of these qualities, others, unfortunately, are not; in both cases they can be developed; in the first one, of course, to a much higher degree. The higher the ambitions of the rider, the more important the possession of equestrian tact becomes. Practice, love of the animal, thinking of him, and experience in riding with better movements in view, will develop this quality more quickly and efficiently than listening to a teacher or reading books. It takes two to play the game of teaching riding; certain things a teacher can teach, others a pupil has to learn by himself with merely the assistance of the teacher. Tact is too illusive to be presented in the form of a table, it is one of those very important intangibles. The easiest way for me to convey its subtlety is by telling the story of the hotel manager who was explaining to the bell hops the difference between politeness and tact. "Suppose," said he, "you enter a bedroom and you see a naked woman; then you say, 'Excuse me, sir.' Now the *excuse me* part is politeness, while the *sir* is tact."

It shouldn't take a person who knows intermediate control more than ten lessons, with a couple of hours of practice between each lesson, to learn the additional points of advanced control (riding an advanced horse) as they are presented in this book. It won't take more time than this providing a person is able and has some equestrian tact. Some, of course, never make the grade.

In a special chapter my pupil and collaborator Alexis Wrangel will tell in detail how to control the horse on the intermediate level, and I myself in another will take up the subject of advanced control, while at present I would like to set down the fundamentals of both these grades of control.

Naturally the first consideration is the horse; that is, his character, the peculiarities of his conformation (as limiting factors), and his balance, as the basis of the mechanics of his way of moving. The first two items we will consider again in the chapter on schooling (we have discussed them both already), but the matter of balance is so important that I would like to give you some additional information about it, even though repeating myself here and there.

The horse's weight is not evenly distributed throughout his body. If you were to take a well-bred horse, put him on two scales, one under the forehand and the other under his hindquarters, and note the distribution of weight at the moment the horse is relaxed, standing with stretched neck, you would see that almost 3/5 of the weight is carried by the forehand. In motion yet more weight will be shifted to the forehand and even·beyond, so that the hindquarters, the seat of propulsion, are free to push the horse ahead. The same thing is extremely well said in HORSE-MANSHIP AND HORSEMASTERSHIP (1945 edition, page 54):

". . . the action, which places the center of gravity near the shoulders and removes it from the hindquarters, greatly favors movement. In fact, the more the center of gravity is advanced, the greater the forward effort of the hindquarters in movement to the front. Moreover, this displacement of the center of gravity tends to cause the horse to move from his base of support, so that the forces of gravity draw the mass forward at the same time that the hindquarters push it in the same direction. In this the leg movements of the horse are extended. . . . In the case where the equilibrium is over the shoulders the hindquarters . . . can only push (the mass) forward and which (the mass) is itself constantly drawn forward by its weight, like the body of a man in a bent forward position. . . ."

The above statements must really be digested and memorized to the point where you will feel an instinctive necessity to let the horse stretch his neck forward, and to follow the balancing gestures of the neck and head with your arms when moving ahead.

As to how to execute this or that movement, for instance how to turn the horse or how to back him, there are certain formulae which will be discussed in the next chapters. But these recipes will work well only providing the horse is schooled and answers correctly to the signals of the rider's legs and hands. And even if the signals are given correctly and the horse is familiar with them, not much good will come of them if the orders are given mechanically without feeling the horse—that is, without what is usually called "equestrian tact." On the other hand, it is perfectly possible to require a pupil to make, let us say, a half-turn on the forehand (on a horse which is schooled to it) after showing repeatedly how the horse turns and without explaining the formula, merely depending on the pupil's feelings and imitative ability. As a matter of fact, this is how I have taught for years. Normally my pupil, merely on feelings, learns to do elementary two-tracks in about half an hour and only then I proceed to add official aids one by one to better the movement. Using this system one never subordinates really important feelings to the much less important mechanical order of the use of legs and hands.

Years ago, when I really didn't know how to teach efficiently, my approach was the standard one; that is, that of telling the pupils beforehand that, in order to two-track one must do this with the legs and that with the hands, which so often resulted in a stiff pupil whose legs and hands were struggling with his memory. I particularly remember one lady who for weeks and weeks was completely lost between two recipes, one for the turn on the forehand and the other for the turn on the haunches. No matter which turn she started, by the middle of it she was beginning to use the formula of the other one.

But if your riding is based on knowledge of what the horse should do, and on your equestrian tact of cooperation with the horse's efforts, then the knowledge of the formulae is important, for they will help you put the final touches on your performance. All these formulae consist of different combinations of three fundamental leg actions and five fundamental rein actions.

LEG ACTIONS

In ideal the desired effect is obtained by merely squeezing with the calves or a light tapping by the calves. The squeeze or tapping increases with the horse's resistance. A pressure with a spur or spurs is the next degree. Kicks with heels or spurs are to be used only if there is a strong resistance.

Leg action #1: Both legs acting just behind the girth, simultaneously and with equal strength. Used when urging horse forward.

Leg action #2: One leg acts just behind the girth. Used, for instance, (inside leg) when making a turn in motion to prevent horse from cutting it.

Leg action #3: One leg acts farther behind the girth to range the hindquarters. Used, for instance, at the turn on the forehand to rotate the hindquarters.

Depending on how they act, the legs may be "good legs" or not:

1) HEAVY legs, which constantly clutch the horse, disturbing him. Heavy legs are often the result of a natural inclination to overuse muscles, or learning to grip before a correct seat, based on balance, rhythm and spring has been established.

2) PASSIVE legs, which are light, and non-disturbing just because they leave the horse alone. Passive legs are often the result of being weak, or having long experience in riding touchy horses which are unaccustomed to legs.

3) PRIMITIVELY ACTIVE legs, which in a coarse manner—seldom in cooperation with the hands or horse's efforts—obtain simple results. These legs often belong to able riders with lack of education.

4) EDUCATED legs, which are "good legs," are able in the shortest time, in cooperation with the hands, to obtain the best possible results with the least expenditure of the horse's mental and physical energy. Such legs are the result of a combination of education plus a highly developed feeling of the horse.

"Good legs" (not necessarily the perfect ones) are required for both Intermediate and Advanced control.

REIN ACTIONS

Rein action #1 (Pic. 57): TWO REINS OF DIRECT OPPOSITION. Both hands being fixed or producing tension to the rear, normally keeping the neck and head straight. Used to slow down, halt or back the horse.

Rein action #2 (Pic. 58): ONE REIN OF DIRECT OPPOSITION. The active hand (the right one in this case) carried slightly outward and then increasing the tension to the rear. Used, for instance, when making a sharp turn to right. This action tends to diminish the speed of the gait. The passive hand must give as much as the active one has taken, unless a certain correction in the attitude of the horse's neck is required.

Rein action #3 (Pic. 59): THE LEADING REIN. The active hand (the right one in this case) is carried outwardly and acts to the right and slightly forward. Used, for instance, when turning the horse on a wide curve. This action doesn't impede the speed. Unless a certain correction in the attitude of the horse's neck is required, the passive hand gives as much as the active has taken.

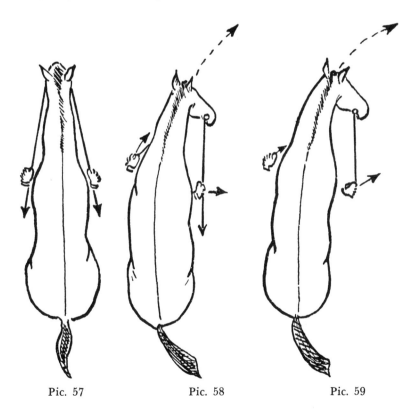

Pic. 57   Pic. 58   Pic. 59

Rein action #4 (Pic. 60): THE REIN OF INDIRECT OPPOSITION IN FRONT OF THE WITHERS. The active hand (the right one in this case) is carried to left across horse's neck, just in front of the withers, and tension is to left rear, or mostly to left, depending upon effect desired. The left rein often assists with leading effect (remaining parallel to the right rein) or as a rein of direct opposition. This action is used, for instance, to keep the horse flat against the wall of the ring.

Rein action #5 (Pic. 61): THE REIN OF INDIRECT OPPOSITION IN REAR OF THE WITHERS. The active hand (the right one in this case) is carried somewhat to the left (but doesn't cross the neck) and produces tension to rear and left, toward horse's left hip. The passive hand normally gives. Used, for instance, to move the horse to the side, while advancing forward (to the left in this case). *In my method this rein is used only to combat resistance.*

There is one more standard rein effect which you will find in most textbooks on riding—that is the "bearing" or "neck" rein. It is used to turn the horse with one hand. This hand is moved forward and upward and then presses one of the reins against the *upper half* of the horse's neck. I used to teach it, then stopped, then taught it again and finally discarded

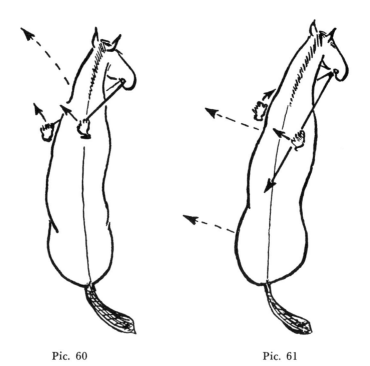

Pic. 60   Pic. 61

it for good from my method. My vacillations were due to the fact that
while it is an efficient way of turning a trained horse when holding the
reins in one hand, it has a quality of unsoundness in it because it turns the
head to the right while turning the horse to the left; this goes against a
fundamental principle of my method—the horse should look where he is
going. Obviously a cowboy or a polo player or a whipper-in needing a
free hand finds this rein effect necessary, but an average cross-country
rider, when forced to ride on occasions with the reins in one hand, can
learn to use this hand so that all the other rein signals can be given to the
horse effectively enough.

In their actions, hands may be:

1) HEAVY, which "ride on the horse's mouth" constantly disturbing
the horse. They usually are the result of a tense, unsteady seat or appre-
hension as to one's ability to control the horse.

2) PASSIVE, which are light just because they "leave the horse alone"
permanently. One will find them in cases of riders who have an easy seat,
but no knowledge of how to ride. On the other hand, in any good riding,
hands should be passive most of the time.

3) PRIMITIVELY ACTIVE, which in a coarse manner, but with feelings, obtain simple results. They are often termed "naturally good hands"
and usually belong to able riders whose long experience is their only
source of knowledge.

4) EDUCATED, which are truly "good hands" and can be defined
thus: "Good hands" are the actions of fingers, hands and arms which
(often in cooperation with legs) in the shortest time obtain the greates·
results with the least expenditure of the horse's mental and physica.
energies.

All the above descriptions of leg and hand actions are as old as the
hills and constitute probably the most unoriginal part of this book. You
will find them in every standard work on riding. I have included them
here just because they are so essential that they cannot be omitted. As a
rule they are presented in a more detailed and hence, to me, more cum-
bersome form. On the other hand, the "two reins of direct opposition" are
usually not presented graphically as they are here.

In military school in my youth there were two cadets who took solemn
oaths that after passing the graduating exams they would never read
anything more in their lives; later they were known in the Russian
cavalry as "the enemies of printed matter." Yet strange as it may seem,
in the civilized United States of today, one can find a similar attitude
toward text-books on riding among those who owe their riding knowledge
merely to many years in the saddle. I have personally seen people make
faces looking at diagrams of actions of legs and hands and saying: "that
is a lot of nonsense—you can't ride that way." But if you were to examine

the riding of the best of such uneducated but very experienced riders you would see that, in a clumsy and inefficient way, they use the same standard aids. You just cannot get away from them and the difference may be only in their application as, for instance, the classical rider uses them to school and ride horses primarily at collected gaits, while the cross-country rider of today is using them primarily to maintain efficient forward movement.

The efficiency of forward movement depends to a large degree on the attitude of the horse's body. If, while moving straight forward, the horse holds his neck and head to the side like a puppy then, obviously, the legs are not going to move forward at their best. To gain the maximum amount of ground with each stride when moving straight the horse must himself be straight from nose to tail. Only in a straight attitude is a straight moving horse in the best position to maintain his balance, the other essentials being also present. For the same reasons, while moving along a sharp curve the horse may accept with his body the shape of the path along which he moves.

A recapitulation of the fundamental principles of forward control gives us the following list:

Feeling of the horse's physical efforts and of his mental attitude.

Consideration of horse's character and physique.

Maintaining the forward balance of the horse when moving ahead.

Soft contact (extended neck and head).

Following arms.

Give and take.

On the bit (extended neck and head).

Flexions.

Three fundamental leg actions and five rein actions.

Different leg and hand combinations based on the above basic actions.

Alignment of horse's body for straight and curved movements.

Bettering of the horse's movement.

If you are familiar with both the theory and practice of all the above points except bettering the movement of the horse, putting the horse on the bit, flexions, plus semi-collection and semi-extension, you know riding on an intermediate level. And if you know them all, without exception, you know advanced riding. You may add quantities of details to this list, but fundamentally there is nothing else to know. The difference may be in degree, and higher degrees are attained not through mere knowledge but through talent and experience. When I was an eighteen-year-old cadet I heard the famous James Fillis saying that at any moment he knew exactly what each of the horse's feet was doing under him. I then thought that the old man must be a liar. Many years later I myself arrived at the point where, when riding horses I was familiar with, I could feel quite a bit of what the hooves were doing. This sort of feeling comes only with experience, and may result in a finesse which is beyond being practical and which only the really educated eye will see.

Years ago I began to make educational movies on riding. One of them is entitled FORWARD CONTROL and illustrates the points which I have just listed. The model (Mr. George Hoblin) rides well and the horse has such lovely movement that every time I see this movie I derive pleasure from it. I know many horsemen who also beam when looking at this horse on the screen, but lately I received a letter from a club where it had been shown, saying that the members weren't interested in the film as it was "too elementary." Which merely means that there is place for a course on the appreciation of good riding as against the pleasure of seeing spills and thrills.

And this appreciation of a good performance of the horse leads me to something which I should have discussed long ago—that is why thirty years ago, when inspired by the Italians to change from old-fashioned riding, I didn't follow the Italian system one hundred per cent. In those days my knowledge of Italian control and schooling was based on rumor that the Italians didn't do any ring schooling gymnastics and expected their horses to find their balance and to learn agility merely by being ridden cross-country and over different combinations of obstacles by non-interfering riders, and on the fact that no book on the Italian method which had passed through my hands discussed schooling of a horse for sport. It looked as if the rumor was right.

In 1936 when in Italy, I visited Tor di Quinto and one of the instructors demonstrated three horses for me. They jumped well but were heavy in hand, rather clumsy, obviously not too pleasant to ride, and the Italian officer discussing them with me said that there was a movement afoot in the cavalry to change their method of schooling by augmenting ring gymnastics.

In the course of my riding life I have experimented here and there, trying to school horses by cross-country riding alone (as almost all of our hunters are schooled), unfortunately minus the Italian hills. In my experience anyway, these horses never formed out as well as horses which in the early stages of schooling were worked almost entirely in the ring. I personally am certain that there is no substitute for ring gymnastics for the development of the horse's balance, movement and agility; one should only be careful not to go overboard in overemphasizing them. They alone can't do the job; jumping low but complicated combinations of obstacles is also important, as is open country when the time arrives for it.

CHAPTER VIII

Elementary Control

In a progressive method of learning to ride, elementary control is meant only for the use of beginners while they learn position. It will work well only on horses of a placid temperament which have been especially trained to work *quietly* when controlled in a very *primitive* but *undisturbing* manner; these horses must maintain, of their own accord, even gaits on loose reins, respond to a *few, simple* leg and hand signals, obey voice commands and put up with the discomfort caused by the clumsy position of the rider. This seems like a large order, but experience shows that most horses would rather be ridden the elementary way and asked little, than be made to do Passage or jump five foot fences.

The extreme simplicity of the *aims* and of the *technique* of elementary control enables the beginner to concentrate mentally and physically on the development of a correct seat; progress in learning is much faster if the student thinks of only one thing at a time.

Actually the fundamental principles of elementary control, with various individual refinements added, are frequently used by uneducated but experienced riders in hacking and even hunting. This, of course, is to be regretted for, while elementary control is an unavoidable step in learning to ride, it hardly can be considered a desirable ultimate aim. I personally feel strongly that hunting should be done on the basis of intermediate riding and that everyone who hunts should make an effort to learn it. Hacking, however, may be a different thing. There, intermediate control is not always necessary in order to have a pleasant ride. Furthermore, in hacking there are many cases where elementary control will have to suffice. For instance: people who do not ride well, do not wish to improve and ride merely for exercise or the pleasure of being outdoors, will be wise to be undisturbingly simple in their control. These people will merely upset their horses if they try to ride the way accomplished horsemen do; a knowledge of one's limitations is very important in riding. Anyone who belongs to this category and has a quiet horse should control him at least in the spirit of elementary riding. From the point of view of the horse, elementary control is definitely better than unsuccessful and hence abusive attempts of the rider to be complicated without knowing how.

As you will remember, in the chapter BRINGING CONTROL DOWN TO EARTH AND FORWARD there is a table which compares the aims and the technique of elementary riding with those of intermediate and advanced. I would suggest your glancing over this table once more before beginning to read the rules of elementary control. (See page 103.)

The table to which I am referring you defines the primary aim of elementary control as *authority* over the horse in primitively executed ordinary gaits, during primitive transitions, halts, backing, turns and in simple, easy jumping. The table further specifies that control over all these movements should be *definite* and *quick,* preferably gentle, but if necessary rough. If the worse comes to the worst it is better to stop the horse, even harshly, than to be taken for a ride.

Obviously, a beginner, or an elementary rider even with some experience, can have authority over the horse through *gentle* means only providing that:

1) the horse is of a placid disposition and has been trained to execute obediently and quietly a few simple routine movements at mere indications of the rider. This routine must be really simple, for the more that is asked of a horse the greater the chances of upsetting him and provoking his resistance.

2) the technique of elementary control avoids a continuous use of legs and hands; avoids even long periods of active aids. On the contrary, the technique should aim at leaving the horse (as much as practical) to work by himself on loose reins and without the influence of the rider's legs; a beginner is unable to ride on *soft* contact of hands and legs. It is only during moments when the rider gives orders that legs or hands should be used. Since such a technique is less disturbing to the horse, he remains quiet and cooperative, and this fact enables the rider to concentrate on his position on the one hand and on the softness of his orders on the other. Riding on loose reins and with passive legs is, by the way, the most efficient means to soften the beginner's torso, his arms and his hands; that is, if he has confidence in his horse.

3) hands are used only to slow the horse down, to halt him, to turn or to back. The action with the hands should not aim at any finer points of riding. Voice commands must always precede the order with the hands, except in turning.

4) the legs urge the horse forward by tapping or kicking; a beginner or an elementary rider is unable to control the horse with a variation of pressures. The legs are used only to move the horse forward at a desired gait, to change to a faster gait and to increase the speed of a gait (one leg is used to turn in place). The legs should not be used for any finer aims. Voice commands must always precede the orders with the legs.

Elementary control is learned simultaneously with the seat. Progress in teaching position largely depends on a certain dexterity of the pupil in the handling of his horse because efficient teaching of position is possible only if the class moves around the ring in an *orderly manner.*

If you were to apply the above-listed principles to different gaits and movements then you would have the following rules of elementary control:

At the halt legs should be relaxed, reins loose. If the horse becomes fidgety, check him with the reins or straighten him with the legs, but hope that merely patting and talking soothingly to the horse will relax him.

To start a walk give a voice command "walk," cluck with your tongue and tap with your legs; if necessary, kick. If you meet with resistance, use the whip gently on the horse's shoulder. During all this urging the reins must be loose.

If the horse walks too slowly, repeat the signals in the same order. If the horse tries to break into a trot say "walk" repeatedly and follow it with checking with the reins. As the walk becomes stabilized, release the tension on the reins and pat your horse.

If the horse breaks into a trot, not because he has misunderstood your commands but because he has became excited, then pat him and talk soothingly to him while checking.

In all these cases be careful not to squeeze or kick the horse unintentionally, and if he walks regularly and quietly leave the reins completely loose.

To start a trot. The method of starting the trot is exactly the same as that for starting a walk, but the legs are used somewhat more strongly and the voice command, naturally, consists of a different word and sharper intonation.

Once the trot is started, establish a steady, ordinary speed by clucking or using your legs or whip if the horse moves too slowly and by checking, patting and talking soothingly if he is moving too fast. Don't forget to pat him the moment he takes the right pace and from then on leave the reins loose and beware of disturbing the horse unintentionally with your legs.

To slow the trot down below the ordinary speed give the command "whoa" and repeat it, following it, if necessary, by checking with the reins.

To increase the speed of the trot above the ordinary, use the cluck, the legs and, if necessary, a little whip on the shoulder. On a sluggish horse maintain the speed of the trot by squeezing with the calves every time you return to the saddle in posting. This is the only case where a beginner is able to urge the horse with squeezes of the legs. At a sitting trot urge the horse forward by tapping with your legs any time it is necessary. The greater freedom of the legs for control is one of the advantages of the sitting trot.

Keep your reins completely loose and your legs passive all the while the horse maintains an even, ordinary trot.

To start a canter from a trot (disregarding the lead) give voice command to canter, simultaneously urging the horse forward with the legs while, for a couple of seconds, checking him with the reins, to prevent him from merely increasing the speed of the trot. Continue to urge him forward these couple of seconds that you are checking him and then simultaneously release the reins and give the final order with one leg—the outside leg (the right leg if moving in the ring to the left).

During the preparation for the canter departure stop posting and sit, in order to be able to use your legs better.

All through this preparation to start a canter the horse's neck and head must be kept absolutely straight. But, as soon as you find that you have time to think of one more thing then, throughout the period of preparation for the canter, keep the horse's head turned slightly to the inside (to the left if you are going to the left in a ring) just enough to see his inside eye. Do this by moving both hands to the outside. This turning of the head to the inside, combined with a stronger use of the outside leg is a preparation for the future canter departure on the desired lead, which is a subject of intermediate control.

When starting the canter use the whip if the voice and leg commands fail; then establish an even speed of the canter by checking or further urging; achieve quietness by talking and patting and then leave your reins completely loose throughout the canter. A beginner or an elementary rider is unable to follow the balancing gestures of the horse's neck and head with his arms. Hence, if these riders attempt to canter "on contact" they are bound either to hang on the horse's mouth if their reins are really taut or, if their reins are slightly slack, the horse will jerk himself against the bit every time he moves his neck and head. The same obtains at a walk and, to a very large degree, on the jump. This is why the first lessons in riding on contact are given at a trot, during which the horse's neck and head is steady. Riding on soft contact is the basic point of intermediate control.

At this stage of learning to ride you should use only one speed at a canter—the rather slow ordinary. Your horse is not schooled to canter semi-collectedly and he may become unruly if you canter him too fast. On the other hand, if the horse knows the *routine* of only one speed, he will canter for you maintaining this speed, by himself, on loose reins.

To change from a canter to slower gaits, for instance, from the canter to the trot, give the appropriate voice-command, repeating it, and check with the reins as lightly as practical, roughly if necessary, to obtain results. Once the new gait has been established, pat the horse and return to loose reins and general passiveness as quickly as possible. Use the same method when in *emergencies* you have to walk or to halt the horse directly from a canter.

All transitions should be gradual, which means that if you are at a halt and you wish to canter you should make a few steps of walk, follow them with half a dozen strides at a trot, and then start the canter. The same rules should be applied in reverse. In other words, if you canter and you wish to halt your horse, you should first bring him to a trot, then to a walk and then to a halt. Abiding by this rule (except in emergencies) you will avoid a great deal of possible roughness.

To make a turn to the right while moving, move your right arm to the right and lead the horse along the turn, acting with the right hand to the right and slightly forward. This is called the leading rein. When making a long turn such as, for instance, a full circle as an exercise, you may need to urge the horse forward with the voice, leg or whip to maintain the speed of the gait. When making a turn or a circle use your leading rein as little as practical. If the horse resists, you will have to lead him throughout the turn, but in many cases an occasional indication will be all that will be necessary and then you may leave the reins loose between the moments when you are repeating your command to proceed along a curve. The above is a very crude form of the "give and take"—which you will learn considerably later.

To make a turn in place, you should use the turn on the forehand which is easier than the turn on the haunches.

If you wish to turn on the forehand, rotating the hindquarters to the left, leave your left leg in its normal position but press it against the horse's body. Then move your right leg about four inches back from its normal position and *tap* (lightly or strongly) with it *throughout* the turn. This action will rotate the hindquarters to the left. With your hands check the horse every time he wants to move forward and keep the reins loose during the moments when he doesn't. When checking with the reins you must keep the neck and head absolutely straight.

To back the horse, use your hands in the following manner: pull on the reins to obtain a step back; the moment the step begins loosen the reins, then pull again to start a second step and give the reins while the horse is making it. Don't back for more than four steps. Don't use your legs while pulling on the reins; in other words, don't simultaneously give two contradictory orders. You can use one of the legs singly to straighten a horse which is backing crookedly or you can use both legs to wake up a sluggish horse before beginning backing.

You can also straighten a crookedly backing horse by using your right rein more strongly (taking his head to the right) when his hindquarters deviate to the right, or the reverse if they deviate to the left. Beyond this especial effort with the hands, the horse's neck and head must be kept straight throughout the backing.

The approach to the jump. With the little knowledge of riding which you possess at this stage, you should not jump higher than three foot obstacles and *never* on horses that are not perfectly stabilized. Such horses will enable you to be absolutely passive, so that you can give exclusive attention to your position and to giving freedom to the horse's neck and head with your hands. If however, on a bad day, a horse suitable for a beginner should lose his quiet approach to an obstacle, then try to establish an even and calm gait by the means described above. If unable to better the horse's approach after trying three or four fences, lower the fence.

As a general rule, your horse must approach an obstacle at an even trot or canter on loose reins. The majority of horses, if properly trained and consistently ridden sensibly, will do this, particularly if the obstacle is not over three feet.

Even if a certain amount of control was necessary to rate the horse during the approach, all the controlling efforts of the rider should completely stop about two strides from the obstacle. From then on and during the jump itself the rider must be completely passive, giving full freedom to the horse to negotiate the obstacle in a natural manner.

The first two months of the normal schooling program described in the chapter THE PROGRAM OF SCHOOLING, are devoted to the stabilization (general and in jumping) of the horse, which is the fundamental training for the beginner's horse.

This is all that there is to elementary control.

Obvious as it probably is to the reader, after having reached this point in the book, that principles of elementary control are the only ones by means of which a novice or an uneducated rider can manage his horse without *abusing* him, this didn't occur to me in the early stages of my teaching career.

I knew that, from time to time, similar principles had been applied on a large scale, for instance, during the Napoleonic wars (a fact which I mentioned in the first chapter), and unquestionably were practiced always by many individuals, probably more often by the English squire than by the scholastically inclined continental gentleman. But to those like me, who early in life were exposed to the academic riding of the 19th century, the concept of riding most of the time on loose reins as an ideal under certain circumstances, would have been an unpardonable heresy; there just couldn't be such circumstances. In spite of my youthful enthusiasm for Italian ideas, a good part of my thinking remained dominated for a long time by James Fillis' philosophy and the essence of Forward Riding escaped me for many years.

James Fillis' book BREAKING AND RIDING, which was our principal text book in the Cavalry School, and which is still reprinted today, is a stimulating presentation of complicated riding; one can find all sorts of ideas in it. You will read, for instance, that "the human voice has a great influence on the horse" and that "I am the resolute enemy of keeping the horse always collected," but such phrases are completely lost among illustrations of fully collected horses doing Piaffe or cantering backwards and innumerable statements like this:

". . . The means for stopping the horse is always the same—namely, raise the snaffle reins while drawing them back with an equal feeling on both reins, so as to bring the weight on the hindquarters; at the same time, close both legs strongly to bring the hocks under the animal's body, and feel the curb reins. *The horse is then between the hands and legs.*"

The majority of my contemporaries still can't get rid of this idea of "leading the horse between the hands and legs," no matter where or when, even when hacking.

I have to admit that I myself do not halt my horse by these elaborate means when I hack, although I know how to do it and all my horses have been schooled to it also. As a rule, when I hack my horse, not as a part of his training but just to enjoy a pleasant morning in the fields and woods, I merely say "whoa," and slightly check the reins to make the horse halt while I am deciding whether to take a path going to the right or to continue straight. And what have I missed by halting the horse this way? Precisely nothing. My horse has halted softly and that is the main thing. Whether he halted with the neck low or high, with the hindquarters under him or not seem to me to be scholastic details which may be important in schooling or in some competitions but which, on this morning, have no connection with my desire to enjoy nature in the company of my horse. Fine riding has its place, but it is out of place to consider it imperative every time one is in the saddle.

I never was James Fillis' pupil and I like to think that he, himself a great master, had a flexible mind and that his teaching would have been accordingly flexible. But this was not the case among his passionately devoted followers, and my teachers made a real fetish of the principle of "riding the horse all the time." This resulted, in my case anyway, in an unhappy horse and in my inability to let the horse really go; a fault it took me years to get rid of.

I wouldn't devote so many lines to the past were it not for the fact that even today some teachers awkwardly combine modern riding with Fillis' principles of constant and elaborate domination of the horse by the rider. Just lately, when addressing an audience of riding teachers and preaching simplification I was criticized by an experienced and unquestionably able riding teacher. And it is typical that the serious riding teacher is rather apt to indulge in complications. Why? I don't know; perhaps because such a teacher knows a great deal but sometimes not enough, or perhaps this is one of the unconscious ways of convincing oneself of one's superiority over ordinary human beings? The fact that some of Fillis' ideas are still occasionally professed, even in cross-country riding, is indisputable.

The method of elementary control as presented in this chapter was not conceived overnight in the quiet of a study. Different practical experiences dictated its different parts at various times, and it was only about five years ago that I put all these parts together into a logical and harmonious whole. I remember very well how it all started: I simply could no longer watch bad riders abusing my horses, hanging on their mouths and unintentionally, of course, jerking them; obviously there was something wrong in my method of teaching. And then I thought, wouldn't it be nice if they all would ride, at this stage of the game, with no reins at all, controlling the horses by voice, as the Asiatic horsemen of 2000 years ago. Going back to the beginning of our era would be incongruous, but I was sure that a happy medium could be found and I began to work in this direction. This chapter is the result of it.

CHAPTER IX

What Is a Good Performance of the Horse

It has already been stated many times in this book that the fundamental aim of intermediate riding is to obtain a *soft, efficient* performance, while the basic aim of advanced riding is to go a step beyond mere efficiency and to obtain a performance of *high quality*. Neither of these aims can be accomplished through mere dexterity of the rider's aids; schooling of the horse on one level or the other is all-important. Perhaps I should elaborate on these ideas by including the following definitions of schooling and riding.

The Aims of Schooling. Schooling aims to develop the horse physically and mentally to the point where he performs *efficiently*—or at his best possible—and is *pleasant* to ride for an educated and therefore discriminating rider. Thus schooling, on one hand, aims at an athletic development of the horse's body and consequently is a *course in physical education,* while on the other hand it teaches the horse signals, obedience, and finally *cooperation.* A good performance of a well-schooled horse exhibits:

1) *Mentally*—calmness, knowledge of signals, cooperation.

2) *Physically*—well-developed balance, strength, endurance, agility, rhythmic gaits and athletic jumping.

The Aims of Rational Riding. Riding should aim to produce a performance on the level of the schooling which the horse has received; in other words, it intends to get out of the horse the best that he is educated to give, within the limit of his abilities.

Both for schooling and for making use in riding of the results of schooling, a knowledge of the mechanics of the horse's gaits and movements is essential. Obviously, before attempting to obtain a certain movement the rider must know its possible good and bad points.

There are thick books written entirely about these mechanics. But out of this immense mass of data only knowledge which may be of immediate and practical assistance to the rider or trainer is presented in this chapter. For instance, my book THE DEFENCE OF THE FORWARD SEAT, contains 142 pages and every bit of it is devoted to the horse's efforts in jumping; it took only seven typewritten pages to cover the same subject in this chapter. This means that all the information given here is absolutely essential. As usual, data presented in such a concise form are hard to read through. Hence this chapter is intended for reference, not for reading. To try to read it would be a mistake, but you will need to refer to it constantly when learning riding or when schooling your first horse; any ambitious advanced rider or active trainer will eventually learn to know its content by heart.

This chapter defines different gaits and movements, points out what constitutes a good movement and what makes a defective one, often tracing the latter to failures in schooling or to bad riding. In such cases, I assume 1) that the horse in question is sound, and 2) that the horse has good average conformation (without being a model).

This book does not concern itself with the conformation or unsoundness of the horse; therefore, it does not discuss faults in gaits, in jumping and in different movements which are the result of a bad physique. But I would like my readers to bear in mind that such consequences of faulty conformation as interfering, paddling, overreaching, rocking, winding, etc., cannot be remedied either by good riding or by schooling.

The mechanics of the horse's movements are interesting to the rider not only from the point of view of the quality of the horse's performance, but also as the basis for methods of controlling the horse; in other words, as the foundation for conceiving formulae for obtaining different movements. In this respect, however, some details of the mechanics leave ample ground for imagination, speculation, and hence disagreement. For instance, what should the horse's position be to start a canter on the right lead? Should his head be turned to the right or to the left? Should his body be absolutely straight or should the haunches be slightly ranged to the right? Observation of a free horse in nature will not give a decisive answer. The same horse on the same day may start successive canters in different attitudes. Obviously, the mechanics are combined with emotions and, in *details,* depend on the reasons for starting a movement. As an inexact illustration, I would like you to analyze the mechanics of your getting to your feet from a chair. First of all, it will depend on how you have been sitting in the chair; then on whether your getting up was unexpected or anticipated; on whether it was caused by alarm, good manners or the simple necessity of moving from place to place. You may have your head turned in any direction, you may or may not use the arm-gestures, etc. The canter departure in nature is just as complicated. In this respect, one may talk about the engagement of the hindquarters, or just the opposite; about the necessity for keeping the preponderance of weight on the forehand; one may stress the freeing of a shoulder or the "loading" of a certain foot, which, by the way, can itself be accomplished in different ways. The Dressage rider usually starts his thinking with the hind legs, the "forward rider" with the forehand; hence there is a divergence of opinions on how a canter on a certain lead should be started.

If the horse does not know any signals, or is simply resisting, then, of course, a certain position may force him into the canter more easily than another would, but even here some horses will more frequently start correctly from a circle; others, when placed obliquely to the direct line of the movement. There are situations when any one of the known positions may be tried by a trainer, when in trouble, on the same horse.

Pursuing the example of the canter, I would like to add a description of the basic stages of what I consider the best way to teach canter departure. I believe that the ultimate aim of schooling is to have a horse responsive to *gentle signals;* force should not come into a finished performance. As you will see later, schooling by the method presented in this book begins on a longe. When going on a longe to the right, with a relaxed mind and body, listening to the trainer's commands, the horse naturally has the head slightly turned to the right; the weight of the longe will do it, if nothing else will; so it is in this attitude that he will make his first circles; in other words, turns, and will start his first canter departures. My first mounted canter will be also on a circle with a radius of at least the full length of the longe (to have it slow and quiet) and, following so far a lightly established habit (without much use of the aids, preferably voice alone) the horse will both circle and begin the canter with the head slightly turned to the right. Eventually, even on a straight line, a pull on the right rein so gentle that it won't even turn the head to the right (in combination with equally gentle legs) will be a decisive order.

All in all, I believe that, in schooling, an appeal to the mentality of the horse and the establishment of a habit through consistent use of the same appeal is more efficient than the efforts of the rider to obtain a certain movement through forcing the horse into a definite position. The very fact that an average horse which has been trained to start a canter on a certain lead from a certain set of aids can be re-trained within a few weeks to start it from a different combination, seems to substantiate my theory.

Of course, the fact that the horse can be easily re-trained does not mean that an appeal to the mentality is all that is necessary; it also means that the mechanics of the horse's movements can be variously interpreted—as I mentioned above.

In the majority of books on riding you will read something like this: "To take the gallop with the right lead, the left hind leg must begin the movement, therefore, if the left hind leg is weighted by the rider's seat it is the one best fitted to raise the mass; if the reins weight the left shoulder at the same time, then the right foreleg is more easily able to extend its stride."

I have many things to say against this traditional interpretation of the mechanics of the canter departure.

First of all, only a well-schooled dressage horse starts the canter from behind. A cross-country horse (even a sufficiently schooled one) moving forward with forward balance in most cases starts the gallop from the forehand, and neither in the hunting field nor in the jumping arena does it matter how the horse starts the canter, providing the departure is smooth and the gallop united. Hence, to you or to me, "weighting one of the haunches" for the canter departure is not necessary.

But I would dare to doubt its importance even in Dressage. Did you ever feel an ache or cramp in one of your legs, when tired after a long ride? And then, forgetting the forward seat, you sat in the saddle unevenly with more weight on one side? Don't you remember that no change took place in the gait, any gait, and it continued straight and even, although, unquestionably, the horse felt uncomfortable. I am certain that an uneven distribution of the rider's weight is annoying and tiring to the horse and I am also certain that switching it consistently in combination with other aids may turn into a signal. But I do not believe that it can influence the horse *physically* to the point where he is forced to behave in a certain way.

You have probably had experience with a horse who, when quiet, always responded to a certain set of aids for canter departure but who, when excited, failed to obey them. Isn't this one more proof that the movement was obtained through a trained horse's cooperation and not through any *forcible* means by the rider?

I personally don't believe in using the weight for the control of the horse. To me, the horse should feel the rider's weight as little as possible in general; this is where the Forward Seat is supreme. But I realize that the weight can be used as a signal and will be effective every time the horse wishes to cooperate. For instance, in very few hours you can teach the horse to turn without any use of legs and hands, merely by switching your weight considerably to one side.

Furthermore, I have my doubts about the decisive influence of "weighting one shoulder and thus freeing the other," by moving both hands to one side or by turning the horse's head to one or the other side. You unquestionably have seen many riders whose horses were trotting straight while their heads were held in a crooked position from an uneven pull on the reins. And, if this unfortunate horse ceases to accept such a rein action as a signal, he will move straight enough, although one of his shoulders is obviously more "loaded" than the other. But again, I know from experience, that loading a shoulder can become a signal.

The average book of the type I have just quoted usually makes a strong point of keeping the horse's body during the canter departure, and when cantering (even slowly), perfectly straight in relation to the straight line of forward movement. This, by the way, is one of the strictest rules of Dressage. Unquestionably, if you wish to take some trouble in schooling, the above rule can be achieved, but this is where the natural mechanics of the horse's body are forgotten for the sake of the artificial precision of manège riding. Obviously, if placed slightly sideways to the direction of movement, the horse will naturally take the lead of the side which is ahead of the other. The same interpretation of the horse's mechanics indicates that no effort should be made on the part of the rider to prevent the horse's ranging the quarters at a *slow* canter. With an increase of speed, the horse by himself will straighten his body, for no effective pushing by the hindquarters (without which there is no speed) can take place unless the horse is straight. Many horses, due to their conformation, will naturally start and maintain a slow canter with the body kept straight; such a slow canter is the nicest in appearance.

But even if it is possible to interpret certain details of the mechanics in different ways, there are fundamentals which can mean only one thing. It is with these basic mechanics that this chapter is concerned.

All the following definitions are conceived as parts of the method about which this book is written; they may not entirely suit another system of riding and schooling.

Here is the list of topics of this chapter in the order in which they are discussed:

1) Ordinary (travelling) gaits.
2) Some of the possible defects of the ordinary gaits due to faulty schooling.
3) Some of the possible defects of the ordinary gaits due to bad riding.
4) Slow gaits:
   slow passive gaits
   semi-collected gaits
   defects and good points
5) Fast gaits:
   fast animated gaits
   semi-extended trot
   the usual defect.
6) The speed of the gaits.
7) Fatigue at different gaits:
   muscular fatigue
   fatigue of the lungs and heart
   mental fatigue.
8) The rhythms of the gaits:
   the walk
   the trot
   the canter
   disunited canter
   counter gallop.
9) The jump:
   what is a good jump
   the mechanics of the jump

the common defects of the jump
changes of leads on the jump
fatigue in jumping.
10) Backing:
    good backing
    poor backing.
11) Half-turn on the forehand in place:
    a good turn
    divergence of opinions
    a poor turn.
12) Half-turn on the haunches in place:
    a good turn
    a poor turn
    divergence of opinions.
13) A turn with movement forward: (circle, half-circle, etc.)
    the mechanics
    a good turn
    a poor turn.
14) Two tracks and shoulder in:
    the mechanics
    divergence of opinions
    good two tracks
    poor two tracks.
15) A flying change of leads.
16) Transitions.
17) A short turn at the gallop.

More information on the mechanics of the horse's movement is to be found in the next chapter and scattered through the book.

Ordinary (Travelling) Gaits, viewed from the side, must show long, even, free, close-to-the-ground strides; such strides constitute *efficient movement.* This kind of stride largely depends on the extended attitude of the horse's neck and head. The horse should move with the neck stretched forward and, on the average, held at about 40 degrees (depending on the gait and conformation) to the ground, and the head held forward of the perpendicular.

Viewed from the front, the horse must keep himself straight from the nose to the tail. His forelegs should move straight forward with no throwing of the feet outward or inward.

Viewed from the rear, the hindfeet should move straight forward, tracking the forefeet.

The rider should be able with *little effort* to maintain an even gait, no matter what the speed or the gait.

All the above points combine to produce efficient movement, which means that all the energy generated at the moment by the horse is utilized to cover ground and none is wasted in nervousness, resisting the rider, high action, disconnected movement, wavering, etc.

Some of the Possible Defects in the Ordinary Gaits Due to Faulty Schooling:

1) *Wavering,* while supposedly moving straight, is nearly always caused by a failure to develop in the horse sufficient "impulse forward." The horse that lacks this impulse stays "behind the bit" and hence wavers.

2) *Unevenness of gaits* (constant variations in the speed) is usually caused by failure to "stabilize" the horse at his gaits or by failure to establish calmness.

3) *Excessive knee action,* while it usually is caused by faulty conformation (for instance, excessively long cannon bones) also may be present when the forward, free swing of the forelegs has not been developed in schooling.

4) *"Cold" shoulders,* which do not act freely, may be perfectly good shoulders (particularly in a lethargic type of horse) the action of which has not been developed through schooling gymnastics.

5) *Stiff gaits* are often the result of a stiff mouth whose resistance to the rider's hand stiffens first the poll, then the neck, then the forehand and finally the whole body.

6) *Disconnected gaits* are gaits which lack synchronization between the beats of hind and fore legs. A disconnected horse fails to move in one piece. Such movement is often the result of working the horse at too fast gaits (particularly at too fast a trot) before the horse has learned synchronized movement at slowish ordinary gaits. Teaching regularity of the rhythm of gaits is one of the basic aims of schooling.

Some of the Possible Defects in the Ordinary Gaits Due to Bad Riding (it is assumed that the horse is well-schooled but badly ridden):

1) *Inefficient strides* due to the rider's failure to have the horse on the bit (or on contact) *with extended neck.*
2) *Uneven movement* due a) to the fact that the rider disturbs the horse; b) to bad cooperation of rider's legs and hands.
3) *Wavering combined with short strides* occurs when the horse is badly "behind the bit," caused by bad cooperation of the rider's legs and hands.
4) *Pulling, with resulting stiff movement,* may be due to the fact that the horse is irritated by the tactless behavior of the rider; it may also be due to the horse being "over the bit." Heavy, slow hands combined with over-energetic legs are the usual cause of the latter.

Slow Gaits may range from merely slow passive gaits with forward balance to different degrees of collection. The first are used at the beginning of schooling and sometimes in cross-country riding; while the latter (as gymnastics) are practiced only in advanced stages of schooling.

In full collection the hind legs advance little under the body and swing out correspondingly little, but they are bent in the hocks, the neck is raised and is arched in the poll, head almost perpendicular to the ground. With this "central balance" the horse moves with shortened, high, light and cadenced steps.

As long as full collection does not lead to the bettering of free galloping and jumping and too much work in it may make the horse nervous and even impair the efficiency of the travelling gaits (by shortening and raising the strides), the trainer of cross-country horses should use semi-collected gaits as gymnastics only. The difference between collection and semi-collection lies in the degree of engagement of the hindquarters (see text on "engagement" in next chapter), of raising the neck and of bringing the head in, and in the degree of the energy of propulsion. (Pics. 62, 63 & 64). In other words, in the degree of central balance, and in the height and cadence of the steps. If, when aiming at collection, you do not attempt to switch some of the horse's weight from the forehand to the hindquarters, do not bring the head all the way in to a perpendicular position and, if you avoid stimulating excessive energy of propulsion, you will have semi-collected gaits. The steps of semi-collected gaits should be shorter, higher and more cadenced than those of ordinary gaits, but not to the degree of full collection. *In any case, the head should be brought in and held in a more or less vertical position through repeated flexions of the mouth* (about one flexion each full stride).

The usual defect of these gaits is nervousness and stiffness, and the usual cause of it is the fact that the horse is gathered by the force of the rider's legs and hands which the horse irritatedly resists. A gradual education permits collection of the horse with very soft hands and undisturbing legs. In such cases, the gait is elastic and the action of the legs rounded.

Semi-collection through flexions is often developed without any special effort by the trainer, in the course of the exercises which consist of changing speeds at different gaits (shortening and lengthening the gait).

The first step towards collection is the *Ramener,* that is raising the neck and bringing the head in by flexing the poll.

Fast Gaits. A fast trot based on free going is called either a *fast* or a *long-striding* one, while that based on collection is called an *extended* one. Dressage, which was always practiced exclusively in small arenas, was never concerned with really fast gaits (except the fast walk). Dressage, however, developed both the trot and canter with an extra extension of the forelegs. In a well executed *extended* High School trot the horse's neck is held high, and the head in an approximately vertical position; the hind legs do not go forward to a great degree under the body (hence the relatively slow speed) but the forelegs are raised up and then extended forward to the maximum. On the other hand in a natural fast trot, the neck and head are held in a normal extended attitude, the hindlegs engage far under the body, while the forelegs lengthen their action correspondingly; the strides are flat. The *extended gallop* (canter) of Dressage was developed in a manner similar to the extended trot; it should not be confused with the gallop of a hunter.

What this book calls the *semi-extended trot* is merely a long-striding natural trot with the neck and head in the position of the *Ramener* (neck held high and the head bent in the poll).

During early schooling merely a faster trot than ordinary is used. Gradually a long stride should be developed. A semi-extended trot, *may* be practiced later as a gymnastic, with some horses. It is a tiring movement and even a simple long-striding trot should be used very discreetly.

THE SPEEDS OF THE GAITS

The ordinary walk approximately	4 miles per hour	
The ordinary trot approximately	8 " " "	
The ordinary canter approximately	10 " " "	
The semi-collected walk approximately	2½ " " "	
The semi-collected trot approximately	5 " " "	
The semi-collected canter approximately	6 " " "	
A fully collected trot (Piaffe) is in place.		
A fully collected canter may be almost in place.		
The semi-extended trot approximately	12 " " "	
A fully extended trot may be slower than the semi-extended one (less strides per minute). The difference is not in the speed but in the size of strides and in the comparative extension of the limbs.		
The hunting pace approximately	18 " " "	
The speed required in the arena jumping and in the cross-country run of the Three-Day-Event approximately	18 " " "	
The speed required in the steeplechase of the Three-Day-Event approximately	24 " " "	

Pic. 62.   Shows a collected canter. (The rider—Mr. Fritz Stecken).

Pic. 63.   Shows a semi-collected trot.

Pic. 64.   Shows an ordinary canter on loose reins—both horse and rider are the same as in the picture of a semi-collected trot. Notice the different distribution of weight of the horse and the resulting difference in action. The rider changes his attitude in each case in order to remain united with the horse.

Pic. 65.   Here is relaxed backing and because it is relaxed the movement is in two beats; each beat is constituted by a diagonal pair of legs. This backing is on an intermediate level—the rider obtains the steps back by means of "give and take" with his hands, maintaining the neck and head of the horse in the normal attitude. Only a schooled horse will back as softly as the horse in the picture does.

Fatigue at Different Gaits.

Muscular fatigue. The walk and trot pushed to the limit are very fatiguing. If a horseman wishes to go fast he gallops. A collected gallop also demands disproportionately much energy from the horse. Hence the selection of the gaits should be directed by the speed required. The very fast walk and trot, as well as collected gaits, should be used as gymnastics only and not as travelling gaits. The very fast as well as collected gaits should be developed gradually; any new movement, bringing new muscles into play, may hurt the horse if used too much at first.

Fatigue of the lungs. (Closely related to fatigue of the heart.) At a walk the horse uses twice as much air as when standing still; at an ordinary trot four times; at an ordinary canter just slightly more than at a trot, and at full gallop more than twelve times as much as when standing. The lungs' fatigue, as well as muscular fatigue, should always be taken into consideration when riding or when schooling. In the course of schooling the "wind" of the horse as well as his muscles should be gradually developed.

Mental fatigue. The horse, if unaccustomed to it, is easily bored by the routine of ring gymnastics. Hence, at first, lessons in the ring should not be over forty-five minutes' duration, interrupted often by relaxing at a walk. This is one of the reasons why some trainers prefer to have one half-hour lesson in the morning and one in the afternoon instead of a whole hour all at once. A tactful trainer doesn't repeat the same exercise too many times in a row.

Concentration and cooperation are things which the horse learns gradually. In this respect a green horse is like a child.

The Rhythms of the Gaits. The seat of the movement being the hindquarters, it is customary to count the beats starting with the hind feet.

The walk is a movement of four beats. The order is as follows:

Either of the hind legs may start the propulsion after the initial step of the diagonally opposite fore leg. If the right hind was the first to push, then the second beat is the right front, the third beat—the left hind, the fourth beat—the left front.

In the course of each stride of the walk, the horse passes through phases when he is supported in turn by diagonal and lateral pairs, and by three legs at once. During the moments of instability (lateral supports) the horse uses the gestures of the neck and head to balance himself. The rider must follow these gestures with the movements of his arms. There are practically no balancing gestures at a collected walk.

The trot is a movement of two beats. The legs move forward in diagonal pairs. Right hind and left front make one beat, while the left hind and the right front form the other beat.

At the trot the horse is supported by alternating diagonal pairs. The diagonal supports give stability to the gait and therefore during the trot the horse doesn't need the assistance of balancing gestures. At the trot the neck and head remain practically steady, and consequently the rider's arms should be correspondingly steady.

The canter (gallop) is a movement of three beats (four beats in full gallop or in an extremely collected one). Depending on the type of schooling the canter may begin from the front or from behind. (The latter in the case of a collected Dressage horse.) In the case of a free-going cross-country horse it starts from the front. The order of the beats of a full stride of a canter (after the first half-stride) on the right lead is as follows: First beat—left hind alone. Second beat—a diagonal pair consisting of right hind and left front. Third beat—the right foreleg alone. In the case of the canter on the right lead the right legs move slightly ahead of the left legs. This should be taken into consideration when placing the horse for a canter departure on a specified lead.

At the canter the horse is supported during each stride in turn by one hind leg, by three legs, by a diagonal pair, again by three legs and by one front leg. During the moments of insufficient stability (single supports) the horse helps his balance by gestures with the neck and head. These gestures must be followed by the rider's arms. There are practically no gestures at the collected gallop.

Between the last beat of one stride and the first beat of the next one there is a moment of complete suspension. It is during this moment that a flying change of leads can take place.

The disunited canter has the following order of beats: if the first beat happened to be the right hind foot then the second beat is the left *lateral* pair and the third beat the right fore foot. It takes an agile horse to correct himself once the disunited canter has begun; hence, it is best to stop the colt and start a canter anew.

Counter gallop consists in making a turn while galloping on the outside lead; for instance, a circle to the left while galloping on the right lead. It is what is commonly called the wrong lead when it is performed unintentionally.

If it is well executed, the horse proceeds with even steps, remaining soft in the mouth and without leaning inward.

An awkward horse will lose his balance to the front and to the inside, hence will move with constantly increased speed, leaning on the rider's hands and also leaning toward the inside of the turn.

While circling at the counter gallop the horse's head must remain turned slightly toward the outside—in the direction of the lead of the gallop.

The Jump.

What is a good jump? A horse which can jump high and broad is not necessarily a good jumper. A high, clean jump may be:

1) Awkward and therefore not safe.
2) Unpleasant for the rider to sit.
3) Difficult to control during the approach.
4) Hard on the stiffly landing horse; such stiff jumping usually leads to diseases of the bones and tendons.
5) The emotional disturbance on the jump may be so great that the horse may require a pause before taking the next obstacle. There are horses which can negotiate a course only if halted or brought to a walk after each jump. In such artificial circumstances they may jump high and clean but cannot be considered good jumpers.

A good jumper in the full sense of the term is the one which:

1) Approaches an obstacle boldly at a quiet, energetic gait, holding himself in a natural, extended attitude (which is the best for jumping).
   Only if the horse is relaxed mentally during the approach does he have a chance to be relaxed on the jump physically, and only a relaxed horse can make an athletic jump.
2) Adjusts his strides himself, the rider being passive (except for occasional "rating") so as to end the last stride on the best line for the take-off.
3) Takes off without any hesitation, loss of stride or undue effort.
4) Is athletic enough to cope with a trappy approach or to compensate for a mistake (if such occurs) in figuring the take-off.
5) Makes the initial effort just powerful enough to negotiate the obstacle (without waste of energy) and doesn't underjump or over-jump it.
6) Uses his body harmoniously throughout the jump.
7) Lands surely and softly, using all the shock absorbers of his body (remains relaxed).
8) Gallops away as quietly as he approached the obstacle, being quickly ready for the next one.

Such a jump can be produced only through good riding of a well-schooled horse which, to begin with, possessed natural abilities for jumping.

The mechanics of the jump. From the point of view of the horse's efforts in negotiating an obstacle, the jump is usually divided into three periods: the take-off, the flight and the landing.

During the *take-off,* the horse uses his forces against the ground to propel his body upward and forward.

During the *flight,* the horse, while consuming the energy of the first period, somewhat regulates and corrects it with "inner motions." But forces developed when the body has no contact with the ground have very little power in them.

During the *landing*, the horse, having regained contact with the ground, uses different forces to enable his body to land a) with an equilibrium which will prevent a fall; b) with an elasticity which will absorb the shock of landing.

More specifically:

During the take-off, the horse has to accomplish the following:

1) He must acquire an angle to the ground with the front elevated.
2) He must accumulate spring in the hocks.
3) He must release the spring, propelling himself upward and forward.

The angle of elevation is produced by a double effort of raising the forehand and lowering the croup. The raising of the forehand is achieved by the upward thrust of the fore legs, while the lowering of the croup is produced by an energetic engagement of the hindquarters. This engagement of the hindquarters, with the weight of the whole horse on them, results in the horse's, so to speak, sitting on them, accumulating the spring in the hocks and in other joints. Then the horse releases this spring by pushing against the ground.

During the take-off the horse makes two gestures with the neck and head. The first one is upward and to the rear and coincides with the thrust of the forehand and the shortening of the horse's back at the moment of utmost engagement of the hindquarters. The next gesture is extending the neck forward and this takes place at the moment of the release of spring and the resulting utmost extension of the back.

In preparation for the neck gestures on the jump the horse stretches it forward a couple of strides before the take-off.

During the flight, the horse has to accomplish the following:

1) Raise the forehand at the moment it passes the obstacle.
2) Raise the hindquarters at the moment when they pass the obstacle.
3) Fold the legs when they pass the obstacle.
4) Give the fore legs a correct angle with the ground before landing.
5) Diminish the speed for the moment of landing.

Strong muscular efforts are possible only when the body is in contact with the ground; consequently, there cannot be any important efforts during the flight. The most that the horse can do while in the air is to regulate his flight somewhat by balancing gestures of the neck and head, also by certain actions of the back and sometimes by a sort of irregular wiggling of other parts of the body. The gestures of the neck and head are the most important of these and they are connected with the efforts of the back. The neck, during the upward part of the flight at first continues the gesture forward, then follows it with a gesture downward, the climax of which is reached at the moment that the forehand passes over the obstacle; the purpose of this gesture is to lighten the forehand. This gesture corresponds with the curving of the back upward so that the horse's body assumes the shape of the trajectory of his flight. During the downward flight the horse's neck and head make a gesture upward which coincides with the caving in of the back. One of the purposes of these actions of the back and neck is to raise the hindquarters at the moment when they pass over the obstacle. The upward swing of the neck during the downward flight also enables the shoulders to extend the fore legs for a landing at the best angle; at the same time this gesture, reaching its climax at the moment when the first foot to land touches the ground, diminishes the speed in the return to the ground and lessens the force of the impact.

Throughout the flight, the muscles close the angles of the legs when they pass over the obstacle and then open them in preparation for the landing.

During the landing, the horse has to accomplish the following:

1) He must absorb the shocks of landing.
2) He must change the angle of his body in reference to the ground.

The shock of landing is absorbed by the joints, tendons and muscles of the shoulders, fore legs and back, assisted by the gestures of the neck and head. The first fore leg to touch the ground is immediately picked up upon landing and so is the second. Both fore legs are in the air before the hind legs come in contact with the ground and there is a moment of complete suspension. By picking up the landing legs quickly the horse diminishes the evil effects of the impact.

The change of the angle of the body in reference to the ground is achieved a) by the upward thrust which each of the fore legs gives in turn upon landing, and b) by the engagement of the hindquarters under the body before they land.

The upward gesture of the neck which began during the second part of the flight reaches its peak at the moment of the landing of the first fore leg and thus also helps to absorb part of the shock. The next gesture of the neck is down and coincides with the shortening and curving of the back upward to enable the hindquarters to engage for landing.

The common defects of the jump. Many defects of jumping may be due to the fact that the horse is not capable either physically or mentally or emotionally. But often the defects of the jump may be traced to no schooling, bad schooling, or consistently bad riding. For instance:

1) *Refusing.* The horse often acquires this habit if, as a result of the bad seat and hands of the rider, he experiences pain every time he jumps.
Consistently demanding higher jumps of the horse than he is capable of performing with ease will also produce a refuser.

2) *Rushing* may develop from a) the habitual nervousness or over-eagerness of the rider who overpushes the horse during the approach; b) from jumping unschooled but bold colts too high too early; c) from jumping before obedience has been established in general schooling.

3) *Climbing fences* (taking off too late and hesitantly) may be the result of heavy, restricting hands or of a failure to develop "flight" in schooling. Failure to develop and to sustain the "impulse" of the approach may also result in "climbing."

4) *A consistently too early take-off* may be caused by failure during schooling to develop the upward thrust of the forehand or by failure to teach the horse to figure his jump economically.

5) *The absence of neck gestures* on the jump is usually the result of heavy hands which never give enough freedom to the horse to make these gestures.

6) *Stiff landings,* which may be so harmful to the soundness of the horse, usually result from the horse being tense physically as a sequel to being tense mentally. The results of rational schooling and good riding should be a quiet horse, jumping in a relaxed manner.

Changes of leads on the jump are often caused by the instinctive desire of the horse to have both hind legs lined up for the thrust of the take-off; obviously, when nearly on the same line, the hind legs can act more powerfully. To even them up during the last stride of the approach the horse has to make the appropriate effort with the leg that is farther back. This effort may carry this hoof slightly ahead of the other and thus the pattern for changing leads while the horse is in the air is set. This lining up of the hind legs requires a certain skill; hence the more experienced the jumper, the bigger the likelihood of his changing legs on a jump of 4' or higher; he may not make any special effort on a lower obstacle. I am far from being certain that the above rather standard explanation of the change of leads over obstacles is the only one, since while studying slow motion pictures I have noticed that more often than not the change occurs during the flight, when the unexpected foreleg speeds up its movement in order to land first.

Fatigue in jumping. Jumping, since it requires a strong physical effort and mental concentration, can easily tire a horse—in both ways. Furthermore, an even slightly unfortunate, hard landing may hurt the horse, as landing on your heels may hurt you. Too many such landings on the same day may start trouble. A judicious trainer will abide by the following rules:

1) He will jump the horse up to the horse's easy limit, at the most three times a week, each time taking ten to fifteen jumps. On the other

Pic. 66 (left).   A turn on the haunches, executed on the intermediate level without any attempts to collect the horse. The horse's head is slightly turned in the direction of the rotation of the forehand and the right front foot crosses in front of the left one, the most important part of the movement for it develops the extension of the forehand. See page 142.

As to the aids: note

1) that the right leg of the rider is applied considerably behind the girth;

2) that the right rein is used as a rein of indirect opposition in front of the withers;

3) that the position of the left arm indicates that it is in the act of using an opening rein;

4) that the position of the left toe shows that the left leg is kept at the girth.

Pic. 67 (right).   This is how "Two Tracks" looks when executed by a free-going horse. The fact that the movement is correct in all its essential details proves that collection is not necessary for the execution of this movement. I would like to stretch the point further and say that as a gymnastic for the development of a jumper a free Two Tracks is considerably more beneficial than a collected one. See page 145.

three working days of the week, he may jump different combinations of really low obstacles, some at a trot, not going higher than 2'6". Primarily because on such obstacles the shocks of landing are negligible, about thirty of them can be taken on the same day.

2) He will not jump a four-year-old higher than 3' 6". At this age the horse is still growing and his bones are not fully formed.

3) He will not jump a schooled jumper more than twice a week and more than ten jumps a day, and will not jump at all for a few days before a competition. The adherence to such a routine will result in the horse having a certain "edge," which he will need for the strenuous day of showing.

The above-described knowledge of the mechanics of the jump is absolutely imperative for anyone who schools a jumper. Only if a trainer can appreciate which of the jumping efforts of the horse are wrong or insufficient can he prescribe the proper exercises to correct them.

Backing (Pic. 65). Backing, if well executed, is a diagonal movement in two beats. The right hind and left front stepping back together, followed by the other diagonal pair.

Good backing is straight, slow, regular and relaxed, with long steps.

Poor backing. If the horse is resisting and consequently stiff, the movement degenerates into four beats, each leg moving separately. It is also uneven, irregular (steps of different sizes) and may take the form of not walking back but "rolling" back.

Half-Turn on the Forehand in Place. This turn is executed from a halt and consists of rotating the quarters to the right or left, whichever the rider chooses, until they have made a half-circle around the forehand and the horse faces in the opposite direction.

A good turn. In a very animated, semi-collected, but completely *relaxed* turn neither one of the fore feet will be stationary, forming a pivot, but while one marks time almost in place the other will be stepping around it. In the training of a cross-country horse this full animation of both fore legs is not essential and it is permissible if some beats are lost because the horse planted his exterior fore leg for too long. But another point concerning the movement of the legs is important—that is, that when rotating the croup to the left, for instance, the right hand leg must engage so as to move ahead and across the left hind. The turn must consist of approximately four clearly defined, well-connected regular steps.

Throughout the turn the horse's neck remains straight and the head either straight or slightly turned to the left, if, for instance, the quarters rotate to the left, only if needed to keep the forehand in place.

Divergence of opinions.

In HORSEMANSHIP AND HORSEMASTERSHIP (ed. 1945, page 103) it is said that during this turn "one front foot is even immobile" and "consequently the aids to be used must cooperate in placing onto this immobile front foot as much of the weight as possible, thus facilitating the movement of the other front foot and of the hindquarters."

This idea of the turn with one of the front feet as an immobile pivot is to be found in much old as well as modern writing. I, personally, can't see it. Granting that the adjective "immobile" is an ill-chosen one and cannot be applied to a pivot which turns, we are still left with a physically unnatural and awkward demand on the horse, that is to turn the foot in place without having casters under it.

Some of the Dressage writers of the 19th century, such as E. Barroil in his book, L'Art Equestre (1889), point out that there are two kinds of turns on the forehand, one with both fore legs moving and the other with one of the fore legs as a pivot. E. Barroil stresses the point that the first kind is used at the beginning of schooling and gradually leads to the turn with the pivoting foot. I believe that even in Dressage the animation of all the parts of the horse's body in the execution of any movement is more important than the mathematical exactness of having the turn really in place. But even if it were generally accepted as one of many perfectionist aims of Dressage, it certainly doesn't make sense when applied to the training of cross-country horses. To me, even for Dressage, the ideal would be that one fore leg *marks time* approximately in place while the other fore leg and quarters circle around it.

A poor turn. In a badly executed turn the resisting horse may move forward, back or to the side. His head may go up and his neck probably will be turned away from the direction of the movement. One of the fore legs, affected by the general stiffness, may stay "planted" most of the time. Being fidgety throughout the turn, the horse may refuse to stand quietly after the turn has been accomplished.

Half-Turn on the Haunches in Place (Pic. 66). This turn is executed either from a halt or from a walk and consists of rotating the forehand to right or left, whichever the case may be, until it has made a half-circle around the hindquarters and the horse faces in the opposite direction.

A good turn. In a very alert, semi-collected, but relaxed turn the hind feet will not be stationary, but will mark time, turning around on a *very small circle* (almost in place). In the training of a cross-country horse a semi-collected attitude is not necessary for this turn and, at least at the beginning of training, the turn should be executed keeping the horse in his ordinary, calm attitude. It is permissible for a couple of beats to be lost because the horse planted one of his hind feet for too long. But the turn can be considered good only, if when rotating the forehand to the left, for instance, the right front leg moves ahead and across the left one. The turn must consist of about four clearly-defined, well-connected, regular, quiet steps.

Throughout the turn the horse's neck and head must either remain straight or the head only slightly turned in the direction of the movement. The contact with the rider's hands must remain soft.

A poor turn. In a badly-executed turn the resisting horse may move forward, back or to the side; his head may go up and the neck will probably turn away from the direction of the movement. The hind legs affected by the general stiffness of the horse may stay planted most of the time and the horse will try to turn in one big sweep instead of taking several regular steps to accomplish it. The front leg which is supposed to cross in front of the other front leg may try to cross behind it.

Being fidgety throughout the turn, the horse may refuse to stand quietly (in the turn from a halt) after the turn has been accomplished.

Divergence of opinions. As to whether one of the hind feet should be used as a pivot, my point of view is the same as it was about the turn on the forehand.

A Turn with Movement Forward (Circle, Half-Circle, etc.).

The Mechanics. The horse in nature is probably never concerned about the quality of his movement, as we are about it when we ride him. A free horse when moving instinctively aims at one thing only: it is to move, no matter what the gait or speed, with the least effort (except when excited). You remember that the horse moves forward not merely by the effort of his muscles but by loss of equilibrium to the front. The horse executes a turn with movement forward on the same principle; that is, he takes such an attitude with the body as will result in a loss of balance forward and toward the inside of the turn. In other words, he overweighs the inside fore foot. If looking where he is going he usually does this by slightly inclining his head and neck in the direction of the turn. Some writers say that turning the head in the direction of the movement which loads the leading fore foot, also impedes its movement. There is no question but that any "loading" impedes *high* action, but I do not think it impedes *flat* forward movement. And even if it should impede it, it would still be practical, for it is the outside front leg which needs more freedom, having more ground to cover.

The horse at liberty may, and often will, especially when frisking in a familiar pasture and when not going anywhere, turn differently; he will take his head very much to the right (when turning left), will curve his spinal column in the direction of the turn and thus losing equilibrium *very much* in the direction of the center of the turn, will make a fast and rather precarious turn. On occasion the horse may turn with the body practically straight and with the head turned just slightly to the outside. Probably every one of these three described attitudes during a turn make instinctive sense in certain physical and mental situations and no one of them is definitely preferable to the horse in the abstract.

On observations of these natural turns, and speculations on their reasons and advantages, are based different methods of riding, one school of thought believing that, for such and such reasons, the loading of the inside front foot is desirable while the other maintains that the freedom of its movement is a more important aim, and so forth. Anyway, at present one school teaches that during a circle the horse's head should be very *slightly* turned to the outside and the other school requires that the head should be *slightly* turned to the inside; both schools give good results.

My method is based on the principle that *the horse must look where he is going;* in other words, he should have his head turned in the direction of the movement. This principle is applied not only in the case of turns or circles but in many other movements as well. For instance, I teach that the head should be slightly turned to the left when starting a canter on the left lead, or when two-tracking to the left, or when making a turn on the haunches to the left; thus the principle is consistently used through-out the method and we shall discuss it further in the chapter on schooling. In all these movements on the intermediate level I also often teach a *straight* attitude of neck and head which is frequently the more practical on this level.

A good turn. If the horse is relaxed and the head and neck move along the curvature, then the horse's body will also accept the shape of the path along which it moves.

On a normal field-turn, which probably will be at least 50′ or 60′ in diameter, the curvature of the horse's body is negligible; to all appearances the horse is straight from nose to tail. Therefore such a turn is not an exercise in *lateral flexibility*. To flex the horse in the sides one must make turns of about 30′ or even 20′ in diameter, and such turns will require bending of the horse.

A circle, being a fully completed turn, is made on the same principle.

A poor turn. In a poor turn or circle the horse may:

1) Lose the regularity of the gait.
2) Lose the proper attitude of the body in relation to the path by turning the head outward.
3) May try to cut the circle with the forehand.
4) May carry the hindquarters inward.
5) May "skid" with the hindquarters outward.

Two Tracks and Shoulder-In (Pic. 67).

The Mechanics. Two tracks can be executed at any gait and is an oblique movement at a somewhat less than 45 degree angle to the direction of the general movement. During it the outside fore leg and the outside hind leg move ahead of and across the inside legs. The head is slightly bent in the direction of the movement. In my method two tracks is not practiced along a wall but only on the diagonal changes of direction through the middle of the ring.

The "shoulder-in" is the same movement only with a reverse position of the head, and more than that, of the neck as well; the whole body of the horse should be bent in the right side when moving to the left (right shoulder-in).

The invention of shoulder-in is usually erroneously attributed to a famous Frenchman, de la Guérinière (who was active in the first half of the 18th century). But in essence it was described a good eighty years earlier by an Englishman, Charles Cavendish, Duke of Newcastle.

In the shoulder-in position the horse is awkwardly placed for movement to the side, but if he doesn't object to it and remains calm, he may benefit by this gymnastic. If you believe that awkward movements should be purposely used in the physical education of human beings to achieve the utmost suppleness, then you will see the reason for the shoulder-in.

Divergence of opinion. I may as well state at the beginning that I believe that except in the hands of superb riders the shoulder-in is apt to do more harm than good. But again I believe in general that all schooling exercises should consist in a gradual development of the horse's *natural, easy, free* movements. In my case even semi-collection (or "natural collection," as Colonel H. Chamberlin prefers to call it) obtained by merely slowing down the gait, and combined with flexions in the mouth, should remain free and natural.

It is very probable that both Newcastle and de la Guérinière, working with a heavy, crude type of 17th century horse, needed the shoulder-in and, being great masters themselves, could extract benefit from it. But then it so happened that the majority of writers and riders have proceeded to use it indiscriminately with present-day thoroughbred horses. I know that only exceptional pupils of mine practice it to the advantage of the horse, and I have seen cross-country horses ridden by international show riders who would have been much better off if the shoulder-in had never been used on them. Many practices of the riders of former days are unnecessary now in view of a different and better horse.

My argument may not hold water when applied to Dressage which, by the way, both Newcastle and de la Guérinière represented. Many exercises which may be beneficial when collection is an ultimate aim are harmful when free-going is the purpose.

I am not alone in my opinion; for instance, in the French magazine, *L'Eperon,* for February 1950, there is an article by René Gogue who, speaking of shoulder-in, and after many apologies to de la Guérinière, points out that only if the horse is carefully prepared for shoulder-in by other exercises can it be of benefit, and says: "It is upsetting to see the number of horsemen who consider that a horse which goes like a crab or which caracols represents the ultimate." I am very sorry that in the matter of this exercise I feel myself obliged to disagree with both Col. H. Chamberlin and the United States Cavalry School and many others who still believe that the shoulder-in is the A.B.C. of making a hunter or a jumper.

When in olden days the first lesson in two tracks consisted in placing the horse obliquely along the wall, his face heading into it, then the difference between two tracks and shoulder-in may not have been so great. But I don't use this method any more and I develop two tracks while moving freely, through the middle of the arena. More will be said about this in the chapter on schooling.

Good Two Tracks are distinguished by the following characteristics:

1) The movement forward is more pronounced than the movement to the side; in other words the horse moves freely to the front.

2) A free movement to the side is greatly helped by the horse being bent in the leading side with the head and neck turned slightly to the side of the oblique movement.

3) The forehand always slightly leads the hindquarters.

Poor Two Tracks may have the following defects:

1) The neck and head being turned to the outside impede the freedom of movement forward and the crossing of the legs.

2) The ordinary speed of the gait is lost, the strides become short, and the two tracks degenerates into side-stepping.

3) A resisting horse, trying to escape the legs and hands of the rider, increases the speed forward and greatly diminishes or completely loses the crossing of the legs.

4) The hindquarters take the lead and the movement forward is shortened.

A Flying Change of Leads.

A flying change of leads can take place only during the moment of suspension (see mechanics of the canter) which comes between the last beat of one stride and the first beat of the next stride.

If the horse is well-collected then the chances are greater that he will change from behind; in other words, that the first beat of the new canter will be marked by one of the hind legs. With proper schooling of the Dressage type, a collected horse may consistently change from behind. A change from the front is considered a grave mistake in Dressage riding. However, if the horse gallops with forward balance and is absolutely *calm,* then the chances are that he will change from the front. A well-balanced (forward balance), well-connected, agile cross-country horse will, while changing from the front, catch up so skillfully with the hindquarters that the change will be perfectly smooth. In such a case there is no reason at all for objecting to it and I consider such a change from the front as a natural result of the forward balance of the horse. But any plunging or other kind of jerkiness during the change, or particularly a change which results in a disunited gallop, should be regarded as a fault.

Transitions.

Transitions between movements and gaits should be quick, precise and smooth. The combination of quickness and smoothness cannot be expected at the beginning of schooling; it is developed gradually. The first aim is smoothness alone, while the rapidity of the change is little by little added to it.

As there are horses who can negotiate only a single jump calmly and which become increasingly upset galloping over a course (cause—bad schooling), so there are horses who will do, let us say, two tracks well by itself but not as part of a program. Any movement by itself, no matter how well executed, has little practical value in the general performance of the horse and it is only in combination with other gaits, speeds and movements that it can be taken as a proof that the horse is prepared to serve in cross-country riding.

Short Turn at the Gallop. In some of the jumping competitions in today's shows (1962), the courses are so tight and have such sharp turns that turning on the curve of a small half-circle may not be efficient enough, particularly in view of the modern vogue for speed. Today I therefore teach a *short turn at the gallop.*

This turn is neither a half-circle (where the hindlegs track the forelegs) nor a turn on the haunches (where the hindlegs remain almost in place); it is something in between. In this turn the curve described by the forehand is larger than the one described by the quarters, and both are larger than the corresponding curves at a turn on the haunches.

In a *good* short turn at the gallop the horse's neck and head remain straight and, during the turn, all the beats of the gallop are preserved. These result from the relaxation and cooperation of the horse. On the other hand, in a *bad* turn, the neck will go straight up, or up and to the side, the mouth will remain open, and the beats of the gallop will degenerate into a scramble.

CHAPTER X

Why Collected Gaits Have No Place
in Forward Schooling

This chapter concerns the mechanics of the horse's movements and, as such, is in a sense a continuation of the previous one. However, instead of describing various movements, it deals with the horse's basic efforts, which are applicable to all movements.

Don't be misled into thinking that because it does not consist of pure practical advice it may be neglected. A knowledge of the subjects which it covers, such as *balance, engagement, mechanics of the horse's jumping,* is of fundamental importance, for on an understanding of them were conceived the Forward Seat, Forward Control and Forward Schooling. But, of course, this subject is for the advanced rider, not for the beginner.

THE BALANCE OF THE HORSE IN MOTION

The balance of the horse in motion was rather briefly described on pages 34-38 and 116-117 and was referred to in other places. Here, writing about it at considerable length, I find that in order to make this text readable I shall have to repeat some of the statements previously made, which is perhaps for the better, for I know from experience that such repetitions are necessary in actual teaching.

When, ages ago, I was learning to ride, I was told by my teachers that the horse is in a state of equilibrium only when the weight is evenly distributed on all four feet—a table, with its four legs, was usually brought up as a good parallel. Somehow it never occurred to most riders of those days that there is nothing in common between the state of balance of a *motionless* table (or a horse) and the fluid balance of a *moving* horse. Many more horsemen today distinguish between the *static* balance of a horse at a halt and the *dynamic* balance of a moving horse. *At a standstill the balance of all animals depends merely on a certain distribution of weight,* while the balance of the same animals in motion is much more complex and depends on various physical efforts (Ill. No. I and II).

The forward movement of all animals is the result not only of the propulsive actions of the legs (the hind legs in the case of the horse), but of a necessary recurrent loss of equilibrium to the front as well. For instance, a man when walking, first shifts his weight forward, taking it

148

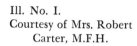

Ill. No. I.
Courtesy of Mrs. Robert
Carter, M.F.H.

Ill. No. II.
Courtesy of Miss Joan Harjes.

Ill. No. I and II. The dynamic balance of a horse in motion depends on his agility and strength.

off the foot which is still on the ground, losing his balance to the front and catching it again on the leg being put down ahead of the body; he aids himself with balancing gestures of his arms. The bigger the steps the more pronounced is the shifting of the weight forward—that is, the bigger the momentary loss of equilibrium to the front. Similarly, the forward movement of a horse consists of continually alternating moments of stability and instability. *Balance is the ability to cope with this phenomenon efficiently.* The same conception of balance is thus described by other horsemen:

1) "The equilibrium of a free horse . . . is achieved at a stand-still by the projection of the center of gravity on the base of support, and

in motion by the uninterrupted succession of momentary losses and retrievals of equilibrium." (From MÉCHANIQUE ÉQUESTRE by Docteur-Veterinaire André, p. 238, published in 1950. The translation is mine.)

2) "The movements of the body over the ground imply displacements of the center of gravity, and consequently, a destruction of the initial equilibrium, which incessantly compels the members to form new bases of support." (From the English translation of a French book, originally published in 1884, THE EXTERIOR OF THE HORSE, by A. Goubaux and G. Barrier, page 478.)

It so happens that horsemen, while always remembering the *base of support*, often forget that a movement is the *disturbance of the equilibrium achieved on that base of support*. Confusion in understanding the balance of the horse in motion is thus rather common.

The mechanics of dynamic balance were known before my teachers were born, but, then as now, many riders would rather believe the traditional tack-room yarns than make an effort to study the theory of equitation.

Now look at illustration No. I and try to figure out why this horse hasn't fallen flat on his nose. The answer is simple: every time the horse was in a similarly precarious situation and was about to fall, a certain leg moved forward into a position of support and was strong enough to do the job. The same reasoning can be applied to illustration No. II. These two pictures indicate that *the balance of the horse in motion depends mainly on agility and strength*.

A well-made, green colt has by nature enough agility and strength to balance himself. However, he doesn't possess these two qualities in sufficient degree to move in perfect balance under the weight of the rider. His legs, which must alternately come into support, are always a fraction of a second too late, and often, even when in the right position to restore balance, they are not strong enough to take care of both the horse's and the rider's weights. Hence a colt is usually too heavy in front and is apt to stumble.

The *basic* aim of schooling is to restore to the horse under the rider the *natural balance* of a free horse. There are several ways of going about it. If you were to do nothing but hack your colt regularly and feed him well, in time, without any special effort on your part, he would acquire enough strength and agility to carry you with ease. If you wish to do the job more quickly and to obtain better results, you would be wise to hack part of the time up and downhill and to jump at least low fences, particularly different combinations of them. But if you wish to solve the problem really efficiently and still faster, you will have to give your colt formal schooling. This will consist not only of cross-country riding and jumping, but of certain exercises as well, such as changing speeds at gaits, for instance.

For several reasons fully collected gaits cannot be regarded as helpful for any type of riding where speed or jumping play an important role. One of these reasons is the fact that the balancing efforts required at a gallop and in jumping are quite different from those necessary at collected gaits. In galloping and jumping the constantly repeated losses of equilibrium are *much greater* than at slow, collected gaits; one may even say that this difference is enormous. Consequently, the skill in using balancing efforts which the horse learns at collected gaits is of no help at all for galloping and jumping. The efforts necessary for the latter are violent by comparison with the gentle ones which suffice for slow gaits. The skill in the use of legs, back and neck required for maintaining balance at a gallop and in jumping cannot be developed by exercises at collected gaits, which do not call for the same efforts from the horse.

At the speed of an ordinary canter (10 m.p.h.) the horse will use his back and neck and head—and will use them still more at the gallop and in jumping. The back will contract and expand, and the neck and head will move up and down, making what are called "balancing gestures." You know that your loins work harder when you run or jump than when you merely walk, and when walking fast you will probably swing your arms. The horse's equivalent of the balancing efforts of human arms is the use of his neck and head, and when walking freely the horse will swing his neck and head up and down. It is only at the trot, the most stable gait of all, that the horse doesn't need the auxiliary balancing efforts of the neck.

The more freely the horse is allowed to move, the stronger are the balancing gestures of the neck and head; these efforts are synchronized with the action of the back. In jumping, all these efforts are very strong and are only diminished if the obstacle is an easy height for the horse and if he takes it at sufficient speed (when "acrobatics" are less necessary).

On the other hand, at slow, short gaits—where the amount of recurrently lost equilibrium is negligible—the horse does not need as much assistance from the auxiliary balancing efforts of the neck and head. This is particularly so at restrained collected gaits, and for that reason, of course, it was possible for dressage riders to establish the rule that "the neck should be erect and stay steady on the withers and shoulders, without moving about." (*Notes on Dressage,* published by the American Horse Shows Association.)

In spite of the fact that in motion a part of the horse's weight is constantly shifted back and forth, one may consider such a thing as the *average* point of the center of gravity of a horse's body. When the horse is ridden on the principle of free going—when he holds himself in an extended attitude and is calm—the *average* point of his center of gravity is farther forward than when the horse is collected. Hence, the former kind of equilibrium at gaits is usually called "forward" balance, while the latter is called "central" balance. By fully collecting a horse it is possible to shift so much weight to the hindquarters that balance will be a "rear" one.

In order to achieve a rapid slowing-down, or an abrupt halt from a fast gait, the horse must quickly transfer part of his weight from the front to the rear. In other words, he has to change his *average* balance from the forward one to at least the central one. And on resuming his former gait and speed, he has to move his point of average center of gravity forward again. *This ability of the horse to play with the distribution of his weight (shifting it forward or to the rear as necessary) is an important element of balance in the broad sense of the term.* This is where the semi-collection judiciously used (on advanced level of schooling) in abrupt slowing down or halting may be useful in training of some horses, but not necessarily all.

It is easy to train a normally cooperative well-made horse to shift his weight readily on voice commands only, in order to achieve an abrupt halt on loose reins. Picture No. III illustrates such a case.

Ill. No. III. A green horse making an abrupt halt. Courtesy of Miss Virginia Delamater.

The horse in this picture was bought from the race track only two and a half months before the photograph was taken. He is still, of course, completely green, but being of a cooperative nature and being trained along sound principles, he already makes a rapid (although still awkward) halt, the rider depending more on the voice than on the reins. The case of this horse, which is quite typical, is the best answer to the argument that work at collected gaits is necessary for abrupt halting, or "coming back" in general. This kind of halting, from the point of

view of the mechanics of the horse's movements, has little in common
with collected gaits (or even semi-collected ones).

Now, why does a calm horse normally perform with "forward balance?" This phenomenon originates in the fact that the horse's weight
is not evenly distributed throughout his body. If a horse is put on two
scales—one under his forehand and the other under his hindquarters—
and the operator waits until the horse is standing in a relaxed manner
before taking the reading, he will find out that about three-fifths of
the horse's weight is on the forehand. This distribution of weight is the
result of millions of years of natural selective breeding with speed as
the aim. The preponderance of weight on the forehand makes it easy
to lose equilibrium to the front—without which speed is impossible.

From this weighing of the horse it is easy to deduce that the average
"forward balance" would be the most natural for horses when they are
calm. (What happens when a free horse becomes excited, you will read
in the section on "Collection.") This distribution of weight also indicates that at an easy, restful halt the horse will have the preponderance
of weight on the forehand.

All this means that the common argument of Dressage riders that
"horses schooled in accordance with the principles of Forward Riding
are heavy in front" really doesn't make sense. In order to perform in a
natural, non-fatiguing, easy manner they should maintain their natural
distribution of weight, and particularly so when performing at speed.

So far I have discussed the problem of balance only when moving
straight ahead. But what about turns? Everything I have said applies to
turning as well. In the latter case the problem becomes even more complex, due to the leaning of the horse in the direction of the turn. This
leaning increases with speed.

Even if we are to consider that the balancing efforts when turning
at speed are fundamentally the same as those required from a horse
when turning at ·a slow gait, they are much stronger in the first case
than in the second one; and the manipulation with the legs necessary
to retrieve the recurrently lost equilibrium must be as fast as the corresponding speed. Thus, although the efforts may be similar in both
cases, the skill in using them is quite different. This is the reason why
small circles at collected gaits do not teach a horse how to handle himself on turns at speed. Practice on very large circles at the speed of an
ordinary canter (about 10 m.p.h.)—and eventually even somewhat faster
—is an important exercise for hunters and jumpers.

THE TERMS "ENGAGEMENT" AND "COLLECTION"

The term "engagement" is usually confusingly used in two senses; it
was thus originally used in this book. A clarification of this subject is
therefore necessary. In one sense it is used to denote the movement of a

hind leg well forward under the horse's belly (as in free or fast gaits); in the other sense the same word denotes a rather short movement of the hind leg forward and correspondingly short movement back from under the body with perceptible bending and unbending in all joints, and particularly in the hocks (as at collected gaits).

Please examine illustration No. IV. It shows the free trot of a completely green colt who had been ridden for only about six weeks. Note the great engagement of the hind leg in its movement forward. Also note that the "disengagement" (backward swing) of the other hind leg is as great; the legs swing like the pendulum of a clock. Then compare this with illustration No. V which represents the *acme of collection—the Piaffe* (trot in place).

You will observe that in the Piaffe the hind legs don't move forward at all under the belly, toward the front of the horse's body; they merely move up and down in the same place under the croup. In this case there is no engagement at all (in the previous sense) and no engagement means no disengagement either.

This is the most conspicuous example of the use of the term "engagement" in the second sense. In all the possible variations of gaits a certain relationship always exists between the swing of the hind leg forward toward the front of the horse's body and its swing back from under the body. At collected gaits, even at the Passage, the hind legs also swing back from under the body. But in this case the disengagement is smaller than at free gaits for the simple reason that the engagement (thrust forward) is also smaller.

Mechanically speaking, the horse's hoof engages when it comes in contact with the ground. Depending, however, on the type of the thrust of the hind leg forward from which this contact has resulted, the leg will eventually exert its propulsion in different ways. Thus it is the manner in which the hind leg moves forward which ultimately determines the character of the movement. The type of engagement which is characterized by a very marked forward movement of the hind legs under the horse's body and by little perceptible flexion at the hocks, produces long flat strides. But, a shorter but energetic engagement, with conspicuous flexion at the hocks, produces short and high strides.

While the hind leg is in the process of engaging—that is, of moving forward under the horse's belly—it is passive. And even for a moment after the hoof has come in contact with the ground, it is passive, as far as propulsion goes and acts merely as a support. At this moment the horse's body is being moved forward by the backward thrust of the other hind leg. But just as the first hind leg on its way back passes the moment of being vertical to the ground it begins its productive work of pushing against the ground. (To add to the confusion in the use of the term "engagement" some horsemen consider it begins only at this moment.) The productive thrusts of the hind legs are aimed backward and thus push the horse forward. The length of the backward thrust is in direct relation to the length of the engagement (in the first sense). The further the hind leg swings forward, the longer will be the extent of its backward push. General Decarpentry writes on page 112 of his book EQUITATION ACADEMIQUE: "The further the hind leg is behind the line of the vertical at the end of its effort, and the more the resultant push acts from the rear to the front, the greater is the extension of the gait." (The translation is mine.)

As long as speed of the gait, at least partially, depends on the degree of engagement forward, the greatest forward engagement at a trot will be at a racing trot. A considerably lesser engagement will produce an "ordinary" trot; a quite small engagement will suffice to obtain a simple, "doggy" slow trot. At a collected trot the engagement *in this sense* is smaller than at the ordinary, free trot (8 m.p.h.) because the collected trot is slower. The Piaffe, being a trot in place, obviously doesn't require any engagement of the hind legs (Ill. No. V); they just mark time in place. If at some moment of the Piaffe the hind legs should begin to move forward under the horse's belly, the horse would be pushed forward and would begin to move ahead, and this would be the end of the Piaffe.

On the other hand, something else very important—which doesn't occur at the ordinary gaits—happens to the hind legs of the horse (and, as a matter of fact, to the whole horse) during the Piaffe. That is the bending—considerably greater than at ordinary gaits—of the hind legs in all joints and particularly in the hocks (look again at Ill. No. V). This occurs because full collection is obtained, first of all, through shifting a certain part of the weight from the front to the quarters (more or less depending on the school), and thus the hind legs are forced to bend in the hocks to accept and carry this additional weight. As the result the back of the horse slopes to the rear, and the croup is consequently lowered. This "lowering of the croup" or "lowering of the hindquarters" (both are proper technical terms) is often also called "engagement," and here is where the misunderstandings take place. While the "engagement" in the sense of the engagement of the hind legs of a free-moving horse (Ill. No. IV) will produce long, flat strides, the "engagement" in the sense of the lowering of the croup (Ill. No. V) will produce comparatively short but high and dramatic steps.

When reading this book bear in mind that the term "engagement" is used in both senses, depending on whether free or collected gaits are referred to.

Now why should shifting the weight to the rear result in high action? It is quite natural, mechanically speaking, that when the hind legs carry so much weight that they are forced to bend in the joints, they

Ill. No. IV. The free trot of a green colt. Ill. No. V. The acme of collection at a
Note the degree of engagement. Cour- trot—the Piaffe (trot in place). Note the
tesy of Mrs. Robert Carter III. complete absence of engagement; also
the "lowering of the croup."

will push more strongly upward than forward. On the other hand, the
greatly lightened forehand can now play upward with ease and will do
so if the rider maintains the energy of movement (impulsion) while not
allowing the horse to transform it into speed. There is nothing new in
what I am saying; in the pamphlet *Notes on Dressage*, published by the
American Horse Shows Association, you may read that at a collected
walk "by lowering the hindquarters the horse lightens the forehand . . ."

The lowering of the croup, in different degrees, is typical of all
manifestations of collected gaits. Normally at the Passage (a very slow,
high, very cadenced trot) it will be smaller than at the Piaffe (in the case
of the same horse), and at a simple, collected trot it may be quite
unnoticeable to the eye. The general principle in this respect is that
the lightening of the forehand is the foundation of all gaits with high
action. *Nothing of the sort* takes place at the free ordinary or fast gaits
at which a hunter or a jumper should perform. The free gaits are based
on the average forward balance and on efforts different from those
used in collected gaits. This is one of the important reasons why
practice at collected gaits is not helpful in schooling hunters and
jumpers. One may even say that long practice in moving with short
and high strides, with the weight shifted to the hindquarters and hocks
bent, will, in the great majority of cases, be detrimental in establishing

in a hunter or a jumper the habit of moving with efficient, long, flat strides—that is, with strides that cover ground without wasting expenditures of energy merely for showiness.

Ideally, it is possible to school a horse so that he will, at the wish of his rider, move either with high (much knee and hock action), well-cadenced, comparatively short strides or extend himself and move forward with long, flat strides, and do both to perfection. In practice, however, it doesn't work this way, and such cases are extremely rare —occurring only with a lucky combination of outstanding horse and great horseman. Obviously it is easier to school a colt for one specific type of work than to make a universal horse out of him. It would seem, however, that a universal horse should be a common occurrence because both free and collected movements are natural to a horse. But there is a hitch to it:

When a free horse moves merely to get from one part of the pasture to another and is *calm* while traveling, he then carries himself in an extended attitude (average "forward balance"), because this is the most economical way to get places. On the other hand, if the same horse becomes excited, he raises his neck, shifts part of his weight to the hindquarters, lowers his croup, bends his hind legs (average "central" or "rear" balance) and begins to move with high, showy steps (collection). In nature this shifting from one type of movement to another works very well. The difficulties in achieving this combination of different types of gaits under the saddle spring mainly from the different emotional backgrounds of the free and collected gaits. It is *not* natural for the horse to produce brilliant, collected gaits when he is calm; in nature he exhibits them only when emotionally stimulated either by love, fright or playfulness. It is quite artificial for the horse to move dramatically without emotional stimulation and to do it merely at his rider's wish. This is, of course, one of the reasons why a rider who is not sufficiently good invariably upsets his horse on attempting to teach him collection. However, a good trainer can obtain full collection without upsetting his horse in the least. To achieve this he has to work very gradually, systematically and tactfully. He has to work so much at collected gaits that they become a habit, completely disassociated in the horse's mind from the natural collection of moments of excitement; at least emotionally, a natural movement has to be turned into an artificial one. This long work at collected gaits establishes in the horse a certain way of balancing himself and a certain way of acting with the legs and the rest of his body, and hence is detrimental to free going, which calls for different balancing efforts and for a different skill in the use of legs, back, neck and head. In other words, it is difficult to have your cake and eat it.

THE RELATIONSHIP BETWEEN THE GAITS AND THE JUMP

The following analysis of the mechanics of the horse in jumping relates to ordinary good jumping in the hunting field, in cross-country competitions, in showing hunters, in horsemanship classes and all other similar equestrian activities in which a good amateur is apt to participate. On the other hand, this text does not take into consideration the unusually talented horses who, as geniuses in jumping, may have their own peculiar techniques. Neither does this text consider the schooling of such horses for international competitions, which is a rather special art.

During the jump the horse finds himself in physical situations not encountered at gaits. Consequently, although he uses the same parts of his body for propulsion and for balance as on the flat, the particular use of them in this case makes a jump a movement all by itself. This is, of course, why:

One cannot make a jumper by schooling a horse exclusively on the flat. It is only practice over obstacles, and particularly jumping exercises, that can develop a jump to perfection. Furthermore, there is such a thing as a talent for jumping—some completely green horses, with little practice over fences, jump better than other horses who have undergone a long and complicated general schooling and had the same jumping experience, but who have no natural ability for jumping.

The most that general schooling can do toward better jumping is to develop the horse's muscles, his balancing efforts (shifting of the weight back and forth), his ability to lengthen and shorten his stride at will (necessary for "placing" for the take-off), and his cooperation with his rider in galloping between obstacles. The actual jumping technique, quite obviously, can be developed through jumping only.

However, some types of schooling on the flat may favor the development of jumping efforts, while other types may be harmful to them. Riding and schooling which allow the horse free play with his back and neck are distinctly favorable for jumping, while restrained, collected gaits with fixed neck and head, and with the rider (using the Dressage Seat) tend to be harmful in the great majority of cases.

Volumes have been written about the mechanics of the horse's efforts during the two short seconds that the average jump lasts. We don't need to go into a detailed analysis of all of them here; I shall discuss only those efforts which are outstandingly important and, as such, should be familiar to everyone who rides over obstacles. As a matter of fact, we can confine our survey almost exclusively to the efforts of the take-off, because it sets the key for the rest of the jump.

Let us start with the balance of the horse in jumping. The photographs numbered VI, VII and VIII illustrate the obvious fact that

Ill. No. VI. The upward flight. The for-   Ill. No. VII. The apex of the jump. The
ward-and-downward balancing gestures   end of the neck-and-head-forward-and-
of the neck and head. Courtesy of Mr.   downward gesture.
Harry de Leyer.

throughout the jump there is complete absence of stability on the
ground. The often referred to base of support is non-existent. The
dynamic balance of the horse over the jump is that of a projectile with
inner forces. During this period he makes efforts with his neck and
head, back and limbs which will enable him to land in a proper attitude
to resume his balance at the gait that follows the jump. The relative
success of these efforts depends only on the *agility* and muscular *strength*
of the horse.

When a man jumps he uses his loins and his back more strenuously
than when he walks or runs, and the swing of his arms is also much
stronger. So it is with the horse; throughout the jump a free horse uses
his loins, his back and his neck strongly. The balancing gestures of the
horse's neck and head (upward and downward) are synchronized with
the efforts of the back. If the neck is held stiffly immobile, the back
doesn't work either. If, for instance, the horse jumps with an immobile
neck held high, the back remains caved-in throughout the flight (Ill. No.
IX). During the jump (over a big obstacle) the back and, correspondingly, the neck and head make five distinct efforts. The two most conspicuous ones are easily observed even by an untrained eye. These are:
1) the upward curve of the back during the upward flight and the
simultaneous forward and downward swing of the neck and head (Ill.
No. VI); and 2) the caving-in of the back during the downward flight
with simultaneous swing of the neck and head upward and to the rear
(Ill. No. VIII).

Ill. No. VIII. The downward flight. The   Ill. No. IX. In jumping, if the horse's
upward-and-backward gesture of the   neck is held stiffly immobile and high,
neck and head.   his back doesn't work either and remains
                                        caved in throughout the flight. Courtesy
                                        of Miss Bonnie Cornelius.

Consequently the first conclusion that anyone studying jumping is bound to reach is that it is important that the mounted horse be in the *habit* of being free to act with his neck and head, because thus he may preserve for jumping the instinctive balancing gestures of the neck and head. And the natural deduction from the above would be that collected gaits, which require a continuously raised neck, and a head permanently held in an almost vertical position, may make the horse eventually lose the ability to use the neck with ease and power when negotiating an obstacle. And, since the jumping efforts of the back occur only when the neck is active, collected gaits cannot be considered helpful to these efforts either.

True enough, we have all seen horses which were schooled at collected gaits and still used their necks and backs in jumping; but such cases are exceptions rather than the rule and depend almost every time on exceptionally good riding, and very clever use of collection in schooling. With an average horse, ridden by an average rider, it will rarely work this way.

As a general rule, only gaits and exercises which require constant use of the back (shortening it, lengthening it, curving it upward and caving it in) in unison with balancing gestures of the neck may be helpful in preserving in the horse his *natural* way of jumping. Such exercises include galloping, riding up and downhill, abrupt changes of speeds and gaits, backing after an abrupt and very short halt followed immediately by resumption of the gait. These, and other exercises, will be helpful only if the rider's hands don't interfere with the actions of the neck ("following" arms), and the rider's weight is kept off the horse's back. But, because jumping is basically very different from the gaits, the above exercises are merely helpful; only actual practice over obstacles —and particularly *jumping exercises*—can develop the jumping efforts of a horse to perfection.

As long as half of the secret of *easy, natural jumping* lies in the horse's use of his loins, back and neck, it is necessary (for purely practical purposes) to discuss these actions a little further. The strength of the neck's balancing efforts depends somewhat on its attitude; the more extended is the neck the more effective are its upward and downward swings, and correspondingly stronger the efforts of the back (Ill. No. X). This is one of the reasons (not the only one) why during the last strides of the approach to a fence the horse, preparing for the jump, stretches his neck and head forward (Ill. No. XI)—when permitted by the rider. This extension of the neck and head comes naturally and easily only if the horse is always ridden on the principle of free going. The *habit* of moving at collected gaits with the neck and head always in a set position may (and in most cases will) become stronger than the instinctive desire of the horse to get his neck and head into an advantageous attitude for use as a "balancer."

But, of course, permitting the horse to stretch his neck and head during the approach to an obstacle is not all that the rider has to do with his arms in jumping. He must also make certain not to interfere with the actual balancing movements of the horse's neck during the jump itself. It is important that during this time the horse be confident that his rider will not interfere with these balancing efforts of his neck. This *confidence* comes only after long acquaintance with his rider's non-interference. This means (and here I repeat myself) that not only while jumping, but throughout schooling and general riding on the flat, the horse must enjoy the liberty of his neck; the rider must always "follow" with his arms the natural movements of the horse's neck. This obviously precludes long work at collected gaits—and how can one develop collected gaits of any quality unless one works at them persistently?

Here I would like to stress again the fact that the loins and back of the horse, as much as the neck, need freedom of action during the jump.

This is where the Forward Seat is invaluable. The horse must be confident that he will be able to use his back when jumping, which means that not only during the approach to the obstacle but during most of the schooling and riding in general he has experienced the freedom of his back. I do not mean to say that horses cannot jump with

Photo by Raine Studios

Ill. No. X. An example of vigorous use of neck and back. Compare the efforts of this horse with those in Ill. No. IX. Courtesy of Bernie Traurig.

Ill. No. XI. Nearing the fence, the horse, if allowed to, extends his head and neck (unless he is moving at a fast gallop with neck and head already extended). This gesture:

    1)   prepares the neck and head for the balancing gestures during the jump,

    2)   assists in loading the forehand for a strong upward thrust,

    3)   helps the horse to raise the croup for a strong and *simultaneous* engagement of both hind legs. See also Ill. No. XVII. Courtesy of Mrs. Raymond Norton, Jr.

stiff backs and correspondingly immobile necks. As we all witness—unhappily all too frequently—horses abused in these ways can by sheer strength and boldness jump and clear big obstacles. I merely wish to point out that under such unnatural conditions horses cannot jump *easily* and *naturally*, and I doubt very much that they can enjoy such jumping.

Now let us look at the action of the horse's legs during the take-off. The old saying that the horse "jumps off his hocks" is only partially correct; he also jumps off his forehand. With two almost simultaneous upward (but not necessarily equally strong) thrusts with the forelegs he raises the front (Ill. No. XII), and with two, also almost simultaneous, thrusts of the hind legs he propels himself forward and upward along the line of the angle to the ground given to his body (partially by the upward thrusts with the forehand, Ill. No. XIII).

To carry a horse over a big obstacle, the thrusts with both the forehand and the hindquarters have to be strong. If you wish to push yourself upward with your hands upon a table, you will first of all put a lot of weight on them, because only then can your arms give a powerful upward thrust. So it is with the horse. To give a strong thrust with the forehand (the push is against the ground) the horse must have sufficient weight on it. Furthermore, to be able, at practically the same time, to engage the hind legs well under the body (in preparation for their thrusts) the croup must—at least during the last stride—be held higher than the forehand (Ill. No. XI). During the last strides of the approach, when the neck and head stretch forward (thus augmenting the weight on the forehand) the croup can then be easily raised higher than the forehand, and (Ill. No. XI) thus the stage is set for both the thrust with the forehand and engagement of the hindquarters. This is another and most important reason why a horse, on nearing an obstacle, likes to extend his neck. And this is the reason why a horse prefers to approach a jump with average forward balance—that is, with the preponderance of the weight on the forehand. On the other hand, the habit of moving at collected gaits, with weight predominantly on the hindquarters (with lowered croup), obviously interferes with the horse's *natural* manner of preparing himself for both the thrust with the forehand and the thrust with the hindquarters (under certain circumstances, however, the horse can also jump like a jack-rabbit).

The engagement of the hind legs in preparation for the take-off differs greatly from their engagement at gaits. While at gaits each of the hind legs engage separately, during the take-off for a jump both hind legs engage simultaneously (this requires a special technique) and are placed on the ground as nearly as possible on the same line (Ill. No. XIV). Failure to line up the hind legs weakens the total strength of their thrusts, and the jump also loses in compactness. Green jumpers often fail to achieve this "lining up" (Ill. No. XV).

Ill. No. XII. The upward thrust (originally against the ground) with the fore-hand in progress. The uneven positions of the two forelegs indicate that each foreleg gave a separate thrust a fraction of a second apart. Note an excellent engagement of perfectly lined up hind legs. Courtesy of Miss Cynthia Banister.

Ill. No. XIII. The end of the thrusts with the hind legs. Courtesy of Mrs. Raymond Morton, Jr.

Ill. No. XIV. Having the hind legs bent in all joints the horse "sits," for a fraction of a second, on his hocks and thus, with the full weight of his body on the hind legs, compresses a spring. In another fraction of a second he will release it, pushing against ground.

Ill. No. XV. During the take-off in jumping both hind legs engage simultaneously and are placed on the ground as nearly as possible on the same line. Courtesy of Miss Stephanie Steck.

The efforts of the horse's hind legs during the take-off are rather similar to those of a man's legs in a jump from a standstill; the man, bending his knees and closing other angles in his body, compresses a spring in his legs and then releases it against the ground. The horse does the same thing with his hind legs; "sitting" on his hocks, with the whole of his weight on the hind legs, he compresses the spring and then releases it against the ground. Neither man nor horse does anything of the kind when merely walking or running. Of course, the stronger the muscles of the hind legs, the stronger the spring. This is where general riding and schooling are helpful—particularly so if the exercises selected tend to develop long pushes, as in the gallop rather than the short ones typical of collected gaits. For instance, trotting and cantering up hill constitute good exercise for developing the muscles of the hind legs. And here is an important detail: In order to achieve a strong and simultaneous engagement of both hind legs and the consequent strong thrust, the horse must have the back, and particularly the loins, unencumbered so that not only the hind legs but the entire hindquarters can take part in the movement (Ill. No. XVI).

There is a moment of the approach to which we often hear the term "collection" applied. This is the so-called "placing." In order to take off at the most advantageous distance from the obstacle, more often than not the horse on approaching a fence has either to lengthen or shorten one, two or three strides ("placing"); or the rider has to oblige him to do it (the former is more desirable). The slower the gait (free or collected), the shorter are the strides; consequently any mistake in placing is bound to be smaller, and it is easier to make the necessary

Ill. No. XVI. Green jumpers are often unable to engage their hind legs so that the hoofs strike the ground on the same line. An experienced jumper may do the same thing when idling over a low fence. Courtesy of Knox School.

readjustments in the length of the stride. This is where it is easy, from a superficial point of view, to make the mistake of believing that a collected canter is preferable for the approach—failing to take into consideration its numerous disadvantages, which I have pointed out. Anyway, jumping at a slow canter doesn't solve the problems of today's jumping. Lately, as you know, speed has been required in many jumping competitions; it is normally called for in hunter classes and usually plays a considerable part in actual foxhunting. Consequently, although we all begin practice over obstacles at a speed slower than the ordinary canter, we gradually increase the pace of the approach. We have eventually to reach the point where the horse can play with his strides and thus "place" himself correctly for the jump—even at speed. The exercise "three speeds at the gallop" is particularly helpful in this respect, because it teaches the horse to change the length of his strides both ways. And one doesn't have to collect a horse to make him "come back." (See the text on collection and semi-collection.)

Everything that I have said above concerning the horse's mechanics in jumping, although true, applies only to the calm jumping of a horse who negotiates a specific fence with ease; the obstacle may be three feet or five feet high, depending on the horse's natural ability and the stage of his schooling. These mechanics, however, may vary from one set of circumstances to another. The fact that jumping is not one hundred percent physical, but involves mental and emotional factors as well, contributes to this variation. A clever horse will frequently figure out the jump better than a stupid one, thus negotiating it with less physical effort. An ambitious animal, in his desire to clear the obstacle, may rise to an emotional pitch which will often produce surprisingly good results, even with an awkward use of the body. Besides

Ill. No. XVII. Only if the horse moves with average forward balance and the rider has his weight off the horse's back, can the whole hindquarters easily participate in the engagement of the hind legs. Courtesy of Miss Martha Albro.

this, both correct "placing" and correct impulsion may be the result of the riding; and the animal may jump with ease or with a forced effort depending upon whether the rider's technique is refined or rough. As a matter of fact, it is quite inaccurate to talk about jumping or about riding in general in terms of black or white. For instance, how many riders in hunter classes do we not constantly see banging their horses' backs while galloping between fences—and yet many of these horses still gallop and jump well. In the same way many horses who have never enjoyed the freedom of using their necks and heads as "balancers" will jump just as efficiently. In these and similar cases, the riders' interference with the horses' natural mechanics is obviously compensated for by either the horses' strength, his boldness, natural agility, experience, habit, or by clever although rough riding. In open jumping (both international and domestic) a common sight is a horse who, while being simultaneously urged forward by the rider's legs and checked by his hands, approaches the obstacle with central balance, neck up and chin in. Some of these horses either quickly extend themselves, if given the liberty to do so during the last one or two strides before the jump, or even jump and clear fences in this seemingly awkward attitude. The reason for this lies in the fact that the horse can execute a jump in different ways, as he can any other movement. The text in the previous chapter that described how a free horse starts a canter explains such facts.

In writing this book I have been influenced by an appreciation of the beauty of an easy fluid performance of the horse. Coupled with this has been the desire to present a method which, although efficient, would involve the minimum abuse of the horse. From the standards thus reached, which may be summed up as those of EASY, CALM, GRACEFUL and COMPETENT JUMPING, the mechanics of the horse's jump as they are presented in this chapter seem to me to be the soundest.

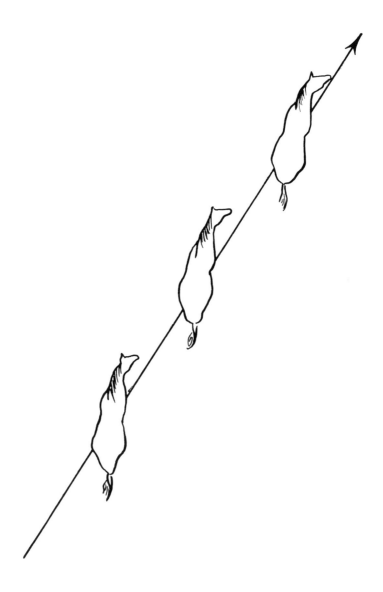

CHAPTER XI

Learning Control on the Intermediate Level

(Preface, by V. S. Littauer)

Of the three chapters on the technique of controlling a horse this one is the most important. Elementary control, after all, should be primarily regarded as a passing stage in learning to ride, or as a substitute for good riding for people who for one reason or another are not interested or are unable to aim at anything beyond a very primitive form of riding; on the other hand advanced control is for those comparatively few who wish to know more than is required merely for hunting and showing satisfactorily.

Intermediate control is especially conceived for riding to hounds and for showing (particularly showing hunters), and, as such, it should fit the need of the majority, for I know of no young boy or girl today who, while learning to ride, does not aspire eventually to participate in one or both of these games.

It is obvious to anyone with hunting or showing experience that technical books on riding usually contain a great deal of material which is superfluous for these two sports. These technicalities of riding are too often beyond the possibilities of an amateur who is not prepared to devote his life to horses. On the other hand, the actual riding in the two games mentioned above is frequently done on an unnecessarily low level; very few will argue this statement. So, in formulating the principles of intermediate control, I was aiming at raising the standards of present riding on the one hand and on the other at doing this in a manner simple enough so that its ideals would be within the reach of everyone. This is the fundamental thought behind this chapter.

Before beginning to set down recipes for the control of the horse on the intermediate level I had to consider the type of rider and horse to whom these would most frequently apply. In my mind this typical rider is a girl in her teens or early twenties who owns a hunter or a jumper, or has a regular opportunity to hunt or show someone else's horse (but it is to be hoped, of course that everyone who is a beginner today will have use for this chapter eventually). This girl is usually very fit physically, brave, loves horses and riding, had her first experience in the saddle as a child, has taken some lessons (as a rule not consistently) perhaps in a camp or, later, in a school, does not know much, but her *character* and *experience* take care of her riding. It is needless to say that this description

169

also fits many women, men and boys. Many of these who would like to ride better, or to improve the performance of their horses, somehow don't know how to go about it, or are ashamed to concede publicly that they have something to learn; it is for them that this chapter is written.

The position of this type of rider is usually strong and has a great deal of acrobatic quality. Hence, if necessary, to change it for the better (they are apt to be behind their horses), it requires merely a couple of hours, and is not a serious matter. The matter of their control, however, is much more complicated, for *efficient* and *soft* control can be present only providing the horse has had at least some schooling, and these people usually ride green horses. They are therefore forced to ride roughly and consequently disturbingly to the horse; which results in a vicious circle. Some of these almost self-made riders, being born with equestrian tact, eventually learn how to handle their unschooled horses with a primitive but effective smoothness, but the majority, of course, remain forever an unwelcome sight to their mounts. Some horses can take it, but many eventually become upset and begin to perform badly. At this late date the owner of such a horse either buys a new one or decides that something has to be done to reform his present one. The really wise riders begin to worry about their own riding. In most cases what such riders need is not so much an improvement in technique of their aids as a better understanding of what riding is all about. They have to learn that a good performance largely depends on schooling.

There is so little that is black and white in riding that even such an obvious, common-sense statement as that a horse to perform well should be at least somewhat schooled, and at least decently ridden, cannot be taken as gospel. Just yesterday I saw a six-year-old horse which, with no schooling at all and badly ridden, was performing well over fences. His owner and rider had raised him, hunted him, shown him successfully in hunter classes and nothing has upset the horse; he performs quietly, on loose reins and doesn't object to being handled roughly when given orders. This horse is a perfect illustration of what I said previously in this book —that it is possible for some people on some horses to hunt and even to show on the basis of elementary control. Of course, one may look at this case from another angle—from the sophisticated point of view of the knowing rider. Then the mere fact that the horse jumps 4′ fences willingly and calmly, on loose reins, is not enough. Yesterday when looking at the free, quiet gaits of this horse, I didn't like them; they were *disconnected* gaits. I knew that they would be rough, crude and unpleasant to me. As to the jump, I was saying to myself when watching the horse go over fences, "give me this horse and I will raise his jumping limit by 6″ in a few weeks." But, on the other hand, I was thinking that this horse ought to be happy, because his uneducated rider controls him in this simple unpretentious manner. What a torture it would be to him if his rider were to acquire all sorts of fanciful ideas and were to attempt to collect him and what not, not knowing exactly how. There are many ways of looking at a thing.

I have already mentioned that when organizing the technique of intermediate control I took into consideration not only riders but their horses as well. A great many of today's hunters and the majority of horse-show jumpers are big, strong horses and, as such, are often ambitious. There is no objection to ambition but, as it happens, it easily becomes overambition and then sheer nervousness. Unfortunately we do not breed horses for character any more. Our best horse is the thoroughbred and he is rarely bred purposely for a gentleman's use. He is intended for the race track where overeagerness may be desirable and is bred primarily for inherited ability to run fast, as well as for certain physical qualities which insure speed. The result is that the horse-flesh of today is truly magnificent. But a quiet, naturally cooperative character has been completely neglected for many generations of horses. As an example of a wonderful disposition having been developed in a horse through selective breeding I would like to mention the Lipizzans. In the carousel of the Spanish School of Vienna you can see eight stallions working together with exemplary docility, while in the stalls they show the friendliness and intelligence of a dog rather than of even a pet horse as we know it. It is far beyond the results usually obtained through friendly grooming and good riding.

Whether you wish to shed tears or not over the fact that so many of our thoroughbreds don't possess this quality, the cold fact remains that they don't. On the other hand, the average well-bred horse of today, although born with a sensitive nature is born a *quiet animal.* It is the senseless behavior of his rider which so often turns him into a nervous one. If horse owners and riders would just appreciate the fact that when a colt, at the age of three, the horse is overimpressionable and should be handled very tactfully for a year or two, only a negligible number of our horses would be maladjusted. This tactful handling merely means that you ask at first very little from a green horse and gradually raise your requirements. You would be wise always to be guided by the golden rule that the less one asks from a horse the calmer he remains. Schooling, and schooling only, will enable you to raise your requirements to a high degree without upsetting the horse. And don't let yourself be misguided by the behavior of the exceptions to the rule.

Now that we have approximately defined the horse and the rider for whom this chapter and, as a matter of fact, most of this book is written, I would like to turn your attention to the essential points in riding to hounds and in show jumping. First of all, when hunting the horse must gallop "economically," that is, using as little energy as possible so as to stay with hounds even in a long run, and when showing, be as fresh approaching the last fence in the show as when taking the first one. In the hunting field efficiency of movement is particularly important at the long gallop; during the short course of the show the horse can exhaust himself only due to wrong jumping efforts over formidable obstacles. Since the gallop and the jump are closely related movements, and the character of the jump largely depends on the type of the gallop during the approach, ease in each of them is fundamentally based on the same factors. The most important of these is approaching a fence, or merely galloping, with average forward balance, with neck stretched (which results in long, flat strides) and in the efficient use of energy in covering ground. But in neither of these two sports can this be successfully achieved merely through having the reins loose, for quite often in the hunting field, and always in the horse shows, precision of control is necessary and riding on *soft contact* becomes imperative.

Soft contact is obviously possible only when the horse is calm. In the usual case a calm horse is the result of schooling plus sensible riding. A sluggish horse will remain quiet, no matter how green he is when he is required to hunt, or how abominably he is ridden; but a sensitive horse will not stand either. The habit of moving with forward balance is conducive to calmness, for this is the natural attitude of a free, calm horse, while a collected attitude is natural for an emotionally upset one. Once the horse has acquired in schooling the habit of moving under the rider at all gaits and over fences in the same manner in which he would do it when free and calm, then you have efficient gaits and jumping, and it will be easy for you (using the legs) to establish a soft contact. When this has been achieved the horse is ready to learn to respond to soft aids, and precision of control becomes possible.

At times, of course, any horse—even a well-schooled one—will resist, and then softness will have to be temporarily abandoned until mental cooperation is restored. Softness is impossible without the mental cooperation of the horse. If you were to analyze such an apparently purely physical characteristic of the horse as a "good mouth," you would find that a considerable part of it is mental cooperation.

Assuming that a certain horse has been schooled to the point where he is capable of performing on the intermediate level, we are left with the question—what should the rider know in order to obtain such performance from this horse? Here is the answer:

1) The rider must be familiar with the technique of the use of legs and hands which obtains different movements on this level of performance.

2) The rider must understand the general spirit of riding on the intermediate level.

Now let us examine these points in greater detail:

Riding on soft contact. Soft contact is obtained by the legs urging the horse forward on the bit; not by pulling on the reins. Responding to the action of the rider's legs the horse slightly increases the energy of his movement, stretches his neck, and thus establishes contact between his mouth and the rider's hands; this is providing, of course, that the length of the reins is correctly adjusted. In this case moving on the bit is somewhat less pronounced than the "fully on the bit" of advanced riding. Being less pronounced, it is much easier to achieve with softness, and this is why it can be the basis of intermediate control. On the other hand, it is much more complicated than riding on loose reins, due particularly to two technical details of riding on soft contact. These are "following arms" and "give and take."

Following arms. Once contact has been established then, in order not to abuse the horse's mouth, the rider's arms must follow the balancing gestures of the horse's neck and head at the walk and canter where these gestures are present. To be able to "follow," the rider must have his arms relaxed in the shoulders and elbows and make movements with his arms (from the shoulders) back and forth following the movements of the horse's neck and preserving a soft contact with the mouth. This sounds simple, but it isn't and an elementary rider cannot be asked to execute it. If the rider doesn't follow and his reins are taut he hangs on the horse's mouth, and if his reins are semi-slack the horse jerks himself against the bit every time that his head makes a gesture forward and down. Incredible as it may seem, the latter case is common even among riders with considerable reputation.

Give and take. It is easy to say that the contact with the following arms must be soft, but even when the rider plays his part well the horse may not play his and may begin to lean on the rider's hands, usually increasing his pace. What do you do then? That is where "give and take" comes in. Every increase of the tension on the reins slows the horse down somewhat (unless the horse's mouth is spoiled, or he is not in the mood to cooperate), and every decrease of tension displaces the bit in his mouth, thus preventing the mouth from becoming numb. An ordinary long, heavy pull on the reins to slow down a horse (without give) will result in the horse's mouth gradually losing its sensitivity and the horse feeling the rider's hands less and less.

A crude form of give and take can be obtained by moving the arms back and forth; a finer one by moving the wrists up and down, and the best one (on a sensitive horse) by opening and closing fingers.

Besides stopping the horse from leaning on your hands at gaits or during different movements, a certain amount of give and take should always be present to prevent the horse from developing this leaning. In other words, a soft contact is the one which is not stiff and has play in it.

Sometimes give and take is not sufficient to keep the horse's mouth soft and either "vibrations" or "flexions" have to be introduced.

Vibrations consist in moving the snaffle to the left and the right through the mouth by a sawing action on the reins. Granting that in some cases a strong "sawing" of the mouth may be necessary, the ideal vibration is executed by merely alternating closing the fingers of one hand while relaxing the fingers of the other.

Flexions are described in the chapter on ADVANCED CONTROL for they really belong to riding on that level, but occasionally they have to be used even in simpler riding—for instance, in the case of a horse with a stiff poll. Different levels of control sometimes cannot be rigidly separated.

Riding on loose reins. About one-third of riding should be done on loose reins, not only at a walk but at all gaits and in jumping. This rests the horse's mouth and contributes to soft contact and soft control. When reading the chapters on schooling you will find out that it is very easy to stabilize the horse at his gaits so that he, by himself, maintains the gait and evenness of speed. Stabilization is the cornerstone of soft control.

Calmness. Obviously, the rider can be soft with his hands while maintaining contact and controlling the horse only if the horse remains calm and cooperative, and this depends largely on the character and mentality of the horse and is really developed in schooling and then maintained through sensible riding.

It can hardly be argued that a horse performs at his best when alert and calm. Efficiency being the basic principle of intermediate riding, calmness assumes great importance, not only from the point of view of softness of control but as a foundation for the economical use of energy as well.

A beginner may disturb a sensitive horse by the awkwardness of his position or by the roughness of his aids, but I would like to assume that those who are going to use this chapter for reference are beyond this stage. However, even a rider with a non-disturbing seat and non-disturbing legs and hands can, over a period of weeks, turn a naturally quiet horse into a nervous wreck. How? By not using common sense. By asking more of the horse than he can do with ease and forcing him into doing it. For instance, if I have a horse which is apprehensive of 3'6" fences and, instead of gradually schooling him to greater heights, I force him today to jump 4' obstacles I will have an upset horse in no time. But you can make a horse jittery even without jumping. A sensitive, green horse would soon become nervous if I were to ride him at a walk one moment, then suddenly put him into a full gallop, then as suddenly halt him, then gallop again, all abruptly and roughly.

In advanced schooling, when the point is reached where the horse easily changes from ordinary to semi-collected gaits, abrupt stops and transitions can be asked of him without upsetting him. Intermediate riding does not include semi-collection; hence to maintain calmness in the horse with a less athletically developed body, transitions must be gradual. Let me repeat here that if you gallop and wish to halt, you should first make a few strides of trot, then of a walk and only after this preparation come to a halt. In order to start a full gallop from a halt you should first walk a few steps, then trot for several strides, then begin a canter and gradually increase your speed to a full gallop. Abiding by these rules will largely contribute to the calmness of your horse.

Even rapid changes in the speed of the same gait are upsetting to the horse. Whenever it is practical an even speed should be maintained. I don't mean to say that it must be slow—not at all—any speed, whenever practical should be kept even, so that the horse has a chance to settle into it. I appreciate the fact that sometimes in hunting, particularly in wooded country, this is impossible, but many other times it is not.

So, all in all, a successful performance on the intermediate level depends at least on some schooling and very much on the calm, sensible behavior of the rider. The more schooling the horse has received, the more and higher the fences you can take and the more abrupt can be your changes of gaits and speeds without upsetting the horse.

The use of voice. The horse easily learns the meanings of different intonations of the human voice; this is why the voice is so liberally used in schooling. There is no reason whatsoever why a soothing voice should not be used in cross-country riding to calm the horse, or sharp words to stop a disobedience. Some riders, however, would prefer to use a gag-bit than to use the voice. This inhibition about speaking to the horse springs from many sources, among which the traditions of the formal riding of the last century (such as carousels and military parades) are probably the most influential. As long as advanced forms of riding aim to exhibit horses schooled to such a high degree that the application of all aids is supposed to be inconspicuous, the rule against the use of the whip, voice and other auxiliary aids still holds its rightful place in Dressage; in the Olympic Games in 1932 a Swedish officer was disqualified for clucking to his horse. But there is no reason whatsoever for objecting to the use of the voice in less artistic or formal types of riding, where efficiency, rather than a ballet on horseback is the aim.

And speaking of aids, it is customary to refer to the rider's legs and hands as "natural" aids, and to the spurs, whip, etc. as "artificial" ones. While this may make sense from the human point of view it certainly doesn't from the horse's. For to him the artificiality of riding begins with someone being on his back. Consequently, the natural impulse of any untrained horse is to object to the rider being in the saddle and to resist the actions of his legs and hands. In resisting the leg the horse often moves against it; in resisting the bit he tries to get away from it. As a matter of fact, teaching flexion of the mouth consists of showing the horse a route of escape (advantageous to the rider) from increased pressure on the bit. So bear in mind that all the signals described below will make sense to the horse and will therefore work only after he has been taught their meaning —this is one of the purposes of schooling.

I have taken particular pains to present the above fundamentals of intermediate riding as simply as I know how, and still I know that a number of riders from the group which I described at the beginning of this chapter will fail to appreciate them. This is not because they are mentally incapable, but because they would like to discard it all as sheer theoretical nonsense which hasn't anything to do with riding to hounds or jumping in a show. They will do so because riding is to them something very different from what it is to me. To them foxhunting or showing is a romantic adventure in which they assert themselves as daring individuals at the top of the social structure. This snobbishly egotistical approach naturally results in their glorying in their personal accomplishments—the horse is a mere instrument to this end. To them, the fact that they have stayed with hounds throughout the hunt on a pulling, bucking horse bolsters their ego and provides innumerable stories with which to impress their friends. Their psychology is part of a certain character and their riding is merely one of the manifestations of it. There is no way of changing them. Good riding as I understand it and as I present it in this book is just not in their nature. This type is familiar to every riding teacher and provides standard shop talk. The average teacher is acquainted with these people because some of them do take lessons, but they take lessons almost in position only—primarily to better their appearance, to acquire a more secure seat and sometimes to learn the knack of not letting a misbehaving horse get completely out of hand. Any attempts at teaching them more fail. Some young inexperienced and optimistic teachers make an effort to convert them; the wise ones leave them alone. I believe in the latter course. Our country at present is full of young people who by their character and mentality present a fertile source for the right kind of material. This source is now so great that I believe what we need now more than ever is more better teachers and more good sound propaganda.

After these little digressions I would now like to return to the main theme of the chapter and let my pupil Alexis Wrangel take over and describe in detail the technical part of intermediate control. He is at the present time learning it and hence will be able to tell you not merely what should be done in different instances but to give you fresh impressions of the reactions of a student; this may be very helpful to you.

THIS PART OF CHAPTER XI IS BY ALEXIS WRANGEL

Capt. Littauer's instructions in roman. My own reactions in italic.

Control in my previous riding experience had consisted in steering my horse and getting him to obey elementary requirements without unduly exciting him. I knew that the horse performed better when its head and neck were stretched forward and free, also that my equine partner usually cooperated willingly when not jerked in the mouth or disturbed by violent leg action. That summed up my knowledge. It was only when I started to study with Captain Littauer that I began to learn a whole gamut of hand and leg signals and their effect on the horse's movements. These signals were based on the horse's physique and mentality, and permitted the maximum efficiency in managing the horse.

Control was made easier by a good position of the rider, but, good position did not necessarily mean good riding. For example, one sees photographs of bad riders looking very well over the apex of a jump, even though their riding up to and beyond the jump is consistently bad. Furthermore, I have met other riders whose position was always correct even though they rode very badly, disturbing their horse by continuous bad control. On the other hand, one occasionally sees riders, who, sitting incorrectly, get a surprisingly good performance out of their horses.

Obviously, the seat is far from being the complete answer to a good performance, (as I learned in the course of my studies) but, other elements being equal, a good seat is one of the fundamental steps toward a perfect performance.

Again, as in the chapter on position, I intend to detail Captain Littauer's instructions as I received them, and follow them by a description of my own reactions and of the difficulties I experienced. I must point out, however, that control cannot be taught only by a series of short recipes of a mechanical nature—such as govern teaching a correct position. The subject of control is much more complicated than the mechanics of the seat; it depends on the rider's instinct and mentality as well as on the emotional and physical state of the horse. It is, after all, not too hard to accustom any part of your body to maintain a certain position and while a knack for achieving it quickly is helpful, practice under a good supervisor eventually takes care of everything.

Control is a very different proposition; it deals with such complicated subjects as the horse's mentality, his nervous system, and the mechanics of his movements. The action of the rider's hands and legs do follow certain prescribed formulae, but the pattern of these formulae changes constantly, and you really cannot tie yourself down to a hard and fast rule as in the case of position.

Equestrian tact governs the application of the recipes prescribed in the manual. Certain general directions were given by Captain Littauer in the course of my studies, but their execution depended finally on my ability to get together with the horse. Only experience through practice rendered this possible. This experience could not be developed really efficiently through hacking and jumping only, but rather in practicing various movements in the ring: stopping and backing; two tracks; turns on the forehand and the haunches, etc. Different exercises which required different combinations of legs and hands, sometimes in cooperation with the horse's efforts and sometimes in combatting his resistances, gradually improved my control.

The more I rode, the more I learned the necessity of trying to out-think and, if possible, out-guess the horse. At first, I did not "give a hoot" what the horse had in his mind—I was more interested in the position of my ankles and the hollow in my back. Correct position seemed the A and Z of riding. But, by and by, I learned to pay more attention to the horse— his state of mind and his actions. Of course I did realize that unless I had a correct position the chances were that I would disturb the horse the minute a change of balance occurred. Many times, when I first sat on a strange horse, I felt awfully uncomfortable—sometimes it was the horse's conformation, at other times an ill-fitting saddle, or sometimes I just had a bad day and felt "off the beam," regardless of what I did, billiards or riding. I came to realize that until I got myself united with the horse, by achieving a reasonable degree of comfort, I was much better just keeping the horse going quietly on a loose rein at a walk, than attempting to do anything else. In the long run this course of action paid handsome dividends.

On other days, and with other horses, I felt fine when getting aboard, comfortable and well in balance, but the horse might not have been out for a long time, and was ready to blow up. Until I learned to wait for the horse to assume a relaxed, natural position, all efforts to achieve correct control failed.

I gained much by trying to put myself mentally in the horse's shoes: if someone were to try to coerce me in any way, at five o'clock, when I get out into the fresh air from closed confinement in a stuffy and boring office, he would meet with a great deal of resentment. Why then, I learned to reason, should I demand immediate and perfect obedience from a horse, after he has come out into a field, following a few days of standing in a stall?

As senseless actions on the rider's part disturb the horse, make him assume undesirable attitudes and spoil his gaits, so the rider's sensible behavior induces that desirable, free-moving and relaxed attitude which is our goal in intermediate riding.

A quiet seat in balance with the horse's movements, plus correctly used, undisturbing legs and hands, will induce the horse to move in his natural, relaxed fashion.

We have analyzed the seat in Chapter VI; let us examine the action of the rider's controlling agents: the legs and hands.

The legs |must at all times be close to the horse, the upper calf maintaining a light contact with the saddle skirts. This frictional grip is part of the rider's position. For control purposes, that portion of the leg from the upper calf down (sometimes down to the heel) is brought into play. The action of the legs depends on the amount of resistance offered by the horse: a light squeeze of the calves is the ideal, under normal circumstances; however, if stronger action is called for then, instead of squeezing, the rider taps the horse's flanks with his calves; this failing, he may resort to exerting pressure with his spurs against the horse's flanks, just behind the girth, and, when that produces no effect, he will give jabs with his spur-equipped heels. In order to spur correctly, the foot must be turned outward, so as to have the knee act as a hinge—the lower leg swinging back and inward in a series of quick short jabs against the horse's sides. The inturned toe or a foot parallel to the horse's side will spoil the natural action of the leg, whether spur or leg is used.

It is assumed, at this stage, that the intermediate rider knows the use of the spurs, and that he is master of his own legs.

There are, however, certain horses which, not accustomed to the use of spurs, will react violently at the slightest touch. In such cases, it is imperative to teach the horse, gradually, the feel and meaning of the spurs. Try using them most discreetly: first accustoming the horse to only a slight pressure of the spur, and subsequently to light taps. It should not take long to accustom any horse to spurs, if patience and tact govern the rider.

Spurs should always be blunt, preferably with short shanks, and they should be used as little as practical.

I recently had the opportunity to school a horse with a rather difficult character, under Captain Littauer's guidance. In the course of our preliminary work, we noticed that the horse was disturbed by even the slightest pressure of the spurs. When I took my spurs off, the horse relaxed and for several weeks I worked him without them. However, as we advanced in the curriculum, certain problems came up when stronger aids than just legs and heels were required.

By then the horse was much calmer and more amenable, so we decided to accustom him to spurs. This was done in the following way: while standing quietly in the ring, with the horse on loose reins, I gradually brought the spurs to touch his sides gently; the instant he moved forward I patted him. That day, I did nothing more than that exercise, repeated many times and, on each successful response, rewarded the horse. The following day, I worked on transitions from the walk to the trot, in the same manner; and a day later my horse obeyed the spurs, as calmly as it had previously answered to the pressure of my calf and spurless heel. Had we decided to have it out with the horse the first day, and forced him to obey the spurs, the problem would probably have lasted for months; as it was, two or three days were enough, and without mental or physical strain for either of the parties involved.

As regards the use of the legs, it should always be governed by that intangible quality called equestrian tact; neither the exact split second when the rider's legs come into play, nor the exact amount of intensity with which they act, can be precisely described; the rider's instinct, fortified by experience, takes care of that. However, the factors which favor the correct use of the legs can be described as follows:

1) Correct timing with the horse's efforts or resistance.

2) Correct strength.

3) Correct cooperation with the action of the rider's hands.

The person endowed with natural ability will develop these through years of riding experience (hacking or hunting), or through a few months or even weeks of correct exercises in the ring, under the guidance of a competent instructor.

The conformation of both horse and rider will facilitate or impede the leg action. A long-legged rider, on a small-barrelled horse, in order to use his spurs or heels, must raise his heels; this is, of course, detrimental to his general position. On the other hand, a short-legged rider, on a big-

barrelled horse, has his legs virtually paralyzed, as his capacity to straddle
is stretched to the limit and, his lower leg, high up on the horse's side, is
pressed permanently against the horse's flank.

*Regarding the varying amount of intensity required in the use of the
rider's legs, I think I shall be rendering the reader a service by relating an
incident in my riding experience:*

*Through force of circumstances, I had ridden constantly for three years
dull, common horses, some of them very spoiled by bad riding. The action
of my legs, therefore, was elementary and my whole equestrian feeling
dulled. One day, Captain Littauer asked me to ride his horse Barnaby
Bright. This creature is an Irish hunter of mammoth proportions: seventeen hands, with an enormous barrel. This giant structure, moreover, is
endowed with an extremely sensitive nature, and much developed by very
fine schooling. Mounting, I felt most uncomfortable; I was not in balance,
and could not get my legs to contact the horse's sides. When I finally
brought my legs into play, in what I thought was a gentle squeeze of the
upper calves, the horse nearly jumped out of his skin. From then on, everything I did seemed to go wrong and, an hour later, when I descended from
this towering, but very much animated monument, I was extremely disgusted with myself.*

*It took hours of riding before I got the hang of Barnaby. I found that
the faintest pressure of my leg was enough for most commands. This, by
the way, was a case when spurs were obviously unnecessary.*

*I realized that experience and common sense govern the rider's leg
action; without them, no amount of advice can be effective.*

Hands. Control at an intermediate level is based on being able to ride
with a light contact between the horse's mouth and the rider's hands. This
contact at times is steady but, even then, light enough to alter in no way
the position of the horse's head or neck nor to impede in any way the forward impulsion of the horse, except when actually wilfully restraining
him.

It is sometimes said that the ideal contact should merely equal the
weight of the reins; in practice this is an unattainable ideal, but a goal
that one should always be striving toward.

There are some horses who, of themselves, like to take a franker hold
of the bit, without actually pulling or being over the bit; others, of a
passive nature, prefer to lag behind.

During the walk and the canter, the horse's head and neck sway considerably up and back and down and forward. Only at the trot are the
neck and head stable. In order to have the feel of the horse's mouth, the
rider must keep the reins lightly stretched, and follow the horse's mouth
with his arms, synchronizing their motion with the gestures of the horse's
head and neck.

When taught position, the rider is reminded to keep his hands well
apart, the left on the left side of the horse's neck, the right on the right

side; then, and then only, can the rider's arms move back and forth in piston-like motion, following those balancing gestures of the horse's head and neck as mentioned in Chapter VI and illustrated in Picture 33.

The pivots of the piston-acting arms are the rider's shoulders and elbows; it is of the utmost importance that these be relaxed—hence the value of correct position (rider firm in balance and relaxed). There should be a straight line of action from the rider's elbow to the horse's mouth; the wrists, though relaxed, must not be bent, as this would break the direct line of action.

A "praying mantis" attitude on the part of the rider's arms is strongly to be discouraged.

At first I found that I was hesitant in taking up the slack in the reins, fearing that I might disturb the horse; the result was that I rode on a half slack rein, under the impression that it was contact. This produced merely a succession of small jerks on the horse's mouth. At the trot, where the horse's head and neck are relatively stable, this did not matter, but at the canter and walk it became apparent as the horse raised its head and neck and felt obviously uncomfortable.

Since I learned this, I have noticed that many reputedly good riders are constantly committing the same error. The nearest way that I can repro-duce, in words, my feeling of a soft, steady contact, is by calling the reader's attention to fishing (and who has not gone fishing at one time or another in his life); when you have cast your line, fishing without a rod, and the slow current of a lazy river has taken up the slack, an ever so light but permanent tension is felt in your hand. This I found to resemble very much the feel of a light contact when riding. In order to follow with my arms the motion of the horse's head and neck, I found that when I re-laxed my shoulders, elbows and wrists the mere feeling of keeping the slack out of the reins at all times automatically made my arms follow through without any difficulty.

All intermediate rein control is based on "give and take."

The hands check or act in some other way—on either one or both reins —until the horse starts to execute the command and, the instant the horse obeys, the hand or hands relax to their original contact or even to slack reins. At no time, except for a fight, is the horse's head or neck raised, nor its balance intentionally disturbed. When the contact gets too heavy, due to the horse's beginning to pull, lighten the contact by a series of give and take actions; when, on the other hand, the horse does not move forward to take the contact push with your legs. *Never try to establish contact by merely tightening the reins.* The contact between the horse's mouth and the hands is established by the rider's legs.

"Give and take" may be accomplished by moving the rider's arms back and forth, in the piston-like action described in Chapter VI, or by the movement of the rider's wrists, or again by the mere opening and closing of the rider's fingers. The intensity with which give and take is applied depends on the reactions of the horse. It varies from a light fixing of the hands, when halting a well-schooled and responsive horse, to sawing on the mouth of a runaway or a jerk in the mouth, intended as a punishment for misbehavior. The "playing off" with one rein, to straighten the horse's head, is also subject to the law of give and take, and so is any action of the rider's hands designed to produce an effect on the horse's actions.

I found that, with practice, very little action of the hands was sufficient to obtain the beginning of a desired movement, and that a succession of checks and release movements, all done in a relaxed and not a brisk manner, was enough in all but extreme cases. The more experience I acquired, the easier and more automatically these give and take movements came, until they became instinctive.

Intermediate control aims at a soft, precise, efficient performance. The formulae listed below are applied in obtaining the required movements. Good results are derived from the *precise* and *tactful* execution of these formulae. The following method of control will work well only on correspondingly schooled horses. It is also meant for schooling horses on an intermediate level. All the movements listed below should be obtained with the indicated precision in schooling and in competitions where a good performance counts. Whereas one cannot expect such precision when hunting or riding cross-country, a horse schooled to precise performance will obey more readily and be pleasanter to ride in the hunting field or anywhere else.

Walk from Halt. Have the reins loose; urge with the legs until the horse moves forward. Establish contact as soon as you can and begin to follow with your arms the gestures of the horse's head and neck.

To increase the speed of the walk, use your legs alternately in rhythm with the horse's stride, i.e., as the left lateral moves forward, urge with your right leg (in anticipation of the right lateral's advance); as the right advances use your left leg.

Using the legs in this seesawing fashion and in rhythm required a certain knack; I found it easier to learn by watching the horse's shoulders: as the left shoulder moved forward, I applied my right leg, and vice versa.

Trot from Walk. Relax your hands, loosen the reins, urge with the legs until the horse breaks into a trot, then establish contact. The swaying motion of the horse's head and neck at the walk ceases at the trot. Consequently, the rider's following-arms motion also stops; however, the hands must remain relaxed, ready to follow any unexpected motion of the horse's head and neck, such as, for instance, when the horse stumbles.

I found that some horses started their trot with a plunging action of the head, and if my hands were not quick enough to move forward and give sufficient freedom, a jerk in the horse's mouth resulted.

Other horses that I had occasion to ride had learned from bitter experi-

*ence that bad riders would always be left behind at the start of a trot,
and would haul themselves back into position by means of the reins. These
unfortunate animals started their trot by throwing their heads up in a
pathetic effort to avoid undeserved punishment. In such cases I found it
helpful to push the horse onto the bit while still at the walk, and maintain
the contact as I broke into the trot, sitting the first few strides.*

The correct speed of the ordinary trot is about 8 miles an hour. It is
important to maintain an even pace and not to permit the horse to go
into a fast trot, except when doing it as an exercise, and then for short
periods only.

To increase the trot. Squeeze with your legs on the downward beat of
the posting trot, as your body returns to the saddle—relax your legs on
the upward beat as you rise in the stirrups—then squeeze again as you
come down and so on . . . keep your action well in rhythm.

If, for some reason, you wish to bring into play a more intense action
of the legs, stop posting and sit, then the action of the legs is no longer
intermittent and may be constant.

Canter from trot, disregarding the Lead. Increase the leg action and
check momentarily with your hands to prevent the horse from increasing
the trot, without, however, raising his head and neck; keep on urging
until the horse breaks into a canter; the instant he does, start following
his mouth with your arms, because the head and neck will be making
balancing gestures. Keep the horse's neck and head straight and do not be
disturbed if he ranges his haunches slightly to the side of the lead. This
is a natural cantering attitude for many horses (exception: fast gallop);
but this ranging must be very slight; do not allow your horse to gallop
sideways.

A smooth transition from the trot to the gallop without interruption of
contact is not an easy matter. The brief but soft checking movement of
the hands has to synchronize with the push of the rider's legs. On a well-
schooled horse, the action of the hands boils down to a very small increase
of resistance on the reins. It is of utmost importance to maintain, at this
point, a correct seat; hunching or leaning the body in any direction only'
disturbs the horse. Stop posting while preparing for a canter departure.

*The instruction to check the horse while pushing with the legs is of
paramount importance. In my case I know that I did not do it at first
sufficiently, with the result that my horse started the gallop by rushing
into it from a fast trot, rather than swinging into the gallop, following a
correct simultaneous application of hands and legs.*

Canter from trot on desired lead. In order to make the horse take the
left lead, apply the right leg somewhat behind the girth—this ranges the
horse's haunches to the left. The left leg keeps steady at the girth and
maintains forward impulsion. Turn the horse's head *slightly* to the left
by a direct action of the left rein. On most horses, use the direct rein;
however, some may react better if you move both your hands to the right,

thereby getting the left rein to act as an indirect rein of opposition, and the right as a mild leading rein; the horse's head is then turned to the left, while the horse's forehand is maintained on the track. After the horse has assumed the correct attitude, the final signal to go into the gallop comes from the rider's right leg; on a schooled horse, mere pressure will be sufficient.

To obtain the right lead, reverse the action of the legs and turn the horse's head slightly to the right.

I found it at first easier to begin my gallop in the corner of the ring. The horse's inside legs have then less ground to cover than the outside legs; the horse has, therefore, more freedom on the inside, and the correct lead is then the easier to take.

To maintain the canter, urge rhythmically with the inside leg. (Cantering on left lead, rider's left leg active; cantering on right, right leg.) In the case of lazy horses you may be forced to act with both legs simultaneously.

The slower the canter the more imperative is this particular use of one leg. For, at a slow canter there is always a chance that the legs on the leading side will become sluggish and will stop moving ahead of those on the other side. The moment the movement of the two sides is equalized the horse will break into a trot.

At the gallop, urging with one particular leg is of no importance.

From the Canter to the Field Gallop. Urge the horse forward with both legs, encouraging him to lengthen his strides; the hands follow the horse's head as the motion of the head and neck become markedly pronounced. With the increase in speed, contact becomes progressively stronger and the rider shortens his reins as he rises in the stirrups and leans markedly forward.

Decrease of Gaits. To decrease your gait from the field gallop to the canter, stop being active with the legs and fix your hands, and the IN-STANT your horse BEGINS to obey—release . . . then fix again, and release again. A deliberate succession of such movements will bring the horse down to the canter, then to the trot, from the trot to the walk, and finally to the halt. The horse should come to a stop relaxed from stem to stern; his spine straight, head and neck in their relaxed, natural positions; the mouth should *not* open.

On the intermediate level of riding, all action is progressive, i.e., from the halt to the walk, then to the trot, then to the canter, and finally to the gallop, with the decrease of gait also in successive order. Nothing is worse for the horse's muscular and nervous system than jack rabbit starts and dead stops from a fast gallop, when neither the rider nor the horse are educated to it. It takes advanced schooling and advanced riding to do it without damage.

With ambitious, pulling horses, fixing the hands may not be enough, and a pull and release action is more effective. In that case, the rider's elbows are drawn back, his shoulders stiffened, his back braced, his chest out; he gives a long pull followed by a short release, another long pull, etc. until the horse slows down. If the horse has taken a strong hold of the bit, a seesaw action of the hands should pry the bit loose and bring the horse to reason. A yet more powerful method is the pulley rein, which consists in fixing one hand firmly on the horse's withers with the rein taut, while drawing the other rein strongly to the side up, and to the rear across the withers.

Change of leads with interruption. Intermediate control does not call for a flying change of leads but merely for a change of leads with interruption,—that is, unless your horse is particularly able to make this change without transitional steps of trot. This exercise is as important in developing skill in the horse as in developing cooperation of the rider's hands and legs. You can practice it during half-circles, half-circles in reverse, and while changing direction diagonally across the arena. There are no special aids to discuss for the execution of this exercise, but there is a certain technical routine to which you must adhere.

Let us suppose that while galloping on the right lead you are approaching point A, where you wish to change to the left lead. Then, approximately twenty feet away from A, you slow the horse into a trot, establish an even, quiet gait and then, at point A use the aids necessary for a canter departure on the left lead. With the improvement of the horse and yourself, reduce the period of the trot.

I have found that on a very well schooled horse this was so easy to accomplish that it was hardly an exercise for my legs and hands. On an insufficiently schooled horse, however, it took me a long time to learn to do it satisfactorily. What usually happened was this: after two or three changes, the horse anticipating them and becoming overanxious about them, would stiffen, begin to pull, would be hard to keep straight, to bring to a relaxed trot and to have start the new canter without a plunge. This exercise on a half-schooled horse calls for a great deal of feeling and great dexterity of hands and legs.

To back. First bring the horse to a halt, then gradually increase the tension on the reins (reins of direct opposition). The instant the horse begins to move backwards relax the tension on the reins, then repeat again. With experience, a pull will correspond to the beginning of the moving back of one of the horse's fore legs and the opposite hind leg; a slackening of the reins will correspond to the actual movement of the horse's diagonal. At no time should the horse raise his head or start backing sideways. The rider's hands and legs form a corridor down which the horse must move. If, for example, the horse attempts to emerge from that corridor by moving his haunches to the right, the rider's right rein and right leg (behind the girth) will compel him to return to the "straight and narrow path." If the horse's haunches move to the left, the rider's left aids come into play. If the horse throws his head up it means that the rider's hands are overactive. This will also be the case when the horse rolls backwards in a disjointed manner; when the latter occurs, the rider's legs must act at the girth and check the horse (reins slack).

I didn't have any trouble learning correct aids in backing on schooled horses. *The reason is simple: there is no cooperation of legs and hands if the horse obeys and backs slowly, regularly and straight; you merely use the hands alone. There is really no difficulty in using them softly at a slow movement when the action of the legs doesn't complicate the matter. Learning control at backing, however, to the point where one can teach the horse this movement, is another story.*

Turns with movement forward. The turn should be large enough to permit the horse to take it comfortably, without in any way losing the forward impulse of the gait at which he is moving.

To turn to the left. When making a wide, sweeping turn use the left leading rein; on smaller turns or when checking the horse on a turn, use the rein of direct opposition—the latter being a stronger rein effect. In both cases the rein should bring the horse's head into position where you can just see the horse's left eye. If it is necessary to maintain the gait while the horse turns to the left, use both legs at the girth. This is under ideal conditions. Now suppose the horse moves his haunches outward. Then your right leg moves back of the girth and acts to maintain them on the track. Or imagine that suddenly the horse moves his forehand inward, attempting to shorten the turn. Then move your hands to the right, preserving the bend of the horse's head. If he attempts to move outward, away from the turn, move both your hands to the left. Whatever formula you are applying, keep your horse moving forward, *your legs active.* Don't let him hang on your hands; if he does, lighten the contact with give-and-take.

When making fast turns, such as when galloping over an outside course of jumps, use the leading rein, the rider's hand moving in rhythm, and leading the horse forward along the path of the turn. When taking a small inside course you will probably have to slow the horse on most turns and hence will need to use the rein of direct opposition, adding the checking effect of the outside rein to it.

In regard to turning with movement forward, during my studies I met with two particular difficulties:

a) If the horse had a rubber neck to the slightest extent I always found myself turning his head to the side much more than was required by the rules; the whole neck and head of the horse forming a sort of hook. It was difficult for me to learn how to remedy it with the legs and an occasional interference with the outside rein.

b) Trying to make small circles on stiff horses normally resulted in their hindquarters skidding to the outside. Knowing that this fault can be corrected by schooling only, my problem in studying control was merely to estimate how small a circle a particular horse was capable of making easily. This feeling did not come at once.

Turns used in learning intermediate control. Certain turns and combinations of turns are used when working in the ring; they are excellent practice for horse and rider—a good way of applying all the recipes used in intermediate control. These movements, which are also used in schooling horses, are the only efficient way to develop the coordination of the rider's hands and legs with the efforts of the horse.

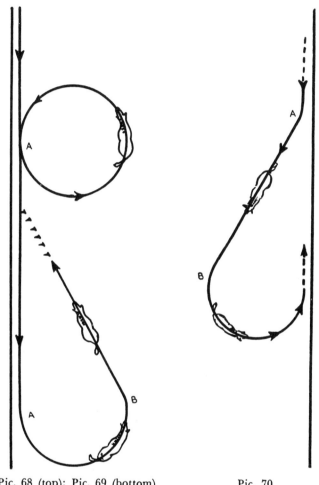

Pic. 68 (top); Pic. 69 (bottom)   Pic. 70

Circle (Picture 68). Moving along the wall at a chosen gait, circle when arriving at selected point A (size of circle depending on gait and the level of the horse's schooling), return to track at same point.

Half-circle (Picture 69). Moving along the wall arrive at a chosen spot, A, and start circling; after completing a half-circle at point B, directly opposite A, head for the wall IN A STRAIGHT LINE; keep the horse moving forward and straight; arriving at wall take track in opposite direction to which you came.

Half-circle in reverse (Picture 70). Moving along the wall, arrive at the chosen spot A; turn outward at 45 degrees to the wall and head IN A STRAIGHT LINE, keeping your horse moving forward and straight to any point, B, chosen conveniently far away from the wall to permit making half a circle; return to the track moving in an opposite direction from that in which you came.

Serpentine (Picture 71). The serpentine is a series of half-circles with a straight, short distance between them. Here is how to execute it. Taking the track along the wall of the ring you arrive at point A (lines AB and CD are the axii of your movement), and start a half-circle to the left, crossing the line AB. You take a straight line for a few strides, keeping your horse straight from nose to tail, then start a half-circle to the right, at the axis line CD—head straight for a short distance, half-circle to the left and so on . . .

Zigzag (Picture 72). Choosing a center line AB, you move along it; then turning at 45 degrees to it, you proceed in a straight line, until you are approximately 6' away from the axis of your movement; you then turn again at 45 degrees and crossing the axis in a straight movement, arrive at a spot 6' on the other side of the line AB, and so forth. As you see, the turns are sharper than when doing the serpentine.

We repeated several times that the horse must be kept straight during a certain phase of the half-circle, half-circle in reverse, serpentine and zig-zag. This is done by urging the horse forward, with both the rider's legs acting in pushing the horse onto the contact, which is a mild form of having the horse on the bit. The rider's hands may come into play, in order to straighten the horse's forehand if he attempts to waddle sideways instead of striding energetically forward; or the rider may merely "play off" slightly with one rein to straighten the horse's head.

Captain Littauer kept stressing the importance of these exercises as one of the efficient ways of learning cooperation of hands and legs; and indeed they are! Having hacked, hunted and jumped for several years I found that I really only started to get at the root of things when I had worked consistently for a while in the ring. However, the benefit of these exercises may be lost if they are applied under adverse circumstances; and I think that I should caution the student, who like myself may try to do them some day on his own. Unless a horse is sufficiently schooled, a succession of signals and different manoeuvres, for example a circle followed immediately by a serpentine, then a half-circle in reverse etc., is apt to excite and upset the horse, and in a few minutes, not only is the value of these exercises lost to horse and rider, but you will have on your hands a serious problem—a mentally upset horse. The correct approach to these exercises is first getting your horse perfectly relaxed, through riding on loose reins and light contact, for the first part of your lesson, without attempting any kind of manoeuvers; then, when your horse is limbered, calm and relaxed, go through a planned program of some 10

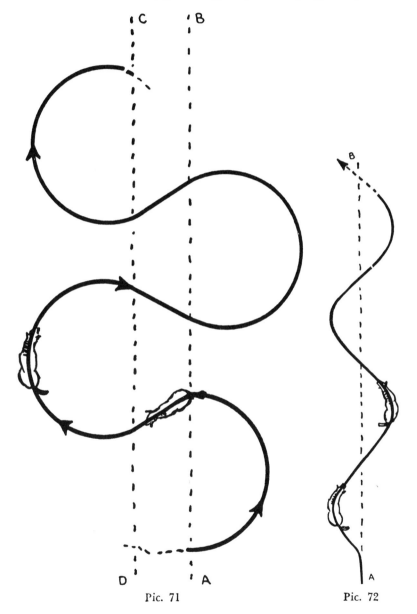

Pic. 71   Pic. 72

to 15 minutes, where these exercises will follow each other in a not too abrupt fashion and will be interspersed with short periods of loose rein riding.

I found that this way of doing things, besides being the most efficient, was also much more pleasant than the drudgery of ceaseless exercises reminiscent of parade grounds. Somehow or other, I noticed invariably that the horse then went about his business in a far pleasanter way.

Changing directions across the ring. We have pointed out that it is important to keep the horse straight during certain phases of the half-circles, half-circles in reverse, serpentines and zig-zags. One way to practice keeping the horse moving in a straight line following any kind of turns, is to work on changes of direction across the ring. To do this, aim your horse at the corner diagonally opposite to the one you happen to be rounding and cross the ring moving straight and forward until ready to turn again. When making this change at the trot, do not worry about which diagonal you may be posting on. You may follow the old rule of posting on the right or left diagonal according to which way you happen to be going; but this is really not necessary, as it is of no help to the horse. However, be sure to change occasionally in order to distribute the strain evenly on both diagonals. For instance, trot five minutes on one diagonal and then five on the other.

This straight movement across the arena, immediately after a turn and without walls to guide you is much more difficult than a novice may think. It took me a long time to master it. If I was too gentle and passive, the horse wobbled; if, when trying to correct the latter, I became too energetic the horse would start pulling and increase the speed. Practically every horse required a different amount of leg. Captain Littauer was encouraging me by telling how on one occasion not a single rider out of a class of fifteen experienced hunters could make an academically good diagonal change of directions across the arena.

Counter-gallop. When the horse gallops to the left on a right lead, or to the right on a left lead, it is called the counter-gallop. There are many practical instances, both in the hunting field and in horse shows, where a horse may be called on to counter-gallop, rather than change leads. For example, when two changes of lead in rapid succession would be indicated, it is preferable to keep the horse on one lead throughout, than be forced to make two flying changes.

To obtain a counter-gallop in a ring from a semi-schooled horse, start on a correct lead and make a half-circle or a half-circle in reverse to get into the false or counter-gallop. When galloping on the right lead maintain the gallop by using your right leg rhythmically at the girth (at the girth and not behind it, as the latter action might make the horse change leads). Galloping on the left lead, use your left leg. Keep the horse's head turned slightly to the side of the lead on which you are galloping (Picture 73). It is the only time when the horse's head and body are bent in the opposite direction to the path of movement.

I found that when jumping a course it did not pay to be too lead conscious, and that unless my horse was actually either off balance or disconnected, it made no difference on what lead I was galloping.

Entering corners. When working in the ring, keep the horse close into the corners, or he will tend to cut them more and more, inching toward the inside of the ring. If he attempts to turn his corner crabwise, use your inside leg at the girth and move both hands to the outside. The inside rein used as rein of indirect opposition in front of the withers must be the stronger; it keeps the horse's head slightly toward the inside while pushing the forehand to the outside. The inside leg prevents the rest of the horse from coming toward the center of the ring. The slower the gait, the closer you can keep to the corners.

Those of our less fortunate readers who have been exposed to riding academy hacks, have no doubt remarked that most irritating habit of these ruined horses to move in a crabwise fashion, away from the kneeboards toward the center of the ring. I have come to the conclusion, after riding many such specimens, that the application of the above recipe will work on them only after hours of tedious work to break a habit acquired by years of being badly ridden.

Turns in Place

Half-turn on the forehand (Picture 74). When making a half-turn on the forehand, the horse's quarters move to the left or to the right, describing

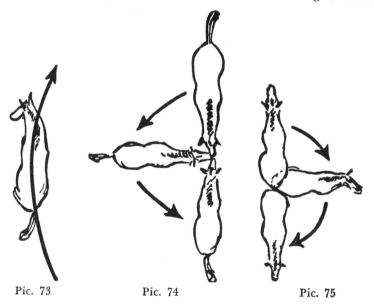

Pic. 73   Pic. 74   Pic. 75

a half-circle around the fore legs. The horse should not pivot on the fore leg, but should mark time with one leg while the other makes a small circle around it. To rotate the hindquarters to the left, apply the right leg behind the girth, and tapping gently, push the horse's hindquarters to the left. As the rider's right leg acts behind the girth, his left remains steady at the girth and acts as a guard to prevent the horse from moving to the left with all his body. The rider's hands are passive, merely maintaining a contact; they act only if the horse decides to move forward—in this case they will check. The horse's body should be straight from nose to tail; however, in the case of the horse resisting the rider's legs, the rider may correct this by turning the horse's neck and head to the right, which will force the horse's hindquarters to move to the left. Under ideal conditions, however, the hands remain completely passive, merely maintaining contact. (To rotate the hindquarters to the right, reverse the aids.) While acting to turn the quarters, the legs also maintain enough impulsion to preserve contact on the reins and to prevent the horse from backing.

I was told by my instructor that the secret in learning to make a successful turn on the forehand depended on not hurrying it, but taking one's time; if necessary waiting 2 or 3 seconds after each step of the horse. Otherwise, if hurried, the horse will start pivoting on one leg or, worse still, will scramble around with all his body.

A finished turn must consist of well-connected, soft and precise steps, but in order to arrive at it, both horse and rider must learn by doing it gradually.

Half - turn on the quarters (Picture 75). This means that the horse rotates his forehand along the circumference of a half-circle whose center is a small area on which move the horse's hind legs. These move, not pivot, one hind leg describing a very small circle around the other hind leg, which merely marks time.

Now for the rider's actions: first, close your legs, to bring the horse to attention and to establish contact between his mouth and your hands. Now, move your hands to the left (half-turn on the haunches to the left); your left rein acts as a leading rein (sometimes direct rein of opposition is preferable), your right as a rein of indirect opposition in front of the withers. The horse's head is turned slightly to the left, but his body is straight. The rider's left leg is at the girth, ready to act if the horse decides to take a side step or begins to turn too swiftly. The rider's right leg is behind the girth; if the horse were suddenly to move his haunches to the right it would ruin the movement, consequently, the rider's right leg must act behind the girth, causing the horse's right hind to move forward and to the left, in the small area on which the hindquarters revolve. When turning to the right, reverse the aids.

1) If the horse tries to back, release the reins and squeeze him forward with both legs.

2) If the horse tries to move forward diminish the leg and check with both hands.

Two difficulties confronted me when making this turn, which I found considerably more complex than that on the forehand: 1) If the hands were the least bit overactive, the horse tried to back and I found it hard to catch that moment in the incipient stage. 2) If I hurried the movement, the horse would simply push its hindquarters outward against my leg and would complete the turn as on the forehand.

As in the turn on the forehand, when learning, the best results were had if I took time out (a few seconds) after each step of the horse. This actually only while learning, for the finished intermediate performance calls for four united steps. My difficulty, then, lay in moving softly and yet without interruption. If I tried the least bit to force the horse around with my hands, the horse's head went up and the neck twisted sideways, or the above listed two evils spoiled my performance.

Two Tracks. The horse moves two tracking when the axis of his body remains parallel to the axis of the ring, but he himself moves obliquely. The horse's head is slightly turned at the poll, in the direction of the movement (Picture 76). When moving to the right, the horse's near fore crosses over and forward of the off fore and the near hind crosses the path of the off hind.

To execute two tracks correctly on the intermediate level, choose a line of movement and move straight along it; then if you choose to move at two tracks to the right, apply the left leg behind the girth (in a series of light taps). The right leg maintains impulsion at the girth; the right hand draws the horse's forehand to the right with a light leading rein effect; the left rein acts as a left rein of indirect opposition in front of the withers and helps to move the horse's forehand to the right. To remain united with the horse you must carry your weight to the right, bearing on the right stirrup. The main points to observe: 1) Do not obtain excessive lateral motion at the expense of loss of movement forward; 2) Have the horse look toward the direction of movement, never the other way; 3) Do not let the action of your hands impede the impulsion given by your legs.

Pic. 76

It was the third point which I found the most difficult to master. Anxious to move the horse obliquely,

my hands exceeded in intensity the action of my legs; the result was that
my horse hung on my hands, impulsion was lost and the horse's body
acquired a twisted and cramped position. A sense of rhythm was im-
perative in coordinating the action of my outside leg with the horse's
strides, while eventually the hands moved merely in a series of light signals.

It took me longer to learn two tracks than any other movement, and
I found it to be really the culminating phase of hand and leg cooperation.
Whereas in turns on the forehand and haunches (also lateral movements)
the horse remained stationary, the forward movement in two tracks made
it difficult to stay with the horse, and yet be free to act freely with hands
and legs.

Approaching a jump. Once the gait and speed at which the rider wishes
his horse to take the obstacle have been set and the immediate approach
to the jump has begun, no restraining, pushing or any other activity must
stem from the rider, except for a squeeze of the calves which indicates
to the horse that he is committed to the jump. Only if the horse begins
to lose impulse is any stronger action of the legs warranted. The rider's
arms follow the horse's mouth, back and forth, in piston-like action;
fingers, wrists, elbows and shoulders should relax. Tension on the reins
should progressively diminish during the last three strides, and be equal
to zero at the moment of the take-off (that is, if you are certain that the
horse intends to jump the obstacle). The rider looks over and beyond the
fence. The exception, of course, is jumping in the hunting field, where
the rider's eyes must be on the ground as well for possible pitfalls—rocks,
holes, mud, etc. He should await the jump in a state of passive alertness—
his position as described in Chapter VI.

The greatest difficulty that I experienced was in remaining passive. I
always attempted to ride the last three strides by urging the horse with my
legs, in some cases even trying to enhance the action of my legs by check-
ing the horse with my reins. Though, occasionally, such tricks worked,
and my horse actually jumped higher, continuous interference resulted
in the horse becoming tense and no longer attempting to calculate his own
approach to the jump. The key to success, I found, was to have the horse
approach the jump in such a manner as if it did not exist at all, looking
over and beyond it, the only indication that the horse was headed for an
obstacle being a certain state of relaxed alertness on the part of the animal.
I found that my control, under perfect conditions, was then limited only
to a squeeze of the calves, while my arms moved back and forth following
the horse's mouth.

Imperfect approach. *Nothing in life is always perfect, nor are the ap-*
proaches to a jump an exception to this rule; they are not always as smooth
and pleasant as prescribed in books. For instance, sometimes on a pulling
horse you suddenly find yourself at the jump, while still restraining him. I
found in that case (and here speaks the voice of bitter experience), that
sudden abandonment of the hold on the horse's mouth, when just a

stride or two away from the jump led to disaster; the horse unbalanced by the sudden release, refused, or worse, catapulted blindly into the jump. I found that the best course of action lay in maintaining the contact (even though heavier than desirable), until the horse rose at the jump,—then following through with my arms endeavoring to give (even though belatedly) freedom to the horse's head and neck in their balancing efforts over the obstacle.

In the case of a potential refusal or run-out, I learned that a slight increase in the contact is a great help. The horse then feels, in a manner of speaking, that he is boxed in a corridor, between the rider's hands and strongly active legs: his only way out is over the jump.

In the course of having had the misfortune to jump, at different times, badly schooled horses, I eventually learned a few helpful recipes to prevent run-outs: for example, when a horse indicates his intention to veer off, while some distance away from the jump, and advances his shoulder to the right, let us say, the right rein of indirect opposition, coupled with the use of the rider's right leg, should straighten out the horse. However, if the run-out is attempted in the last few strides, a quick action of the left direct rein, and of the left leg, should swing the front and the croup into line. At the jump-off, on hesitating horses, the rider should give a powerful push, which in the last decisive second may mean the difference between a jump and a run-out or refusal.

However, the full answer lies in riding schooled horses and not having to resort to any such expedients. A run-out should be an exception and not a rule.

Galloping away from the jump. Upon landing, stay off the saddle. Do not restrain the horse until he has taken two or three strides and regained his balance; it should not be done earlier. Interference with the horse's recovery of balance on landing will make him nervous and he may begin to rush his fences or to throw the head up when landing and lose the good quality of his gait.

It was a long time before I started to pay attention to what happened after a jump. The pleasure of having cleared the obstacle successfully made me feel careless for a few seconds afterwards—most vital seconds, as I subsequently learned, for they are the time when the horse readjusts himself to the violent change in balance. I found that with my weight well off the saddle and a light contact, the horse stretched his neck and easily rebalanced himself in a few strides.

Jumping over easy courses. On starting, select your pace and attempt to maintain it throughout the course with the least possible variations; though certain obstacles may require to be taken faster (wide jumps) and others somewhat slower (in-and-outs, jumps situated at difficult angles and after sharp turns), the transitions in the speed should be gradual and never brisk. Attempt to make all turns as sweeping as possible—and come in straight at the obstacle; once committed to the approach of the jump, look over and beyond it—this will keep you from being tempted to calculate the approach yourself, thereby usually interfering with the horse's own calculations. Do not look back to see whether you have knocked the obstacle, but keep your eyes on the course ahead. Do not anticipate what may or may not happen at any one jump; commit your horse and stay still with the weight well in the stirrups; act only if you feel that the horse is about to rush or that the forward impulse is dying down or that the horse begins to waver. Upon completion of the last jump, do not stop your horse like a polo pony; stop as gradually as space permits. On an intermediate level the passiveness of the rider is essential. In advanced riding, when competing in the show ring over difficult courses, the hands and legs of the rider will be more active, the horse then being ridden more on the bit.

As regards the uniform speed to be maintained while riding a course: I found a somewhat useful, though approximate, simile in comparing it to a song—though you may sing certain parts of it slowly and others fast, the time frequently remains constant. I found that though on occasions an ever-increasing pressure of the legs was necessary to clear an obstacle, usually once the forward impulse was established one had merely to maintain it at its proper pitch.

Cross-country riding on the intermediate level. One of the aims of intermediate riding is efficient and pleasant riding in the field. In order to achieve this, we must work part of the time in the ring, where our own study and the schooling of the horse are made easier by a relatively confined space; but as we progress, more and more time must be applied to riding in the field. There we must strive to put into effect the results of our work in the ring; a quiet, relaxed, forward-moving horse, his head and neck free to perform their balancing movements, which the horse is now especially called on to use as he moves over the uneven terrain. Certain rules of field riding must be borne in mind:

1) Distribute your gaits evenly; do not indulge in a sharp succession of short periods at different gaits, this will make the horse nervous.

2) Alternate your gallops and trots with long periods of walk on loose reins.

3) Choose your terrain with consideration for the horse; avoid stones and hard uneven surfaces, if forced to move over such—walk.

4) Do not ride on contact only; allow periods of canter and trot on a loose rein.

5) Start and end your ride with a ten minute walk, first to limber your horse, and lastly to cool it off. If the horse is really hot, the cooling-off walk should be longer than ten minutes.

I found field riding as relaxing for myself as for the horse. After too much work in the ring, I found myself at times getting tense and feeling that my horse also was losing the game. Long periods of walk, trot and canter and some galloping in the field were then a pleasant and efficient tonic for the horse and myself.

Cross-country jumping. Cross-country jumping should be as deliberate and as relaxed as when jumping in the ring. Though the pace may be occasionally faster, it should never be allowed to degenerate into a pell-mell scramble over fences. Obstacles should be approached at right angles and with a good clear approach, whenever possible. Maintain a light contact on the horse's mouth and follow carefully all movements of the horse's head and neck with your arms.

In jumping cross-country one must pay great attention to what is on the other side of the fence (if you can see it in advance); landing on hard pavement is hardly a tonic for the horse's legs, and it's much better to pull up and lose some time than to risk an injured tendon.

I love cross-country jumping; to me it is the ultimate pleasure in riding. When, after working under Captain Littauer I had occasion to ride and jump across country on a schooled horse, I finally realized what great a difference it made when horse and rider were one—the former bold but obedient, the latter efficient and authoritative. Months of scholastic work in the ring pay here their ample dividends and here it was that I understood that I had really learned something after much rigorous and, at times, not very lively work in the ring.

Going up and down hill. We can bring under the heading of cross-country riding going up or down steep gradients—both involving for the horse radical changes of balance. Just as in jumping, the horse requires, at such times, complete liberty of his balancing apparatus, the head and neck, and also the freedom of his motor, the hindquarters. We have described in Chapter VI the seat required from the rider; his control can be described in one word—*passivity.* There is not an awful lot you can do profitably when the horse is sliding down a sharp gravel slope; except to check him in order to prevent his "rolling." Climbing a steep hill, the rider will concentrate on keeping his weight off the saddle; if necessary by grabbing the horse's mane and standing in the stirrups. The reins should preferably be loose.

Rearing. A horse prone to rearing often has a sensitive mouth. Therefore, when the rider's hands become the least amount overactive, such a horse will be inclined to rear, particularly if his usual state is that of being behind the bit. If this happens, lean forward, grabbing the mane, loosen the reins completely; the instant the horse's forehand comes down to earth, urge strongly with your legs. The horse cannot easily rear while turning, hence you may anticipate rearing by sharply turning the horse around one or more times.

Bucking. A young horse "full of beans" and one who has been confined a certain time in his stall will, upon emerging into fresh air, be tempted to buck. If given his freedom and spurred on, the bucks will increase in violence; therefore the best cure is anticipation and prevention. To get rid of the bucks: longe a frisky horse before mounting. When mounted, start with a long walk, keep contact with the horse's mouth, then follow with perhaps a five minute jog, sitting in the saddle; do this preferably in the paddock before coming out into the field. When bucks do occur, sit down deeply in the saddle, leaning slightly back. Bring your hands up (with a jerk, if necessary), in order to get the horse's head up; the horse can buck freely only when its head is down; hence, in anticipation, keep the horse's head up when you feel that bucks are "around the corner."

Run-away. A run-away, other than one caused by bolting through sheer fright, is often the fault of the rider. There is a speed of the gallop beyond which the horse gains such impulse and momentum that he is sometimes carried away emotionally by the great pace. A rider should learn to "feel" the speed of the gallop beyond which it is not safe for him to let his horse go and to check him before he reaches it. It also happens to the person who keeps an uninterrupted pull on the reins while at the same time squeezing the horse with his legs. The bit pressing continuously and on one part of the horse's mouth, deadens it; the horse takes a firm hold and we are off. The run-away can usually be antici-pated and thereby prevented—however, if it does happen, deal with it as shown under the radical method of decreasing gait . . . space permit-ting, attempt to get the horse galloping in an ever decreasing circle until brought to reason. Half-halts may be useful in preventing the horse from acquiring undesirable speed.

Half-halt. Close the fingers on the reins and move the hands quickly and forcefully upward; follow quickly with a "give." This causes the horse to raise its head and neck and transfer to the rear the weight put forward excessively on the shoulders. Half-halts should not be used in jumping. Though some talented riders do place the horse for the take-off by means of one or several half-halts, and then release him at the jump as one would release a coiled spring, this practice makes the horse dependent on split-second timing by the rider and he no longer can figure out by himself the correct approach to the jump.

In the case of a rusher (though the only cure is, of course, complete re-schooling), half-halts can be successfully used in the following manner: some 20′ in front of the fence, one or more half-halts should check the horse sufficiently to prevent him from boring down into the fence in a fast and dangerous fashion. This, to repeat again, is something worth-while in the case of emergencies, but in no way to be used systematically as we so often see it done in shows.

Voice Command. An important auxiliary to the use of the rider's hands and legs is the voice. A "whoa" or a click of the tongue are powerful aids when dealing with a horse that is used to being spoken to. Use your voice soothingly to calm, harshly to reprimand, authoritatively to bring obedience. A soothing voice may also be a reward—a harsh sound a warning to behave!

It happened many times in the course of my riding studies that I was much helped in achieving this or that result by using my voice. On several occasions I was fortunate to avoid open rebellion where even expertly used hands and legs would have had quite a time.

Punishment and reward. There is no fixed rule regarding punishment; when and how severely to punish is determined by equestrian tact, that unknown quality about which we spoke at the beginning of the chapter. Avoid punishment whenever possible, but when you have definitely ascertained that punishment is necessary, do it in a dispassionate way, do not fly into a tantrum; when you lose your temper you lose control of your actions, and usually lose the battle.

The rule about rewarding is much simpler. Reward always when the horse has done what you have asked; a piece of sugar or a pat on the neck will accustom the horse to obeying your hand and leg signals; with willingness all work will be done more efficiently and much more pleasantly.

I was lucky that in the course of my equestrian studies all my teachers, though differing radically on many aspects of riding, unanimously agreed and assiduously preached, "REWARD YOUR HORSE WHEN HE HAS DONE WELL."

Both reward and punishment must follow quickly the right or wrong behavior of the horse.

I am not one of those fortunate people who have their own horses, and who can apply one particular method of riding and schooling to them. These lucky ones are able to enjoy the results of a year's work on one horse. While studying with Captain Littauer I worked different horses for periods of weeks or days at a time; many were riding academy specimens, much abused by previous bad riding, and the process of bringing them to an even half-way responsive attitude so as to be able to learn control on them was a major problem.

In order to resolve this problem, it was occasionally necessary to do things quite contrary to what you may find prescribed in this chapter. I mentioned this to Captain Littauer when we were assembling material for this book, and I said: "Captain, if we are going to tell people to do things which we have previously warned them against, we shall bewilder them." This was a point to consider. On the other hand, we both felt that those exceptions to the rules with which we are frequently confronted should be mentioned. For instance, many readers may have been invited for a day's hunting, and had to mount strange horses with whims and habits very different from those to which they were accustomed. Or there may be times, when vacationing somewhere or other that we are given the opportunity of riding an unfamiliar horse for a couple of weeks. In such or similar cases, it is impossible to re-school the horse and adapt him to our way of riding, even though, in the long run, our method may vastly improve him. Therefore, compromise may be necessary to a greater or lesser extent, depending on the ways of the horse.

The main problem being, in such cases, to get on terms with the horse, and derive pleasure from riding him in as short a time as possible.

The aim of intermediate control is a performance at which, as we have constantly repeated, the horse remains relaxed, not requiring more than mild leg signals and soft hands—this is our ideal. But when confronted with unschooled, spoiled, upset horses no rules can be laid down, except the one given to me on many occasions by Captain Littauer: "First and foremost attempt to achieve a non-belligerent attitude on the part of the horse." Some readers, when reaching this part of the text, will remember particularly unpleasant devils that they have had the misfortune to straddle at times in their riding careers. We will discuss in the following pages these unpleasant specimens, assuming that we are not planning to re-school them but merely hope to arrive in as short a time as possible at a reasonable degree of understanding with the horse. This in no way deviates from Captain Littauer's system, but merely stresses the fact (and this is the main purpose of these pages), that all methods must be flexible enough to allow for exceptions.

I once mounted a horse which, as soon as he felt my weight on his back and my legs at his sides, immediately assumed a heraldic attitude and pranced in lather for the next couple of hours; the lightest of contacts (I held the rein in two fingers) seemed too much, the mere inkling of a leg signal seemed to irritate this Bucephalus to the point of madness. A couple of days later, I saw the same horse cantering quietly for his owner who sat back on the cantle, his legs stuck far out along the horse's shoulders, the reins slack; when he wanted to give a signal, he jerked the reins this way or that and again allowed them to sag. To my amazement, this seemed to work perfectly.

The next time I mounted the horse I tried this method; it produced immediate results. The instant I reverted to the conventional rational seat and brought my legs to the girth, things began to happen! Evidently the horse had become accustomed to carrying the rider's weight on his kidneys—the moment the rider transferred his weight forward, the horse took it for a signal to rush on. Accustomed to a completely loose rein, he could not understand, and consequently refused, even the slightest tension on the reins. The horse's owner carried his legs forward, in an attitude so often seen in old English hunting prints. Occasionally these legs swung back and kicked; they never pressed or gripped the horse's sides. Consequently, even a light contact grip annoyed the horse intensely. As the owner did not jump or ride across country, but merely hacked along roads and paths at a walk, trot and occasional canter, his seat and control, bad as they were, were quite sufficient for what he wanted.

Efficient riding on an intermediate level requires no more than a snaffle bridle, but many times we see over-collected horses, burdened with heavy double bridles, whose looks alone suggest that they are pullers. Attempt first and foremost to get such a horse to stretch his neck, walk him on loose reins, dropping the curb reins entirely. If the horse stretches his neck and lowers his head try jogging, then trotting with loose reins; if the horse's head and neck remain stretched and low, you have won your battle. The chances are then that at a canter and gallop, providing nothing untoward happens, the horse will continue in the position in which we desire him to be, and which being the natural and the easier for the horse to assume, he will readily maintain. However, to this course of action there may also be exceptions. For example: some time ago I had occasion to mount such a horse for an afternoon of riding. The instant I was mounted, the horse collected himself into a bundle and took strong hold. I tried a walk on loose reins and after a short while did succeed in obtaining a walk with outstretched neck. There, however, my success ended, for no sooner had I requested a trot than up went the neck, in went the chin, and the horse, with a churning trot, pulled like a steam engine. The correct solution to the problem was, of course, many, many days of walking on a loose rein; and a complete gradual re-schooling of the horse. This was out of the question; the day was cold and I cherished but little the thought of freezing for the next couple of hours walking a horse which I would never have a chance to school anyway. So I tried a last expedient: choosing a small enclosed field, only a little longer than a schooling ring, I set my horse into a canter. He immediately took hold and increased his speed, but instead of meeting the resistance of my hands, he met nothing but the slight pressure of contact. Evidently surprised, he kept on going fast, but his head dropped a little and I felt the muscles of his neck relax somewhat. A dozen circles and his neck was stretched, the gallop was slowing down considerably, and the reins were only slightly stretched. A quarter of an hour later I was trotting along the road on loose reins. This is not a method of curing a pulling, over-collected horse; it is not even an expedient worth considering on 99% of horses, but if it works with the 1% on which misfortune may some day plant you, then use it by all means.

I believe in and practice Captain Littauer's method of riding and schooling. I derive much pleasure and obtain good results from it when I try subordinating its rules to common sense and to my imagination, but I do not (and Captain Littauer constantly advises this himself) use these rules as I would a manual for the lubrication and maintenance of my automobile.

For instance, I may some day ride a horse, relaxed and stabilized, but with the habit of holding his head turned to one side. Were I, through forceful control, to attempt straightening it, I would, most likely, meet resistance and upset the horse. Better to spend the day riding pleasantly and forget about straightening the horse's head. Now if this horse were given to me for a few months, then I would work on remedying this defect by suppling the horse in the stiff side of the body by means of circles, half-circles, and in the stiff side of the mouth by "playing" with the rein on that side—by the application, in other words, of rules from the book. I may be invited hunting and may straddle a horse which gallops and jumps under a strong pull. Attempt to ride him on a light contact and I would be carted all over creation, But, were I to buy this horse, I would spend three months or more stabilizing him and working over cavalettis until, I hope, eventually the horse would jump as described in the chapter on schooling. Then I am sure the horse would jump better and be a far more pleasant conveyance.

To cite all the exceptions to the rules would be impossible or, at best, a most tedious business, nor is it the purpose of these pages to do so. My intention is to repeat again that studying a method of riding must be done thoroughly and one must be finally convinced of its superiority, as I happen to be convinced of the superiority of the method described in this book; but the application of the system to horses must be guided at all times by feeling, common sense and imagination; all three prerequisites to dealing with any kind of being, whether of the human or animal variety.

CHAPTER XII

Advanced Control

While intermediate control strives for the soft, efficient performance of a hunter or jumper, advanced riding aims one notch higher and lays great stress on the *quality of the horse's movement.* This means excellent gaits, really skilful turns and transitions, and truly athletic jumping.

A description of what constitutes a high quality of movement you can find in Chapter IX. Now a few words about its practicability. It is obvious that if a horse is schooled with the quality of its movement always in view, a superior mount will be developed. Such a horse should have a better chance of winning in jumping competitions, but is not necessarily a better hunter than a horse schooled on the intermediate level; that is, as far as the actual negotiating of a country is concerned. While a horse which is schooled to move softly and efficiently should be a very adequate hunter, it will take a discriminating and well-educated rider to appreciate in the hunting field the superior qualities of an advanced horse.

Even the statement that a horse schooled on the basis of advanced riding will have a better chance of winning is true only if he is competing against less well-schooled horses of equal abilities. No matter how excellently a horse is schooled, if he is an animal with little natural gift for jumping, he will have small chance against a green but talented competitor.

All in all, I believe that advanced riding—that is, advanced schooling and correspondingly advanced control—is a waste of time in the case of poor horses and is unnecessary for those human beings who are not interested in the finer points of life in general. If, upon taking up advanced riding, you expect spectacular results from schooling any kind of a horse, you will be disappointed. The finer your aims are, the more carefully you should consider the material with which you propose to work; that is, you must thoroughly analyze the possibilities of turning a particular horse into an athlete, as well as estimate your own abilities to accomplish the job. But if your aspirations are not so lofty, and you are looking merely for a somewhat better quality of performance than that on the intermediate level, then, even if your horse is not a perfect specimen, and even if you are merely an average rider, you can achieve something of a better order. You may not obtain magnificent gaits or consistency over 5' courses; but the gaits of your horse will be lighter and more pleasant than merely soft and efficient ones; and, although the jumping limit of your horse may be only a 4' fence, he will take it more acrobatically than a horse trained on the intermediate level.

Obviously, advanced control is very closely connected with advanced schooling. The horse will respond only to what he knows and the fine efforts of an advanced rider will be wasted on an insufficiently schooled horse.

Summing up what has been said, it can be concluded that advanced riding cannot very well be recommended to everyone. To many people it is of no interest and of no necessity. And from the point of view of the horse, all people who do not make a sufficient effort to develop their riding technique should confine themselves to simpler riding, which is less likely to hurt the horse. Trying to use finesse without knowing how, usually results in abuse of the animal. Advanced control and advanced schooling will be worthwhile as ultimate aims only for the following categories of riders:

1) Those who own very good horses and who desire to compete against equally good ones. Today in this country, as you know, there is a great abundance of magnificent horse-flesh. Schooling is, of course, the soundest way to get ahead among equally able horses.

2) Those who love riding for riding's sake, who have good—or even merely decent—horses, who perhaps hunt, or perhaps show, but, in whatever mounted sport they participate, do it for riding's sake, rather than for the game, and value a finished performance of the horse.

Putting aside these general considerations, and looking for the actual differences between intermediate and advanced control, we find three main ones:

1) Riding the horse, *at times* fully on the bit (in contrast to the merely soft contact of intermediate control).

2) Obtaining halts and reductions in speed by the means of flexions (instead of merely the give-and-take of the intermediate level).

3) Developing the horse's balance to the point where he can change easily from an extended to a semi-collected attitude (intermediate riding merely asks for soft increases and decreases of speed without any *radical* change from forward to central balance).

These three principles, putting the horse on the bit, flexions, and semi-collection, considerably alter the technique of control. While later in this chapter I shall describe how they apply to specific movements, here, in general, is how they are obtained:

Putting the horse on the bit. Let us assume that you are trotting on soft contact. You have obtained it by urging the horse lightly with your legs, not by pulling back on the reins. Now, let us suppose that you will urge still more with your legs. The horse will probably try to increase his speed, but you will prevent him from doing so with your hands. Let us further suppose that you will do it so tactfully that the horse is not going to pull, but will merely ever-so-lightly increase the tension on the reins by stretching his neck. I grant you that this is a great finesse; that is why it belongs to advanced riding. Attempts of an inadequately prepared rider to put the horse on the bit will result in an excited, pulling horse, and eventually in a dead mouth.

But imagine you have done it all very tactfully; then this is what has happened under you: the urging with your legs activated the horse's hindquarters; this energy, travelling through the horse's back has reached the neck, stretched it and the horse has taken a slightly firmer hold of your hands; the movement of the hindquarters and forehand has become united; now the horse moves in one piece. Thus moving on the bit, synchronizing the action of the hind and fore legs of the horse, improves the gait.

On a very well-schooled horse a rider can even drop the reins and for a dozen strides or more, the animal will continue to move as *connectedly* (not collectedly) as on the bit. Approaching an obstacle on such a horse, the rider can connect him a dozen or so strides before the jump and then gradually diminish the tension on the reins to zero and the horse's body will still be, at the take-off, perfectly synchronized.

When putting your horse on the bit you should consider the following matters:

1) The horse must take the bit with the neck and head stretched and mouth closed. Exception: semi-collected gaits; about them, later.

2) If the horse has started to pull or to increase the speed of the original gait it means that you are using too much leg.

3) If the horse tosses his head, or opens his mouth or brings the chin in, at the same time slowing down the gait, it means that you are using too much hand.

4) The difference in the feeling to your hands between riding on the bit and riding on contact should be slight; where you should be looking for the difference is in the movement of the horse.

It is easy enough to lay down laws that the horse must be ridden on *soft contact* in intermediate riding and *be softly on the bit* in advanced riding. It is true that a good rider can achieve either on any decently schooled horse at a walk, trot and canter; a fast gallop, however, presents specific difficulties.

At a gallop the natural inclination of a strong, ambitious horse often is to go faster than his rider desires (particularly when in company) and such a horse will constantly have to be restrained. Of course this will rarely happen in cases of lazy or weak horses who need urging; horses of a placid disposition, who easily obey rider's orders or keep an even hunting pace of their own accord; or horses whose *cooperation with their riders has been developed through schooling.*

And there is another important condition—movement. As I have already explained, movement is a series of states of lost and regained equilibrium. The faster the movement, the more pronounced is the loss of balance to the front and it takes a very skilful horse to retrieve it sufficiently and in time. Hence, unless the horse's balance (in the widest sense)—in other words, his ability to switch his weight as necessity requires—has been developed to a high degree in schooling, a fast galloping horse will have a tendency to be heavy in front, and hence to lean on the rider's hands.

To sum up: it is important to remember that having the horse softly on the bit depends more on the degree of *schooling* of the horse than on the dexterity of the rider.

Flexions (*direct and lateral*). Flexion is a relaxed retraction of the lower jaw as a result of increased tension on the reins. Flexions can be *direct* or *lateral*.

Direct flexion is a retraction of the lower jaw in the vertical plane in response to increased tension on both reins and is used in slowing down, halting, semi-collected gaits and, sometimes, in backing.

Lateral flexion is a retraction of the lower jaw combined with a turning of the head to one side in response to the increased tension on one rein. It is used during short turns.

What is to be gained through flexion can be summed up in one word: *softness*. Here is why:

Let us suppose you are trotting and wish to obtain a very gradual halt and you don't care how long the transitional period from trot to halt takes; then, by means of give and take, you can obtain a soft halt. But supposing, for one reason or another, you wish to make an abrupt halt; then your increases of tension on the reins will have to be considerable and they may throw the horse's neck up, open his mouth and, in general, stiffen the whole animal. In an emergency this may be acceptable, but it cannot be considered a soft halt. But if your horse has been taught flexion, then as a result of increased tension on the reins (to a certain point), he will flex in the mouth, causing a resultant flexion in the poll and the reins will slacken instead of tightening; and after a couple of flexions, the horse will halt.

For the same reason flexion is helpful in slowing down and is very necessary at semi-collected gaits; but the latter will be specifically discussed later on. Some horses, however, will learn an abrupt, soft halt without flexions.

In "Dressage," where perfection of flexion is necessary, a curb bit is imperative. But what can be considered good flexion for field riding can be very well obtained on the snaffle, and the fact that there is no curb in the horse's mouth greatly simplifies the rider's technique.

The technique of obtaining flexion on a horse educated to it (it naturally cannot be done on an untrained horse) is as follows:

Let us assume that you are walking and wish to halt softly and rather abruptly. You increase slightly the urging of your legs so that, at least momentarily, the horse takes the bit and then you increase the tension on the reins. The moment the horse has relaxed his jaw, you give the reins, repeat the procedure once more, increasing the tension on the reins to the point where the horse knows that not merely a flexion but a halt is required from him. Then perhaps you will need to do it a third time while the halt is already in the making, and you will have a soft, relaxed and comparatively quick halt.

The technique of slowing the horse by means of flexions is exactly the same; and how the horse is educated to flexion you will find in Chapter XV.

One of the common faults in flexing is *overflexing,* otherwise called "dropping the bit." It is a common occurrence in the case of horses with sensitive mouths, who were taught to flex before being taught to move forward on the bit or at least on contact. In such cases sometimes even a light pressure on the bit (particularly if it is a curb) will cause the horse to drop his whole neck and head abruptly. The chin will come far in; you will hear the dropped bit dangling in the horse's mouth and you will have under you a horse which is behind the bit; in such a state, he is uncontrollable. This is one reason why I suggested urging with the legs before attempting to flex the mouth with the hands; it is a precaution against overflexion. But, on horses which move well on the bit and which do not overflex, flexions can be and, in many cases, should be obtained by the hands alone.

When a horse is on the bit the degree of tension on the reins at different gaits varies in direct ratio to the speed; in other words, the horse takes a stronger hold of the rider's hands at the gallop than at the walk. And if an increase in tension on the reins, over and above that normal for whatever speed the horse is travelling at, causes the horse to flex, then it means that he has an ideal, obedient, educated mouth.

But such an ideal state of affairs rarely exists in life, and my prediction is that, while it will be easy for you to halt a horse from a walk or to slow an ordinary trot down by means of flexions, you probably will never be able to decrease the speed of a really fast gallop by these refined means alone. At least the first part of slowing a fast gallop will lack flexions, and they may appear only after the original pace has been considerably cut. I am pessimistic about this, because the horse is in high spirits when galloping fast and will not be very attentive to light variations in the tension on the reins; also because the momentum of a fast pace and the strongly pronounced forward balance of it are not conducive to a quick, soft slowing down. It is really at semi-collected gaits that flexion will come easiest.

In 19th century books on riding great stress is put on the high position of the neck during flexion, and on an almost vertical position of the head as the result of flexion. Today, one will aim at achieving something similar at semi-collected gaits; but it has nothing to do with flexion at ordinary gaits. During such gaits the neck and head are stretched and although they will change their positions while flexing, this change should not be too radical. However, if your slowing down or halt is very abrupt then, in order to execute it, the horse will have to bring his hindquarters under and, as a result, the neck will go up and the head may assume an almost vertical position.

Lateral flexions. The technique for obtaining lateral flexion is practically the same as for the direct one. Some horses will have to be urged with the legs, others not. The difference lies only in using one hand instead of two.

Lateral flexion softens a movement along a very sharp curve (as when making a circle of only 20′ in diameter), because in order to move softly along such a sharp curve the horse must bend. His body must assume the shape of the curve and this is greatly facilitated by lateral flexions in the direction in which he is moving.

Lateral flexion may require the use of the legs in the majority of cases, for it should not be accompanied by a slowing down of speed. Practically, it is used only at semi-collected gaits, for only at such gaits would one attempt such small circles. Hence lateral flexion is merely an exercise in the physical development of the horse. It is only once in a blue moon that you may have practical use for it; for instance, on a short turn in horse show jumping, and then only providing that there is enough room to stretch the horse's neck before arriving at the next obstacle.

Flexion is very closely connected with moving on the bit, and I think that the easiest way to make you appreciate this is by giving you the whole picture of the relationship of legs to hands on different levels of riding. This relationship is based on the rule that the more the rider urges the horse forward the more effective must be the means of making him "come back."

In elementary riding, where the horse is partly urged with the voice and in general urged only to move at slow ordinary gaits on loose reins (stabilization), there, obviously, a voice command to slow down added to a plain check on the reins will be sufficient to get results.

In intermediate riding, where the horse is urged forward on contact and is kept on it to obtain an efficient movement, "give and take" becomes necessary to maintain softness and to regulate the gaits.

In advanced riding, where the horse is put on the bit (to obtain a high quality of movement) by somewhat stronger legs than in intermediate control, and hence gains in impulse, a more effective means of checking the horse softly becomes imperative—hence flexion.

Semi-collected gaits. In Chapter III, THE SEARCH FOR BALANCE, I have pointed out that a free horse, when excited, raises the neck, flexes the head at the poll and shifts weight in varying degrees to the hindquarters. This distribution of weight and a specific tuning of the muscles (due to this attitude) result in high, cadenced movements. In nature they are movements produced by an emotional state; in riding we call these collected gaits, and the difficulty in obtaining them arises from the fact that we want the horse to execute them *animatedly but coolly*, and as a result of the rider's orders and not of his own excitement.

A collected horse is in central balance and thus, having a lighter forehand than when in forward balance and the hindquarters staying more under the croup can be extremely skilful at all sorts of turns, lateral movements and transitions at slow gaits. Hence manège Dressage is based on collection. However, in cross-country riding and in jumping, where galloping and the negotiation of obstacles require forward balance, collection is of no practical use except in the schooling where it is used for gymnastics. To be exact, I suggested the use of it, not in the form of full collection, but of semi-collection. What the difference is between full and semi-collection you will find in Chapter IX, WHAT IS A GOOD PERFORMANCE OF THE HORSE? and how semi-collection is developed is described in Chapter XV, THE PROGRAM OF SCHOOLING.

When used discriminatingly *in combination with free movements*, semi-collection is a wonderful exercise for developing the longitudinal flexibility of the back, the pliability of the horse in general, and the knack of shifting his weight at will—in other words, his balance.

The present attitude of the great majority of my pupils is such that anything that requires a great deal of slow work on detailed refinements is not received enthusiastically, particularly if such work is not obviously connected with fast riding across country and over fences. Lack of enthusiasm in anything precludes success. Semi-collection, which is used in the *advanced* level of riding and schooling, as it was originally presented in this book, is the most debatable of these items. Since semi-collection does not (with a few exceptions) contribute sufficiently towards riding in cross-country competitions, in shows, or to hounds, I no longer insist today, as I once did, on eventually studying it.

I find my new policy more practical, because experience shows that most people fail to learn collection—even semi-collection—and abuse and upset their horses in attempting it. The main aim of my teaching is to make competent jumpers and cross-country horses, and I believe that obtaining final results is more important than rigidly following a certain teaching or schooling program. I would much rather see a relaxed jump of a horse without the benefit of semi-collection, than a stiff one as the result of the misuse of it. Whatever my tenets on the subject may be, I am ready to disregard them here and there to achieve better riding and better performance.

But I still believe in the discriminating use of semi-collection in slowing down and halting, and even making a "few steps" of it as I originally suggested it in the text. Some horses definitely require it, while to some others it may come so easily that even an intermediate rider will be able to apply it here and there with ease and without disturbing the horse, thus obtaining refinements, if not practical advantages.

Here I feel a few lines should be added, further defining the term semi-collection. Collection, as you know, is based on transferring a certain amount of weight from the forehand to the hindquarters. Depending on the amount of weight transferred to the rear, the collection may be of different degrees. A part of the technique of lightening the forehand consists in raising the neck and bringing the head to a position more or less nearing the vertical. This raising of the neck and bringing the head in is, as a matter of fact, a lesson preparatory to full collection, and is called *Ramener* in French; there is no generally accepted English equivalent for it. *A "few steps" of semi-collected gait really means nothing more than limiting oneself to the Ramener without forcefully transferring weight to the rear.*

In abrupt halting or slowing down, however, a cooperative horse will of his own accord switch a certain amount of weight to the rear by sitting to some degree on his hocks. Since he does it by himself, it means that it is natural; this I presume, is why General Chamberlin in his book TRAINING HUNTERS, JUMPERS AND HACKS talks about "natural collection." This is also why I refer, in my original text, to *"semi-collection or natural collection."* This is rather confusing; all I intended to say was that in semi-collection the rider's efforts do not go beyond the *Ramener,* but that under certain circumstances the horse may naturally transfer some of the weight from the forehand to the quarters.

The *semi-extended* trot is a long-striding trot with the neck and head carried in the position of the *Ramener.* Today I use it very seldom, —again, because I do not believe that in the majority of cases teaching a horse to carry the neck high and the head in is helpful in developing a *calm gallop* and a *relaxed jump.* This carriage of the neck and head indicates excitement when a horse is in a state of liberty; under the rider it will still carry this association, and to this may be added the likelihood that an unskilled rider in the process of inducing this carriage in the horse may upset him. Systematic, judicious training can eventually produce collection in a calm horse, but such a degree of artistry is not within the reach of the averagely good rider.

On the whole, although a semi-extended trot may look dramatic and be admired by the audience, a simple lengthening of strides, the horse remaining in forward balance with an extended neck, is a sounder exercise for the majority of hunters and jumpers. In the latter case the lengthening of the stride primarily indicates obedience to the legs, and the subsequent shortening of the stride, obedience to the hands. Thus this exercise develops obedience to the aids. This obedience permits the practice of the exercise known as the *three speeds at the trot,* whose chief virtue is that it leads to the *three speeds at the canter.* The latter has actual practical value, for the horse can place himself (or be placed) for a correct take-off only if he can lengthen or shorten his galloping stride.

Please note that even in the original text I minimized the importance of semi-collection by requiring only "a few steps" of it and by stating that it is "an exercise only."

Also, in that part of the original text dealing with how to obtain semi-collection (page 277) I say: "The main point to watch is not necessarily the engagement of the hindquarters, or a somewhat arched position of the neck and head, but the repeated flexions (about one in each stride) which insure the softness of the movement."

Accordingly, a few words on my present attitude toward flexions become necessary. In this respect I am very adaptable. If a horse comes back softly without flexions but with a natural, relaxed attitude of the neck and head, I do not insist on teaching them; but I have no objection to a horse naturally flexing, if this does not result in his staying behind the bit for too long a time. If the horse has a stiff poll and I wish to relax it, I make an issue of teaching him flexions. In other words, in this case I follow the general principle of my schooling—that is, of achieving final results rather than of pedantically following a preconceived program. I always, so to speak, try to play by ear.

Now, how to achieve a semi-collected movement: the technique of obtaining it at a walk, trot or canter is the same; but it is easiest at a trot. At a walk you will usually find that the horse does not have sufficient impulse; at the canter, he may have too much; and at both these gaits he will have a stronger inclination to switch his weight forward than at a trot.

Suppose you are moving at an ordinary trot and you desire to change to a semi-collected one; the first thing to do is to stop posting and bring the horse down to a slow trot, lightly on the bit or on contact. Then you should urge the horse forward with your legs to activate the hindquarters, and with your hands receive the energy thus produced, not allowing it to be transformed into an increase of speed. Meeting the resistance of your hands, a horse who has been taught flexions should flex. In the course of this process, the neck will rise somewhat and the head will bend in the poll. The moment the horse has flexed you give with your hands and immediately urge with the legs once more, again obtaining a flexion. After you have repeated this a few times the horse's neck will rise considerably and the flexions, which follow each other about once every stride, will keep the head in an almost vertical position. Once this attitude has been assumed, the horse's legs will begin to act more upward than forward and you will have a semi-collected gait; in order to maintain it, continue to urge, at the same time checking with flexions.

I again repeat that you should use collection as an exercise only, usually not more than for a couple of dozen strides. Every semi-collected period must start from a free movement and end by a free movement; only if this rule is observed does the exercise have any value.

When obtaining an abrupt slowing down or a halt by means of rapidly switching the horse's weight from the forehand to the quarters, the rider must move his torso back (decrease the angle forward) to preserve his

unity with the horse. This has all been described in Chapter VI, LEARN-
ING THE FORWARD SEAT.

During early schooling and when working at semi-collected gaits, the
rider's position will require the long schooling adjustment of the stirrups, and at the semi-collected gaits the torso must be vertical to the
ground. This is the case when for a score of strides the Forward Seat is
changed to a Dressage one. It should be turned back to the schooling
Forward Seat the moment a free movement is resumed. On a schooled
horse it is not necessary to lengthen the stirrups in order to obtain good
semi-collected gaits.

While it makes no difference how you hold your reins, or how you use
your hands when flexing the horse's mouth merely to soften the slowing
down or the halting, you will be better off to abide by certain rules for
semi-collected gaits. These rules are:

1) Don't held your reins in a "driving" position. Hold them the usual
way: see Chapter VI.

2) Don't hold your hands widely apart; there will be no neck and head
gestures to follow, anyway. Keep about a fist's width between your hands.

3) Hold your hands vertical. To obtain flexion, bend your hands from
the wrists downwards; to release the tension on the reins afterwards,
bend the hands upwards. On a horse with a well-educated mouth this can
be obtained merely by a play of fingers.

4) The arms, as usual, should be bent at the elbows, elbows slightly
ahead of the hips and, whenever possible, there should be a straight line
of action from the elbows to the horse's mouth.

Being on the bit, flexion, collection, are very much abused terms.
People who are unable to ride on loose reins, and who have not the
slightest idea of what soft contact is, talk freely about riding on the bit
and collecting their horses. Never having felt a soft, educated mouth in a
horse and not having soft, educated hands themselves, they don't realize
that they are merely riding pulling—hence abominably stiffly-moving—
horses. Many people think that collection means just an arched neck,
that flexion is merely dropping the bit; and quite often horses which are
pulling are referred to as being on the bit.

These misconceptions are a hang-over from 19th century teaching
when, in Dressage, these three fine points of riding were taught to rank
beginners, because without them there was no Dressage type of riding;
and anything different was not considered riding at all. There still are,
in fact, people who think this way.

Transitions. If your horse has been schooled to move on the bit, to flex
and to execute semi-collected gaits while you, yourself, know the technique of obtaining these three things, then you will be able to obtain
extremely smooth transitions in which the original gait is good almost
to the last stride and the new gait is good from the first stride. This, of
course, is an ideal; but you can come very near to it in practice.

Here is an account of the necessary technique: let us suppose that you are at an ordinary trot and wish to obtain a halt. You make certain that your horse is lightly on the bit; then, very gradually, increase the tension on the reins and, just before the horse actually begins to slow down, you urge him with your legs while, with your hands, you obtain the first flexion. Then again urge with the legs and again obtain a flexion. By now the character of the trot changes; the ordinary trot has been replaced by the first stride of a semi-collected trot; another urge with the legs, another flexion with a slowing down check attached to it, and the semi-collected trot has become really slow; another very short stride of it and the horse comes to a halt in a semi-collected position, standing squarely.

If, after the original slowing down and the first flexion, you would attempt to maintain the new slow trot and keep it energetic with your legs and soft, through repeated flexions, you would have a semi-collected trot, obtained through a perfect transition.

If, after halting the horse, you wish to resume the ordinary gait, then, while standing still, gradually give the reins, at the same time very lightly applying the leg, so that the horse stretches his neck in proportion to the rein given; and when you feel that the horse with extended neck is taking the bit, you make your first step forward. This having the horse on the bit from the first stride (or almost the first) is the secret of a good transition from a slower to a faster gait. On the other hand, semi-collection with flexions is the secret of the perfect terminating of a gait or slowing down.

A horse performing in this manner presents a beautiful picture to the eye of a connoisseur, as any athletic and plastically moving animal would. But it has little practical value in the hunting field or in the jumping ring; first, because what can be done at slow gaits cannot be done at a fast gallop, and secondly because in these two particular sports the rider has no time for niceties. But just the same, I think that changing from forward movement on the bit to a semi-collected movement with flexions is a wonderful gymnastic for the horse and greatly improves his suppleness and balance. Once the horse has been schooled on these principles and is ridden by an advanced rider then, although the rider may not consciously apply them in some sort of a jam in the hunting field, subconsciously he will use finer means than an intermediate rider, and the horse will respond more athletically than a horse schooled on the intermediate level.

I hope you have not received the impression that all advanced riding is done on the bit with flexions and semi-collection. Please don't stumble into this pitfall. First of all, about one-third of any type of riding should be done on loose reins (more than one-third in elementary riding). A horse is not an automobile; he needs rest. Precise riding with good movement is tiring. Furthermore, of the remaining two-thirds of the riding, one-half should be done on the basis of intermediate control; that is, when schooling. In hacking, hunting or jumping, the occasions when you will ask your horse to perform on an advanced level will be rare and the duration of such periods should be short. It is only during competitions, such as the training test of the Three-Day-Event of the Olympic Games, that you will apply the principles of advanced riding consistently.

Besides refinement of gaits and transitions, advanced riding includes the elaboration of several movements. Here they are:

Backing. 1) While in intermediate riding backing is only done after halting a horse from a walk, in advanced riding where, by means of flexion and semi-collection an abrupt, soft stop can be made, the horse can be backed from a trot or canter immediately after a very brief halt; and the gait can be resumed with a minimum of time for transition. If you remember, in intermediate riding all the changes of gaits are gradual; so if you are cantering and wish to halt, you must first go into a trot and then into a walk; hence no matter what the original gait, you will always be at a walk before halting. You should be as gradual when resuming the gait. Attempts to do the whole thing—halting, backing and resumption of the original gait—on an intermediate horse, as abruptly as advanced riding calls for, would result in a struggle with a horse which is physically incapable of doing it.

2) Advanced riding calls for the ability to back any odd number of steps; no more and no less.

If you make an odd number of steps, such as five or seven then, at the end of backing, the horse must stand not squarely, but with one diagonal ahead of the other, or with one fore leg ahead of the other.

Turn on the haunches. The turn on the haunches can be executed either at a walk or at a canter; the latter, which is called a "Pirouette," is a part of advanced Dressage, and hence is not a subject of this book.

In intermediate riding the turn on the haunches is executed either from a walk or from a halt. Due to his knowledge of how to collect himself, an advanced horse can make a very quick transition from a trot or canter to a walk; and hence it can be said rather inaccurately that an advanced horse can make a turn on the haunches either from a trot or from a canter (the actual turn is at a walk).

Besides this, the differences between the turns on the haunches at the intermediate and advanced levels are in the execution of the turn itself. In advanced riding the half-turn on the haunches must consist of four definite, well-united steps, the hindquarters not pivoting but animated, one of the fore legs crossing well ahead of the other. All this can be achieved more easily if the horse is in a semi-collected attitude, head slightly turned in the direction of the movement.

Obviously, such a turn has no practical value except for the physical education of the horse. But a horse whose skill has been developed to this point will be a much more agile animal in the hunting field or elsewhere, even when no such thing is demanded of him.

The technique of making an advanced turn on the haunches (rotating the forehand to the left, let us say) is as follows: Upon bringing the horse to a walk or a halt, increase the tension on the left rein to turn the head slightly to the left (if possible through a lateral flexion); then, moving both your hands to the left, rotate the front of the horse in this direction, helping with continuous tapping of the right leg behind the girth—this will help to turn the horse and will prevent the right hind leg from getting out from under the body; keep the left leg at the girth to regulate the turn—use it if the horse turns too fast, or side-steps to the left. In the course of the turn try to obtain a couple of flexions—lateral ones will, of course, satisfy any academician; but just ordinary direct ones will be much better than nothing.

Half-turn on the forehand. While the turn on the haunches is a valuable exercise, the turn on the forehand is not, and it is used only to teach the horse to yield the quarters to the action of one leg applied to the rear of the girth. Once the horse has learned this, the movement soon loses its importance in schooling but may be asked here and there in actual riding for turning the horse in a spot where there isn't much elbow room.

If, for one reason or another, you would like to execute it very accurately, then you should use the aids the same way as in intermediate control, adding a couple of flexions and a slight turn of the head to the side toward which the quarters are rotating. This turn of the head to the left, in combination with the quarters rotating to the left, will bend the horse in the left side and so will make the movement lighter and will enable the rider to keep the forehand from moving in too large a circle.

Semi-extended trot. At the intermediate level there are three speeds of the trot: slow, ordinary and fast. In advanced riding, while the ordinary trot remains the same, the slow one *occasionally* takes the form of semi-collection, while the fast trot *sometimes,* and only for short periods, assumes a semi-extended form.

The semi-extended trot is slower than the fast trot, but the period of suspension of the limbs is greater. It is unquestionably a stimulated movement and, as such, is a close relative of semi-collection, with a neck correspondingly high and head in. The difference in technique is as follows: while to obtain a fast trot you merely push the horse forward on the bit and with the hands watch for possible breaking of the gait; in order to obtain a semi-extended trot you must first of all place the horse in the semi-collected position and then extend the stride.

This is a very difficult movement to execute softly, unless the horse has a natural impulse forward and a natural tendency to extend the forehand.

Again, this is merely a gymnastic which can be used for the improvement of the ordinary gaits; it is in a better travelling trot that you should see the effect of bringing the horse to the point where he can do a semi-extended trot.

Two tracks. The difference between the two tracks on the intermediate and the advanced level is in the quality of the movement. The long, free steps of two tracks are primarily developed through the use of a certain method in schooling which is described in Chapter XV. However, they will even be better through the mere fact that the legs and hands of an advanced rider will work in greater synchronization with the efforts of an advanced horse than those of an intermediate rider can with those of an intermediate horse.

Of course, on an advanced horse you can execute two tracks at a semi-collected trot; it will be effective and it may impress many of your friends. But I am almost certain that the steps will become short, possibly the horse will acquire a tendency to lead with the quarters and, at any rate, it will cease to be an exercise for a hunter or jumper. This is typical of most movements practiced on the Dressage principle; the practical value for a cross-country horse is replaced by mere showiness.

Flying change of leads. As in the case of two tracks, a good change of leads is developed in schooling, and cannot be obtained by a merely fine use of aids. Intermediate riding calls for a change of leads with interruption, advanced riding for a flying change of leads—just one change. The difference of aims on these two levels is imposed in this case not by the limitations of a horse at the intermediate stage, but by those of the rider. A horse which can change leads with an interruption consisting of one stride of trot is five minutes away from a flying change, but his rider may not be. There is no new technique to learn, the aids remain exactly the same; but the time in which to switch them is shorter and the synchronization must be perfect.

There is no use in saying that you should apply your aids for the change of leads a fraction of a second before the suspension period of the canter begins; thinking of it will merely make you stiff and you will lose the feel of the rhythm; it is all in the rhythm and you will acquire it only through practice.

Having the horse on the bit when approaching an obstacle. This is the only difference in technique in jumping on the intermediate or the advanced level. The difference is so negligible, as far as the rider is concerned, that it is almost theoretical. An ambitious horse approaching a fence will, of his own accord, increase the tension on the bit. On the other hand, when riding a sluggish horse, any sensible intermediate rider will urge the horse forward to the point when the tension is stronger than a soft contact; that is, if the horse doesn't jump at his best on loose reins.

So then, where is the difference? The difference lies not in the technique of riding but in the degree of schooling. In the case of an advanced horse, moving on the bit will mean connecting the hindquarters with the forehand, while an intermediate horse may increase the tension on the reins while continuing to gallop in a discombobulated manner.

What I have said here applies only to single or very widely spaced obstacles; the technique of riding over courses is described later in this chapter.

In summing up, I should like to underline the fact that the better execution of different movements in advanced riding does not depend on a special technique, but is merely due to the following points:

1) The horse, being on the bit, is connected and has a highly developed impulse forward.

2) Through exercises which rapidly take the horse from extended to semi-collected gaits and vice versa, the horse's balance is developed to the point where he is master of his own body no matter what he does.

3) Flexions soften all slow movements.

4) A rider who has schooled the horse to the stage where he employs these three things has very good cooperation of his legs and hands with the efforts of the horse. Anything that he asks has a fine touch to it.

Elsewhere in this book I have warned my readers against too rigidly accepting rules for the technique of riding and schooling horses, and I should like again to repeat this advice.

Educated riding is a combination of *science* and *art*. Some people, with a tendency to be very academic in everything they do, judge riding, among other things, merely from the point of view of certain scholastic conditions, shuddering at anything that is irregular. Therefore these people are liable to see details only, and pronounce their judgment of the whole on the strength of these details. Some of these people, glancing at a rider will say: "He rides badly because he hasn't got a straight line of action from the elbow to the horse's mouth"; or: "He sits badly because he doesn't hold his legs far enough back"; and the fact the horse may be performing beautifully under his rider remains unexplained. These people may not even notice the latter, for they judge the whole performance on the fact that the rider's legs are not in an academically good position.

I, personally, appreciating the scientific part of riding and devoting this book primarily to it, because it is the part which can be taught, am very much for individual artistic expression. If someone were to obtain a magnificent performance from his horse, neglecting most of the advice in this book, I would be the first one to appreciate it. Rules are not made for geniuses. The trouble is that the artistic part of riding does not allow itself to be analyzed or imitated; it is the property of an individual. And even if one is born with it, his natural talent will not manifest itself from the first day in the saddle, but only after education or long experience. One of the practical aspects of education is that it shortens the time of necessary experience. Therefore it seems sensible to start by learning the scientific part of riding; to stick to it if one has no special talent and to give a full expression to individualism when, in certain cases, art seems to be more powerful than knowledge.

The big question is how one will recognize whether or not he is talented. There can, of course, be no definite rules in this respect; but as a leading thought, let me say the following: In any art, at the moment of production or creation, a real artist submerges his ego in his achievement; he forgets everything but what he is trying to do—becomes that thing itself. The true artist identifies himself completely with his subject to the point of absolute self-forgetfulness. The Oriental artist realized and formulated this basic truth long before it occurred to the then less thoughtful, less sophisticated Westerner. Centuries ago, the Chinese painter maintained that to paint, for instance, a bamboo blowing in the wind, you must not only carefully observe all the outward appearances of the bamboo, you must also *imagine* you are a bamboo planted on a mountain-side and blowing in the wind; if you are painting a heron you must think yourself into that heron so that you feel and think as that heron does. Otherwise art is empty and dead, a mere recording of outward forms. Translating this into terms of riding, it means that while the rider remains exclusively interested in himself; that is, in how *he* looks in the saddle, in how *he* makes the horse take the jump, in how *he* holds his hands, he will remain a rider and only a rider—not even an artistic one. In order to be a horseman he must forget himself, identify himself with the horse, feel that it is he, himself, who has changed leads at the canter or taken the jump; only then will there be that complete union and harmony which produces true art.

Advanced control in jumping. I may as well begin by stating that advanced control doesn't work miracles in the hunting field or over outside courses. Of course, the combination of an advanced horse and of an advanced rider will make a superior performance, no matter where; but the law of diminishing returns is also to be considered.

The mechanics of the jump, the principles of jumping and the making of a jumper I have discussed in other chapters. Here we are merely concerned with the matter of riding the horse between fences. This subject is very controversial and I should like to present its different angles.

Riding over courses. Throughout this book I have been calling my readers' attention to the fact that hunting and showing over easy jumping courses can be done very satisfactorily on the basis of intermediate riding, as the latter is defined in this book. As a matter of fact, the results would be not merely satisfactory but considerably above the present standards of our hunting and showing. But, in the majority of cases, the intermediate level of riding will be insufficient for high and complicated open jumping classes or the international competitions, which are usually called military, although more and more civilians participate in them. There, in order to be a *consistent* winner, advanced riding is necessary. Why?

The *ease* with which a horse negotiates a series of obstacles depends on certain conditions of the course:

1) *Height and breadth of the fences.* The greater the natural jumping abilities of the horse, the higher will be the limit of the obstacles he can be schooled to jump with *ease and hence consistently.* A 3'6" fence may always be a strenuous jump for one horse, while a 5' one might be comparatively easy for another. But generalizing, it may be said that *3'9" to 4' obstacles are easy* for a big, strong hunter (even an unschooled one) while a *5' fence requires a strenuous effort* from almost any horse. This one foot of difference is really tremendous. The horse by his nature is not a high-jumping animal: I have discussed this in Chapter II. Advanced schooling, which makes the horse more athletic in general, raises somewhat the height of his jump.

2) *The size of the jumping ground.* If the fences are far apart, as in the majority of cases in the hunting field, and as on the outside courses in hunter classes or when very few jumps are set in a small arena, it is one thing. But when this small arena is packed with complicated obstacles, it is a different story. In the latter case the problem does not consist merely in jumping but in the very skilful way it will be necessary for the horse to handle himself between obstacles. He has very little space between fences in which to re-establish a balanced gallop with correct impulse and the length of stride which will be required for the next fence. And, according to whether the obstacle ahead is broad or a high vertical one, his balance and pace will have to vary, while impulse is maintained. This alternation of broad with vertical obstacles, if they are really large, greatly increases the jumping difficulties, requiring constant changes in the manner of approach to a fence and in the way of jumping itself. Obviously, in the hundreds of thousands of years of its wild existence, the horse never was faced with complicated courses. A fallen tree, or a brook here and there which could not be passed by, would be the most that he would have to negotiate on the prairies which he inhabited. His body developed accordingly.

The physical education which the horse receives in advanced schooling enables him to face with confidence all the intricacies of complicated courses, particularly if he is ridden by a rider who has mastered the little finesses of advanced riding.

3) *The presence or absence of sharp turns.* The problem of galloping the horse evenly over fences set against the wall of the arena is comparatively easy. To change the pace often, because of turns, and still to have the right impulse at the take-off for a jump close after the turn, is a complicated matter for any horse. To be able to do it the horse has to be more than merely a good jumper and a good athlete; he has to be a highly specialized acrobat. Schooling, as presented in this book, takes your horse in this direction.

4) *The speed required.* In hunter classes, merely a hunting pace is de-

manded; you may vary it somewhat, depending on what pace is the most natural for your horse, and still make a winning performance. In international competitions speed is often scored, the obstacles remaining formidable; and one has to face these conditions no matter whether one's horse's natural inclination is to jump from a fast or a slow gallop. Furthermore, the dexterity of the rider's legs and hands alone will not be able to keep the horse calm and soft when galloping fast; here schooling is all-important.

5) *The presence or absence of trappy combinations.* When this book was originally written there was a vogue for so-called "jumpable" courses. A triple in-and-out, consisting of three identical vertical obstacles, equally spaced, to give the horse a comfortable stride between fences, would be a fair example of the latter. Lately (1962), however, "trappy" combinations seem to be in the air: An example of such would be a triple in-and-out in which the middle obstacle, for instance, would be a broad one, and the distances between fences would be unequal— one too short and the other too long for a comfortable stride. It is obvious that in such situations, the rider, who by walking the course is able to figure out in advance the best way to negotiate it, has an advantage over the horse, who is faced with it only when he jumps it. This is an example of a case where my basic theory that the horse should be the more important member of the partnership does not fare too well.

All in all, the difference between jumping in the hunting field or over outside courses, and jumping in a small arena *crowded* with complicated obstacles, is as great as the difference between a collected and a free, fast trot. These are both trots, but the efforts of the horse differ greatly in each case, as well as the techniques used by the rider to obtain these two manifestations of the same gait. A successful technique for jumping in classes of our military type has seldom anything to contribute to cross-country riding. This point is often missed and unfortunate attempts to imitate international winners are fairly common.

If you were to visualize clearly how these different conditions of jumping competitions affect the horse, you would see that while the comparatively passive riding of hunters can be made into a practical rule for everyone, in complicated and high open jumping classes this can only be an ideal within the reach of a few. If your horse is very able physically and mentally, has been schooled to a very high degree, and you are a very well-educated and naturally talented rider, then this ideal can be approached very closely. For instance, a number of members of the United States Army team have attained it during the past twenty years. To put it simply, they rode over international courses as if they were simple hunter courses. And it wasn't merely an exhibition of beautiful riding; their performances were winning ones. A thorough schooling of horses and riders was the backbone of the riding of our military team.

On the other hand, if a horse has merely an unschooled jumping talent and the rider is merely a money winner with great experience and no education, then their performances over difficult courses will have to be based on constant *forcible* riding. For instance, if the horse is over-eager (a high jumper must be eager) and tries to approach an obstacle too fast for his own good, his rider cannot check his unschooled horse by merely somewhat increasing the tension on the reins. He has to pull really hard on the horse's mouth, which, of course, raises the neck, opens the mouth and caves in the back. Furthermore, if this checking has occurred far away from the jump, the rider usually cannot afford to give his horse freedom once he is slowed down. For the horse still has several strides in which to plunge forward, probably in a discombobulated manner, and to plough through the obstacle. Consequently, the rider, with repeated checkings, holds the horse back to the last stride and only releases him when he feels that the line of the take-off has been established; then he has quickly to release the reins and strongly urge the horse with his legs. This technique is called "placing." The normal result is that, although a horse may jump high and clean, his efforts are seldom plastic or natural, and the abuse of the horse from the rider's seat, hands and legs is ever-present. It is truly marvelous that there are some dozens of horses in this country whose character and physique are such that they can take this abuse and a moment afterwards walk quietly out of the arena on loose reins; furthermore, some stay sound for years. But don't forget that these are exceptions and don't expect your horse to be one: it is safer not to.

Of late, I more and more often meet horse-show goers who are completely disgusted with our open jumping classes and refuse to look at them any more. I think that in their wholesale condemnation they go overboard and miss the pleasure of seeing a couple of truly good performances in every class, at least in big shows. Furthermore, there are some riders in these classes, very few to be sure, who, year in and year out, win ribbons on unschooled horses, some of which would simply run away with average riders on their backs. In spite of the ugliness of their uneducated riding; in spite of the ugliness of the performance of their horses; in spite of the fact that these riders do nothing, or little, which I recommend in this book, one has to admit that they have something. And this something is not experience alone, for, while a few are good, many others remain a mess forever. So it is not merely experience; it is talent also. It is the kind of talent of which I spoke earlier in this chapter, and one can only be sorry that the business considerations of these riders' professional lives do not allow them time to school their horses. I have run into so much of it in my own practice. So many people who possessed able horses were willing to give me no more than two or three months to get them ready for showing; fortunately I could decline these cases; some cannot.

But while most of these professional riders have commercial excuses for their rough riding (I hope that they are looking for an excuse), some of the members of the international teams ride almost as roughly, and have none. They have plenty of time to concentrate on schooling their horses and on developing the finesse of their own technique and they, presumably, have the advantage of a good equestrian education. While some people are over-critical of their roughness, others, impressed by their victories, try to imitate them. I think, in both cases, there is a loss of balance.

One can hardly ride over complicated courses at an even pace. Sometimes a short stride is necessary before a high vertical fence, while a fast gallop with increased impulse may be required for a broad obstacle; and the fast pace will have to be slowed down considerably for making a sharp turn. This all means that the rider has to assist his horse by changing his pace, while maintaining the impulse: If this is done far away from the jump and the horse allowed to go free, once the necessary pace has been established, it is called "rating." Its success depends as much on the technique of the rider as on the degree of schooling which the horse has reached. Besides being cooperative and calm, the horse must have highly developed impulse forward and be equally developed in "coming back"; in other words, he must be very flexible longitudinally. Only if this longitudinal flexibility is present will the horse be able to decrease and increase his stride, almost on a dime, at the rider's will. Furthermore, the horse must be obedient and cool in order to maintain the new pace from the point of rating to the obstacle.

But what if the horse is not obedient? What if a couple of strides after being rated he should need another rating, and then another; so that there may be only one stride left between the last rating and the take-off? Then you have nothing else but "placing"; so it seems to me there is a definite relationship between rating and placing; and the difference is mainly the result of the degree of schooling, although it may also depend upon the principle on which the horse is schooled.

The principles of free, natural jumping successfully applied to a schooled horse will manifest themselves as follows:

a) Some clever horses will learn to rate themselves (the rider being passive) in the hunting field or over easy courses. Other horses (in these two sports) will require minimal assistance from the rider.

b) On complicated courses all that will be necessary will be a couple of mild checkings far away from the obstacle, after which the horse may be allowed to go free during the rest of the approach. This, of course, in the case of a horse which has attempted to approach an obstacle too fast.

If, on the other hand, the horse is approaching a fence too sluggishly, then the rider will be able, with strong use of the legs, quickly to give the necessary impulse, while yet far away from the fence, and then merely to sustain it until the jump. Or he may gradually develop the correct impulse, by progressive squeezing during the last half dozen strides of the approach.

Speaking of "rating" Colonel H. Chamberlin in his book TRAINING HUNTERS, JUMPERS AND HACKS (English edit. 1946, page 133) says:

"The most pleasant characteristic of an excellent hunter or jumper is his willingness to be rated. If trained for a year or more according to preceding chapters before he is called upon to hunt a difficult country, or to jump a full-sized course of imposing obstacles, rating will be possible. . . . The numerous frenzied and uncontrollable horses seen in the hunting field and show ring are a sad commentary on their trainers."

So, all in all, a good performance depends, of course, mainly on schooling; this cannot be argued. But the principle of free-going to which I fully subscribe (for to me it is the most pleasant to ride, to watch, and obviously is the least abusive to the horse), is not necessarily the only possible principle on which a jumper can be schooled to win.

In the late forties the Mexican Army team has gained a top position among international winners, riding and schooling their horses on principles completely different from those which I teach. And, by the way, there are few things as diametrically opposed to each other as the reasoning behind the schooling of jumpers by the cavalry school at Fort Riley and the logic behind the Mexican way.

The fundamental idea of the former is thus expressed in the Fort Riley manual (Edit. 1945, part II, page 233):

". . . The main and most difficult task of the trainer when riding over an obstacle is to 'let the horse alone.' . . .

"Too often riders believe that they are assisting their horses over obstacles by using their hands and legs in various ways other than those to be described. The idea that one can 'place' his horse for each jump over a course of big and imposing obstacles is erroneous. Many really brilliant riders have tried it, but without complete success. The horse must do the jumping and the less he is bothered, except to encourage and rate him, the better he will do."

This, in its essentials, is what I teach; but the statement that a horse cannot be successfully placed time after time was proved wrong by four years of Mexican victories. The Mexican riders approach the jump at a slow (sometimes collected) gallop *always full of impulse* obtained through a series of strong urgings forward combined with as strong checkings. About one stride before the jump (sometimes earlier) the Mexicans, with truly artistic precision, release the coiled body-springs of their horses. Thus their horses go over vertical fences with a very steep trajectory and do it efficiently, helped by great acrobatism developed in general schooling as well as over fences.

In spite of the consistency of the Mexican winning, and my personal admiration for the skill of the riders, I am all for the Fort Riley method, although I may disagree with some details of it or with some explanations they give for it. On the other hand, the reasoning of the Mexicans as applied to international competitions, particularly in small arenas like Madison Square Garden, is clear to me. They are not the first to have used it successfully; some of the French, Germans, as well as riders of other nations, have applied it with good results in the past. I, myself, was brought up on the idea that the horse must be led, "between the legs and hands" up to the moment of the take-off and that the last three strides of the approach must be particularly controlled. This principle is as old as the hills. It is not this idea, but a superb execution of it that is impressive in the case of the Mexicans.

But weren't the free-going performances of the United States Army team in the thirties, when the riders were first led by Colonel H. Chamberlin and later strongly dominated by his ideas, as impressive? And do you remember how consistently successful the Germans were about fifteen years ago, using yet another method? I have already mentioned the fact that in my lifetime I have witnessed the rise and fall of half a dozen methods of jumping in horse shows, and, in my opinion, in every case the marvels worked by a certain system could be largely attributed to a fortunate combination of riders and horses directed by an outstanding horseman. One brilliant exponent of a method has seldom been immediately succeeded by another as brilliant; hence the success of methods fluctuates. Remembering all this, it is rather difficult to be impressed by mere victory, while it is easy—for me, anyway—to be enthusiastic about a method which results in natural, plastically beautiful performances which do not abuse the horse. I have no doubt that the majority of real horse lovers will join me in my feelings. But, all of us being different, many, of course, will disagree with my point of view. Among the latter will be those who merely like the spectacular and violent, and who just want to see horses tackling mammoth obstacles, no matter how.

While some of what I have just said was included here merely to broaden your horizons, the following paragraphs are for your daily reference:

1) Don't lose perspective and don't confuse the technique of riding in international competitions with the jumping that you will do in the hunting field or in amateur shows. By no means try to imitate the former, for it is based on a lifetime spent in the saddle, plus inborn talent, often a thorough equestrian education and exceptionally able horses. Furthermore, you cannot possibly get to the bottom of an international rider's technique (I am talking about a good one) by merely looking at him performing. Of course you will see some obvious disconnected points of it, but not the subtle connecting links. If you are interested in it, you have to study it; it will take you a long time and it may be worthwhile; but just mimicking it will result in the same mess that you may observe in every show displayed by riders who have fallen into this very pit.

2) The difference between riding courses on the intermediate and advanced levels consists in the following facts:

a) an advanced horse is more supple in actual jumping as well as during the approach and hence, if necessary, can be handled with greater precision during the latter;

b) an advanced rider, having better developed cooperation of legs and hands with the horses's efforts, can lead an advanced horse toward the obstacle with greater finesse than an intermediate rider could do on an intermediate horse.

3) Whether you are an intermediate or an advanced rider all your hopes should be placed on schooling and not on the last-minute dexterity of your legs and hands. It is only when you feel that the horse needs assistance that you should help him with your aids. On the other hand, I do not preach complete passiveness. Quite often, on the strength of having cleared a few jumps passively, the rider continues to be inactive on later fences, on which the horse does require correction; the result is knocked-down obstacles. *Ride as passively as practical and at times as actively as the circumstances may require.*

CHAPTER XIII

Modernizing the Ideal

The equestrian events of the Olympic Games consist of three classes:

1) DRESSAGE, which is a competition in almost the highest achievements in classical riding: "Grosse Dressurprüfung," as the Germans call it.
2) PRIX DES NATIONS—arena jumping.
3) THE THREE-DAY EVENT, which is an all-around test for a cross-country horse. This test consists of the following three phases:
   a) *First Day:*—Schooling Test. In an arena 195 feet by 65 feet, marked with letters to point out the changes in movements. Time limit—12 min.
   b) *The Second Day's Test* is divided into these continuous phases:
      A-Phase—4 miles on roads and trails. Time allowed 27 min., 17 sec. Penalty assessed for overtime. Rate, 8 m.p.h.
      B-Phase—2.3 miles over Steeplechase Course with 10 to 12 jumps. Time allowed, 5 min. 5 sec. Penalty assessed for overtime, bonus given for under time. Rate 24 m.p.h.
      C-Phase—10 miles on roads and trails. Time allowed 68 min. 11 sec. Penalty assessed for overtime. Rate 8 m.p.h.
      D-Phase—5⅓ miles Cross-Country with 30 to 35 varied obstacles at 4' and ditches with width of 13'. Time allowed, 18 min. Penalty assessed for overtime and bonus given for under time. Rate, 18.7 m.p.h.
      E-Phase—0.6 miles on the flat. Time allowed, 3 min. Penalty assessed for overtime. Rate 13 m.p.h.
      The total distance is 22.3 miles. The total time allowed is 2 hours, 1 min., 18 sec. Average rate horse must go is 11 miles per hour, or a fair gallop for the entire 22.3 miles. He must be in condition for the Jumping Test next day.
   c) *The Third Day*—Jumping Test. This is held in a stadium. The course is about 0.8 miles, with twelve varied obstacles not higher than 4'. A water jump 12' in width is included. Rate of speed, 433 yards per minute. Penalty assessed for overtime.

These conditions vary somewhat from one set of Olympic Games to another.

You may remember that in previous chapters I have pointed out the Three-Day Event as a possible ideal for an ambitious American amateur rider. This chapter is devoted to the discussion of this ideal. As you see, *The Third Day* is simple enough and I don't expect anybody to object that it is too much for a non-professional rider. *The Second Day* may be much too strenuous for many and require so much conditioning that, in its unabridged form, it may be considered impractical for amateurs. But it is very easy to modify this. For instance: the steeplechase can be cut out; the distance of the cross-country run can be reduced; the number of jumps cut down, their height lowered somewhat, etc., and still one would be left with an excellent test for a hunter. My personal objections revolve mostly around the Schooling Test which, in my opinion, over-emphasizes collected gaits and slights the "ordinary" ones, which a hunter will actually use. To understand how such a program was conceived we have to go back at least to the beginning of this century.

Fifty years ago continental Europe still had several large militaristic states with huge standing armies; a sizable part of each army was the cavalry which was still, on occasions, nostalgically referred to as the "Queen of the Battlefields." When one takes into consideration the fact that, traditionally, the officers' corps, particularly of the cavalry, was to a considerable extent drawn from members of the privileged class, then it becomes obvious that all the European equestrian competitions, including the Olympic Games, were bound to be dominated by military thinking. The first riding competition in the Olympics took place in Sweden in 1912. Two classes out of three were conceived for officers' chargers; these classes were the "Individual Dressage" and the "Military," which is now known as the "Three-Day Event." The third class was, as it is today, the "Prix Des Nations"—arena jumping, which represented not the business but the sport of the cavalry. As long as the "Individual Dressage" and the "Military" classes were designed primarily for cavalry officers, it was quite appropriate that the Emperors of Germany and of Austria-Hungary should present the challenge cups. There wasn't a single civilian among the competitors.

Those were the last days of the old-fashioned armies and the cavalry was still expected to charge in closed formation or to file by in brilliant parades, resplendently dressed and at smart collected gaits. For all these closed-formation manoeuvres, with their quick, precise swinging around of the flanks, turning in small areas etc., collected gaits were essential. But all this was just a part of what the cavalry should have been able to do. Besides an easy manoeuverability in thick columns, it should possess endurance to withstand long marches, speed for certain occasions and jumping ability, which may sometimes be useful. In my youth these latter requirements were beginning to predominate and quite often, on parades, we passed the reviewing general at full gallop with lances lowered as in a charge. But even then, to be able to restore quickly the precision of formation at suddenly diminished speed, at the end of the parade grounds, collection was necessary. All these requirements were combined, in the Russian army anyway (it was probably the same in other countries) in a competition which, in our case, was cumbersomely called "The test for an officer's horse actually used in cavalry ranks." It included an endurance test, a steeplechase, arena jumping and a training test; the whole thing lasted three days. In its conditions this test was very similar to the "Military" Class of the 1912 Olympics, which, in a revised form, is familiarly known to us as the Three-Day Event.

Then what was the Individual Dressage class? It was also a competition for officers' chargers, but more of a parade type. In its aims it was on the ambitious side and it gave an officer the opportunity of showing what he had done with his horse in his spare time. The chronicler of the Olympic Games, Dr. Gustav Rau, in his book, DIE REITERKÄMPFE BEI DEN OLYMPISCHEN SPIELEN (pub. 1929), on page 29, says about the Individual Dressage in Sweden:

"The conditions require nothing more than would be required of a well-ridden officer's charger. For one saw in the competition many well-ridden horses, but on the other hand no horse whose performance could be called an Event, no horse which moved with the complete submission and in the perfection of a really schooled horse, absolutely light in the hands and legs of the rider, always in the best position, collected, with arched neck, with highest cadence and greatest lightness. One saw also no rider who was a completely accomplished technician . . ." (the translation is mine).

Although the class was open for civilians, only officers actually took part in it. The competitors were not members of highly specialized army horse show teams; neither in Russia nor anywhere else, I believe, was there a group of officers taken out of the regiments and assembled eighteen months or so before a competition exclusively for the work of preparing themselves and their horses for an international tournament. In those days in Russia, a month or so before an international event the army would hold trials among officers *active* in their regiments; the best of these would be sent abroad. This is why the Individual Dressage didn't exhibit the highest standards of riding, although the conditions of the class were rather simple. Such movements as Piaffe, Passage, Change of Leads in two or one tempos, which in Berlin in 1936 were a part of the program, were not required; on the other hand, the program included five jumps all lower than 3'6" and an obedience test during which the horse should be made to walk past objects at which he had previously shied. Each nation was permitted to enter six individual competitors who did not form a team, and received prizes individually; hence the class was called Individual Dressage. In the Games of 1912, for instance, Sweden entered six riders, while Russia was represented by only one.

Beginning with the Games of 1920 this program underwent considerable change, finally becoming a class for everything that may be required of a manège horse, short of going into real High School, while jumping and the obedience test were dropped. Thus the class became far above the possibilities of a regular officer active in the ranks of cavalry regiments; it became a class for specialists in classical riding who could devote almost all of their time to this art. And in the Games of 1928 in Amsterdam this class was won by a civilian, Baron von Langen (Germany). In that year, for the first time, team prizes, as well as individual, were given.

In the Games of 1912 (as well as of today) there was another Dressage class which was a part of the competition called "Military." The manner in which the conditions of the class were described supports my thesis. In all the manuals on the Olympic Games, it is merely said that the latter test is the same as the Individual Dressage, excluding the figure of eight, with or without changes of leads, flying changes of leads, jumping and obedience test; the jumping, of course, was taken care of during the cross-country and arena jumping phases. In other words, there was a relationship between the two classes, both representing the same ideals, but one being more elementary than the other. The accent, of course, was on collection. For armies which still paraded at slow paces, in tight ranks and expected to charge in the same manner in war, precise, collected gaits were of practical importance.

Very soon after the beginning of the first World War, we, in the then very active Russian cavalry, understood that there was no place any more for slow gaits, for parade-like charges and, discarding our curbs, we extended the strides of our horses. The aims of the dressage of the Military Class ceased to make much sense to us—after the first mounted charge against machine guns.

Now, with the abolition of horse cavalry in this country, which unquestionably will be followed by the rest of the world, it would seem that riding in the Olympic Games should completely lose its military aspect and become a competition in civilian types of riding. Since the latter differ from the military, some of the conditions of the classes in question should be changed. For instance, from the point of view of a lieutenant commanding a platoon in a parade in 1900, it was of the utmost importance to have a horse schooled to stop on a dime, to gallop at times practically in place, and so forth; if his horse were unable to do all this, he would not be able to keep his proper place in the formation with the precision of a wooden soldier. Today's counterpart of this officer is a young man or woman who hunts or jumps in shows and to whom all the above requirements are absolutely unnecessary, while they have their own ideals for which to strive. From their practical point of view the program of the Dressage test of the Three-Day Event, in spite of all the modifications it has undergone in the fifty years of its existence, still preserves too many essentials of the past. It seems to me, that for the up-to-date amateur rider, in the United States anyway, the development of fast, free gaits in a hunter or jumper and the easy manoeuverability at these free gaits, is much more important than the ability to make a small circle at a collected gait. I know that some will not share my tendency to relegate collection to second place; hence I think I should further explain my stand.

The word *collection* is often very loosely used; you hear people say that they collect their horses before the jump or in a trappy situation in the hunting field, etc. One in a thousand of those who use this word so easily, really collects his horse. The best of the rest merely refer to the ability of their horses to change their balance by gathering themselves, which is known as "coming back" and which requires only a simple technique on the part of the rider. The majority think that they collect their horses when they slow them down by a strong pull on the reins, which arches the neck stiffly and often forces the resistant mouth open. To remind you of what truly collected gaits are, here is a quotation from the rules of the Olympic Games:

"*Collected Walk:* The horse should move resolutely forward with his neck raised and arched. The head approaches the vertical position. The hind legs are engaged, i.e. brought well forward under the body. The pace remains a *Walk* with the normal succession of beats. The collected walk is slightly slower than the ordinary walk, each step covering less ground but being more elevated owing to the fact that the joints are more bent. The mobility is, therefore, greater without the steps being hurried.

"*Collected Trot:* The neck should be raised permitting the shoulders to move with greater ease in all directions, the hind legs being well engaged and maintaining the energetic impulsion notwithstanding the slower movement. The steps of the horse are shorter but he is more mobile and lighter. [About the term *engagement* see page 154.]

"*Collected Canter:* The horse's shoulders, being unconstrained, should be free and mobile and his haunches should be active and vibrant. The muscles should be more relaxed without the impulsion being diminished."

I hope you realize that the putting into practice of these wonderful words—"greater mobility without the steps being hurried," "shoulders moving with greater ease in all directions," "the active and vibrant haunches," etc. could be accomplished only by a highly schooled rider riding a highly schooled horse. But I wonder how many of these perfect teams will be able to do all this in the excitement of the hunting field or during a gallop between obstacles at a horse show; and you will have to argue hard to prove that it is necessary for cross-country riding and jumping. On the other hand, as I have already pointed out, some of it is an excellent gymnastic in the schooling of a hunter or a jumper, providing it is not over-emphasized. Hence the presence of collected gaits in this schooling test is absolutely logical; it is their quantity with which I cannot agree.

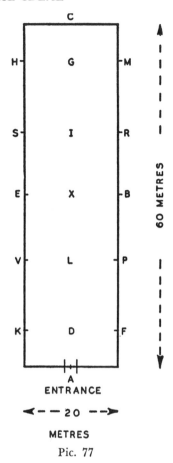

Pic. 77

Now, keeping the above definitions in mind, glance through the program of the schooling test of the Three-Day Event as it was in England in 1948.

Here is this program:

	Enter at the canter.
1. At G	Halt. Immobility of horse. Salute, move on at ordinary walk.
2. At C	Track to the right.
M to K	Change directions.
3. At K	Collected walk.
4. At A	Turn down centre.
D B G	Counter change of hand on two tracks.
5. At G	Ordinary trot (posting).
6. At C	Track to the left.

F H M	Change of directions at utmost extended trot (posting).
M to K	Ordinary trot (sitting).
K M H	Change of directions at utmost extended trot (posting).
7. H to A	Collected trot sitting.
8. At A	Turn down center.
D E G	Counter change of hand on two tracks.
9. At C	Track to the right.
At B	Halt. Back 4 paces. Move on at Collected trot (sitting).
10. At E	Small circle 6 metres diameter at collected trot.
11. At S	Collected canter (O.F. leading).
12. At B	Small circle 6 metres diameter at collected canter. Returning to B, collected trot.
13. At A	Ordinary canter (O.F. leading).
14. E C F	Extended canter.
15. At F	Collected canter.
16. At A	Turn down center.
At X	Collected trot (sitting).
At C	Track to the left.
17. At E	Small circle 6 metres diameter at collected trot.
18.	Returning to E. Collected canter (N.F. leading).
19. At B	Small circle 6 metres diameter at collected canter. Returning to B, collected trot.
20. At C	Ordinary canter (N.F. leading).
21. H E K F	Extended canter.
22. At F	Collected canter.
23. At B	Turn left to X.
At X	Halt. Move on at ordinary canter (O.F. leading).
24. At E	Track to the right.
At C	Halt. Back 4 paces. Collected canter (O.F. leading).
25. M to X	Two tracks right.
26. At X	Straight forward on center line.
At D	Collected trot.
At A	Track to the left.
At F	Collected canter (N.F. leading).
27. B to G	Two tracks left.
At G	Straight forward on centre line.
28. At C	Track to the left.
At H	Ordinary walk.
H X F	Extended walk (utmost extension).
At F	Collected walk.
At A	Turn down centre.
29. At G	Halt. Immobility of horse. Salute, leave the arena at the walk.

If you were to do the very boring job which I have just finished, that is, of tracing this program on the map of the arena and counting the relative distances covered by collected, extended and ordinary gaits, you would find out that the ratio between collected and ordinary gaits is almost three to one. When you think that this is the test for the work which is part of the training of a cross-country horse, it simply doesn't seem to make sense. Perhaps this is where one can find the explanation of a surprising remark made to me by one of the contestants a few days before the competition—"I have no doubt about the performance of my horse in the cross-country test, but he does the schooling movements rather poorly." In one of the Olympic Trials at Badminton in England a number of riders who placed poorly in the schooling test made cross-country performances of high quality, while others did just the reverse. For instance, one English rider placed 27th in the dressage and 5th in the cross-country performance, another correspondingly moved from 35th to 17th place, etc. If such cases are possible, it would seem to mean that this type of schooling is not essential, that it doesn't do its part in preparing horses for the field and that it is a superimposed structure.

Before the Olympic Games in Berlin in 1936, the Italians succeeded in persuading the International Equestrian Federation to make some modifications in the rules governing the schooling test of the Three-Day Event, namely (here I quote Captain Piero Santini, who stated these modifications in his book, THE FORWARD IMPULSE, on page 25):

"1) *The suppression of the collected gaits,* and the resulting acceptance of the forward balance, which logically results in

"2) The substitution of the expressions *'pas ralenti,' 'trot ralenti'* and *'gallop ralenti,'* which imply only a diminution of speed (and no high action or change in the horse's *natural* balance), for *'pas rassemblé,' 'trot rassemblé'* and *'gallop rassemblé' ('rassemblé'* meaning collected), which involve high action and balance on the quarters.

"3) The suppression of all direct passing to the trot and gallop from the halt, in favour of progressive transition from the halt to the walk, from the latter to the trot and from the trot to the gallop."

It seems that this agreement was not very definite and was arrived at against the opinion of some nations, for in the German Program of the Games the word "collection" was retained; neither were the Italian suggestions listed in the Program of 1948.

There is a practical limit to the use of collected gaits when training a cross-country horse. Too much collection may have evil effects on the efficiency of travelling gaits (particularly in the case of a semi-schooled rider), which, after all, are the gaits which a hunter or a jumper will use the most. If worked too much at collected gaits, a horse may begin to lose the length and flatness of the stride and, instead of using all his energy to cover ground, his action may begin to acquire a certain undesirable height, which is sheer waste of energy.

All these theoretical considerations lead me to the following practical suggestions:

a) If you expect to participate in the Olympic Games or official horse trials, then don't argue but prepare your horse for what is required.

b) If, on the other hand, you use this program merely as an *ideal* which you hope to reach with your horse, then the schooling test should be modernized in the following ways:

1) Replace at least half of the collected periods with ordinary gaits.

2) Don't strive for full collection, but for semi-collection.

3) You do not have to collect your horse when you do two tracks; a free two tracks with long ordinary strides is a more beneficial exercise for a cross-country horse and a jumper than a collected two tracks.

4) Retain one small circle at a semi-collected trot and one at a semi-collected gallop in your program but also make larger circles at an ordinary trot and canter, just as you would turn in the field.

5) Don't do any backing from collected gaits, but show how your horse halts from ordinary gaits, backs and resumes the original movement. In this way (particularly at a canter) backing develops *coming back* and is an important exercise for hunters and jumpers.

6) Retain a couple of diagonal changes of direction across the arena at an extended trot (semi-extended, to be exact). But also show how your horse makes the transitions from a slow trot (not a collected one) to an ordinary and then to a fast one (not extended) and back to the ordinary and to the slow. This is a fundamental exercise for the development of the longitudinal flexibility of the horse's body. Do the same at the canter.

In the extended trot the great impulse of the hindquarters, being somewhat checked by the rider's hands, results in the full extension of the forelegs, while the speed is not necessarily fast. A *fast trot* is a flatter, quieter movement; it is just a fast trot with long strides. It is the counterpart of a *slow trot* which is a slow, quiet trot, with short, flattish strides. Both extended and collected trots, being extremely animated, are not quiet movements which one would use cross-country.

7) Introduce in your program a *counter gallop,* which means turning or circling, for instance, to the left on a wide arc while galloping on the right lead. This is a wonderful balancing gymnastic. I know several very successful trainers of jumpers who would drop, if forced to, all other exercises but would keep this one.

8) Introduce into your program about three jumps to be taken as part

of the routine of gaits and movements. One obstacle to be taken at a trot, one at a canter and one as in a *handy hunter* class, that is: approach the jump at a walk; from the saddle remove the upper bar of the fence, withdraw about 25 feet, then take the fence. Neither the cross-country nor the arena jumping phases will enable you to show how pleasantly obedient and quiet your horse is approaching the fence and going away from it.

9) During the latter part of your ring schooling it would be a good idea to lay out your arena on not absolutely level ground; your hunter will rarely be working in perfect conditions. A very gradual slope somewhere in your arena will tell much more about the balance of your horse than all the collected gaits put together.

You do not have to construct such an arena; just choose a suitable ground, measure it and mark it with letters. (I recommend an oval arena 125' x 250'.)

At first I planned to end this chapter by giving a sample table of a modernized test for schooling. And then I decided against it, for I am afraid that some of my readers may take it rigidly as the only possible form of the *ideal*. This rigidity, in riding anyway, I wish by all means to avoid. It's the spirit of schooling rather than pedantic rules which I would like to stress in this book. In the chapter on schooling you will find a description of all the movements which may enter into the composition of such a program. Dozens of such programs, long and short ones, all varying from each other, can be made and your understanding of schooling will benefit greatly if you try your hand at making up a couple of them yourself. Try them out. And, if you do, then, I am quite certain that my criticisms of the Olympic Games program will make more sense to you.

It is reasonable to assume that many of my readers who have read this book thus far would come to the conclusion that I hold a grudge against Dressage. Those who think so would be mistaken; I am very fond of Dressage as an exhibition of the supreme form of classical manège riding. I have not had the leisure to become really proficient at it myself but still, even here in the United States, I once schooled a horse to a rather high degree, have played with a couple of others and would go out of my way to witness a good Dressage performance. As a matter of fact, it is the Dressage class above all other classes of the Olympic Games in Berlin in 1936 which stands out in my memory. But, admiring it, I know its limitations and fail to see what the possible connection can be between it and cross-country riding.

This year, in Madison Square Garden, the Spanish Riding School of Vienna gave an exhibition. I watched them with great interest, several times at the show, as well as in practice before the opening, and tried to pick up something in the technique of the riders or in the movements of the horses which would be of value to my work. Unfortunately there was nothing. But I know of at least two riding teachers (I am certain they were not alone) who took their pupils to watch the performance which they considered (aside from the different jumps in the air) as perfect basic training for any type of riding. I cannot see it in this light at all and when I heard the following story about the White Horses it seemed to me to epitomize all that I felt about the anachronism of their performance. It seems that the rather limited Horse Show orchestra was asked to play a Bizet composition arranged for an eighty-six piece orchestra because the Lipizzan stallions could not perform at their best to any but old-world airs.

Granting some exaggeration to the story, I understand that Colonel Alois Podhajsky (head of the Spanish Riding School of Vienna) desiring to have everything perfect, merely wanted to have music which was particularly appropriate to the movements of his program; his horses, of course, would perform disregarding the tune played. But just the same, the fact that there was a careful selection of music makes the whole thing very remote from a foggy morning in the hunting field.

While the ideals suggested thus far in this chapter and set down twelve years ago are still practical for many riders, I find that my own ideal has become a further modification of them; hence this additional text.

The Complete Test For Hunters

I rarely have occasion today (in 1962) to use semi-collection in my teaching, because it usually seems quite unnecessary. Practically all my better pupils (human as well as equine), even outstanding winners in important shows, are consistently successful without using it—performing exclusively on the principle of free going. And the conditions of modern life are such as to confirm the practicality, for the usual rider who shows or hunts, of training his mount according to the unadorned Italian method of schooling a field horse.

In spite of this situation, I still feel that semi-collection as a part of schooling on the advanced level should be retained in the book, if only to remind the ambitious horseman with extra time to spare that there is such a thing. On the other hand, I now believe that natural calm gaits should perhaps be stressed even more than they were in the original text. I came to this practical conclusion several years ago, and already in 1956 proposed to change the formula of the Three-Day-Event still more radically than I had in the first part of this chapter. Eventually some of my pupils and I worked out a new substitute formula, which we originally called the *Complete Test for Hunters.*

While the *Complete Test* was at first designed with the hunter in mind, non-hunting communities can adapt its conditions to prove the versatility and pleasantness of a horse which may be primarily a *jumper;* riding departments in boarding schools and colleges, and commercial riding schools can put on a *Complete Test for Riders* with phases planned and judged to test the rider's rather than the horse's skill and efficiency in different situations; the phases of the test can also be adapted to a *Complete Test for Junior Horses,* which play the various roles as country hack, hunter, jumper or horsemanship horse. All these variants of the *Complete Test* have been successfully tried.

Judging of the *Complete Test* should not be by a mechanical count of points, but the horses should be judged on the same principle on which working hunters are judged, while the judging of riders should follow the pattern of judging in horsemanship classes. Otherwise the result may be similar to what happens frequently today in recognized *Horse Trials* where the second phase is apt to take the form of simply open jumping across country and as such contributes nothing to bettering riding standards.

The *Complete Test* consists of three (or four) phases:
1) Program Ride (a combination of schooling exercises)
2) Cross Country (a hunter trial type course)
3) Working Hunter Horse Show class (as found in better shows).
To these three phases a fourth should be added in the case of testing a hunter. This is:
4) Group phase with hounds (as found in the hunting field).
For detailed description of how to conduct such a test I would like to refer to a booklet, *The Complete Test for Hunters,* written by Mrs. Robert E. Cater III, M.F.H., Groton Hunt.

The Description of THE COMPLETE TEST FOR HUNTERS
ON INTERMEDIATE LEVEL
THE FIRST PHASE—THE PROGRAM RIDE

The first phase of this competition, The Program Ride, is so different from the Dressage test of the Three-Day Event that I would like to include here one of the many possible variations of it, as an example of the spirit in which I believe such programs should be conceived.

Here is a sample of a program ride, conceived for the intermediate level:

Enter at A at an ordinary trot; trot on the middle line through X to C. at C track to the left and continue ordinary trot (around the arena) to B. at B make a gradual halt and then execute a half-turn on the haunches; resume the ordinary trot and trot to E.
at E make a large half-circle (45′ in diameter) maintaining the speed of 8 m.p.h.; trot to A.
at A make a gradual halt and back four steps; resume ordinary trot; trot to G.
at G fast trot to C (preferably lengthening the strides and not merely increasing their frequency; however, it should not be the extended trot of dressage).

at C ordinary trot to H.

at H slow trot to K (as slow as you can make it without collection).

at K ordinary trot to G.

at G change directions across the arena to H, negotiating obstacles 1 & 2 at a trot.

at H continue ordinary trot to C.

at C gradually start an ordinary canter and canter (around the arena) to E.

at E a large half-circle (about 65′ in diameter) change leads when nearing the wall (flying or with an interruption of the gait) ; continue canter to B.

at B slow canter (as slow as you can make it without collecting the horse) to C.

at C resume ordinary canter; canter to H.

at H continue canter diagonally across the arena to G, negotiating obstacles 2 and 1.

at G continue ordinary canter to K and, if the horse is on the outside lead, then change leads (flying or with an interruption of the canter) somewhere near A.

at K gallop (about 15 m.p.h.) to B.

at B ordinary canter to A.

at A ordinary trot to K.

at K make a gradual halt; back four steps and walk forward on loose reins, to prove that your horse is still calm; walk to H.

at H pick up your reins; walk to C "on contact."

at C halt; make a half-turn on the haunches, then resume the walk and gradually start an ordinary canter; canter to G.

at G change directions to X, negotiating obstacle 1 (slow down the ordinary canter) and at about X change directions again over obstacle 3; continue canter to M.

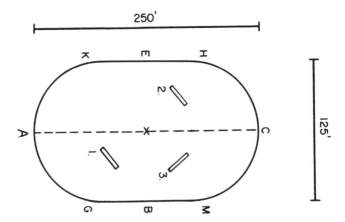

at M slow canter to C (as slow as you can make it).
at C make a turn (preferably a short one) to the middle line and continue slow canter along the middle line to X.
at X halt for about five seconds, then start an ordinary trot; trot on middle line to A and leave the arena.

The important points to note in this program are:

1) The size of the *oval* arena, which is 125′ x 250′, permits the contestant, without being cramped, to exhibit a good ordinary trot (8 m.p.h.), and ordinary canter (10-12 m.p.h.) and even a gallop of about 15 m.p.h. (The official size of the arena for the so-called Dressage tests is approximately 65′ x 195′ and is too small for a big hunter to exhibit the beauty of his free movements, while the square corners of such an arena further cramp him.)

2) That a few jumps are included in the program; first of all to underline the fact that the schooling test and the movements of which it is composed are part of the education of a horse destined to jump under varying circumstances. This presence of fences in the *Program Ride* tests the calmness of the horse or the skill of the rider in negotiating unexpected obstacles and may prove conclusively whether the horse in question is pleasant to ride over fences and whether the rider is skillful enough to control his horse when it is, unexpectedly, introduced to a jump in the midst of different movements on the flat. This is quite different from merely rolling over an outside course. The height of fences in this schooling program should be 3′-3′ 6″ for the intermediate level.

3) Although in Dressage very small circles (20′ in diameter) at slow collected gaits are an important part of the exhibition, in the case of hunters (either field or show) wider turns at the *speed* at least of the ordinary trot and canter are clearly more important. Consequently, the circular movements should have diameters of at least 45′ for the trot and 65′ for the canter. A short turn at the canter (which is not a circular movement), frequently encountered in show jumping and hunting, may also be included in programs for the intermediate level.

4) In accordance with the definition of the Intermediate Level in this book, neither collected nor semi-collected gaits are included in the program. All the movements in the *Program Ride* must be of the kind which are actually and efficiently used in schooling a hunter or a jumper. The inclusion of the collected Dressage movements (both short-striding and extended) in the official Dressage test represent a part of the versatility test which the Three Day Event is. The *Complete Test* should represent a considerably narrower, more specialized program. Making a specialized horse is within the reach of many more riders than making a universal one. The *Complete Test* aims at raising the standards of many, rather than at achieving outstanding results with a few.

Phase II—Cross-Country

This consists of galloping (at a hunting pace) across country, over a hunter-trials type of course, which takes advantage of the natural terrain, while the obstacles should be neither artificial nor tricky but, typical rather of the local country.

The Intermediate Cross-Country course should be under two miles long, with two "Hold Hards." In these, the horses are required to come to an abrupt halt (as if in an emergency) and to stand still for about 30 seconds. If the test takes place in hot weather, the horses may be walked in a circle, if necessary, to recover their wind, after they have stood quietly for the prescribed length of time. Horses which come unduly overheated to the finish line are penalized. This rule is particularly educational for those would-be horsemen who will take any chance with the horse's condition merely in order to win. The pace should be a sensible hunting pace; excessive as well as insufficient speed is penalized; a horse that doesn't slow down in bad or slippery going is also penalized. In short, this phase is not a steeplechase and not only should the horse show calmness throughout, but the rider should exhibit the cool common sense of a horseman who takes into consideration distance, going and weather, in relation to his horse's condition. Thus the spirit in which this phase is conducted differs radically from that of the recognized Horse Trials, in which speed in the cross-country phase is rewarded by bonuses.

The obstacles in this phase should, of course, be varied and their height for the intermediate level should be 3'-3' 9". The negotiation of obstacles should be judged by the same standards by which a working hunter is judged. On the other hand, in *Horse Trials* neither the style of jumping nor the manner of the approach is judged and thus the door is open for this phase to become a kind of cross-country open jumping— a form which, unfortunately, such competitions occasionally do assume.

Phase III—Working Hunter Class

In this phase the horses are competing in a normal show-ring type of working-hunter class and thus this phase can serve as schooling for regular showing. With this in view, the elementary level of this phase may be even simpler than anything one finds at a horse show. In cases where the *Complete Test* is designed to test riders, this phase should take the form of horsemanship over fences. In the *Horse Trials* the corresponding phase, Arena (Stadium) Jumping, is conducted along the lines of open jumping (although the fences remain low) with F.E.I. rules.

Phase IV—Group Riding

This phase has been included in the *Complete Test for Hunters* because the horses' manners must be observed in company before the judges can determine which are the pleasantest conveyances to hounds. Many horses that behave well alone become upset and hard to handle in company. Not only other galloping horses, but hounds often excite a horse that may be rather quiet under other circumstances. Even when hounds are not available for this phase it still provides a necessary test for a hunter.

When hounds are not used, horses can go through different exercises in company, on the flat and over fences, all devised to test the calmness of individual horses when they are passed by others, when they have to wait for their turn to jump, when they have to turn away from the group, etc. This subject is described in greater detail in another addition to this book—*Special Exercises for Hunters.* (See pp. 309.)

The test of calmness in company may also be regarded as a must for a *Complete Test for a Junior Horse* which may be asked to hack in company, compete over fences in hunter and junior jumping classes, perform in horsemanship classes and follow hounds as well.

From the point of view of bettering the standards of riding, the above type of test, I am certain, is the most practical for today. This does not mean, however, that it will remain such forever. Changing conditions of life will unquestionably change the attitudes of horsemen, and a test that makes common sense at present may not suit future developments in riding.

CHAPTER XIV

Almost Anyone Can Learn Forward Schooling

Why *Forward* Schooling? Why not merely Schooling or Dressage? I suppose such a question will spring to the minds of many of my readers; hence the above title requires explanation.

This chapter does not concern itself with schooling in the abstract; it doesn't describe schooling in general terms, claiming that it suits any kind of riding. The schooling presented in this book hasn't anything to do, for instance, with Polo or High School; it has for its goal a very specific type of riding: that is hunting, jumping, and a superior type of hacking. It intends to develop the horse physically and mentally for cross-country work, where the horse must be agile and soft while moving (most of the time) with forward balance. The latter is the reason for the name Forward Schooling. Not only in its name but in its essence it is in harmony with the two other parts of my method—Forward Control and the Forward Seat.

On the other hand, in this country, under the term Dressage, a type of schooling is usually understood which is primarily based on collection (central balance), no matter how elementary the schooling is. (About Dressage, see also Chapter IV.)

People usually react to the word "Dressage" in two ways. Those who are really not horsemen at heart and merely wish to "raise hell on horse-back" (excuse the phrase) will consider it as something which belongs to the ring, perhaps to junior equitation classes, but has by no means anything to do with jumping or cross-country riding. Another group of riders, composed of serious horsemen with an old-fashioned education to which they tenaciously adhere, will maintain that Dressage is a *general* physical education for the horse, valuable no matter to what use he is to be put. A few riders will even maintain that Dressage is excellent for jumpers.

"Jack of all trades, master of none" applies to a horse as well as to a human being and, if he aims only at producing a specialist, the trainer will have an easier time and will reach his goal more quickly. So Forward Schooling aims at making superior hacks, hunters and jumpers and nothing else. Such an approach to the physical development of an athlete would be considered standard in all other sports. No one would expect a champion golfer to be a winning tennis player or swimmer. Granting that a generally well-developed body is a great asset in any sport, in order to excel in any one particular thing one has to undergo special training. Never have I seen such a clear illustration of this point as when on the S.S. *America* at the same time as the United States Olympic Teams travelling to England in 1948. The members of different teams, runners, discus throwers, wrestlers and others, spent a good part of each day on deck practicing their own various sets of exercises to develop different muscles, different swings of legs or arms or what not. In this respect in riding, a step-child among the sports, there still exists mental confusion on the subject of schooling the horse; I suppose primarily because there is vagueness in the general understanding of how the horse uses his body.

Of course if one has a great deal of time on his hands (which it seems few have these days), then why not give the horse a sort of Liberal Arts education, followed by a specialized one as a post graduate course. The horse may even gain from it; but only in exceptional cases will the results make up for the extra time spent. The law of "diminishing returns" works even in riding. This idea of a general physical education as a preliminary to a specialized one occasionally takes grotesque forms such as, for instance, the old belief that early experience at the plow is good for hunters, although obviously the muscular efforts made in hunting are not the same which are made when plowing.

All the exercises recommended in this book have as their basic aim free, efficient movement and so they attempt to develop those muscles of the horse's body which produce long, flat strides. Superficially, it is permissible to say that the better the horse's development in general, the better he will jump; therefore a great deal of work on collection is necessary. However, the muscular training which produces short, high steps has little in common with that which results in the long, flat strides of a hunting gallop and its closely related movement, the jump. As a matter of fact, it is rare when a Dressage horse gallops well.

On the other hand, some work on semi-collection may be advantageous in the development of the horse's agility, and you will find a description of this work here.

The fact that many movements of Dressage are included in Forward Schooling without aiming at their perfection, makes it rather customary to call the ring part of Forward Schooling—"Elementary Dressage." Superficially, of course, schooling movements devoid of finesse in their execution can be called elementary. But if one looks more deeply into the matter, and in his work actually connects all the simply executed ring movements with jumping and cross-country work, then there is nothing elementary about Forward Schooling. It is all by itself and its comparison with Dressage is bound to result in mental confusion. Fortunately, Forward Schooling is much simpler than Dressage, but it is as *complete* and *final* as the latter.

So, all in all, the schooling program presented in the next chapter is a program of practical schooling for a cross-country horse. It aims at making a hunter or jumper a well-balanced horse, a good mover, a good jumper and a pleasant, strong, agile, cooperative horse to ride. In my estimation it is also the best method of preparing junior horsemanship horses for hunting seat equitation classes. As it is presented here it is stripped to the bone; everything that could be considered non-essential has been eliminated; you simply cannot make it shorter and simpler and still claim that you are schooling a horse.

In presenting my method of schooling I assume that you have read this book thus far and are especially familiar with the second chapter on the mentality of the horse, with the three chapters on control and with the chapters on the mechanics of the horse's movements. In this last, as you remember, I defined the aims of Forward Schooling as the physical and mental education of the horse; of course, primarily the physical, and then the mental to the point where the horse cooperates with the rider. Schooling does not consist of making a pet out of a horse or merely giving him good manners. It means taking an awkward, green horse and turning him into a strong, well-balanced, strong-winded, agile animal, who carries his rider with the ease with which a human athlete would carry a burden.

In the cavalry school, where I was a cadet, schooling was not taught. Upon graduating I knew advanced riding, that is, how to obtain a good performance in all sorts of movements from a schooled horse. But the subject of schooling floated in my mind in the haziest form. In those days the fact that it should be a logical system of gymnastics escaped me and such a movement as two tracks I would have easily considered trick riding if I hadn't been told (with little explanation) that it was a part of schooling. So, meekly obeying, I was repeating that two tracks is a good exercise, not being able to see why, nor understanding its place in the process of development of the horse's body.

It was only in New York, around 1930, that it became clear to me that schooling is inseparable from position and control and that even the type of seat used depends on the type of schooling. Once I realized this, I was in trouble. The seat that I had adopted was a modification of the Italian seat, but Italian schooling, which primarily consisted in letting the horse develop by himself while being ridden over difficult terrain, always seemed to me inefficient; I couldn't accept it. The excellent book on training by Colonel Harry Chamberlin had not yet made its appearance; James Fillis' book was obviously too old-fashioned, as were all other books of the period, and all by myself I was unable to conceive an entirely new and really efficient method of schooling cross-country horses. So, for a while, I was at a loss. Then I had a piece of good luck; the Chilean Army team came to New York, having at its head Captain Eduardo Yanez, not only a great rider, but a man with an exceptional equestrian education and with a very clear and logical mind. As a result of innumerable talks together, and watching him in the saddle, the plan of Forward Schooling began to take shape in my head. My first program appeared in 1938 in my book MORE ABOUT RIDING FORWARD and parts of it were almost entirely dictated by Captain Yanez; for a couple of years before it appeared in print I had already been lecturing with it, while my equine pupils demonstrated. On the strength of its practical application I improved the program somewhat in my next book, BE A BETTER HORSEMAN, and I am doing so again in this one.

It has been a source of constant regret to me that I never could figure out how schooling horses professionally could be turned into a living, a work which I have wanted to do in preference to all others. Even before I took a piece of paper and a pencil to calculate the possibilities in such a business I was facing a problem which I have still failed to solve, that is how a poor rider can successfully ride a schooled horse? Here I do not refer to a merely quiet, docile, well-mannered animal which jumps easy courses consistently, no matter what the rider does on his back; such horses are commonly referred to and sold as well-schooled ones. A really schooled horse (an athlete) sold to a person who does not know riding well will at first, at least, give him more trouble than pleasure for, being responsive, he will react too sensitively to clumsy aids, will become bewildered by their frequent lack of meaning and, since he will be very agile, when excited or irritated may be much too quick for the security of an indifferent rider. All in all, only a schooled rider can enjoy a schooled horse. This, of course, considerably limits the possible market.

And finally, schooling cannot be done cheaply; it requires a skilful, intelligent rider; no such high-class man would work for less than twelve or fifteen dollars a day (after all, he is on a par with the skilled artisan) and he couldn't properly work more than three horses a day, which in round figures means that schooling a horse would cost about $1000, plus another $700 for board, shoeing, etc., while the horse is being schooled. When this, even without any profit, is added to the initial cost of the horse, then the whole thing becomes impractical. It becomes impractical primarily because of the fact that the majority of prospective buyers don't know what a schooled horse is and would rather pay less money for a supposedly schooled horse who has been given some sort of manners and jumped over fences by cheap and primitive labor. This sort of "fixing" of a horse, particularly of a good horse, can be done for $150 or $200 and the tag of a schooled horse attached to him, with very few people recognizing the difference. (These figures are, of course, ludicrous in 1974.)

Realizing these market difficulties I abandoned my pet project and as a close substitute have tried to specialize in teaching how to school horses. Thus the rider and the horse could progress simultaneously, while the cost of the course would be amply covered by the student's pleasure in improving his riding.

It would be foolish to expect that the majority of the great number of people who find their way into the saddle at one time or another would be horsemen at heart; of course not. Hence it would be naive to hope that they all would be interested in schooling. But, the number who are is still surprisingly small. It would seem that all the riders who have time enough to hunt regularly and money enough to own beautiful hunters, as well as the intelligent horsemen among the horse-show riders, would be interested in having their horses perform really well. But this is not the case either; I know of no group of riders which is in its entirety interested in riding per se. The real horsemen are scattered all over the country; you will find them belonging to different social and riding groups and doing different types of riding. As an illustration of the comparative lack of interest in schooling I would like to give you the statistics on the rental of three of my films: "Forward Control" rents twice as well as "Forward Schooling," while "The Forward Seat" has a three times bigger circulation.

So, you may say, if this is the situation why should I worry about schooling, teach it or write about it? This is precisely what I was told when, thirty years ago, I pioneered with the Forward Seat. The best that well-wishing friends could tell me then was something like this: "Why do you insist upon the Forward Seat? Nobody wants it, anyway. Why don't you just swim with the times and make money by doing so?" I firmly believe that the time has arrived when the best among American horsemen are ready to become interested in schooling. Another ten or twenty years and it will be as firmly established as the Forward Seat is today.

Of course, thirty-five years ago, when the American riding scene was virgin soil, one couldn't introduce schooling and make a go of it; preparatory work had to be done. Now, the latter has been accomplished, or almost accomplished, and schooling is bound to interest many, as any constructive accomplishment fascinates Americans in general. Many of my readers have probably noted articles on schooling which have appeared in different periodicals during the course of the last fifteen years; undoubtedly these were written and published because schooling is in the air. Unfortunately all of these articles which I came across were written on the basis of old-fashioned Dressage ideas and as such, being too remote from the actualities of American riding, succeeded merely in producing learned arguments in the form of letters to the editor.

Schooling can be practiced in many different ways to fit different human characters. It can take the form of a rigid routine in which one systematically moves from one point to the other; or it may be treated as something extremely flexible with all doors open for one's imagination. Take your pick, depending upon your character. A judicious use of any sensible method should bring good results. This last statement is very well illustrated by the fact that many internationally winning teams which have succeeded each other in the laurels have schooled their horses in different ways.

Personally, not being pedantic, being bored by routine in life in general, and believing in the conquering power of the human imagination, I present my program of schooling as something very fluid. If you happen to be a different kind of person and prefer to accept the program which you find in the next chapter as a mathematical equation, go ahead and do so and you will still obtain good results. But if you prefer merely to be given indications, and then to be left alone to analyze the performance of your horse, to figure out for yourself how to correct the defects of his performance, how to turn a merely good movement into a really excellent one, etc., then if you are successful you will get a still greater joy out of it. Even, perhaps, by discovering something new, you will contribute to the progress of riding.

Long ago I came to the conclusion that the greatest obstacle in the way of progress in riding is the reluctance of so many riders to think. Consequently, all my teaching is based on efforts to stimulate thinking among my pupils. My experience has proved that I was correct and that only if riding is done with the head as well as the breeches do real horsemen result. Hence, I would like you to accept my program of schooling as merely a skeleton upon which to base your own ingenuity.

Earlier in this book I have stressed the point that one must be an advanced rider to school a horse; it is unquestionably so if one aims at considerable results. But, on the other hand, advanced riders being in the minority, such an approach to schooling considerably reduces the number of people who could enjoy it and profit by it. Hence the important question is whether a merely intermediate rider can school a horse. Yes, he can, but schooling and its aims must be simplified somewhat, as follows:

1) Eliminate riding fully on the bit.
2) Replace semi-collected and semi-extended gaits by gaits merely faster and slower than ordinary.
3) Eliminate small circular movements which require semi-collection.
4) Eliminate flexions. Efficient "give and take" will suffice.
5) Eliminate flying changes of lead.

With these simplifications you will still be able to make a good horse. On the other hand, practice in schooling will eventually teach you advanced riding.

The program of schooling which is to follow is meant for really green, but mentally and physically sound horses (as green colts usually are). Only with drastic modifications can it be applied to the reclaiming of spoiled horses; these are cases all by themselves. Reclaiming ruined horses is a lengthy, discouraging and rarely completely satisfactory procedure. Its hopefulness or hopelessness depends on the fundamental character of the particular horse, on his age, and on how firmly his bad habits are established. While schooling a green horse usually proceeds in a comparatively uniform manner, the reclaiming of each spoiled horse is a case by itself.

To illustrate how tedious such work can be and how little one can hope for from it in some cases, even if successful, I would like to tell you a story of my own experience. In the early thirties one of my pupils had, among several horses which she showed, an open jumper, *Arnoldean.* This mare was good enough to compete in Madison Square Garden, but was hot, was becoming more so from year to year and was getting harder and harder to control, in spite of being bitted with increasing severity. I had many arguments with the owner, insisting that for a while the horse should be taken out of competitions, quieted down and re-schooled. Being many years younger, I was considerably more optimistic than today and was convinced that the job could be done. So, one of the hot arguments, in which I insisted that *I* certainly could do the job, ended by my purchasing the horse, really merely to have a chance to prove that I was right. I began by removing from her mouth the complicated paraphernalia which she carried, replaced it with a plain hunting snaffle and almost went out of the window of the ring. This was the beginning of a long walk (and nothing more than walk) which lasted six months. At the end of it she walked quietly on loose reins; but so does a normal green horse when first mounted. In approximately another year she became a good hack and I rode her all over the countryside on loose reins (snaffle) at all gaits. I even could quietly take an occasional obstacle on her; but the very sight of a horse-show ring or even of a course of jumps would make her frantic. I used this horse to illustrate the chapter on schooling in BE A BETTER HORSEMAN. The moral of this tale is that, if it is possible, you should keep away from ruined horses; and remember that two months' work on a green horse is worth six months' efforts in reclaiming a spoiled one.

But if, unfortunately, you have a spoiled horse and have to make the best of it, you still can use my method in your attempt to reclaim him. Only such cases have to be treated individually and the schooling program rearranged for almost every one of them. If your horse is like the majority of spoiled horses, then he is probably very excitable, pulls, rushes his fences, jumps them stiffly and perhaps dangerously, etc. To cure all this you *must* stabilize the horse (2nd month in the program) and it is very possible that that is all that your horse really needs to be an enjoyable mount again. But, if the horse is too far gone, you may not succeed or the reclaiming may take much too long to be practical. But, if you have succeeded in calming the horse then, becoming more discriminating, you may find out that your horse isn't balanced well or isn't agile or that his strides are too high and too short. In such cases concentrate on only a couple of defects at a time; choose exercises in the program which will counteract these faults and work on them. The moment your horse improves in these two presumably most glaring defects take up the next two most important faults and so on. Thus, little by little you may cover the whole program of schooling, but in an order of your own which suits your case.

As an illustration of such use of the schooling program I would like to describe one of my recent experiences. I was asked to ride a certain horse for a few days in succession to determine whether he should be sold or whether anything could be done to improve his performance, which was extremely clumsy. He was a heavy-weight hunter of very decent conformation who had been hunted one season at the age of four and by spring was not only jumping but even moving with a neck like a giraffe turned up to the skies and at gaits of his own invention. My friend had acquired him for about ten per cent of what he had brought the year before, and had stabilized him within half a year, so that the horse was moving very quietly with his neck in a natural position—but there was one hitch. Once the horse was quiet it became obvious that whoever had ridden him for this one hunting season had done a thorough job in dulling his sides and his mouth—they were really dead. When I mounted him and squeezed him with the full strength of my legs till I was blue in the face the horse didn't even move an ear. Neither did he move when, attempting to back him, I leaned back with my body, adding its weight to the strength of my arms and finally pushed my feet forward to use as a brace. The obvious problem was that, although to combat his clumsiness he had to be put through a course of gymnastics, it was impossible to make him do all the necessary movements in a *relaxed* manner when there was no response either to the hands or the legs. In the course of the first ride, after trying every trick of the trade that I knew, I came to the conclusion that my first problem was to explain the meaning of the aids to him and that the approach should be through his brains rather than through his mouth or sides. The second day I armed myself with a whip and a few lumps of sugar and quickly met with disappointment—the horse wouldn't eat sugar! So this day didn't get us anywhere and upon dismounting I switched some of my responsibility to the groom, telling him that by to-morrow the horse simply must eat sugar—and he did. The next day my pupil mounted him and we began, perhaps illogically, with the half-turn on the forehand. While my assistant was rather gently using one leg to rotate the quarters I, from the ground, was helping with the whip, tapping the horse's side just behind the rider's active leg. Then came the sugar. This was the exercise in obedience to one leg. For the next exercise we chose backing, to teach obedience to the reins of direct opposition. Again, while my pupil was rather gently and hence hopelessly pulling on the reins I, tapping his fore legs with my whip, would force him to make one step back. Then would come a pat, another gentle pull, another tapping with the whip, another step back and perhaps a piece of sugar. The next day I was doing it from the saddle with the help of whip and sugar, but without any assistant and in another two days it became clear that signals could be taught to him and if so, then he could, in a relaxed manner, be put through all the exercises necessary to rid him of his clumsiness.

There is one bright side to the work of reclaiming horses; that is that once you succeed in calming and relaxing the horse, the rest of the schooling can proceed at a faster tempo than with a colt. Assuming that a spoiled horse will be at least six years old, hence formed physically and having the knack of carrying a rider, you won't have to worry so much about straining his body as when schooling a *growing* horse.

Putting too young a horse to work is very common. I could give a very long list of outstanding authorities on riding who all agree that actual schooling should not begin before the horse has reached the age of four and that he should only take his first 4' fence when nearing five. Putting the horse to work earlier is taking the chance of crippling an immature horse both mentally and physically. On the other hand, if the trainer proceeds slowly while the horse is yet a youngster it is likely that he will be still sound and calm when nearing twenty.

Such statements can be found in practically every worthwhile book and as far back as the 17th century. So unquestionably everyone who owns a horse has heard it at least once. But this is one of the facts which is more conveniently forgotten than remembered. The reason is to be found in the common traits of the human character. Suppose an average rider buys a three-year-old horse; one of the questions that worries him is "will this horse jump?" His limited knowledge of horses and riding, and his probably non-existent knowledge of schooling, will result in his being convinced that the horse can jump only if he actually sees him jumping on the day he buys him. Hence a dealer is compelled to jump his colts much too early and he even cannot afford to take time to do it gradually. The average rider, no matter how good his resolutions may be, once the horse is bought, usually can't wait to see how the horse will go for him in the hunting field or in the horse show and thus arises one of the commonest abuses of this animal.

There is one more thing, and a very important one, pertaining to correcting horses (not full reclaiming) which I would like to discuss. Many people own horses which do not behave in a really obnoxious manner but merely have some irritating defects. For instance, a horse may have a stiff poll; a rubber neck; an arched, overflexed neck; a mouth stiff in one side or a generally hard mouth or an oversensitive one; stiff sides, short gaits, etc. I wanted very much to write a special chapter on how to remedy these imperfections without going through the full program of schooling. Unfortunately this cannot be done; I don't believe that anyone can give sensible advice in such cases without seeing and analyzing the individual horse. While schooling colts is a rather uniform process, correcting the bad habits of old horses is very irregular. I am often asked questions on how to correct such habits and I always decline to answer, saying that I personally must see the animal. Just the other day a lady asked me what she should do to correct such and such a fault in her horse's jumping. As usual, I said that I would like to see the horse but, feeling that she was disappointed and that I should prolong the conversation I, in my turn, inquired about the age of the horse and was very glad I had asked the question, because the answer was "twenty-four." So, in order to avoid hundreds of such possible misunderstandings, I am not going to tackle this matter in this book. The schooling program, however, contains all the necessary data and it is up to you to use your imagination in applying them to your horse.

Jumping, in this chapter, as in this book in general, is not presented as a separate subject but rather as an integral part of the schooling of a hunter and jumper. Obviously jumping, as a series of movements of the horse's body, is as closely related to ordinary gaits as these gaits are to each other. The quality of the jump, the gaits, the turns and other movements is the result of the degree to which the horse's balance, strength and agility have been developed; and all of these factors in their turn are influenced by the conformation and the emotional qualities of the particular horse. Hence it is really absurd to think that all the jump that the horse has can be gotten out of him by merely jumping; basic general schooling must precede the actual exercises over obstacles. There is nothing new about the idea that through basic schooling the body of the horse is developed to the point where he can use it efficiently in jumping, but it may sound novel to many readers, for in this country this fundamental rule is rarely observed. In the majority of cases no basic schooling is given to a jumper and he is expected to develop his natural jumping abilities merely through jumping fences. This primitive method often does not even include an assortment of fences to develop different jumping qualities. The thing that may be bewildering to a layman is the fact that by this cave-man practice horses are made which leap far over very high obstacles. Even if you consider that this procedure sometimes includes poling with electric shocks or a light blistering of the horse's legs (enough to make him afraid of touching the bars), it still makes jumpers who win ribbons and hence are valued by many. The results of such brutal but quick "schooling" are practical because the quality of our horses, and therefore their natural ability, is very high while the conditions of the average jumping classes are not conceived to promote good jumping but rather merely high and clean jumping. If you don't care whether your horse is so upset by the whole thing that he jumps like a lunatic, that he leaps so stiffly that every landing hurts him and consequently he has seventy-five chances out of one hundred of being buried before he reaches seven years; if, furthermore, you don't mind if he is unpleasant to ride and if his jumps are difficult to sit and ugly to watch, then, of course, you will not agree with my reasoning which is, as you already know, based on the desire to have a mentally and physically relaxed horse who performs naturally and athletically. To a horseman all this is clear, but to a layman or a beginner such terms as a natural or athletic jump are empty sounds; he doesn't know what a good jump is, he is merely impressed by the height of a huge leap. And even to some experienced riders with elementary mentality the humane and artistic approach to the horse's performance is "just boloney." And to prove that it is boloney they will cite you horses who, at the age of twenty, go quietly, stay sound and win ribbons after a life-long jumping career which began with practically no education. And these are not stories. There are such horses, numbering probably something like five per cent of those competing. These are the horses which impress the novice in the game, for he sees them perform year after year while, naturally, he never hears of the great majority which are dead and buried. I have pointed out already that this book does not concern itself with exceptional riders, neither does it take up the cases of exceptional horses. It deals with the average and the hope of my method is to raise the standard of the average performance.

I suspect that the feeling against my method as regards jumping may be quite general in certain groups of riders such as, for instance, owners of open-jumpers and, consequently, I would like to point out that my approach is not a purely personal one. As a matter of fact, one may say that it is international in certain equestrian groups; it is (in its fundamental principles) what Colonel Harry Chamberlin taught in the United States and what riders of his caliber practice in other countries. As I have pointed out already, many details of artistic riding and schooling can be and should be greatly simplified for the use of amateurs, but many of their fundamentals cannot be discarded.

A year ago a very interesting book entitled CONCOURS HIPPIQUE, written by Y. Benoist-Gironière, was published in France. Its subject is very specific—jumping in horse shows, and its form is very original. The author makes various statements which he submits to sixteen outstanding riders of different countries (our Colonel Earl F. Thomson among them) for comment and criticism. On page 32 we read (the translation is mine):

"Before undertaking work over obstacles let us be sure of good (basic) schooling . . . to make an unschooled horse jump with a rider is to go out to meet trouble and to provoke resistances which are frequently permanently compromising."

And here are comments on this statement by three internationally known horsemen:

1) "Preliminary schooling is of first importance. Certain pre-war teams which we know well and which had very great success owe the better part of their victories to it; it was the basis of them. This schooling which is to be undertaken with a young, green horse should put him forward on the bit, balance him and render him absolutely supple and obedient to

the hands and legs. This work done, it will be possible to ride him agreeably in competitions on a snaffle and not on a full bridle, martingale, pulley or other forcible means which are always harmful." (Commented by Colonel Haccius, Vice President of the International Equestrian Federation. Former member of the Swiss International team.)

2) "This is absolutely correct; the difficulties encountered in competitions are almost always the result of incomplete schooling." (Commented by Colonel Lombardo di Cumia of the Italian International team.)

3) "This phrase should be written in letters of steel on all jumping courses . . . basic schooling is necessary everyday. Lack of schooling was the reason why many good jumpers couldn't be used with success." (Commented by Colonel Jose M. Cavanillas, captain of the Spanish International team.)

Any logical thinking about the horse's jump is bound to bring one to the conclusion that the main components of a good performance over an obstacle are:

1) A quiet, relaxed but alert approach.
2) Boldness based on assurance.
3) Ability to figure the take-off.
4) Powerful thrusts with the forehand and hindquarters.
5) Acrobatic use of the back, neck and head.
6) Efficient folding of the legs.
7) A quiet, relaxed going away after landing.

Out of these items the quiet approach and landing, the strong thrusts and the acrobatics largely depend on the basic schooling which develops the horse's cooperation, relaxation when ridden, balance, strength and agility. When teaching your horse to jump you must constantly have in mind the components of a good performance and what produces them.

There are several points which we should discuss before beginning to examine the schooling program; one of them is the use of force when working and later when riding a horse. Naturally, at least at the beginning of schooling in general, and during the first lesson of every new movement in particular, because the horse does not understand what is wanted of him, or because what is asked requires more effort than he cares to make, he may resist. A talented, tactful, experienced trainer will probably succeed in avoiding open revolt and will greatly diminish the amount of even mild resistance, but still some will take place; no matter how good the teacher, on occasions his pupil will misunderstand him. In combatting these misunderstandings and resistance the trainer, of course, will have to enclose the horse between his legs and hands and with the various combinations of these aids, as described in the chapters on control, force him into the execution of this or that movement. Such moments are bound to occur not only at the beginning of schooling but even in the advanced stages of it. Their number can be tactfully diminished but they cannot be completely eliminated; the question is only whether the combination of aids which *forces* the horse into the execution of a certain movement should be regarded as an ultimate in schooling, and later in riding, or whether the lessons should aim toward replacing force with the *lightest signals* to which the horse can be trained to respond. For instance, in the canter departure on the left lead (in the case of a cross-country horse) what is better as a *final* aim? Is it better that even a completely schooled horse should start a canter on the left lead only after the rider has closed-in both legs to establish contact, then with his left hand turned the head slightly to the left, at the same time moving both hands to the right, and ranged the quarters somewhat to the left with his right leg? Or, is it better when, while going free on contact or loose reins a *slight* touch with the left rein, so light that it will not displace the head, and an urge with the right leg, so light that it may not range the quarters, will be a *memorized signal* sufficient to make the horse start the canter on the left lead? In other words should schooling aim at a constant, *forceful domination* of the horse by the rider, or should it attempt to establish the *cooperation of the horse?*

I believe in the latter. I believe that a good rider is not merely a man who, by means of physical dexterity, is always able to place the horse in this or that position in order to obtain this or that movement, but is also a person who has access to the mentality of his horse. Granting that great Dressage or jumping performances on an international level cannot be expected on the strength of the horse's mental cooperation alone, I believe that a normally good performance in the hunting field and in amateur shows is more easily achieved by putting stress on the horse's mental cooperation. Only great riders, riding really well-schooled horses, can ride forcibly without contracting the horse both mentally and physically. Average riders (with whom this book is concerned), riding merely decently-schooled horses, are much better off if they don't try to imitate the best equestrians, and realize their own and their horses' limitations. As a matter of fact, all great riders make constant use of the horse's cooperation and this is one of the reasons why in truly great Dressage performances the spectators cannot see the activity of the aids; they are too mild to be easily observed. But this mental cooperation is rarely spoken of in our age, probably because ours is a mechanical era and comparatively few amateur riders of today are interested in the horse's mental processes. Our modern humanitarian approach to the animal may, paradoxically enough, not always be a really understanding one.

As an illustration of how strongly cooperation can be established in the horse I would like to tell you of what happened to me just yesterday. I have a huge Irish hunter *Barnaby Bright* who, for various reasons, had not been ridden for eighteen months and, pleasantly loafing at pasture, had had plenty of opportunity to forget everything he had ever known. Lately he had been mildly exercised a few times and three days ago I mounted him to see how much schooling he still remembered. On the first day, during the whole half hour that I rode him he had a constant and strong inclination to send me to hell but, on the second day, bribed by a piece of sugar for every well-executed movement, he went through his whole program; this, by the way, is somewhat more than is required in the schooling test of the Three-Day-Event; he did two tracks at the trot and gallop and even the four changes of leads in four strides in response to slight efforts of my legs and hands. The most amazing thing to me was his semi-collected trot, which he did brilliantly on very light contact. During it I could even drop all tension on the reins and he would still go semi-collectedly for the next five or six strides, after which I could feel that he was thinking of stopping it and was asking me—"isn't it enough?" Then, all that was needed was to re-establish contact, urge him forward onto it with the legs; he would flex and would continue again for a few steps on loose reins, with little aid from my legs, practically by himself. And all this after eighteen months of probably not thinking of being ridden.

This excellent memory which the horse possesses is the ally of a good trainer and the enemy of a bad one. The horse will remember unpleasant experiences as easily and as tenaciously as pleasant ones. So beware.

I know from practice that anyone with merely moderate abilities can school a horse by emphasizing mental cooperation. I also know from the same personal experience of a teacher that the same riders if they don't make use of the mentality of the horse, and try to dominate him by mechanical aids alone, have unhappy, stiffly-moving and often resisting horses under them. The fundamental aim of my method is the gradual turning of the often necessarily forceful riding of the early lessons into obedience to mild signals, the horse performing "on his own."

I realize, of course, that in some cases the above described refinement of riding is impractical; I personally was familiarly acquainted with one such case—the army or, to be more specific, the Russian cavalry of fifty years ago. Since the bulk of the ranks consisted of troopers who were not sportsmen, who were taught riding for war and not as an art or even a game, and who actually didn't have any time to think of riding or to practice it outside lessons and riding in military formation, riding in the army could not be taught on the principles on which this book is based; there, naturally, the forceful aids had to be dominant, and a truly good performance could not be aimed at.

Some riders, not in sympathy with my method in general, and particularly those who were brought up in the spirit of precise Dressage, will probably object to what I have just said, maintaining that the comparative passiveness of the rider and freedom of the horse will result in lack of precision in the execution of different schooling movements. They are right; they will. And this brings us to the second fundamental point of my method of schooling.

All the schooling movements which you would find in the program are merely the means to develop a cross-country horse or a jumper; they are not an aim in themselves. For instance, when two tracking, you are merely giving the horse an exercise which will tend to develop the engagement of the hindquarters and the extension of the shoulders, as well as general agility—all of them important in jumping. But you don't practice two tracks just to obtain perfection in this movement. Such perfection is the aim of the supreme form of *ring riding*—Dressage; it has nothing to do with the preparation of a horse for the field. *In any movement all the value of the gymnastics is exhausted long before perfection is reached.* The same goes for the obedience of the horse; one naturally wishes to have a cooperative horse, but an automaton is unnecessary. For instance, in the Full Dressage of the Olympic Games, while standing still the horse must be absolutely immobile; if he turns his head to the side or moves one of his legs a few inches it is considered a fault. Obviously this doesn't mean anything in cross-country riding.

Aiming at complete precision in the execution of schooling movements can, besides being unnecessary, also be an evil. For, as an example, *perfection* in the flying changes of lead can be obtained only through full collection. So if one wishes to reach perfection in flying changes of lead the horse must be worked a great deal at a collected canter and so much of a collected gait may give the horse a habit of moving with comparatively short, high steps. Thus the main aim of preparing the horse for cross-country and jumping—efficient movement—will be defeated. When following my program of schooling never lose track of the main aims and never confuse important things with mere details.

The above two points: 1) The horse's cooperation and 2) considering ring exercises merely as gymnastics to develop efficient movement, are the most important for you to remember. Besides them there are others, rather common ones, which are to be found in many books on schooling. They are:

1) *Be tactful.* Don't ask anything while the horse is upset; for teaching the horse a new movement choose a moment when he is in a cooperative mood. Never provoke a struggle, and do everything to avoid one when you feel it coming. Always be a sympathetic teacher and not the conqueror of a brute.

2) *Be patient.* Try all sorts of means of explaining to the horse what you want of him (of the two you have the more brains and this is your part of the game). When the horse refuses to comply with your orders the doubt should flash through your mind, "perhaps I did not explain clearly enough to him what I wanted;" you simply must learn the horse's language.

3) *Be moderate.* Never forget to consider the horse's mental and physical fatigue; each lesson is a step in the gradual development of the

horse and every lesson must be only very slightly more difficult than the preceding one.

4) *Be analytical.* When resistance is encountered try to determine its causes; perhaps a certain day is an "off day" for the horse, or some of his muscles hurt after too much of some one exercise on the previous day; or possibly he merely does not concentrate, or he is really ill, etc. Each one of these conditions will require different action on your part. Get in the habit after dismounting of reviewing the lesson in your mind.

5) *Be persistent.* If your analysis leads you to believe that there are no legitimate causes for the horse to misunderstand or to resist you, then coolly, but stubbornly insist on the execution of what you wish.

6) *Be grateful.* Give the horse frequent rests; never fail to recompense him either with patting, or soothing words or a rest or a bit of something tasty each time he cooperates.

7) *Be just.* Never punish a horse merely because you are irritated; if it is necessary, punish severely at times, but never angrily. If on a certain day you feel generally angry with your horse, then the best you can do is to forget about schooling for that day. Punishment should be the result of cool judgment and not of hot emotions. Both punishments and rewards must be administered very rationally; only then will the horse learn to know what is good and what is bad in his behavior.

Here are two more points to discuss before we reach the program; they are the seat and the equipment. Naturally, I expect you to use the forward seat, but I also hope that you are not going to use it pedantically. If at certain periods of schooling you should require a strong use of the legs, lengthen your stirrups (the forward seat for schooling). If, in teaching a certain movement, change of leads for instance, you should feel you could do better if seated loosely, do so, etc. Don't try to a have a picture seat but rather a workman's seat; your seat is a means and not an end.

Your equipment should be a plain hunting snaffle and nothing else. It will suffice for semi-collection with flexions. Don't use a full bridle for schooling unless you are a *very good* rider. For schooling a cross-country horse it is a too complicated, a too refined and an unnecessary instrument. If, after you have schooled your horse on a snaffle, you should find that he is hard to control in the hunting field, then put a Pelham or a full bridle on him, but merely as a stronger brake. There is no special technique in using the full bridle just for this purpose. This is the only case when with some high-strung horses a full bridle will be necessary even after being schooled and well-ridden according to my method, while you will never have use for martingales or other gadgets.

Many riders use martingales on the slightest provocation; some merely because they believe it dresses up the horse. I personally belong to the category of those who are ashamed to use one. It always seems to me that the presence of a martingale betrays the fact that one either failed to give a correct attitude to the horse's neck in schooling, or that one has bad hands. As a matter of fact, I pride myself on the fact that I do not remember the day when I used a martingale for the last time. Looking upon it purely practically, the question resolves itself into the following points:

1) In order to accomplish anything in improving the horse's head carriage a *standing* martingale must be adjusted so short that the balancing gestures of the horse's neck are impeded. A long standing martingale is only good for saving the rider's nose.

2) The ordinary adjustment of the *running* martingale is such that it pulls the reins down the moment the rider uses them and makes the hands heavy.

3) Horses very often throw up the head to fight against the martingale. Lately I had a class in which three riders were mounted on horses with bad positions of the neck and head and hence with martingales. In half an hour I removed the martingales and in two days every one of these horses (all young ones) was moving with neck and head extended forward. In these two days I succeeded in calming these horses through softening the hands of their riders.

Once in a while, of course, one meets with exceptions.

To all the suggestions to be found in this chapter I would like to add one more, which I have left for the last because I think it the most important and did not want it to be lost among the others: *Occasionally stop to consider what your horse thinks of you.*

A short while ago I was giving a course in schooling to a few of the best riders in a women's college. These girls, one at a time, showed me the horses on which they had been working for two or three months. The routine of presentation of every horse began with the rider telling me her horse's past history, her analysis of his character and physique and what she was doing to improve the horse.

Among these horses was a five-year-old thoroughbred possessing (as I later learned) remarkable jumping ability; he had arrived at the college two months previously as a completely upset horse. To use an appropriate expression, he was "walking on his eyebrows." Obviously his jumping ability had been his undoing and he had probably been forced to jump anything in sight at the age of three and had accordingly become a nervous wreck. It had taken the student all of two months to calm and stabilize him and, naturally being impatient, she was rather angry with her horse and, among other things, said to me, "he is a fool." Then her very wise instructor (Miss Harriet H. Rogers) interrupted her and said: "He is not a fool but he thinks that all human beings are."

Now, in the spirit of all that has been said, I am about to present the program of schooling. This program, conceived for an average horse, may not entirely fit yours; you may have to change the time schedule as well as the order of exercises, so, as I suggested, instead of following this program rigidly accept it rather as an indication and adjust it to suit your individual problem. It assumes that the horse to be schooled is at least nearing four years.

CHAPTER XV

The Program of Forward Schooling

This chapter is entirely devoted to an explanation of the schooling program for your horse. When using this program the following points are to be considered:

1) This program in its entirety is for hunters and jumpers; in the case of country hacks all the jumping, with the exception of stabilization over 2' obstacles, can be eliminated. You need to preserve the latter as your horse may have to jump a tree fallen across the path or some such thing. Long, fast gallops are also unnecessary for a hack and in his case the level of execution of all exercises can be somewhat lowered.

2) The division of the work into nine periods of a month each is an approximation which is expected to suit the average horse schooled by the rider with some schooling experience. You may find that in your case as little as seven months or as much as twelve months may be required to cover the program without upsetting your horse mentally or crippling him physically. But even if nine months happens to be the best time for you, you may find that switching an exercise here and there from one month to another brings better results. If your actual work shows that this is so, do it by all means. And, I repeat: in general, don't consider the program a rigid rule; it is meant to be merely a guide in your thinking about the gradual physical development of your horse.

3) The titles opposite each month refer to the new exercises introduced in the course of it; only in some cases do these titles fully describe the work of the month, but they may help you to memorize the general plan of schooling.

4) Only the newly introduced exercises are mentioned in each month of the program; in actuality movements introduced during a certain month occupy less time than the work on bettering those already learned.

5) Before beginning each new movement read the description of it in Chapter IX on What Is a Good Performance of the Horse, and the technique of its execution in Chapters XI and XII on Learning Control on Intermediate Level and Advanced Control.

While following this program always keep in mind the general philosophy of schooling which you will find in Chapter XIV on Almost Anyone Can Learn Forward Schooling.

6) This program is conceived for a horse about four years old.

7) The whole program should be executed on a regular hunting snaffle; no martingales or other supplementary contrivances should be used.

NOTES ON THE PROGRAM OF FORWARD SCHOOLING

1ST MONTH (LONGEING).

Longeing. Schooling begins on a longe, teaching obedience to voice commands for a walk, trot, canter, halt, slowing down or increase of speed. These are the first lessons in cooperation. If, when mounted a month later, the horse is already obedient to the voice, then when riding him along the wall of the ring the rider will be able to control him primarily by voice commands without poking him roughly in the ribs or pulling heavily on his mouth. It will take time for the horse to learn the mild leg and hand signals and the efficient way of teaching them is with the help of the voice, gradually transferring the horse from it to legs and hands; everything should be done to establish obedience to regular aids without dulling the horse's sides and mouth.

The technique of longeing is very simple. First you have to explain to the horse that you wish him to go around you on a circle of the radius of the length of the longe. You can do this by leading the horse on a large circle and little by little lengthening the longe and, with the help of the whip pointed toward the horse step away from him. Or you may ask someone to help you by leading the horse around while you stand in the middle of the circle. Teaching this may take you twenty minutes, or, if you are awkward about it or the horse resists, a couple of days. You may have a little extra trouble with some horses who will go willingly to one side and not to another. When longeing to the left hold the longe in the left hand with the whole arm leading the movement. At first you will need the whip to urge the horse forward simultaneously with giving the voice-command. To prevent the horse from cutting down the circle point the whip toward the shoulder. If the horse disobeys your command to slow down or to stop, quickly shorten the longe and moving toward the horse hold the whip in front of his face. Probably in about ten days you will require the whip rarely and it will be lying at your feet in case of need. The horse should respect the whip but not be panicky about it. Hence it is good practice to accustom him to it by gently patting his body with it at the beginning of the first half dozen lessons.

Never start your lesson if the horse, feeling fresh at first, bucks and romps around you. Don't punish him for this but let him get it out of his system; then start to work. But if, during the lesson, the horse, for instance, gallops when you want him to trot, disobeys your voice and the signal with the whip pointed in front of his face, then give him a jerk with the longe.

In short, that is all. You don't have to hold your leading arm precisely in a certain position or your whip at a special angle (some writers make a terrible fuss about such things); the essential is to establish understanding between you and your horse. In other words, primarily to use your brains and have sympathy for your pupil.

Longe on the cavesson. A halter is too loose, while attaching a longe to the ring of the bit of a bridle spoils a horse's mouth and makes the jerks with the heavy longe too severe.

In about two weeks, when the horse walks, trots and canters quietly and evenly around you, begin crossing bars laid on the ground. As soon as the horse responds to this without any excitement gradually raise the bars to about 1'6".

When longeing over a fence, a circle is too small (even at the full extension of the longe) to give a *green* horse a straight approach long enough for a comfortable take-off. Therefore, when longeing over obstacles, adopt

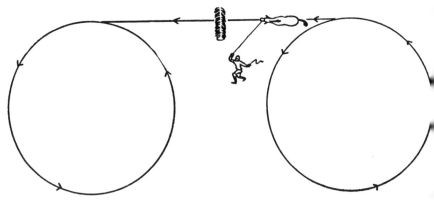

Pic. 78.   Longeing over fences. (*See text*)

the following procedure: first, to stabilize the horse at the gait, make two or three circles about 20' away from the jump on the take-off side. Then let the horse go straight for the last 20', running parallel to him yourself and keeping slightly ahead of him, leading him forward with the longe. It is particularly at the moment of the jump itself that the longe must be ahead of the horse; otherwise you will pull him back, although by rapidly letting out the longe you can considerably diminish the ill effects of this. Don't stop running as soon as the horse has cleared the obstacle. Run another 20' or so, and then either gradually stop the horse or make a couple of circles to return the horse to the quiet movement of the approach (Picture 78).

And what about jumping in a chute or free in a small ring? I think any kind of free jumping is good for the horse and I do not use these two methods, simply because when the horse is completely free I rarely can (with my voice) regulate his gaits and speeds. On the longe this is in the hands of the trainer and the exercise becomes a stepping stone to the next lessons in stabilization, while on the obstacle itself the horse is completely free. But I have seen quite a few horses which performed completely free in a small ring, obeying the trainer's voice commands. They were doing all the gaits, changes of directions, and jumping calmly at any gait indicated by the trainer. If you can do this with your horse, so much the better.

When teaching a young horse to jump on the longe bear in mind that you do it partly because his natural balance under the weight of the rider has not yet been restored even at ordinary gaits, and you cannot expect him to jump athletically when mounted; this will have an opportunity to develop later when general schooling has improved his balance. Hence, at an early stage the most that you can do mounted is to teach the horse to approach fences (bars on the ground) quietly. A correct mental attitude is the basis for future physical efforts.

In many cases I am unable to start the schooling on a longe. Many of my junior pupils lack the strength to handle a young playful horse on a longe, while others are soon bored with longeing, as they are naturally eager to work their green horses mounted. Since the young green horses acquired by junior riders have almost always already been ridden, longeing can in these cases be skipped and voice commands and early cooperation can be taught from the saddle. An adult, however, who has acquired a truly green horse, will certainly benefit by starting on a longe.

In the case of a colt which is apt to be fresh when first mounted it is important that he either be turned out before the lesson or that an adult longe him in order to get the bucking out of his system.

Hacking to cool off. Each of your longeing lessons, with the frequent pauses for rest, should last from half an hour to forty-five minutes and if your colt, which I assume is already broken to the saddle, is in good physical condition I would suggest mounting him after longeing and taking him outside, preferably in company with an old and quiet horse, for a relaxed walk. But in such cases avoid as much as possible using your legs and hands; remember the horse doesn't know their meaning yet.

Mounting, leading, etc. You should make use of the rest periods to teach the horse to stand absolutely quietly when you mount or dismount; to stand calmly while you are holding him dismounted; to walk by your side without fuss when you are leading him and so forth. It would be nice to teach your horse to follow you when free for, after all, this month is the time when you lay the foundation for a friendly relationship between you and your horse.

2ND MONTH (STABILIZATION).

Stabilization. To stabilize a horse means to teach him to maintain *by himself* even gaits on completely loose reins. This is a very important point to achieve. A horse stabilized at gaits somewhat slower than ordinary ones, will later on obediently maintain higher speeds on very light contact. Stabilization is the basis for a future soft mouth, which consists in certain physical responses based on mental cooperation. Cooperation established so early in the game will be rarely forgotten by the horse.

While stabilization at a walk and trot is taught along the walls of the arena, stabilization at the canter, a couple of weeks later, would be wisely begun on a large circle approximately the size of the longeing circle or slightly larger—going nowhere the horse will probably canter quietly. Stabilization is achieved on the strength of voice commands learned the previous month.

Stabilization of the approach to the obstacle is taught simultaneously and is begun by approaching the bar on the ground, gradually raising it; if lucky, you may reach the height of 1'6" or 2' at all gaits in the course of this month. Don't fail to see the woods for the trees and remember that your aim at this period is not a clean or a high jump but merely a quiet approach. If, for instance, when your horse approaches a 1' obstacle at a trot he merely trots over it instead of jumping, so much the better; for this means that the horse, being relaxed mentally, recognizes the height of the fence and does not waste energy on more effort than is necessary to negotiate it. At this stage you are not teaching the horse to jump but merely to approach obstacles. Don't slight this part of schooling and you will never have pulling or rushing horses. Work over Cavaletti may begin during this month.

It is very possible that in your community the horse is started jumping in a very different way and hence the above method may seem very strange to you. But just the same I would suggest your giving it very careful consideration, for it is the one on which practically all modern authorities agree. Colonel H. Chamberlin, for instance, who made or influenced the making of many outstanding international jumpers says:

"After about two weeks' jumping instruction on the longe, mounted work over the same obstacles that were employed for leading and longeing may begin. When mounted, the trainer, beginning at the walk, rehearses thoroughly all work previously done on the longe. This is done despite the fact that the colt, when on the longe, by this time may be cantering over small obstacles about two feet high. The points of most concern, when mounted work starts, are: allowing absolute liberty to head and neck; maintaining the same speed and gait before and after passing an obstacle; and approaching the centre of each obstacle perpendicularly. The rider should hold with one hand either to the pommel or to a strap around the horse's neck, in order to prevent being displaced and so alarming and hurting the colt through jerking his mouth or jarring his back. *The reins, without exception, should be loose and floating when the colt actually crosses the obstacle.* In fact, the reins should be floating *at all times in these early lessons."* (TRAINING HUNTERS, JUMPERS AND HACKS, English edition 1947, page 126.)

Many years ago I witnessed the Chilean Army Team work their horses before the show in Madison Square Garden. Two or three of their horses were made to do the following exercise: while galloping to an obstacle at a good clip the rider would drop his reins about 40' away from it and either say "whoa," at which command the horse would stop in front of the fence, or cluck with his tongue, and the horse would go over it. The little control of the hands which these horses required resulted in their free-going and consequently natural way of jumping. This was in the middle thirties, when the Chilean Army Team was winning a great deal.

When stabilizing the horse don't use your aids in the standard manner; your horse does not know them yet. Instead, remember that during the longeing the horse has learned to know two kinds of punishment: A jerk with the longe for going too fast, and a crack with the whip or a touch with it for refusing to go ahead. Utilize these punishments when mounted, but do everything possible to avoid having to resort to them often. Then your practical method of stabilizing the horse will come to the following: let us assume that you wish to start a trot; you give a voice command, if the horse responds, you pat him, if not, you repeat the command two or three times, each time raising your voice; if there is still no response you use the whip lightly, preferably on the shoulder. When the horse refuses to slow down from the voice you tighten the reins for a couple of seconds and if still there is no response you punish him with a slight jerk. The advice to punish always sounds cruel in print and, in the hands of a stupid trainer, it may actually be so. But you will be surprised how rarely you will have to punish the horse if you use your ingenuity in explaining clearly to him what you wish.

It would be wise, in the latter stages of stabilization at a walk and trot, to practice changing, at first gradually and then abruptly, your schooling position to a galloping one, accustoming the horse to such sudden redistributions of the rider's weight as is sometimes necessary in actual approaches to the fence. A horse accustomed to this will not rush madly forward the moment you begin the gallop and change your seat accordingly.

Transfer from voice-commands to hand-and-leg signals. Stabilization is closely followed by another lesson, the transfer from voice-commands to hand-and-leg signals. This is achieved in the following manner: for instance, you wish to change from a trot to a walk; in the tone of voice to which the horse is accustomed you say "walk" and at the same time gently pull on the reins. If there is no response, repeat "walk" as many times as necessary, simultaneously increasing the tension on the reins. Don't forget to pat when the horse obeys. Another example: Suppose you wish to start a canter from a trot; you give a voice-command, if necessary repeating it a second and third time, raising your voice each time, and at the same time you slightly urge with your legs. Gradually the horse will associate certain voice-commands with certain leg-and-hand actions and you can begin to lower your voice little by little and eventually to drop it entirely.

If you are a good teacher and can explain your wishes clearly to the horse then you will succeed in replacing the voice by very *mild* leg-and-hand signals. Normally your first hand signal will be varying tension on both reins to slow down or stop the horse, while the first leg signal will be the signal with both legs used simultaneously to urge the horse forward into a walk or trot.

Guiding lesson. During the same month you begin to teach the horse to turn in obedience to the action of one rein (leading rein) making *very wide* turns, circles, half-circles or changing directions diagonally across the arena; these constitute what are called "guiding lessons."

Outside of the short moments when there is tension on the reins because you are giving an order, riding during this month should be on loose reins, because the main aim of the month is stabilization of gaits.

Stabilization of a "rusher." If you have the bad luck to own a horse which rushes his fences and you would like to teach him to approach the obstacles quietly, then, as a rule, the usual routine as applied to colts must be changed. The method used will have to be different for the reason that many horses which rush fences may be absolutely quiet and even stabilized at gaits. Rushing fences may be a habit which does not match the rest of the horse's performance and a horse perfectly sensible in general may, due to unfortunate experiences, lose his head the moment he sees an obstacle. In this case you have to take up teaching a quiet approach to fences as a special problem. For this purpose you may use Cavaletti, which are described later in the chapter (fifth month), or you may resort to the following method: start a trot, aiming at obtaining a slow, sleepy gait on loose reins; then start to move toward a very low obstacle, perhaps merely a bar on the ground and, the moment the horse increases his speed, take him away on a circle (a wide one), sometimes to the right, sometimes to the left. At the end of each circle, when again approaching the fence, watch for the slightest increase of speed: if it comes, make another circle. (Picture 79) You may have to make twenty or thirty circles before even stepping over a bar on the ground. The circles, I repeat again, must be wide, something like 60′ in diameter; small circles may excite the horse. The fence, without wings, must be placed in the middle of the ring, thus enabling you to circle to the right and to the left, sometimes after approaching rather closely to the obstacle. The monotony of these circles can be broken by halts or halts with a few steps of backing at that time in the circle when you are facing the jump. In very bad cases you may have to confine your first lessons to a walk or you may start every lesson with one. In many cases Cavaletti are the efficient way of correcting a rusher who is generally stabilized except on jumps; at least they may be very helpful at the beginning of the course, while circles, halting and backing may be added later to an approach to a normal, single fence. In any case, unless you have real luck, reclaiming a bad jumper is a tedious and disappointing business and in his case the normally simple problem of stabilization of the approach to an obstacle may turn out to be a complicated one.

Halts. Don't forget to halt the horse frequently; it will save you a lot of trouble later if, from the beginning, you establish the habit of standing

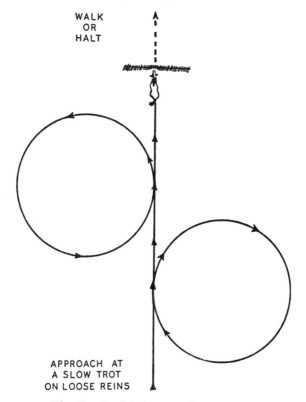

WALK
OR
HALT

APPROACH AT
A SLOW TROT
ON LOOSE REINS

Pic. 79.   Reclaiming a rusher. (*See text*)

quietly. Therefore adopt the routine of standing still for about ten counts or longer, if the horse is fidgety. *Frequent halts should remain on the program throughout the schooling,* unless your horse is of a sluggish nature.

Especially at the beginning and, as a matter of fact always, halts should be gradual. This means that if you wish to halt the horse at a trot you first bring him to a walk, make a couple of strides of it and then halt. If you halt from the canter, include a moment of trot followed by a moment of walk. Emergency halts, of course, are not governed by the above rule.

COMMONSENSE HORSEMANSHIP

With the improvement of the balance and agility of the horse the transition gaits can be shortened in their duration and, during the last months of schooling, when the horse knows semi-collection, the transition gaits can in some cases be eliminated altogether without jeopardizing the softness of the horse. In such cases an abrupt stop will come naturally without your asking for it. The horse will do it for you by himself just because he is equal to it, perhaps without even flexing at the poll.

Longeing. It would be a good practice to longe the horse for about twenty minutes before mounting him. Thus you can get rid of all the bucks the horse may have in him on certain days and establish cooperation before putting your foot into the stirrup. Throughout your schooling here and there you may resort to the longe. You will find it useful at times when, for one reason or another, the horse needs merely light exercise; or when the horse hasn't been worked for a few days and is extra fresh and a pasture is not available where he can be turned loose to work off his excess energy. In this respect I don't think it is wise in general to mount fresh horses and give them the experience, which can easily turn into a habit, of misbehaving while mounted. This is not the time to show your boldness but rather your understanding of the horse's nature and your clever use of this understanding.

You might also occasionally like to longe the horse over obstacles, even during advanced stages of schooling. There may be many reasons for this. Sometimes, for instance, a horse, after being jerked inadvertently several times on the jump may start jumping with the neck stiffly up. A longe may help you to restore his natural balancing gestures.

Hacking. At this period your hacking should be at a *walk only* and on loose reins whenever possible. It is so important to implant in the horse's mind that going out is not an exciting business. If your horse becomes nervous when alone then hack as long as necessary in company with an old, quiet horse.

Don't think that you are wasting time by hacking at a walk; it is a very important gait in the schooling and conditioning of a horse. A fast walk hardens tendons, flexes and relaxes all the joints, develops calmness and can be kept up for some time without unduly fatiguing the horse. No matter how far along you are in schooling, a walk is never to be neglected.

3RD MONTH (IMPULSE FORWARD).

Riding on contact. Loose reins whenever possible are gradually replaced by riding on *soft* contact. The contact should be so soft that while it is being established it does not slow down the horse. Sometimes the voice or the legs may be necessary to prevent slowing down.

When first changing from loose reins to contact, sneak up on this contact so gradually with your hands that neither is the gait disturbed nor the position of the horse's head and neck changed in the slightest. The same conditions should prevail when changing from contact to loose reins—the horse should continue to maintain the same attitude, gait and speed.

When teaching the horse to go on contact, continue to ride about one-third of the time on loose reins. As a matter of fact, it is a very good rule to adhere to throughout your schooling and later in your riding; it rests the horse's mouth and keeps it soft.

To establish contact when riding a sluggish horse an almost constant use of legs will be necessary (until the impulse forward is developed). The legs should be used merely to establish contact and to keep the horse alert, but not for increasing the speed; this should remain the ordinary one.

Impulse forward. After approximately two weeks of riding on soft contact begin to develop impulse forward, which means quick, energetic but *quiet* response to the rider's *mild* legs. Teaching this requires tact and can hardly be satisfactorily explained in print. It is something like this: suppose you wish to increase the speed of the trot; you have given a mild signal with your legs and the horse has not responded. By no means begin to use the legs harder and harder, ending with a series of kicks—it will eventually dull the horse's sides. Instead, the moment that there is no response, give the whip; then repeat the procedure several times if necessary. In my own experience I don't remember a case where I did not succeed in obtaining good results within fifteen minutes and without exciting the horse in the least. A daily repetition of the lesson should establish a decent, although at first awkward, impulse forward within approximately ten days.

Don't confuse impulse with speed. Impulse is keenness, alertness, energy of movement, willingness to go forward; it may or may not be transformed into speed. A fast movement may have impulse, which means energy of action combined with reserve energy, or it may not. On the other hand, a slow movement may have plenty of impulse. In the case of a schooled horse, impulse can be controlled with soft hands. While in the case of a badly-ridden, unschooled horse it degenerates into mere pulling.

During a movement with impulse (as always) the neck and head must remain extended; to be exact, the neck should naturally come up a little but the head must remain out.

Moving forward on the bit. When impulse forward is added to riding on contact then you have a horse which begins to move on the bit.

Again, don't forget that a cross-country horse must take the bit with the neck and head extended (not arched and with the chin in). The tension on the reins should still be light but somewhat stronger than when riding on comparatively passive contact; at first the horse may resist by tossing his head or by trying to jerk the reins out of your hands. Considering the discomfort of the horse, the periods on the bit should be very short at first; one long wall of the arena is plenty. Riding on the bit greatly improves the movement by making the horse move *in one piece,* for the horse takes the bit as the result of the increased energy in the action of the hindquarters.

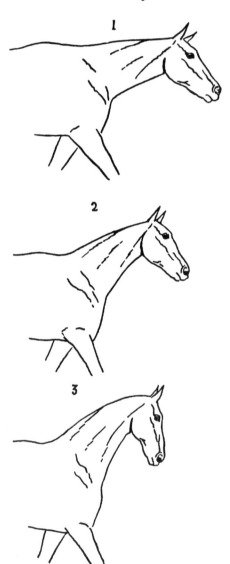

1. The average attitude of the neck and head that the colt should have at the beginning of the schooling and for some time afterwards.

2. The carriage of the neck and head that the horse should gradually acquire through schooling.

3. An incorrect carriage that a field horse should never have except during short periods of semi-collection in schooling.

Pic. 80

You may have the feeling that already during the first lesson the horse has taken the bit, but he will not have taken it. The horse may increase his leaning on the bit, but it will be a long time before the impulse starting in the hindquarters and travelling through the back and neck will reach the mouth, thus uniting the horse without disturbing his *relaxed attitude*. As a matter of fact, during all your nine months of schooling you will be preoccupied with moving on the bit *energetically* and softly. And it will take you a long time before you will be really able to feel it yourself.

Years ago I had a very able pupil who upon learning advanced riding and schooling, spent one summer training three hunters. She was schooling them almost every day, of course greatly concerned with teaching them to go on the bit. It was late in the summer when one day, while I was watching her school one of her hunters, she suddenly stopped and said to me: "You know, something very wonderful has just happened to me. For the first time I have really felt what having the horse on the bit means." I am recounting this little incident not to discourage you but to caution you—there are many degrees of being on the bit, beginning with a worthless one and going on to very valuable ones. Having the horse on the bit energetically and at the same time softly is one of the finesses of riding on the advanced level. On the intermediate level, soft contact or having the horse mildly on the bit is all that is required.

Coming back. The development of the impulse forward and of going on the bit must be taught simultaneously with an obedient, *relaxed* slowing down, which is called "coming back" and which is obtained by means of "give and take." Don't fail to observe this rule, for if you should push the horse more and more ahead without developing coming back at the same time, you are taking the chance of making a puller. If you are tactful in teaching the coming back then, during the next month, while increasing and decreasing speeds at a trot the horse by himself may begin to flex in the mouth when slowing down. Coming back exercises, usually practiced at a trot, should include frequent walks and halts.

Entering the corners. This is an exercise which primarily teaches the horse obedience to the "rein of indirect opposition in front of the withers"; although this rein is not used alone but in combination with the inside leg and with the outside rein acting as a leading rein.

This exercise can be efficient only if the corners of your ring are right angles; an oval ring does not present the problem. At first you perform the exercise at a walk and in the following manner: suppose you take the track to the right along the wall; when you are about 15′ from the corner the horse normally begins gradually to leave the wall to cut the corner on a smooth arc. Prevent him from doing this by moving both your hands to the left to press the forehand to the wall and use your right leg to keep the body at the wall. In this case your right rein acting as a rein of opposition in front of the withers will not only keep the forehand at the wall, but will also slightly turn the head to the right— the attitude which you wish to have when turning to the right. When you have prevented the horse from cutting the corner lead him into it, entering it as deeply as it is possible while preserving enough room to make *a free, relaxed turn*. It is very important to teach this combination of the reins to the horse at an early period of schooling, as it will be used quite often in different movements such as the canter departure, sometimes circling, etc. In an oval arena teach this by making the horse move flat against the fence.

Canter departure disregarding the lead. In early schooling a calm canter departure, with a horse holding his neck and head stretched forward and *straight*, is more important than obtaining a specific lead. Attempts to do the latter as early as the third month of schooling may make the horse tense.

Jumping (boldness). As to jumping, the big item is still the approach and the next step you take is not toward raising the height (although you may gradually raise it by half a foot) , but toward the establishment of a *quiet and bold* approach to obstacles of different shapes and colors. If these are kept low, well within the present abilities of the horse, then the fact that the bar is red, or that it is a picket fence instead of the so-far familiar post-and-rail, will rarely make the horse nervous or inclined to refuse. The necessity of showing a new obstacle to your horse is thus eliminated (which is extremely important) and your horse learns to face any kind of unfamiliar obstacle boldly; some day in the hunting field this will give you great satisfaction and make you proud of your horse. As a part of this work, frequently change the position of your fences. Don't use solid fences (see next month's text).

Hacking. You should not work the horse every day in the ring; there is no question but that the ring-exercises are boring and fatiguing to the horse and he may begin to resist just because of this. Work four times a week in the ring and on the other two days take him for a walk with an occasional trot in the fields and woods. And I hope you have a pasture; for if you have, you will have a happier and more cheerfully working pupil.

Counter Canter. See text for the 5th month.

4TH MONTH (AGILITY).

Now the horse has been mounted for two months; he has gained in strength and begins to acquire the knack of carrying you. This strength supporting this knack means better balance. But, of course, the retrieving of natural balance under the weight of the rider is far from achieved. It will take all of nine months; and all the exercises in this program are helpful toward this end. The growing general agility of the horse will be particularly helpful. But when I say "general agility" the phrase is so truly general that it doesn't mean much. More specifically it consists primarily of three kinds of agility: longitudinal flexibility, lateral flexibility and ability for skilful lateral displacement.

Longitudinal flexibility means the ability to shorten and extend the back and neck. Its presence will make the balancing efforts on a straight line much more effective. Lateral flexibility is the ability to bend the spinal column laterally. It will help the balancing efforts on turns. Exercises in lateral displacement, developing sidewise movements, will help balance in both cases.

Increase and decrease of speed at a trot. The first exercise in longitudinal flexibility is very simple: While trotting at an ordinary speed you increase the speed somewhat, for about half of the ring, then return to an ordinary one and then slow down to a really slow, doggy trot to which you sit. At first the increase and decrease of speed should be so negligible that the exercise does not become a gymnastic and is merely a lesson in cooperation. As a matter of fact you have been doing almost the same exercise already when developing the impulse forward and the coming back. So that in a way, this exercise is a development of your work of the preceding month. But now, in about a week, you begin to increase and decrease the speed more abruptly, aiming at greater differences in speed. Gradually, by the time you reach the sixth or seventh month, and if you ride on advanced level, your fast trot is already a semi-extended one and your slow trot a semi-collected one, while the ordinary one always remains the same. When this level is reached in this exercise then it has really become an exercise in longitudinal flexibility.

Longitudinal flexibility is a very important factor in jumping, for during the jump the horse contracts and extends his back quite drastically. On this longitudinal flexibility will also depend the ability of the horse to adjust his stride for a correct take-off.

Circular movements. Exercises in lateral flexibility and agility consist of different circular movements. The three to start with are circles, half-circles and half-circles in reverse; all of them large, the circles being about 50′ in diameter.

You should practice them all together, and in combining them you should also include a straight change of directions diagonally across the arena. Thus you keep the horse alert, guessing what the next order will be and the lesson becomes a development of the guiding lesson as well as an exercise in lateral agility.

Now that your horse probably moves decently on soft contact and even begins to move on the bit, it should be easy for you to keep him straight from nose to tail when moving straight and make him bend his body to accept the shape of a curve when moving on a circle. Of course, the circles are still too large to be a powerful exercise in lateral flexibility, but this is the beginning. Next month you will make them somewhat smaller, then again smaller and finally, during your seventh month, you should arrive at a circle just 20′ in diameter to be executed at semi-collected gaits. Rather large circles, but at fast gaits, are as important exercises as small ones at semi-collected gaits. (The latter at the advanced level only.)

Circles requiring occasional use of one rein of direct opposition teach the horse obedience to this rein effect.

Work on small curves, at slow gaits, bending the horse from the nose to the tail so that the curve of his body corresponds to the shape of the path along which he moves, is an exercise in lateral *flexibility*. But work on large curves at speed does not require the bending of the horse; the latter is even detrimental when speed is involved. On the other hand, working on large curves, at speed, poses problems which moving along a small curve at collected or slow gaits does not.

First of all, at speed, the loss of equilibrium to the front is greater than at collected gaits. Then, at speed, the inclination of the whole body towards the inside is also greater. These two factors require of the horse greater agility in the constant restoration of the equilibrium lost both forward and to the side. So work at speed on large curves becomes an exercise in *agility* rather than in *flexibility*.

In the hunting field, and today in many jumping competitions where speed is required and the courses are of the hunter type, *agility* rather than *flexibility* at turns is necessary. On the other hand, in the tight and tortuous courses of open jumping, and of those of some recent horsemanship classes, *flexibility* may be of importance.

I say that flexibility merely *may* be of importance, because many horses who began their work on large circles keeping themselves straight (but in early lessons when the head may turn to the side of the turn) eventually preserve the same attitude when skilfully making turns along a small curve. This straight attitude being on the whole advantageous in jumping tight courses (for jumping soon after a turn), the question arises whether the development of *agility* in schooling a horse is not more important than that of *flexibility*. In my present opinion (1962), development of flexibility for flexibility's sake should be pursued only when the horse in question really needs it. For riders with such horses, the original text of the book on this subject should remain, but this addition should be noted.

Half-turn on the forehand. The first exercise in Lateral Displacement is the half-turn on the forehand executed from a halt. It teaches the horse to yield the hindquarters to the action of one leg used a few inches behind the girth. Obedience to this use of the leg makes it easy to keep the horse straight later during backing and in many other movements; furthermore, it prepares the horse for future two tracks which is a powerful exercise in lateral displacement.

Because the horse's hindquarters are much more easily displaced laterally than the forehand, the half-turn on the forehand has little value as a gymnastic; it is rather a movement which teaches a leg signal. In teaching the half-turn on the forehand try to keep the reins loose most of the time and swing the quarters around step by step, pausing for a few seconds between each step. In other words, give as gentle as practical a push to force the quarters to make one short step to the side (help with the whip if necessary); check any possible movement of the forehand with the reins, then relax your leg and the tension on the reins and pat your horse. Make the next step as soon as the horse relaxes. The half-turn should be accomplished in approximately four steps. Don't forget that the horse's *neck and head must remain straight.*

Of course, the half-turn on the forehand, as everything else in schooling, should be practiced in both directions. Don't make more than one turn in the same place; always move between two successive turns. Half a dozen spread throughout the day's work should be enough. But when encountering difficulties you may want to make a dozen, executing them close together.

Jumping. As to jumping, I have a reasonable hope of believing that after two months of stabilizing the horse's approach to the jump, the habit of going toward the obstacle quietly has already been established. If you have not raised the fences above the height recommended and have not disturbed the horse on the jump with your seat, legs and hands, then I am certain that this is the case.

Once a relaxed, quiet approach has become a habit, you can take the next step and begin to develop a powerful jump. This is done at first over low but always broad obstacles taken at a trot; and this is why. Simplifying the matter, one can say that the efforts of the horse on the jump consist of a combination of three factors: impetus of the speed of the approach, push with the hindquarters, and acrobatics (balancing gestures, etc.). At an ordinary trot, deprived of the impetus of the gallop, the horse has to depend on the strength of the push, and the broader the jump the more strength is required. Later, when the obstacles reach the height of about 3'9", acrobatics will also come into the picture. Your first broad obstacles should not be higher than 2'6" and not wider than about 3'. But you must vary them, continuing to develop a bold and quiet approach toward unfamiliar fences.

With the above gradual and logical procedure you won't need any wings except on especially unfortunate occasions. The better teacher you are, the more rarely will such occasions present themselves—in ideal never.

A very much argued question is whether solid fences should be used or not in schooling jumpers. I am against them, and not merely for the obvious reason that they are dangerous for both horses and riders. The usual argument for them is that the horse learns to respect an obstacle and hence makes an extra effort to clear it. This, of course, is true. But

it is also true that the majority of horses learn to be afraid of jumping
at the same time and so begin to approach fences in a mentally tense
state which, as I have pointed out many times, results in physical tension and consequently in an unathletic jump. There is no question but
that there are horses which will make a clean performance only if they
have been made afraid of the jump through its solid construction or
through poling. I am convinced, however, that the majority of horses,
if properly schooled, will not refuse, run out or knock down fences consistently, for the simple reason that it is less trouble to take a fence clean
than to run out, refuse and be punished or be hurt in knocking down
the obstacle.

There is a big difference between jumping solid fences in the hunting
field where the horse is stimulated and alert, and jumping them alone
on the familiar training ground where the horse, being bored by the
routine, can easily go to sleep and become careless.

One more argument: There is no question but that the average international jumper jumps cleaner than the average hunter, but the former
doesn't jump solid fences in competitions.

I am convinced that the majority of those who resort to solid fences
do so either because they don't know how to school horses or don't have
time to school, and so are left with solid fences as a means of making
the horse go clean—by scaring him over the obstacles.

Hacking. Hacking during this month should be done mostly at a walk;
the periods of trot should be short and its speed never faster than the
ordinary one. And remember that you must return to the stable with a
cool horse. If your horse is inclined to shy don't get angry, don't punish
him without analyzing the reason and treating it from the psychological
point of view.

5TH MONTH (SEMI-COLLECTION AND SEMI-EXTENSION—WITH SOME HORSES
ONLY).

Semi-collection (trot). For a whole month you have been doing the
exercise in longitudinal flexibility—the increase and decrease of the
speed at a trot. Another two or three weeks of it and, all going well, you
probably will be able to make rather sharp transitions from an ordinary
to a slow trot and perhaps even omit the ordinary and change directly
from fast to slow *without upsetting the horse.* If, for one reason or another, this doesn't work well, postpone these rapid changes of speeds for
another two or three weeks. But if your horse responds to the transitions
quietly, there are more chances pro than con that when sharply slowing
down he will bring the hindquarters under, will raise his neck somewhat
and will flex in the mouth and poll. Once the horse has acquired a soft,
collected attitude it is a matter of the tact of your legs and hands to
preserve this attitude while moving forward for a few steps. If you suc-

ceed in this you will have a semi-collected trot. The main point to watch is not necessarily the engagement of the hindquarters, or a somewhat arched position of the neck and head, but the repeated flexions (about one in each stride) which insure the softness of the movement.

If a soft, obedient "coming back" through give and take has already been achieved during the previous weeks of the exercise in longitudinal flexibility, then there is a good likelihood that the first flexion will come (as easily as I described) during your first order to slow down abruptly. However, nothing in riding works one hundred per cent and perhaps, due to the poor conformation of your horse or to his resisting mentality, or because of insufficient dexterity of your legs and hands, flexions may not develop; instead of slowing down softly, the horse will stiffen both in the poll and in the jaw, throwing the neck and head upward. The next ten minutes will tell you whether this was a passing misunderstanding or whether it is going to be a major resistance. If it turns out to be the latter, then you have to give special lessons in flexions.

Flexions (direct). If flexions require special attention it may be worthwhile to start teaching them dismounted; this is very easy. Place yourself on the left side of the horse in front of the shoulders; take the two reins in the right hand about six inches from the rings of the bit, and begin to pull toward the hands of an imaginary rider in the saddle. The pull at the beginning should be very gentle and should be gradually increased in tension until the horse relaxes the lower jaw; then drop the reins and pat the horse. If the horse refuses to flex even from a strong pull and merely brings the chin in while keeping the mouth firmly closed, then by light upward jerks raise the neck and head, take the reins one in each hand and make a gentle see-sawing motion. In case the horse tries to back when you ask him to flex, place him in a corner of the ring with his quarters to the fence. If you have the ability to explain to the horse what you wish of him, the above lesson shouldn't take more than ten minutes. Then mount and repeat the lesson while the horse is standing still. In this lesson squeeze with both legs every time before asking a flexion; this will prevent the horse from moving back and may, by pushing him on the bit, make it easier to obtain the desired result. If the horse overflexes or "drops the bit" by, making a big and quick nod, increase the pressure of legs and diminish the tension on the reins when asking the next flexion.

The third lesson in flexion should consist in obtaining flexions while changing from a walk to a halt. The horse must flex just before halting; in other words, a halt must be achieved through flexions, thus insuring its softness. But this may not happen at first, and the horse may only flex after he has halted. This should not disturb you, for a few days of work will straighten out the matter.

The fourth lesson should consist of changing from a trot to a walk through flexions, and the fifth lesson of flexions used when changing from a faster to a slower trot. Considerably later (probably in one month) the horse will be ready to flex when slowing down at the canter.

In general, in all the slowing down, halting and backing (that is, in all cases when the tension on the reins is increased), flexions should be present as the natural outcome of this increased tension. On the other hand, when moving forward, the horse should flex continuously only during the short periods of semi-collected gaits, which are obtained with an increased tension on the reins. As you know, the semi-collected gaits are used as gymnastics only; in actual riding, the horse must move with neck and head extended and you don't wish to lose this attitude through overdoing flexions and semi-collected gaits. Therefore, you should re-member a very important rule: *After every semi-collected period, or after backing or halting or slowing down with flexions, make certain that the horse resumes his ordinary gait with the neck and head stretched for-ward.* A well-schooled horse will stretch his neck with the first strides of the free movement forward.

Semi-extended trot. While trots faster and slower than ordinary are developed simultaneously, when the horse is ready for semi-collection and semi-extension, it may be necessary to choose which to start with, so that the one will not interfere with the progress of the other. As a rule, over-ambitious horses do better if semi-collection is taught first, while lethargic animals benefit from the stimulation of extension, and consequently it is advisable to teach them extension before attempting the extreme slowing down.

If, when trotting fast, you were to increase the pressure with the legs, at the same time increasing the tension on the reins in order to prevent the horse from trotting still faster, and if all this were tactfully done, you would be able to lengthen the strides through further pushing of the hindquarters and the corresponding extension of the fore-limbs with-out gaining much in speed.

Don't make more than a full ring of an extended trot, slowing down somewhat along the short wall. Normally periods of extended trot should not be longer than a diagonal change of directions or one long wall of the ring, if your ring is of the size of Olympic Games requirements (ca. 65' x 195'). Half a dozen such periods a day are sufficient.

Increase and decrease of speed at the canter. If your horse is by now well stabilized at the ordinary canter and will not get upset if you should increase the speed, then begin the standard longitudinal flexibility exer-cises at the canter by increasing the speed to somewhat faster than ordi-nary and decreasing back to ordinary. Perhaps toward the end of this month you will even be able to decrease the speed to slower than ordi-nary without breaking into a trot. The slow canter, largely depending on the balance and agility of the horse, may not come out well for another month or so. But once it does you are around the corner from semi-collection (for some horses only), which your horse knows already at a trot.

For a while, to keep the horse cantering slowly and without breaking the gait, you probably will have to use your legs and hands quite strenuously. To avoid dulling the horse's sides and stiffening his mouth your periods of semi-collected canter should be very short—not longer than half of the long wall of the ring. After each such period canter a full ring on loose reins. As I have already suggested on several occasions, skip semi-collection and semi-extension when schooling on the intermediate level.

Canter departure on a specific lead. I assume that until now, when desiring a specific lead, you have always started the canter either on a circle or on a turn of the ring, and that the fact that the canter started on the correct lead was not so much due to obedience to certain aids as to the physical position in which the horse was placed. However, the association of your aids with a certain lead unquestionably has taken place in the horse's mind and now it is merely the matter of emphasizing this association. There may be many ways of teaching the horse the canter departure on a desired lead while moving on a straight line; I would suggest the following procedure:

While cantering, let us say on the right lead, change directions diagonally across the arena and somewhere between the center and the next wall, stop the canter, trot a few strides (as few as possible) and begin the canter on the left lead just at the moment when the horse is reaching the wall and about to take the track to the left (Picture 81). Due to this turn and the habit of cantering on the left lead when going to the left, you will probably obtain the correct lead, so pat the horse and walk him immediately. After a walk for something like one length of the long wall, resume the procedure. Gradually make your interruption of the canter and new canter departure earlier and earlier so that eventually it will take place in the center of the ring, while you are moving straight. By now it will be almost entirely in response to your signal, although the association in the horse's mind of the canter departure with turning upon reaching the wall will remain a help. The next lesson will consist of eliminating all the assistance of the association of place with the movement by starting a canter on either lead while moving straight along the middle line of the ring.

Another way of teaching a canter departure would be by starting a half-circle at a *trot* and beginning the canter just before reaching the wall (Picture 82). In my work I usually use the first method because it saves time by teaching two things at once—the canter departure and change of leads. However, if too much cantering upsets your horse at this stage of his development, then you would be wise to start your canters from a trot at the end of a diagonal change of directions (Picture 83) or

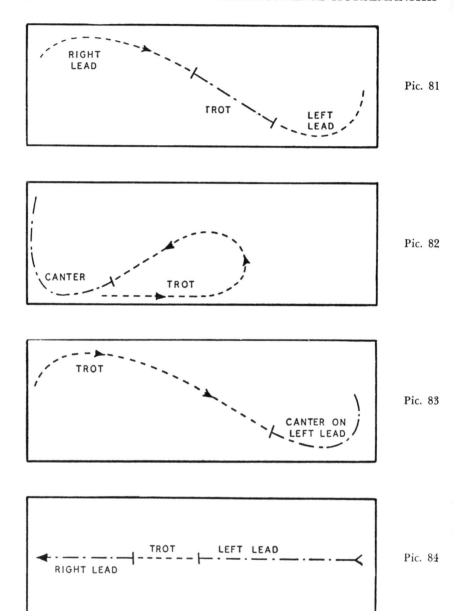

Pic. 81

Pic. 82

Pic. 83

Pic. 84

Teaching canter departure on a specific lead.

from half-circles begun at a trot. Beginning with this for a few days may be an easy introduction to the lesson as I originally described it. Eventually the canter departure on any given lead, or changes of lead with interruptions, should be made on a straight line. (Picture 84)

Throughout these lessons your attention should be concentrated on having the horse move straight and in a relaxed manner.

Serpentine and Zig-zag at a trot. Serpentine and Zig-zag (see Pictures 71 and 72) are variations of circular movements and, if compared to an ordinary circle, are of interest in the development of the lateral flexibility of the horse because they require constant alternate bending instead of continuous bending in one direction. The short curves of the Zig-zag also require a quick engagement of one or the other of the hind legs (always the inside one).

Both of these exercises also lighten the forehand and lighten it progressively as the changes of direction gradually become more abrupt.

The execution of these movements at a trot leads to their execution at a gallop; in this case, the counter gallop being involved, the exercise becomes an even more important gymnastic.

The counter gallop. The first lesson in counter gallop should consist in merely making a corner of the ring (if your ring is at least 65' wide) while maintaining the outside lead. For instance, take the track to the right, start the canter on the right lead, change direction diagonally across the arena and keep on galloping on the same lead while making the first turn after reaching the opposite side of the ring. Then walk your horse and pat him. As soon as it comes out softly, make two corners, then four. Within two or three weeks you will be able to make a large circle.

Or you may start teaching the counter gallop by merely galloping on curves with a large radius. Large half-circles or half-circles in reverse may also be useful.

The speed of the counter gallop should be somewhat slower than the ordinary speed at the canter. During the counter gallop the horse must remain relaxed and soft in the mouth; he will if the size of curves are large enough for his present ability.

The counter gallop is one of the exercises for the improvement of the horse's balance and general agility; it also helps to put the horse on the bit. It is a forceful exercise and I know at least two internationally-known trainers of jumpers who consider it as one of the most important ones.

There is a certain relationship between the counter gallop and the *flying* changes of lead. If the flying changes are taught first then the horse may easily take up a change of lead as resistance every time the counter gallop is asked. This schooling program takes this fact into consideration.

Counter canter (counter gallop). Almost all of my junior pupils begin to participate in easy jumping competitions before their horses are completely schooled; one can hardly stop them from doing so. This poses certain problems, one of them being turns between obstacles.

In many cases a horse will change the lead during a jump, and thus the following situation may arise: A horse going to the right, and galloping on the right lead when approaching the last fence on the long wall, changes the lead on the jump, and consequently finds himself on the outside lead when making the turn (I assume the horse cannot yet execute the flying change of leads). If he is not at ease making the turn on the outside lead it will require quite a few strides after the turn, for him to reestablish a good balance, and if the next fence is near the turn he may approach it badly and will be at a disadvantage at the take-off. Many jumping competitions are lost because of inability to negotiate turns skilfully.

Taking this into consideration, I now teach, whenever possible, the *counter gallop* (counter canter) early in schooling—earlier than I originally placed this movement in my schooling program. With completely green horses I teach it as soon as I start the work at a canter. At this time the horse, not yet schooled to the signals for canter departure on the desired lead, will start the canter in a hit-or-miss fashion as far as leads are concerned. And if it so happens that he starts on the outside lead I ask a much longer canter than if he were to start on the inside lead. Since the colt is too awkward to attempt to change leads, and is prevented by the rider's legs from losing the gait, it is easy to keep him at the counter canter. It should be repeated daily until he is comfortable at it.

This early counter canter, coinciding with the lessons on stabilization of the canter, should be practiced as much as possible on loose reins.

Only after the colt canters with equal ease on either the outside or inside lead, do I begin to teach the canter departure on a specific lead. This procedure in schooling enables my pupils to show their incompletely schooled horses with greater success.

In cases, however, of schooling horses with a couple of years of experience of being ridden, teaching the counter canter is much more complicated. By then they are usually in the habit of cantering always on the inside lead, and will try to change back into it, either by interrupting the gait or by making a flying change. In such cases the counter canter has to remain in its original place in the program of schooling. Thus the program has the counter canter in two places—one for completely green horses and the other for semi-green ones.

Jumping (acrobatics). In jumping you continue to work on a quiet approach to all gaits, on developing boldness by jumping low obstacles of different descriptions and on developing flight by jumping wide obstacles also of different forms and colors. Depending on the progress of your horse, in the course of the month the height may be raised (by from 3″ to 6″) and the width may be extended (perhaps by 1′).

There are many ways of achieving the above aims. As it actually happens, there is no way which can be considered universal. Different methods may suit different horses. In this respect I would like to discuss "Cavaletti," the very name of which implies their Italian origin. I describe them here, for I particularly would like to recommend them as a means to develop in your horse an *acrobatic* jump, which is the main object of this month's work over obstacles.

The Cavaletti consist of several bars (perhaps seven) on the ground in the middle of the ring, placed at intervals to fit the stride of the *trot* of a particular horse. Begin by placing the bars 4′ 3″ apart, and subsequently alter the spacing to suit your animal's stride. It is important to have all distances equal. Flank the last bar with standards.

The Cavaletti should at first be crossed at a walk and afterwards at a trot on *loose reins,* the rider remaining in a jumping position. As soon as the colt calmly negotiates the Cavaletti at a trot, raise the last bar (the one that is flanked by standards) to about 6″ (perhaps at first at one end only). When further raising the height, pick up the next-to-the-last bar and place it also on the same standards, thus giving the horse a take-off area of at least 8′6″. In the early stage of schooling the jump should be about 2′6″. After negotiating the Cavaletti, move straight forward for about 75′ before turning alternately to the right or to the left; always turn on a wide arc and return (again making a wide turn) to your starting area, something like 75′ away from the Cavaletti.

It is very important to present obstacles to the colt as a part of the *routine of a trot.* Normally, therefore, don't start a trot at the last moment of the approach nor drop back to a walk immediately after a jump. Continue, instead, on an even rather slow trot for about five minutes and in the course of this repeatedly cross the Cavaletti.

The Cavaletti are made progressively more difficult by raising or broadening the fence or by shortening or lengthening the take-off area. After raising your fence to 3′ or higher, you will normally enlarge the take-off area (so not to cramp the horse) by moving the standards somewhat further away from the grid (perhaps 1′ for every additional 3″ to 6″ of height; perhaps little more, perhaps less). It is important that, at the beginning, the size of the take-off area be comfortable for the horse.

Besides helping to calm your colt's (or a ruined jumper's) approach to an obstacle, the above-described simple use of the Cavaletti gives other important results:

1) Practically all horses while negotiating the Cavaletti (if calm) lower and extend their necks. Thus a horse acquires the habit of approaching

fences with the neck and head in the best attitude to make strong "balancing gestures" during the jump.

2) The distance between the bars on the ground can be adjusted to cause the horse either to lengthen or to shorten his stride. While the latter may sometimes be desirable in the case of too eager a horse, the

Pic. 85

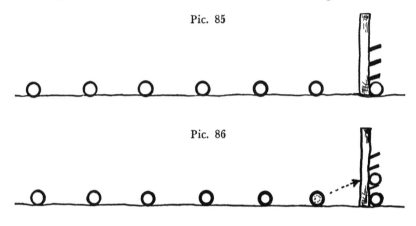

Pic. 86

Cavaletti.

normal adjustment for a calm horse must be such as to lengthen his stride somewhat. This gives the horse the habit of making the last strides of the approach more alertly, while consistently maintaining the rhythm of the gait.

3) If the take-off area is correctly adjusted for the height of the fence and for the individual peculiarities of the horse, then the horse is given practice in taking off at the distance which for him is most advantageous. Accumulation of such experience will tend to develop a habit.

4) When jumping at a trot, the horse, being deprived of the impetus of the gallop, is forced to use his muscles more strenuously and, on higher jumps, even to resort to acrobatics ("use himself").

For the most efficient use of Cavaletti, in later schooling, over higher fences, the trainer must analyze the jumping defects of his horse and arrange the Cavaletti so as to promote more efficient efforts. If, for instance, the horse has a tendency to take off too late, climbing fences (while going at them boldly), the trainer should widen the jump and lengthen the take-off area enough to force the horse into making a broad jump, but he should be careful not to make the take-off area so large that the horse will be tempted to take an additional short stride and come in too close. If, on the other hand, your horse consistently takes off too early (without rushing) it usually means that he does not know how to give a sufficiently strong upward thrust with the forehand, either because of muscular weakness or because of clumsiness. To correct this defect: a) the fence at the end of the grid must be vertical and high enough to require from the horse a thrust with the forehand, b) the take-off area must be wide enough to give the horse room for a normal take-off but too short for an early one, c) the jump should neither be so high nor the take-off area so small that the horse may consider the situation hopeless.

To recapitulate, by means of Cavaletti you can develop in your horse:

1) stabilization of the approach to the jump;
2) lengthening or shortening of the strides of the trot during the approach;
3) lowering of the neck and head during the approach;
4) the thrust upward with the forehand during the take-off (short take-off distance);
5) the thrust upward and forward with the hindquarters during the take-off (a long take-off distance);
6) the use of the back and the neck during the jump.

One cannot make a jumper exclusively with the use of the Cavaletti, since they can be negotiated at a walk and trot only; the horse has no opportunity to learn how to figure the approach at a gallop, nor to acquire a knack of jumping from that gait. Consequently, jumping multiple in-and-outs will eventually be an absolute necessity.

In reclaiming ruined jumpers (those who rush fences and are so upset emotionally that they are physically stiff and jump in bad form) the Cavaletti often work wonders. The technique of using the Cavaletti in such cases is fundamentally the same as the one described above for schooling colts, but with the following differences:

1) Calm walking, on loose reins, even merely over bars on the ground, may at first be impossible, and the horse may have to be controlled all the time while ridden over the Cavaletti. In order to break the rush forward, the trainer may even be obliged to halt the horse before, in the middle of, or immediately after the Cavaletti. And even after a quiet walk over the bars has been achieved, it may take a while before it can be duplicated at a trot.

2) For a while one should jump only with the help of the Cavaletti.

3) It may be necessary to change gradually from the Cavaletti to ordinary fences by removing the bars on the ground, one by one, leaving the last bar before the jump to the last.

Hacking. Assuming that the horse by now is well stabilized at the ordinary canter in the ring I would suggest your adding the canter to your hacking, both on loose reins and on soft contact.

You should hack alone as well as in company with other horses and in the latter case make a point of being sometimes ahead and sometimes behind the others.

6TH MONTH (TRANSITIONS).

Short, simple programs. A good performance doesn't consist merely in good gaits and individual, well-executed movements. Quick, precise, *soft* transitions between gaits, speeds and movements form an important part of the horse's performance. You have been working already on some of the transitions when, for instance, decreasing and increasing the speed at a trot and canter or when interrupting the canter to change the lead. Now the time has come to ask more of the horse by assembling everything that the horse has so far learned into a program of three to five minutes' duration, to be executed for precision's sake from letter to letter, as in the schooling test of the Olympic Games. And do not forget to include about three obstacles, distributing them throughout the program. See the Program Ride in the *Complete Test for Hunters,* Chapter XIII.

Half-turn on the haunches. The half-turn on the haunches develops the mobility of the forehand, prepares the horse for future two tracks and teaches correct response to the combination of a leading rein (sometimes of direct opposition) with the rein of indirect opposition in front of the withers. It also prepares the horse for the short turn at the gallop.

You can teach the half-turn on the haunches either in place or with movement forward; the latter method would be better on horses with a tendency to back when learning the turn. If teaching in place, begin only after a few seconds of relaxed standing still and make the turn in sections, halting and patting the horse after each step; the turn must be accomplished in four such steps, each step covering 45° of an arc. Be certain that the tension on the reins is negligible and release it completely upon halting after each step. Once the horse executes it very quietly, connect the individual steps. If you have decided that, in the case of your horse, teaching the half-turn on the haunches while in motion is better, then do it either along the wall at a walk (as in the first method), merely eliminating the original halt as well as the halts after each step, or do it by making a series of circles (at a walk), each successive one being smaller than that preceding it, and finally achieving the turn on the haunches. During such a turn the horse will be moving forward more than is desirable and the hindlegs will describe a circle perhaps three or four feet in diameter. Little by little you will be able to cut down the amount of movement forward. If your horse has a lot of natural lateral flexibility, then the method of diminishing circles may work well even when used during this month. But if your horse is stiff in the sides he will be very awkward in making the small circles (even at a walk) which we have not reached yet in our program of schooling. In such a case (if you insist upon this method) you will have to postpone the turn on the haunches until better lateral flexibility has been developed.

Personally, I have never had to resort to circling in teaching this turn and have never had difficulty in getting it in place at the wall, sometimes after halting, other times while moving. Furthermore, I don't necessarily like teaching it from a circle, for quite often this requires too much tension on the reins. I have described it here only as a sample of how differently sometimes the same movement can be taught. Even if never actually used by you this method can serve you as an example of how to use your imagination while teaching your horse.

Backing. Never teach backing before the horse is decently on the bit, as it may put him behind it, nor before he has learned flexions, as in that case he will back at every increase of tension on the reins (when teaching flexion in place). However, with ambitious horses, reluctant to slow down, you may need to teach backing four to six weeks earlier.

Your first lesson in backing should consist of about four steps back after a halt from a walk, followed by a resumption of the walk. Second lesson—the same thing from a trot. Third lesson—the same thing from a canter. There may be only a couple of weeks in time between the first and second lessons but it will probably take a month or more before backing can be executed softly from a canter and followed by an immediate resumption of the gait with the neck and head stretched forward.

The horse must back in response to the give and take of your hands, keeping the head and neck in the normal relaxed (stretched) position.

If you encounter resistance and the horse requires a very strong pull on the reins to force him to make a step back, you should ask someone to help you. This assistant, holding a whip, should place himself in front of the horse and tap him on the legs every time you gently increase the tension on the reins. In such cases a couple of steps at a time will suffice and the horse should be patted after every step. If tactfully done this lesson can be explained to the horse in a couple of periods of from five to ten minutes each (on two successive days). If you can think of a better way to explain to the horse that you wish him to back merely from a *slight* increase in the tension on the reins go ahead and try it; the essential thing is to teach backing without pulling hard on the horse's mouth; the method makes no difference.

Few things in schooling can be achieved in a mechanical manner. The trainer must always think of ways to get around whatever resistance is encountered. As an example: some horses, when taught to back with the help of an assistant will step back from his whip, throwing up the neck and head. In many cases this could be overcome by the assistant offering the horse a piece of carrot, thus inducing the horse to stretch out his neck in reaching for it, and only after this happens beginning to tap the horse's legs with the whip, giving the carrot only after two or three steps back have been taken.

Short Turn at the Gallop (see definition in Chapter IX).

This turn should be taught only after the turn on the haunches (first in place and then at a walk) has been mastered by both horse and rider. To teach it, place two standards about 40′ from each other at one end of your schooling field; let the pupil gallop toward these so as to make his turn on the inside lead, going toward the left standard if he is on the right lead and toward the right standard if on the left. During the last two or three strides before the standard, he should reduce the speed abruptly and then make a 180 degree turn within the standards at diminished speed. The moment the turn has been made, the original speed should be quickly restored, the pupil galloping back toward the starting point. Little by little move the standards closer together, eventually placing them perhaps only 20′ apart, or even less.

The rider should not try to turn the horse with one rein, but instead he should use his aids as in the turn on the haunches—that is, swing the forehand around rather than simply make a small half-circle. The horse's neck and head and body must remain straight throughout the turn; the bending of the horse in the side and curving of his neck and head which may be required in making really small circles at slow gaits, should not be present in this case. This turn can be made at a counter canter, rather awkwardly, in most cases.

Two tracks. In the course of this month you can also begin the preparatory work for two tracks. To accomplish this you must do the following: walk briskly down the middle of the ring on loose reins and, after repeating it to insure long strides, the third time begin to use one of your legs somewhat behind the girth (as in turn on the forehand), to push the horse to the side, still keeping the reins loose. You should expect that in the course of a walk of approximately 150′ the horse will deviate to the side by about 10′ to 15′ only. This may seem too little to you but it is sufficient for the first lesson. The main point is that the horse continues to move forward with long, free strides, his neck and head in their normal, stretched attitude. As with all other exercises, practice it in both directions, working the horse more in the direction of his stiff side (if he still has one).

In a couple of weeks the horse, understanding your leg and becoming more agile, will deviate considerably more, still *preserving long strides.* By then your horse will already know the half-turn on the haunches and you will be able to improve your two tracks by riding the horse on soft contact and leading his forehand by your hands (as in the turn on the haunches). The neck must still remain stretched, the head slightly turned in the direction of the movement. The important thing is that the strides must continue to be long. In other words, the horse must always move more forward than sideways. Only then is this exercise of any value to your jumper. It is beneficial in two ways: when two tracking to the right the horse has to make an exaggerated engagement of the left hindleg and a strong extension of the left fore. The reverse takes place when two tracking to the left. Your jumper needs agility of the hindlegs when engaging them for the take-off, while he needs the extension of the forelegs for a safe and soft landing. This, by the way, is one of the reasons why we value long, sloping shoulders in a jumper.

One caution: never teach this oblique movement along the wall, as it was always taught in the past ("travers" and "renvers"); this shortens the horse's steps and, although such an oblique movement, particularly at a collected gait, may be very effective as a spectacle, its short steps make the exercise useless for a cross-country horse.

Today, in 1962, I no longer consider that *Two Tracks* is of real importance in making hunters and jumpers. It is, however, an excellent exercise for developing the cooperation of the rider's legs and hands in controlling both the positive and negative efforts of the horse. I use it today mostly for this purpose—that is, for educating the rider rather than the horse. I have retained the original text, however, for the use of those people who may disagree with my present point of view.

Serpentine and zigzag at the gallop. These exercises involve the counter gallop, for if you make a serpentine or zig-zag maintaining the same lead you will be half of the time on the counter gallop. Both of these exercises are wonderful gymnastics and after your horse knows the flying changes of lead these two movements offer you an opportunity to check how obedient he is to your signals (by not trying to change the lead).

The curves should be always kept large enough for the horse to be comfortable; they should be diminished only with progress in the horse's balance and agility. The horse must remain soft during the counter gallop.

Stop the horse every time he changes the lead and begin the movement anew; pat him if he keeps the lead.

Change of leads with short interruption. This obviously is a development of the former lesson of making changes with long interruptions. I am devoting a few lines to it just to emphasize the fact that the approach to the future flying change must be gradual; if it is not, you will upset the horse. If your horse is excited during the trot between the two gallops, anticipating the new departure, then you should replace the trot with a full stop, a stop long enough for the horse to relax completely. After such a relaxed halt has been obtained, walk a couple of steps, then trot for two or three strides and only then start the canter on the new lead. It may take you several days to straighten the thing out.

Jumping. In jumping, as in everything else, most of this month's work consists in perfecting things previously learned. The new item on your agenda is teaching the horse to "figure" his take-off at the gallop—the gait which he will actually use in the hunting field and horse shows.

When I was young, riders tried to teach horses this "figuring" by controlling the horse's last three strides and then giving him the order to jump. In the great majority of cases the results were unsatisfactory because forcible control was upsetting to the horse and, although the take-off might take place on the correct line, the jump itself would be stiff. Furthermore, the horse was becoming dependent on the rider's placing him and very few of us can go over a serious jumping course without making one or two mistakes in placing the horse.

Now, teaching the "figuring" of the take-off, we create a certain condition which automatically develops this knack in the horse while he enjoys full freedom when approaching the fence. As in everything else, there are many ways of doing it and no way can be recommended without knowing the horse in question; perhaps the particular horse that you own will require some adjustments of any method which I may suggest. But, as general suggestions of what to do let me give the following:

1) Build a quintuple (five-fence) in-and-out. Start with all rails on the ground; walk and trot the horse over the combination on loose reins, maintaining an even, rather slow speed by occasional checking; keep yourself in a galloping position. If the horse takes this calmly then begin to raise the fences—the last fence first, next the preceding one, and so on. The first rail goes up the last. When all fences are 2′6″ the distances between them should be 18′ to 20′ (Picture 87); this should give one full stride of gallop between the fences. Canter quietly to the combination on *loose reins* with the legs doing no more than maintaining the necessary impulse. With all the training which your horse has previously received

Pic. 87

I don't expect him to refuse or run out; but if he does, then start with still lower fences. Your horse may take off too early or too close on the first fence. This doesn't matter, since the correct take-offs for the following fences are indicated by the distances between them. So you are bound to have four good take-offs against one bad one; the score is in your favor and time will develop the habit. When raising fences you have to increase accordingly the distance between them to suit the stride and the comfortable take-off of your horse—he must have a free stride between fences.

Upon reaching a height of over 3′ don't use more than four fences, and when eventually you come to 4′ fences a triple in-and-out will be sufficient, with distances of 24′ between obstacles.

2) When the take-off over the quintuple in-and-out which I described has become regular, begin to vary the combination. For instance, your first fence may remain a 2'6" vertical, the distance between it and the next fence allowing for one stride; the second fence is again a vertical but a few inches higher; after it there is an increased distance which allows two strides and the third fence consists of parallel bars about 3' apart and 3' high. After it the space again permits of only one stride and the fence is a vertical of, let us say 3'3". You may play with this set-up, making all sorts of combinations, mixing the heights, the type of jumps and the distances. (Picture 88 illustrates a combination where all fences are 2½' high.)

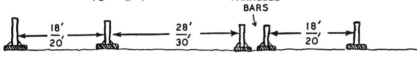

Pic. 88

Your first gallops to the combination of jumps intended to teach "figuring" must be slow. But with the improvement of the horse's technique you should increase the speed, providing that it does not excite the horse.

When making different combinations you must keep in mind all the peculiarities, good and bad, of the jump of your horse, and particularly notice whether he is inclined to take off too early or too late, and arrange combinations yourself to correct the particular faults of your horse.

The correct figuring of the take-off does not merely depend on the horse's ability to calculate it mentally but also on possession of the necessary skill to put this calculation into practice. This means that the horse must be able to lengthen and shorten his strides at will. This is where all the exercises in longitudinal flexibility pay off.

Some naturally clever and longitudinally flexible horses will learn to take off correctly practically without any special work. But if natural abilities are lacking then, as a rule, it is not the physical but the mental side of the matter which may give you the more trouble. A French proverb says "When one is dead it's for a long time; when one is stupid it's for ever."

Hacking. You probably began your hacking in company with an old and quiet horse, later you have done most of it alone, perhaps sometimes in company with a couple of friends. Now, as a step toward future hunting, I think you should look for opportunities to hack in large company. When hacking with a group of horses, make a point of being sometimes at the head and at other times in the middle of the crowd or behind it. If your horse behaves equally quietly in all three positions you are lucky. Being gregarious by nature, he probably will hate to be the last, particularly if the distance between him and the other horses is 100′ or more. There is nothing that you can do with your legs and hands to correct this; it is a case of uncontrolled emotions and there is no rule that can be given you to overcome this difficulty. But again, if you have studied the character of your horse, if you know his peculiarities, you may know what to do to combat this mental obstacle. You cannot do it just with the aids, your approach must be that of a psychologist. (See "Special Exercises for Hunters" at the end of this chapter.)

Many horses easily acquire the habit of working quietly in company. Some temperamental horses learn it only with time and practice. Others never do, no matter how well they are schooled; these may perform very well individually but be impossible in the hunting field. There is nothing that can be done about such cases; some horses are adapted to one type of work, some to another. This factor is often not taken into account, although horsemen have talked about it for ages. As early as the middle of the 17th century the famous English horseman, William Cavendish, Duke of Newcastle, said in his book:

". . . if the horse is fit to go a Travelling pace, let him do it, if he is naturally inclined to make Curvets, he must be put to it. . . . If none of these suit him, he will perhaps be good for racing, hunting, or for coach or cart. . . . He that is qualified to be a bishop is not fit to command an army; nor he that is fit to be a secretary of state to be keeper of the seals."

This is why when buying a hunter I think it is wise to search first for a suitable mentality and only secondly for a good conformation—always hoping, of course, to find a horse which combines both.

7TH MONTH (THE ULTIMATE IN RING GYMNASTICS).

In a way, you are now reaching a critical moment in your schooling. This is because the time is approaching when you will have to analyze the performance of your horse and decide whether he does all his exercises athletically enough for his future work as a hunter or jumper. You are not through with schooling yet; cross-country work is still ahead of you. Furthermore, you will be repeating the exercises he already knows for a couple of months and the execution of them is bound to improve. But, considering all this, you must decide whether you have to make a special effort to achieve more refinement in the execution of some of the movements. When contemplating this subject don't be carried away by the beauty of perfection; never lose sight of practical ends. As I have already said, all the benefits of physical development derived from these exercises are exhausted long before perfection of execution is reached. If you were planning to be a Dressage rider it would be different; then the very aim of your riding and of the competitions in which you would take part would be a *perfect* two tracks, a *perfect* change of leads, etc. In our case all these movements are not ultimate aims in themselves but are merely the means to develop a strong, safe, pleasant hunter or a dependable jumper. However, the performance of your horse may not be even; due to some mental or physical peculiarities he may execute some movements better than others. You may consider it necessary to equalize them and now is the time to do it.

In Chapter IX on What Is A Good Performance Of The Horse, I have described the good and the bad in different movements. In ideal you have now reached the good and to avoid too much repetition I will be brief in my description of how your horse should perform during this seventh month.

Emotional state of the horse. Whatever has been achieved during the previous six months should not have been at the expense of disturbing the horse's natural calmness. Today your horse should do two tracks, change leads and perform other movements in the same quiet state of mind in which he walked on loose reins half a year ago. And even more than that, for now you should be able at will to increase the alertness and impulse of the horse to a reasonable degree without upsetting him in the least. This increase should be merely the turning on of a tap, and as easily turned off. If you haven't achieved at least seventy-five per cent of this ideal (in an individual performance, anyway) you have failed in your schooling.

Physical state of the horse. Your horse today must be as sound as on the day you began to work him. While it will be easy for you to notice any change for the worse in his emotional state, you may be apt to over-look the beginning of unsoundness until it begins to make the horse lame. Hence I believe in having a consultation with your veterinary every two months, even though, to your knowledge, there is no reason to worry. Even if the doctor doesn't detect anything wrong he may, taking into consideration the points of your horse's conformation and his age, suggest reducing the amount of jumping or galloping or circling, etc. As a precautionary measure the advice of a veterinary is particularly im-portant if your horse is less than four years old.

Balance. Now, after six months of work, the horse has enough strength, agility and knack of carrying a burden to move under you with good bal-ance. The early stumblings have disappeared completely and, more than that, the horse doesn't feel awkward and heavy on the front; his gaits, turns, stops and changes of speeds are now skilfully done and give you in general a feeling of lightness combined with firmness of foot. Each of the exercises (including jumping) that you have practiced has con-tributed to the development of this balance.

A further improvement in balance will take place during the next two months when you will be working in the open, particularly when you begin to ride cross-country over varied terrain, up and down hill and so forth.

Ordinary gaits. All the ordinary gaits by now should be efficient, the horse moving forward with long, flat, free, regular strides. Furthermore, at all gaits the actions of forehand and hindquarters are harmoniously *connected,* the horse moving in one piece. This connected movement is exhibited by the horse not only when he is urged forward on the bit, but even when he is ridden comparatively passively on contact, perhaps even when on loose reins. Ordinary gaits are not spectacular but they are the "backbone" of the horse's performance.

Semi-collected gaits (as an exercise only). These gaits are now energetic but soft, the horse flexing every stride and walking calmly on loose reins if desired, immediately after the termination of each semi-collected period. The above qualities should exist already, at least at a trot; at a canter you may be still two or three weeks away from the goal.

Semi-extended trot (as an exercise only). Now, at the semi-extended trot, the horse does not move at his full speed but engages his hindquarters considerably and energetically extends his fore limbs, thus pushing every stride ahead of his body. This is a strenuous and stimulating movement; be careful not to overdo it.

Fast gallop. You really haven't had a fast gallop yet. You will start it in a month when you begin to work cross-country. So far, during your hacking you shouldn't have cantered faster than what the horse can do in the ring—which isn't much of a speed. But, just the same, it is faster than the ordinary canter and I hope it is absolutely quiet; it should be. Up to now you shouldn't have dared to increase the speed of the gallop beyond the point at which the horse remains calm.

The halt. At a walk, of course, for a long time you have been able to halt the horse abruptly; also at a semi-collected or a plain slow trot. It still probably takes something like 10′ to halt the horse from an ordinary trot, and probably not less than 20′ is required to come to a halt from an ordinary canter. That is, if you wish to do it softly. In an emergency, by using your hands harshly, you can always halt the horse much more quickly. But even when aiming at softness the formerly long intermediate periods of going from a canter to a trot, from a trot to a walk and from a walk to a halt are now considerably abbreviated.

The horse halts squarely and stands quietly for any length of time, although not necessarily as immobile as a monument. You have achieved the above results merely by making frequent and tactfully executed halts.

Transitions. All the transitions between gaits and movements are now sufficiently rapid, precise and soft. For instance, it probably takes you now no more than two sections of a fence (something like 20′) to change from an ordinary to a semi-extended or fast trot, no more than two strides of a trot as interruption when changing leads at a canter, and about 10′ to make a transition from an ordinary to a semi-collected or slow trot. The main thing is that during at least seventy-five per cent of these transitions the horse remains soft—let us hope so anyway.

You may find out that by now it is easy for your horse to start a canter from a walk. And if he does it without throwing his head up and without making a small upward bounce at the departure then include it in your program.

Naturally, the main test for the smoothness of transitions remains in the execution of a program which includes all the movements learned. By now your program is already approximately on the level of the training test of the Olympic Games; as a matter of fact, you can try to execute it. If you should consider doing so I would suggest your re-reading Chapter XIII, MODERNIZING THE IDEAL—and altering the program, replacing most of the collected gaits with ordinary ones, and adding two or three jumps.

When schooling a horse you ought to change the program quite often, presenting constantly unexpected combinations to the horse. But if you are working on a program for demonstration purposes you should do just the opposite—that is, make up a definite program and repeat it every day. The horse's memory and cooperation will be valuable in softening the transitions.

Circular movements. Gradually decreasing the size of your circles, in the course of this month, you should be able to make small circles merely 20′ in diameter, both at the semi-collected trot and semi-collected canter (as required in the Olympic Games). To insure softness during such a confined circular movement you should teach the horse "lateral flexion" which is a side retraction of the lower jaw in response to the increased tension on one rein. (With some horses only. See text on Flexions.)

I hope the lateral flexion will come as naturally as the direct flexion may have with your horse. But if it doesn't you may have to give the horse a couple of dismounted lessons. I doubt that it will be necessary; but if it is, the technique of teaching lateral flexions in hand is identical with the teaching of direct flexions. There is only one difference—one rein is used instead of both.

Don't make many of these extremely small circles, for a circle of about 40′ in diameter, made at ordinary gaits, is a sounder (although milder) lateral flexibility exercise for your future hunter.

When making small circles watch for the relaxed attitude of the horse. This is possible only if the size of the circle is diminished very gradually, in accordance with the progress of the horse. If not, the horse will become heavy in hand, will lose the regularity of his gait and will throw his hindquarters outward, will "skid" with them. A slight skidding can be controlled with the outside leg without further stiffening the horse, but not a big skidding, which is the result of asking more of the horse than he is yet capable of doing.

Serpentine and Zig-zag at a trot and canter, and half-circles and half-circles in reverse at a trot should also remain on your daily program, as lateral flexibility exercises; but now you may wish to use the last two also at the canter as an instrument for changing leads or for the counter-gallop. These half-circles may help you in obtaining your first flying changes.

Turns in place. I expect your horse now to know by heart both the half-turn on the forehand and half-turn on the haunches, and to execute them on soft contact in place and, if required, to stand quietly before and after.

Two tracks. I am certain that your two tracks at a walk is good, that you have begun to execute it at a trot and that there you still have difficulties: sometimes the horse doesn't move forward enough and his hindquarters begin to lead; at other times he loses the obliquity of movement and makes a few steps of mere change of direction. But probably another two or three weeks of it will straighten up these matters.

If the horse begins to lead with the hindquarters turn the horse's front with your hands more in the direction of the movement; increase the speed of the gait by using the leg on the side of the direction of the movement (its action will also decrease the movement of the quarters in this direction), and diminish the action of the other leg which has moved the horse too much to the side.

If the horse's defense consists of losing the angle of movement by increasing the speed, then halt him, give him the correct angle, make a few steps of two tracks at a walk, maintaining this angle, and then continue it at a trot, keeping the latter slow.

If your horse happens to execute the two tracks particularly well, just for fun, you can execute, without any special lessons, what is called a counter change of hands at two tracks. It consists of making about six steps to the right (this is the number of steps required in the Olympic Games), then six steps to the left, then again six steps to the right and so forth. The only difficulty you will encounter in this movement will be in changing from one direction to another without leading with the hindquarters during the first couple of strides. To overcome this make one straight-going stride in between. This exercise is unnecessary in making hunters and jumpers; it is in Dressage that a big point is made of it. But as long as an imperfect execution of it is easy, you may enjoy doing it. Also, for the same reason and to no special advantage to your horse, you might like to do *ordinary* two tracks at the canter; neither will this require special lessons or special technique.

Backing. Probably by now your backing after halting from a walk and trot is good and you may have begun to back after halting from a canter, resuming the gait immediately afterwards. This is a powerful exercise in coming back, engagement of the hindquarters and impulse forward. In general, it develops great agility and is one of the most important exercises for a jumper.

Don't attempt to start a canter immediately after the last step of backing because your horse, *not being collected,* doesn't have his hindquarters under him, and the canter departure from such a comparatively extended position is bound to be awkward and strenuous for the horse's hocks and loins. Upon completing backing, walk the horse forward for about one full stride and then begin the canter; that is if your horse knows the canter departure from a walk; otherwise you will have to make another stride or two of a trot.

If you were ever to have the good fortune to see the military teams of different nations work their horses before an international competition you would notice that this exercise (almost immediate canter departure after backing) is very important with most of them.

Changes of leads (flying). I expect that by now your horse is able to change quietly and softly with a very short interruption—with luck, flying.

Just one flying change is all that cross-country riding requires. You may for fun teach your horse to make several consecutive changes, but this is sort of extra-curricular and of no importance. The important points are that the horse should go free (while changing leads), straight, and maintain the regularity of the gait, not plunging after changes. You will probably reach this flying change in the course of this month.

As I have already pointed out in the chapter on advanced riding, there is no special technique involved in the flying changes of lead and success in getting your first change depends on asking it on the day when you feel your horse has acquired enough skill to respond to your demand. This skill, as you know, is developed by gradually cutting the number of intermediate trotting steps between the original gallop and the new departure. In the course of my life I have obtained the flying change of lead with many horses at the first asking. The trick is in knowing the day.

Jumping (simple courses). The general schooling and the exercises over obstacles which you have been doing for the last six months now should be apparent in the performance of your horse in the following ways:

1) Alert calmness combined with boldness.
2) Even, relaxed gaits during the approach.
3) Impulse forward not necessarily combined with speed.
4) Obedience based on knowledge of signals, and on the habit of cooperation.
5) Correct figuring.
6) Strong flight.
7) Skilful acrobatics.

In developing the jumping technique of your horse you have for a long time been using several obstacles in different close combinations, where the whole set-up aimed to promote nothing more than one specific jumping effort, although there were occasional exceptions to this rule. Now, a course is something very different: every obstacle in the series is intended to require some different quality in jumping or in galloping to an obstacle or galloping away from it; it is in this respect that a course is a test for the horse's ability to solve various jumping problems. Hence, a well-constructed course consists of a series of different problems in jumping, and during the gallops between fences. This last element, the galloping, is extremely important and many horses which can leap high lose their heads completely if they are galloped over even as few as three fences, particularly if the latter are far apart. An illustration of this is to be seen in every open jumping class.

Your first course should be laid out on flat ground outside the ring; it should consist of approximately eight different obstacles; it must have a couple of changes of direction on wide, comfortable turns and it should take about two minutes to gallop over it.

And what if you don't have a field in which to set up an outside course, and unfortunately have to do all your jumping in a comparatively small, enclosed arena? Here is the unpleasant truth: throughout the description of the program of schooling I have been assuming that those of my readers who wish to undertake schooling had adequate facilities. These consist of country for hacking, of open fields for galloping, of a large enclosed (not necessarily covered) ring in which you can work alone for at least an hour a day. An outside course is just one of the requisites, but it is an extremely important one in making a hunter or a real jumper. However, a decent jumper for small arena competitions can, of course, be made by practicing over courses crowded into a riding ring. In this respect no special advice can be given without knowing exactly the individual physical limitations of your surroundings. Just make the best of them.

Corrective jumping. Although from now on jumping courses is your main jumping problem, jumping exercises over single broad obstacles, Cavaletti, etc., remain on your program. The necessary resumption of your old work of one type or another will be indicated to you by the performance of your horse over courses. When going over them you should note the defects of your horse's going or jumping. Very possibly your horse will begin to lose calmness or flight or the use of the back and neck, or correct figuring; any one of these faults ought to mean that you stop going over a series of obstacles and return for a while to the work of one of the previous months. I am certain that in the course of the next three months this will happen two or three times, and each time it will take something like three days to restore the horse's original performance. If you are slow in detecting the appearance of a fault, it will take you considerably more than three days to correct it. Above all, be careful not to lose the alert calmness and the resulting relaxation in jumping.

Among the faults in jumping which may have been appearing for a while, and which became conspicuous when you began jumping courses, may be (I hope not) the following:

1) Your horse, although jumping correctly in every way, may knock down fences too often, even though they are well within the range of his ability. This may be the result of insufficient effort; in other words negligence, or a physical inability to fold the legs, or because of not looking at the top of fences.

Insufficient effort. Insufficient effort may, in many cases, be corrected by adding an iron pipe, $1\frac{1}{2}''$ in diameter, to the obstacles. If you place such an iron pipe on a level with the top bar of the jump and about 6'' in front of it, you will induce the horse to take off earlier and with greater strength. This is called *passive* poling (Picture 89).

Pic. 89.   A light iron pipe placed on the take-off side about 6'' in front of the top bar will make horse stand well back when taking-off and jump higher. Use when a horse with well-developed flight becomes careless.

Pic. 90

In case the horse knocks the jump down, usually by the hind legs dropping too soon, place the iron bar on the landing side of the jump. The most effective part of the iron pipe is the unexpected and startling sound it makes when hit.

The fault of dropping the hind legs is often the result of the rider either being left behind or not giving enough freedom to the horse's neck and head. So, before using the iron pipe, make certain that you yourself are not at fault.

Insufficient folding of the legs. If the insufficient folding is merely due to negligence, then passive poling may take care of it. But if it is the result of slow-acting muscles which haven't learned the knack of getting the legs out of the way quickly, you are facing a difficult problem. A triple bar, requiring from the horse a progressive folding of the legs, seems to be the most effective means of correction, particularly in combination with passive poling (Picture 90). Another way is to jump low fences up and down slopes (Picture 91).

Pic. 91.   Jump up-and-down-hill fences if the horse doesn't fold. A low triple
bar will enable an awkward horse to fold gradually.

Mere poling, passive or active (active poling means hitting the horse's legs with a pole by raising it in one way or another), may take care only of cases of sluggishness but not of physical disabilities. In the latter case it may make the horse jump higher but will not teach him to fold. Because of more effort he may clear the fence but his legs will still be hanging down.

Not looking at the top of the fence. Some horses, approaching the fence, don't look at the top of it as they should, which doesn't mean at all that in order to do so the horse has to raise his neck. This, by the way, is the reason why I have nowhere recommended putting a bar on the ground a couple of feet in front of the obstacle to make the horse take off earlier. This "take-off bar" (on which I was brought up), while working well with some horses, makes others look down instead of up. If it is necessary to teach the horse to look over the top of the fence use post and rail fences, concentrating two or three bars near the top and having nothing below them (Picture 92).

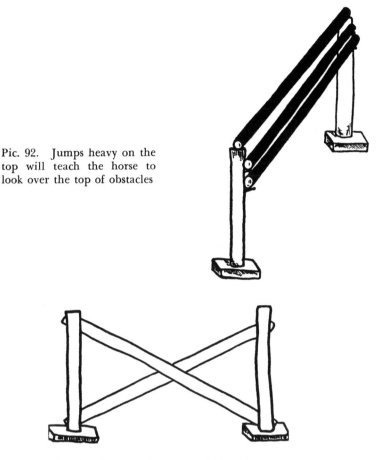

Pic. 92. Jumps heavy on the top will teach the horse to look over the top of obstacles

Pic. 93. Use cross bars to teach jumping over the center of the obstacle.

2) *Jumping the obstacle off center.* If your horse begins to jump close to one post or the other instead of jumping over the middle of the fence, use a cross bar jump, or place some frightening object on the side of the jump toward which he usually swerves (Picture 93). Be certain to take care of this fault as soon as it appears and before it becomes a habit.

3) *Jumping bias.* To correct bias jumping use low parallel bars and take them diagonally at a gallop. Jump this obstacle at the slant opposite from the one at which the horse likes to take it (Picture 94).

Rapping (poling). Poling does not have to take the cruel forms which it sometimes does. Intelligent rapping will help some horses. As a permanent part of a system it is used only by those who don't know how to make a jumper.

Lt. Col. Lombardo di Cumia of the Italian International Team lately said in print:"Rapping should serve to make a horse, who already jumps correctly, jump a little higher, but should never be used to train a horse who is jumping badly." Major Jan de Bruine, captain of the Netherlands International Team wrote recently: "Perhaps I am mistaken, but I do not believe in poling. I have made many faults after having been rapped by a 'professor' while I have made clean courses without being poled. Passive poling on the other hand, is very useful and is understandable to the horse."

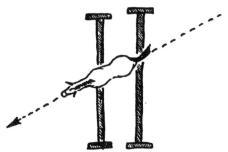

Pic. 94.   Diagonal jumping at a gallop will correct the defect of jumping side-ways. The obstacle must be of a broad type.

These two quotations express very well my belief on the subject. But if in the case of your horse, poling is necessary, then there is a serious question—should it be done over high or low fences. A French authority, Y.Benoist-Gironière, says: "Poling should be done on a medium-sized obstacle and not over mountains." And Major de Menten de Horne of the Belgian International Team says that the obstacles for poling should be: "even small." While Count de Maille, one of the outstanding civilian riders of France, has the following opinion on the subject: "I say very small." (The foregoing quotations are from CONCOURS HIPPIQUE, by Y.Benoist-Gironière, Paris, 1949.)

One of the obvious inefficiencies of active poling is the fact that the horse learns to associate it with one or two men (necessary to do it) standing at the fence; consequently to be done effectively, it has to be operated from far away by a pulley. As you probably know, poling with electric current is now regarded favorably by many.

I personally try all sorts of means to make the horse alert and careful of the fences before I resort to poling. There are many ways of doing it and it presents an open field for your imagination. For instance, if you ask someone to stand at the fence and when the horse is about 30′ from it to grasp one end of the upper bar, raise and lower it into position again rapidly, the horse will overjump the obstacle. Again, if you do this too often the horse will associate a man standing at the fence with the raising of the bar.

Hacking. Obviously, you will stress in your hacking whatever happens to be the most difficult. If your horse doesn't like to remain behind other horses you try to make him to do so, and if he is restless when alone, thinking of his friends left behind in the stable, then you hack him alone, developing the habit of being without the herd. As to the new additions to your hacking program I think by now a low jump can be taken here and there. It will constitute a practical application of something learned in the ring and a preparation for future cross-country jumping.

8TH MONTH (WORK IN THE FIELDS).

The new part of the work of this month consists in practicing exercises already learned in different locations on large, flat fields. The main purpose of this is to teach the horse to work in different surroundings, for otherwise the habit of performing well only in your own back yard can easily become established. I usually combine it with hacking in the following manner:Leaving the stable I hack for about twenty minutes at a walk and trot to limber the horse and then stop in a suitable field for something like ten minutes to execute a program consisting of all or some of the movements my horse knows. Then I resume my hacking, rest my horse, and in about twenty minutes, in another field, again repeat some of my ring exercises, in a program or singly, whichever is necessary, and so forth. The next time I do this work I take a different direction to do the same sort of thing in different surroundings.

There may be two reasons for your occasional return to work in the ring:

1) The physical condition of the fields; for instance, the grass may be too tall or the ground too soft—after all you don't want to chop up someone's fields—and there may be other purely local reasons.

2) You may wish to return to the ring to correct a defect which has suddenly appeared in some movement, or to execute your program with *precis on,* which is possible only in a ring marked with the usual letters or other signs.

All in all, the work on schooling exercises in the open will probably be limited to a couple of days a week, because galloping, jumping over courses and corrective jumping, as well as corrective riding in the ring, will take a great deal of your time and of the horse's energy.

Galloping. For a long time you have been cantering in the ring and while hacking. From the very beginning the speed of your approximately ordinary canter has been regulated by the behavior of your horse, which means that you have gone only as fast as was practical for preserving the calmness of the horse. At first it was somewhat slower than the ordinary canter and I hope that little by little you have been able to increase the speed to somewhat faster than that of the ordinary canter. I also expect that you have gradually lengthened the duration of the canters, being guided by the increasing stamina of your horse. By now your horse should be able to canter for about seven minutes at a speed of something like ten or twelve miles an hour without any harm to his health. Up until now a faster or a longer gallop would probably have been taking chances. But, from now on, you should make a point of increasing the speed to eighteen miles an hour, and at the very end of the ninth month it will perhaps be easy for your horse to keep up this speed for as much as ten minutes. Not knowing your horse and his present condition I have to be rather indefinite in giving you speeds and durations of gallops; all the above suggestions are on the safe side.

In consideration of the fact that your horse is still young and has not yet reached his greatest possible development in agility, balance and strength, these first gallops in the open country should take place on large, *level* fields free of stones and holes. The length of your gallops is limited by the horse's breathing and general fatigue, and the speed by his excitability. During a faster gallop the horse must take a firmer hold of the bit.

Jumping. Gradually your courses should become more complicated and this process should proceed along the following lines:

1) Increase the number of changes of directions and gradually narrow the angles of some of the turns.

2) Alternate long approaches to obstacles with short ones.

3) As usual, all obstacles should be different in construction, some should vary in color and now they should be arranged in more difficult combinations than in the previous month. For instance, your normal triple in-and-out, with distances allowing for one stride between fences, can be changed now to a combination of the same obstacles with one stride between the first and second and two strides between the second and third fences. Later you may require your horse to jump this obstacle in both directions. And still later one of these vertical fences can be replaced by a broad jump. This is a typical example of how combinations of fences are made progressively more difficult.

The number of your fences on the course may now be something like ten or twelve; the majority should be about 3'3", with three or four of them raised to 3'9". The courses should still be set on level ground, without wings, the fences being 20' wide. The horse should not be jumped over the same course more than twice if he negotiates it well. This doesn't mean that every two jumping days you have to change the course entirely; but about one-third of it should be replaced with different fences, and you should change your route.

You shouldn't be in a hurry to increase the complexity of your courses. You have not only this month but the following one in which to do it.

9TH MONTH (WORK OVER VARIED TERRAIN).

When you reach this month you should plan your jumping and the work on schooling exercises, in the open and in the ring, so that about two days a week are left for work across country. I do not mean to say that on these days all of your two hours are to be spent galloping up and down hill; such gallops, depending on the stamina and temperament of your horse, may consist of one period of ten minutes or two six-minute periods, or some other combination. In any case before your gallop or gallops, you have a long preliminary period of limbering up your horse—something like half an hour; then you have a cooling off period on your way home—at least twenty minutes; then you may find it wise to make some specific relaxing exercises after the first gallop, if your horse has stiffened; or you may think it necessary to take over again one or two fences singly (several times perhaps), fences which were particularly bad during the gallop. Besides all this you will have to give the horse a long rest of, let us say, another twenty minutes between the two gallops on the day when you may have decided that two gallops of six minutes each are preferable to one gallop of ten minutes (all these durations of the gallop are approximate). All in all, two hours will be fully occupied by the preliminaries and the follow-up of your few minutes of galloping.

For this work you should choose a part of the country which offers a variety of terrain—fields, woodland paths, hills, fences, streams, etc. For the first two weeks of this month you walk, trot and occasionally canter the horse slowly over this country, taking fences at slow gaits, aiming to establish calmness as a preparation for gallops over the same terrain. During these two weeks you continue with fast gallops on level fields (see previous month), thus conditioning the horse. As I have already pointed out, your aim is a hunting pace, which is approximately eighteen miles per hour (and it is also the pace of most European jumping competitions and of our hunting classes over the outside courses); but this does not mean that you begin with this speed. After two weeks of preparatory walking, trotting and cantering you begin your gallops cross-country with a speed of approximately twelve miles per hour; you increase it as much as possible while preserving the horse's calmness, and you gallop only as long as the horse remains calm. It is very possible that you may find that for some time three gallops of four minutes each are more satisfactory for your horse than one gallop of ten minutes. But even if your horse should work with perfect calmness at a speed of eighteen miles per hour, you still should not maintain this speed throughout your gallop. You must vary the speed as a part of your transition work and occasionally you should even stop and walk or trot your horse for half a minute before again resuming the gallop. Not for one second must a fast-galloping horse have the feeling that all the brakes are off. In other words, you should prepare your horse mentally for the actual work in the hunting field or over outside courses. The fact that your horse gallops quietly when alone is sufficient for the latter case, but is not enough for the hunting field. Therefore, occasionally you must do the same work in company. When riding with a couple of friends you may suggest interrupting the gallop at any time to bring the horse to reason, thus working toward establishing the habit of calmness in company. No such thing can be done later in the hunting field. These gallops cross-country not only prepare the horse mentally for his future work, and condition him physically, but also further develop his balance and general agility.

As already mentioned, all the lengths of the galloping periods I have given are approximate, but they were worked out as simplifications of those in the Three-Day Event. There the cross-country run at a speed of about nineteen miles per hour is 5½ miles long and has over thirty obstacles, which means that the gallop lasts about eighteen minutes— this occurs approximately one hour and a half after taking a steeplechase course of a little more than 2 miles. It normally takes from two to three years to prepare a horse for this contest and, naturally, all the horses selected possess superior physical abilities.

Jumping. In its essentials the work over courses remains the same as in the previous month, the courses gradually becoming more complicated. In the course of this month some of your fences should be raised to the height of 4'.

End of the Schooling Program

As you see, the schooling program, even simplified as it is, is a long one and, while it is all new to you, you should not become confused by the many directions along which the physical development of the horse is supposed to progress from month to month. Just re-read the notes on the schooling program as you go along.

Now you are ready to begin to hunt or to show. I wish to underline the word *begin* because, although your horse has had the basic schooling for these games, he hasn't had the experience of working in these special surroundings; furthermore, his conditioning is still not sufficient to withstand a full day of hard hunting, nor has he yet had practice in negotiating the really high fences necessary to win in any class that is listed on the program of a show. But what he needs from now on is not more schooling but merely practice, with perhaps an occasional return to schooling when things begin to go wrong.

Horses don't stay schooled unless they are consistently well and sensibly ridden. Stupid riding in a couple of shows or in a couple of hunts may upset the horse so much that it may take one month of corrective schooling to get him back to where he was.

A well-schooled horse sold to a poor rider can become unmanageable in the course of only a few weeks. This all means that a schooled horse is a superior instrument only in the hands of an intelligent and educated rider. And, vice-versa, a good rider can demonstrate his skill only on a schooled horse.

Schooling, as described in this program, even when used by a good rider in training average horses, does not guarantee one hundred per cent success. With casual approximation one can say that full success can be expected with only seventy-five per cent of the horses. The emotional make-up of some horses is such that they can never learn to go calmly when galloping fast with a large field, while the physical or mental limitations of others will preclude them jumping really big obstacles. But, just the same, schooling will improve even these cases, and a potential runaway will be merely nervous at times and a potential refuser will learn to negotiate average field fences easily.

As I have pointed out many times, schooling doesn't aim to make a horse who merely stays with the hounds or wins ribbons. It is intended to make him *pleasant to ride,* that is, keen and cooperative, in the hunting field or in the horse show, and to develop him physically to the point where he can *participate in these games for many years without being crippled* by work which is too much for a physically undeveloped horse.

Unfortunately, our normal horse shows don't have any schooling competitions, hence the fascinating game of schooling a horse is at present a solitary one. Judging by my own reactions, this situation should be very disturbing to other trainers of horses, since we all like to demonstrate what we are able to achieve. In my case this takes the form of torturing my friends; a process which often backfires and tortures me, for so many nice people for whom I ride don't know a thing about riding. A demonstration of really good ordinary gaits (one of the main aims of schooling) , or of athletically negotiated 3'6" fences leaves them standing with blank faces, while a scramble over a 5' obstacle or two tracking like a crab makes them "oh" and "ah." This, by the way, is one of the reasons why I mentioned in the seventh month of the schooling program a few extra-curricular movements like the counter-change of hands at two tracks and a series of flying changes of leads on a straight line; unnecessary as these movements may be in schooling a hunter or jumper, an exhibition of them is bound to boost your own morale.

And speaking of yourself, I believe that these nine months of schooling a horse will make a real rider out of you, even if the first product of your efforts turns out to be far from perfect. Schooling a horse is really the only way to understand the meaning of all the formulae of control. One learns the use of a certain combination of legs and hands only when he tries it on a horse who does not understand it. It is through the mis-understandings of the horse and his various types of resistance that one fully learns the cooperation of legs and hands with the efforts of the horse. But, as I have frequently said, only so much can be done with the legs and hands alone. Most good riding and schooling is done with the head. It is your understanding of the mentality of the horse and an imaginative approach to his emotions which really wins the day. The experience of schooling even one horse is most valuable in this respect. Horses don't read books, but a clever rider can establish a common language with his mount and with its help translate to him what he himself has learned through reading.

I also expect that this chapter has opened up new vistas in riding for you, showing you that this sport does not consist merely in physical skill, but that it also contains many mental problems which can hold one's interest in riding long after a youthful fascination with purely physical activities is gone. I know so many people who dropped riding in their middle life just because the mature side of it was never presented to them.

As a footnote to the description of the schooling program I am giving a sample of distribution of work during a lesson. I assume that this lesson takes place exactly in the middle of the course—the end of the second week of the fifth month. I also assume that you have reached the working time of one hour and a half a day, that on this particular day you have decided to work the full time in the ring and that the horse did not have to be longed before mounting.

As usual, this program of a lesson is not a rule. It merely tries to em-phasize certain important points, such as frequent and rather long rests, frequent halts, frequent changes of subject in order not to bore the horse, riding a great deal on loose rein, ending the lesson on a new exercise.

10 min. Walk, mostly on loose reins, to limber up the horse, with about two turns on the forehand, a couple of circles and as many half-circles and half-circles in reverse. Four halts.

5 min. Ordinary trot, at first on loose reins, later on contact. Serpentine and Zig-zag (one of each) and circles, half-circles and half-circles in re-verse (one or two of each). Two diagonal changes of directions. Three halts.

3 min. Walk on loose reins to rest. Two halts.

3 min. Ordinary canter, at first on loose reins, later on contact. Two changes of lead (while changing direction). One halt and about four circles (on the right and on the left leads).

5 min. Walk on loose reins to rest. Two turns on the forehand.

5 min. Increase and decrease of speed at a trot with a couple of halts. On contact and sometimes on the bit.

5 min. Walk on loose reins to rest. A couple of halts.

3 min.   Ordinary canter on loose reins and contact. Two changes of leads. One halt and several circles.
5 min.   Jumping wide obstacles at a trot. About six jumps.
10 min. Dismount to give your horse a complete rest.
3 min.   Increase and decrease of the speed at the canter with two halts. On contact, and short periods on the bit.
5 min.   Walk on loose reins to rest. Two halts.
5 min.   Increase and decrease of speeds at a trot with the emphasis on semi-collection and semi-extension. Mostly on the bit, with two long halts.
5 min.   Walk on loose reins to rest.
10 min. Work over Cavaletti; about ten jumps (starting with a very low one). At first cross Cavaletti at a walk (without jumping), later at a trot without and with jumping.
5 min.   Walk on loose reins to rest. Two turns on the forehand.
3 min.   Counter gallop.
90 min. Dismount and cool off the horse in hand.

SPECIAL EXERCISES FOR HUNTERS

The schooling of a jumper and the schooling of a hunter differ in some respects. First of all, while a future jumper is prepared for an *individual* performance in an arena, a hunter is schooled for cross-country work in *company*.

As you know, habit is a dominating factor in the horse's life; therefore a hunter prospect should be given ample opportunity to become accustomed to working with other horses. Hacking in company is not enough; a future hunter should also often practice his ring exercises together with other horses. Exercises such as stabilization, Cavaletti, multiple in-and-outs, jumping single fences, halts at all gaits, backing, turns in place, changing gaits, even increase of speed, should be frequently practiced in a class-ride form, with rigidly kept distances between the horses. In the early stages of schooling, a future hunter must be given experience in cantering or jumping behind other horses, with yet others galloping or jumping behind him. Regular work in company will in time develop the precious habit of remaining calm while performing in a group.

As helpful practice, I would suggest occasionally asking the class to disperse, the riders working individually, moving in various directions and at different gaits, working in the center of the arena as well as along the fence. Any horse intended eventually to perform in company needs to acquire the habit of remaining quiet when meeting horses moving in the opposite direction; we all have seen many horses which would shy away or even rear on encountering other horses, particularly if the latter were moving fast.

But even the regular class work comprised of the usual schooling exercises, whether in the ring or in a field, is not sufficient. Certain emotional situations, peculiar to foxhunting, should be imitated in the ring or in the schooling field, and eventually across country, thus, accustoming future hunters to the specific conditions in which they will work. For instance, your colt must learn to remain calm when, for one reason or another, he has to wait his turn at a jump or when other horses pass him at a gallop. These and similar situations can be approximated by what I call "exercises for hunters." The exercises for hunters (as any class work) can be practiced only if there is somebody to give directions. It is to this person that the description of the routine of conducting the exercises is addressed.

Exercises for Hunters.
  Exercise #1.

Direct your class to walk along the fence of the ring, keeping their distances of two or three lengths of a horse (about two or three sections of a fence). When the class is moving along in an orderly fashion give the command: "Begin passing at a trot." At this command the last rider moves out of the line, starts a trot and passes (on the inside, of course) the whole line of riders. Once he finds himself ahead of the leader, he moves towards the fence, and breaking into a walk assumes the position of the leader. The rider who was second from the rear as soon as he is passed by the one behind him trots out and begins passing also and the remainder follow suit in succession. Thus, at any given moment, some riders are walking on loose reins, along the fence while others are trotting, preferably on loose reins also, passing the walking riders.

The progressive development of this exercise consists in passing a trotting class at a canter, and finally, a cantering one at a gallop.

This exercise is an old favorite with riding teachers and is used by them for bettering the technique of the rider's control; the exercise is merely routine to all good school horses.

  Exercise #2.

Start your class riding at a walk along the fence of the ring. Make the class take a numerical order, thus dividing them into odd and even numbers. Give the following command: "each even number pass the horse ahead at a trot"; at this command all even numbers should simultaneously start a trot and each rider pass only the horse which is ahead of him (as usual on the inside). The moment this is done all the even numbers should resume the walk. You now have the whole class walking along the fence and, let us hope, maintaining the usual distances of two lengths of a horse. When distances are easily kept (on loose reins at times), it means not only that the riders are in control of their horses but that the horses are calm and cooperative. Your next command is: "each odd number pass the horse ahead at a trot." Repeat this exercise for as long as necessary.

As soon as this exercise is mastered at the walk and trot, make your class move at the trot, passing at the canter. If it is practical to go still further you may make the class move at a slow canter (slower than ordinary) and pass at a faster one. For passing at a canter you should double the distances between riders. Even a good-sized ring (125' by 250') is too small to perform this exercise at a canter if the group is larger than about six. Your schooling field is the place for practicing it.

Exercise #3.

Have your class ride at a trot toward a low obstacle. When the leader is about 75' from the fence, give the command: "odd numbers take the obstacle at a trot, even numbers make a wide circle (following their leader) to the right and then go over the obstacle." You should of course alternate circling to the right and to the left. The odd numbers after negotiating the obstacle, gradually drop into a walk, thus waiting for the other group to join them. The even numbers, after making the circle, take the jump, also single file (now keeping double distances), and after the jump they resume the trot, catch up with the other group, take their respective places in the class and drop into a walk. Now, your next command should be addressed to the whole class—"everyone trot." While the class is trotting you order the necessary turn to approach the obstacle again (perhaps this time from the other side). Then you ask even numbers to go straight at the obstacle and odd numbers to make a circle before taking it. Later the same exercise should be done at a canter, and later yet, over a raised obstacle. This exercise really should be practiced in a large field and not in the ring, particularly if the class is a large one.

A variation of this exercise would be to ask the odd numbers to jump while the even numbers pass to the left or right of the obstacle, the class forming up again on the other side of the jump.

You can also make a long fence, one part of which is lower than the other. In this case your command to the class which approaches the fence single file at a trot or canter, would be "odd numbers jump the higher part of the fence and even numbers jump the lower one; on the other side of the obstacle resume your places in the class."

Exercise #4.

Ask your class to trot or canter toward an obstacle and at about 75' in front of it form a line parallel to the obstacle either to the right or the left of the halted leader. As a variation, the class may halt in a bunch; wait until all the horses are absolutely calm and then begin to call individual riders to take the jump singly at a trot or, if you think preferable, at a canter. The individual horses must leave the group willingly; those which don't should be punished. While one horse jumps, the others should be standing calmly. Little by little your class will be lined up or bunched up on the other side of the jump, probably something like 150' away from it; you then order them to resume the gait, forming the usual single file. Have your class make the necessary turn to approach this or a different obstacle again; repeat the routine.

As in the case of all the other exercises, this one may be varied. For instance, you can order all the even numbers to jump and only the odd ones to line up 75' before reaching the obstacle. After the even numbers have negotiated the obstacle and have either lined up on the other side of it or are walking away, in a class, with doubled distances between horses, you should order the odd number group to take the jump in their turn, either singly or in a class.

The number of exercises for hunters can be considerably enlarged. You only need to think of the various difficulties which you or your friends have experienced when hunting and invent exercises of your own to cope with the specific situations which bother your horse. For instance, you can duplicate the situation when a field, forced to ride single file along a woods path, has to halt for one reason or another and each horse wait his turn to jump.

Caution: Obviously, horses which are apt to kick should not be included in group exercises. Also, horses which have a marked tendency to refuse or run out should not take part in exercises over obstacles where a halt before the fence or passing of the jump is required.

While recommending these exercises, I fully appreciate the difficulty of putting them into practice among almost any group of riders except those practicing in riding schools or the riding departments of private schools and colleges, where regular schedules are maintained. In the average hunt club, for instance, it seems to be next to impossible to organize even as few as half a dozen riders who will school together regularly. However, if you wish easy, safe, pleasant hunting, this is the only way to go about training your horses, unless you are one of those lucky individuals who possess horses so calm and sensible by nature that in the hunting field they will behave like ladies and gentlemen without any emotional conditioning for fast work in company, and will do their work quite decently even without any schooling.

CHAPTER XVI

How to Teach Riding (General Considerations)

This is an introduction to the next three chapters in which I discuss my method of teaching riding.

I do not believe that riding can be taught efficiently by anybody to anybody on any horse and in any place. Any method can be practiced successfully only if the teacher, pupils, horses and equipment meet certain requirements; this chapter is devoted to an analysis of these requirements.

THE TEACHER

It may seem strange to the uninitiated that the statement that the *teacher must be an up-to-date rider* should be necessary. But, since the rating of riding teachers in this country started only recently, and so far is confined to the field of physical education in women's colleges and schools, one has to admit reluctantly that many join the profession without having a satisfactory preparation for it, some of whom undertake teaching purely as business. I actually know riding teachers who ride sitting on the horse's kidneys, with legs stuck forward, hands at their stomachs and whose control of the horse is as absurd. They don't even represent a good old-fashioned type of riding and merely exhibit a complete lack of knowledge of it. The ignorance or lack of discrimination of a large part of the potential clientele unfortunately enables some of these teachers to make a business success.

Sometimes simple but correct riding, which has been learned superficially, lacks a thorough understanding of why one behaves at certain moments in the saddle in one way and not in another. This sort of riding is not enough for the teacher. Teaching is imparting one's knowledge and, consequently, the *teacher must know why he is doing this or that.* In other words, besides being a rider, the teacher must know the theory of riding; for teaching to ride consists in explaining to the pupil what to do and when and why, on the one hand, and training his body to the point where he can do it, on the other. This knowledge of riding, in my estimation, is even more important than riding itself. As he grows older, the teacher will gradually lose the excellence of his performance in the saddle; but there is no limit to his accumulation of knowledge for the benefit of his pupils.

Theoretical and practical knowledge of riding are not all that is required from a teacher; he must have the *ability to impart this knowledge*

313

to his pupil. I imagine that many are born with this talent, but unquestionably it is developed with experience. I can frankly admit that today in one lesson I can teach more than I did in four or five lessons twenty-odd years ago, when I first began teaching in the United States.

I know of many others who, like me, have progressed in the efficiency of their work, and it seems to me that in all cases it was possible due to two reasons: 1) *analytical self-criticism, and 2) a method.* Almost from the first day of my teaching I developed the habit of looking back for a few moments over each lesson which had just been completed. While doing so I was trying to analyze the mistakes which I had made, at the same time never sparing compliments to myself for the good part of my work. As to the method: I do not mean that a teacher should be pedantically inflexible—not at all, just the opposite. He must possess a keen mind which will enable him to see at a glance the emotional and physical conditions of his pupils and horses, and to be directed by them during the lesson. But I also know that the easiest way to teach riding is to pronounce the letter B only after the letter A has been learned. I have often witnessed how hopelessly desperate both pupil and teacher become, and how fruitless the work, when lessons have no connection. One lesson must logically lead to the next, and the *teacher should constantly improve his method.*

Probably the most difficult quality for a teacher to have is the *ability to go ahead with the times.* Riding, as everything else, is not stationary. New ideas spring up in different parts of the world. As in any other field, many of them are just fancies, but some present an improvement upon existing theories. A true knowledge of riding, plus an open mind, will enable one to discriminate and to improve. Unfortunately this is seldom the case, and many of us die professing what we learned fifty years before. In the history of riding our century has shown more rapid progress than almost any other period. Many of us have not been quick enough to follow it; this is largely responsible for the conflict of ideas we are now witnessing.

Now about the character of the instructor—of course there is a set of, so to speak, recognized "bedside manners," such as *patience, cheerfulness* and *an encouraging attitude.*

Patience is tremendously important; cheerfulness is always pleasant; but frequently over-encouragement merely makes pupils lose all sense of what is really good. I believe that sincerity is more productive than flattery. Be prompt in telling a pupil when he did something well, but never hesitate in telling him when it is bad. If one works methodically, avoiding asking more from the pupil than he can do, the word "bad" is rather seldom necessary. It is important for a pupil to learn to discriminate, and it is the teacher's duty to teach him to do so. I have found out that tactful, analytical criticism is resented by only a few. These cannot learn riding.

Many of us love to ride for an audience and get a great kick out of performing for an admiring pupil. There is no harm in it, but long ago

I came to the conclusion that the spirit of—"Look at me, look how wonderful I am," is not a sound one for the teacher to have. Of course a teacher must mount to demonstrate and, naturally, for a long time his riding is bound to be very superior to his pupil's. But the time comes for the teacher to say, at least to some of his pupils: "This is how well I can do it, but you are younger and abler than I am, you will do it better in time." It is a great thing for the teacher to be proud of the riding of his pupils. A good teacher produces occasionally a better rider than he is himself.

THE PUPIL

Pupils present a wide range of abilities; many were not born to ride well, some will make good riders, and only a few will become outstanding ones. Riding teachers are not magicians; the most that a teacher can do is to develop to the maximum the *natural abilities* of his pupils.

A potential rider possesses the following qualities: *suitable physique, boldness, sympathy for the horse, a quick mind, and the ability to work hard, logically and patiently.*

A good teacher will use the rider's physique to develop a strong seat (the basis for good hands), and strong, sure use of legs. Boldness, as well as being necessary for hunting and jumping, will make possible quick, correct thinking in tight places. Sympathy for the horse will enable the pupil in time to understand him, to feel him, and to "converse" with him; a logical mind is necessary in schooling horses; and no one can accomplish much unless he works.

Working, as I understand it, does not mean merely taking lessons. I do not believe that one can learn to ride through merely riding around a teacher while being constantly corrected by him. Consequently *my method of teaching requires "home work."* During the lesson I explain what to do to obtain a certain movement, and why; I show the easiest way to go about it; I repeatedly correct my pupil until he knows when he is right and when he is wrong. After this he should work by himself for two or three hours, training his body so that he can execute with ease what I have taught him during the lesson. This achieved, he is ready for the next lesson. I begin it by asking him to show me how well he has learned the previous one; depending on the results, we either go ahead or repeat the former lesson, and I again insist on "home work." A pupil who is unable to work by himself is hopeless.

I have obtained the best results since following this method. The most inefficient, expensive and the most common way of trying to learn riding is to take lessons twice weekly and never go near a horse between times. Then, hour after hour, you hear the instructor repeating like a gramophone, "heels down, straight back, relax," and so forth. This may be a good way of earning a living for the instructor, and for the pupil to have a good time; but it is neither teaching nor learning. Of course, a beginner can do his home work safely only if he is provided with a small enclosed ring, with an absolutely dependable horse and with somebody to keep an eye on him without attempting to teach him.

The theoretical knowledge that one must possess to become a good rider is quite substantial. It is difficult for the pupil to remember everything he has heard during lessons and this is why he *must read;* he must practically memorize certain passages in some books. Among riding students the reluctance to read is common and its presence considerably diminishes the speed of progress in learning.

So, as you see, "home work" must be both mental and physical. Responsibility for progress in learning to ride is equally divided between the pupil and his teacher. It is up to the pupil to train his body and to learn the theory of riding, and it is up to the teacher to direct his pupil's efforts efficiently.

If the pupil does not progress in a satisfactory manner, there is normally a natural tendency on his part to blame the teacher for the failure, and as natural and perhaps as sincere an attempt on the part of the teacher to put all the blame on the pupil. Either, of course, may be the case, just as substantial progress may be the result of only one party working well. But really efficient teaching takes place only when both teacher and pupil possess the necessary qualities described above and apply them in their work.

HORSES

The fact that one cannot learn riding on one horse is obvious, but there must be a *system* to the changing of horses; the change of horses should follow the pupil's progress.

The horses on which a pupil is taught position (whether he is a beginner or a rider who is changing his seat) should require a minimum of control. Their gaits must be easy and even, and they should keep a slow trot and slow canter (alone or in a class) almost by themselves. In the same manner they should jump low obstacles.

It is absurd to try to teach position on horses that stop or pull or become excited or refuse to stay along the wall, etc. A beginner cannot be expected to control the horse while learning position; all his mental and physical efforts should be concentrated on himself. Only if he is given such an opportunity can he progress rapidly.

Rarely can one buy a "ready-made" horse for beginners, but making one is easy and merely consists of the two first months of schooling—teaching voice commands on a longe and stabilization when mounted (see the chapter on THE PROGRAM OF FORWARD SCHOOLING). If the horse in question has a placid nature (and all beginners' horses should have) such a horse can begin to work under beginners in two months. Practice will improve him in the course of the next half year. Once such a horse has become a perfect instrument for teaching position he becomes really valuable to the school. Anything which may upset him should be avoided. Hence he should never be used for better riders who may be learning control and will, therefore, be trying to use aids or make him execute more complicated movements. A beginner's horse must know one routine only, that is ring work and hacking at slow, even gaits on loose reins, obeying voice commands.

Once the pupil has acquired a decent position, knows elementary control and the time has arrived to begin to teach him intermediate *control,* he should be transferred to a different set of horses—schooled ones. These horses must know at least all the simple movements, *responding correctly to the aids.* They should not be upset by the heavy legs and hands of a green rider.

When the pupil has learned (more or less mechanically) the cooperation of legs and hands, he should be introduced to horses equally well schooled but more sensitive who, in a mild way, will object to heavy handling. On these horses the student will learn to *feel* the amount of legs and hands required in various movements. Proper exercises and methodical work will develop "good legs and good hands." To develop strong legs in particular the pupil should ride over-lazy horses, and to develop softness of hands, he must ride over-ambitious ones; these, of course, are special cases.

The next step is to teach the pupil to school a completely green horse. I believe that schooling should be taught to every *able* rider, for it is the only way to give the polishing touches to his control, feelings, and full understanding of riding.

A poor teacher will find innumerable excuses against having such a variety of horses and, true enough, if the teacher is bad he won't have any use for two categories of horses mentioned above. He will never need green horses, for he probably will never develop his pupils to the point where they are ready to learn schooling, and even if asked by an outsider to give such a course, will not know how to do it. Furthermore, he won't even have use for the schooled horses on which control should be taught, for most of his pupils will remain perpetual beginners while, to him, good control will mean nothing more than to be able to "master" a difficult horse in a very primitive way. In many cases he will not even have beginners' horses, for he has never learned how to organize his teaching and his remarks like "keep your heels down" will be forever hopelessly entangled with directions such as "more right leg and left hand."

So the presence in a riding school of different groups of horses on which different elements of riding are taught is a recommendation in itself.

Quite often failure to organize efficient teaching is not the fault of the teacher but of the circumstances in which he finds himself. For instance, many colleges and schools have no riding stables of their own although they may have a riding teacher on their staff. The physical education department makes some arrangement with a local stable for the use of their horses. In such cases the very same horses are hired out to towns-people who may ride very differently and many very badly. This is where even the best teacher is under too great a handicap to teach efficiently.

TEACHING GROUNDS

The most inefficient way to *begin* teaching a beginner is "on the road." The familiar picture of such a pupil dragged along on a lead rein and trying to post under the count "up, down, up, down," always makes me sorry for both the horses and human beings involved. The pathetic thing about it is not merely the unnecessary physical effort put into it but rather the fact that the whole course in riding started in this way cannot amount to much.

I believe that there is only one way to begin the course of lessons—that is in the ring. Of course, a covered ring is the best for schooling riders and horses; a covered ring makes the work independent of the weather and permits it to be systematic. But, this being impossible in most cases, an open ring will do. It may be of different dimensions, but if one has to teach both beginners and advanced riders and school horses in the same ring, then the size of the Olympic Games training test arena should be considered; it is 65 feet by 195 feet, with right angled corners.

The ring should be laid out on even ground and if used for beginners, should have at least a 4' fence around it for the safety of the pupils. On the other hand, for advanced riders and for schooling horses, a mere 6" board (as on a polo field) is all that is needed; for these latter cases one requires a defined arena only to help pupils to move straight, not to go away too far from the teacher and to work, in general, with a certain precision of control.

For the sake of this precision of control about a dozen letters should be painted on the walls of the arena, just as it is done in the Olympic Games. During the lesson in control, all the commands are executed upon reaching a specified letter. If, for instance, the instructor has given the command to start the canter at the letter A and the pupil has succeeded in executing it only after he is far past the letter, then it is obvious to him that his control was poor. These letters are also necessary when practicing programs in schooling horses.

As a rule, horses under beginners cut corners. To prevent this, while your beginners don't yet know control, you should place a post in each corner, about 8' away from either of the two walls, and the horse should be made to go between it and the wall; horses quickly acquire the habit of doing it by themselves. An oval arena eliminates this difficulty.

The equipment of the riding ring should include a large variety of fences. This variety is primarily necessary for schooling horses; for teaching pupils, a dozen fences will suffice, and the full dozen you will only use when your pupils have reached the stage of learning how to take courses. If your ring is too small for such courses they ought to be set up outside it. Unfortunately, as a rule, an outside course means a permanently set up series of jumps. This does not make sense either for schooling horses or for teaching humans. In both cases the courses must be often changed, depending on the current aim, progress or encountered difficulties.

If the jumps were too heavy, I would be the first to think twice before dragging them around, and would probably unconsciously invent all sorts of reasons for the same course remaining for another week. Obstacles should be light and easy to assemble.

As for wings—you need none. If, on a very unlucky day, something like wings may be helpful you can always make them up out of spare posts and rails.

Even if your ring is roomy enough to set up a course for beginners you need a large outside field in which to set up long and complicated courses for your advanced riders and for schooling horses. It will be fortunate if such a field is not level, so that your horses and pupils learn jumping up —and down—hill with an occasional "drop."

Country for hacking is, of course, essential in making cross-country riders and horses and, if there is a hunt nearby which your advanced pupils, human and equine, can join occasionally, you are ideally situated.

EQUIPMENT

It is imperative that you have forward seat saddles. Knowing how expensive it is to equip a whole stable with new saddles I have hesitated to say this, but, unfortunately there is no way out. A good hunting and jumping seat just cannot be taught on anything else.

In a stable of, let us say, twenty horses I personally would not have use for more than three full bridles which I would need on rare occasions for teaching the use of the curb to *very* advanced riders. For hunting those horses which become emotionally upset when galloping in company I would recommend a Pelham. All my regular teaching and schooling of horses is done on a snaffle and I firmly believe that you and your pupils and your horses will be better off if you follow suit.

Martingales are *absolutely unnecessary* to me—unnecessary for my horses and, if I am successful in my teaching, unnecessary for my pupils. But I would keep a couple in my tack-room—one standing and one running and I would put them on occasionally to demonstrate to my pupils their ill effects.

When teaching position to beginners one of my first concerns is to stabilize their legs. In this period of learning I don't want them to use their legs for control; hence they all should ride with a short, straight crop in hand—just a wooden stick about 2′ long and thick enough to grip easily. When I give the command "trot" all pupils should repeat it loudly to their horses and if they meet with no response they should urge the horse with the crop *using it on the shoulder.* A riding school must have many such crops.

Many ideas and even actual paragraphs of this chapter appeared in an article written by me in 1941 for "Official Individual Sports Guide," published for the National Section on Women's Athletics, by the American Association for Health, Physical Education, and Recreation.

CHAPTER XVII

How to Teach the Forward Seat

This chapter is about a method of teaching position. I assume that my readers are familiar with the theory of The Forward Seat and hence do not discuss its details but merely analyze its main principles to make the appreciation of the teaching technique easier.

Do you have a method or are you just swimming along while your charming personality keeps your pupils happy? And in general what does one need a method for? Is it possible to adhere to any program when dealing with a great variety of human types? Perhaps a combination of knowledge of riding, common sense and flexibility is more important than a teaching method? You have probably taken part in such discussions and, if not, you certainly will after reading the following pages.

A good method is a logical, *flexible* sequence of lessons which achieves the best results with the majority, with the least danger to their health and with the minimum of effort. Of course it is based on the knowledge of riding, and common sense is needed to put it into practice. I know of so-called riding schools where learning position is a never-ending process which can be terminated only either by the pupil's changing his interest or by the considerations of his pocketbook. I know of others where position is taught in fifty to sixty riding hours. Did you ever count how many hours it takes you to get seventy-five per cent of your pupils to the point where, as far as their position is concerned, they do not need serious criticisms at a walk, trot, canter, gallop, or in jumping up to 2½' or 3'? Can you do it in twenty lessons? Several teachers whom I know can. How? Through the use of a highly developed method. How does one develop a method? Through a combination of knowledge, practice and thinking. Now, can I invite you to think with me in analyzing an approach to creating a method?

A good working position has the following characteristics:

1) The unity of the horse and of the rider in motion.
2) Non-abuse of the horse either by the rider's weight or by his aids (in our case, not the use of the aids but merely their position is considered).
3) The rider's security in the saddle.
4) The aids in a position to control quickly, efficiently and softly.

In order to have all these elements happily combined a pupil must develop certain physical qualities. These are:

1) Correct design of position.
2) Such a distribution of weight in the saddle that his line of center of gravity coincides with that of the horse.
3) Balance in motion.
4) Springiness of the body to absorb the shocks of locomotion.
5) Rhythm of moving with the horse.
6) Mental—and hence physical—relaxation.
7) Grip.

To prevent any possible misunderstanding I feel that I should define these points.

1) Correct Design Of Position (In Profile) may be summed up as follows:
   a) The rider is placed close to the pommel.
   b) His legs are bent in the knees; heels are pulled down.
   c) He is inclined forward from the hips, more or less, depending on the gait and speed.
   d) His back is straight, shoulders open, head up.
   e) He keeps his arms bent in the elbows so that each forearm forms with its rein a straight line of action from elbow to the horse's mouth.

   Correct Design of Position (From The Front) may be summed up as follows:
   a) The rider has his weight evenly distributed on both stirrups.
   b) His toes are out just enough to bring the upper-calves in contact with the saddle.
   c) His grip ends with the upper-calves and the rest of his lower-legs is away from the horse.
   d) He looks straight between the horse's ears.
   e) His hands are about one foot apart.

2) Correct Distribution Of Weight means that, upon acquiring a correct design of his position, the rider places enough weight in the stirrups so that the line of center of gravity of his body will coincide with that of the horse. The efforts of loading the stirrups more or less, depending on the gait and speed, are in harmony with:
   a) corresponding increase or decrease of the inclination of the torso forward,
   b) greater or lesser angle in the knee.

   The ability to maintain a correct distribution of weight *in motion* largely depends on the balance and rhythm.

3) Balance In Motion is the stability of the rider in the saddle without any gripping and regardless of disturbing shocks of locomotion. Bal-

ance is the result of innumerable small compensating movements of the body and *primarily of the torso*. The effectiveness of unconscious balancing efforts largely depends on relaxation.

4) The Spring In The Rider's Body is the result of the angularity of his attitude and of sufficient weight in the stirrups from which, acting as from the floor, the rider can give impetus to the spring accumulated in the angles of the ankles, knees and hips. A straight body has no springs in it and hence the longer the stirrups the less spring the rider has. Semi-relaxed joints make the spring effective.

5) The Rhythm Of Moving With The Horse is a result of innumerable, unconscious movements of the body, and *primarily of the torso*, which help to preserve in motion the fundamental unity of the rider and the horse. It largely depends on a correct design of the rider's position, his correct distribution of weight and his balance. However, an average beginner learns the rhythm of the posting trot long before acquiring the above qualities.

6) Physical Relaxation does not mean sloppiness. In riding it means a state of the rider's body when it is neither slack nor stiff but continuously alert, ready to follow the quick and often unexpected movements of the horse. This condition exists only if mental relaxation is present.

7) The Grip is a muscular effort which brings into hard contact (of varying degrees) with the saddle, the lower-thighs, the inner surfaces of knees and the upper-calves. An effective grip depends on: correct design of leg position and on the strength of the muscles involved.

Table V shows how the presence of these seven elements affects the fundamental points of a good position. You may disagree with my point of view as expressed in this table and might like to change the check marks around. That would be fine; for the purpose of this chapter is not to give you a ready formula to follow but to stimulate you to create your own efficient method. With it, perhaps, you will teach position in seventeen hours instead of my twenty.

I repeat again that you may distribute the marks "very much" in a different way than I have, but even then the main lesson of the table will still be the same; that is, that the unity of the rider and horse, non-abuse of the horse, and rider's security all depend on all seven fundamental characteristics of the rider's position. This can be argued only unintelligently; for instance: we all know riders who sit really badly and who, in spite of their precarious position (especially while jumping) fall rather rarely. On the other hand, we all can think of riders who have a correct position and in spite of it find their way to the ground quite often. The possible deduction from these observations is that the whole column on "security" is wrong, while the real explanation of the above examples lies in the different conformations of the riders. A lightly built rider with long legs and a short torso is bound to have more security than a rider with short legs and a long heavy torso. In such discussions we really talk about the pupil's natural abilities. The following table, as all the thinking in this chapter, presupposes an averagely able pupil.

For this average pupil the logic of this table works as follows (we shall discuss the first line of the table):

1) A rider who has a correct design of position has a foundation for unity with his horse in motion, since he sits in such a way that in order to distribute his weight correctly he merely has to put sufficient weight in the stirrups.

2) A rider who has a correct design of position has a foundation for non-abuse of his horse since he keeps his weight on the part of the horse's

TABLE III

	Unity	Non-Abuse of the Horse	Security	Efficient Aids
Correct design of position......	x very much	x	x	x very much
Correct distribution of weight..	x very much	x very much	x	
Balance in motion............	x very much	x	x very much	
Spring....................	x	x very much	x very much	
Rhythm...................	x very much	x	x	
Physical relaxation...........	x	x	x very much	x
Grip......................	x	x	x very much	

back which is most suitable for carrying burdens. Furthermore, he is non-disturbing to the horse with his legs, and has the best chance to be non-disturbing with his hands.

3) A rider who has a correct design of position has a foundation for maximum security since he has his body in the best position to utilize balance, grip, spring and rhythm in motion.

4) A rider who has a correct design of position has a foundation for an efficient use of aids, since his lower legs are sufficiently back and close to the horse's sides, while his hands are sufficiently forward and apart.

A few minutes of thinking about the above table may give you two or three very interesting ideas. For instance: in the column on "security" the words "very much" appear four times. This fact seems to indicate that the grip does not have to be taught early, and may be regarded as a polishing touch to an already sufficiently secure Seat. This is welcome news, for the early teaching of grip invariably stiffens pupils and slows down progress. Now the question is how most efficiently to develop in the pupil's position all the elements on which will depend his future good riding. Although superficially it may seem that there are one thousand and one ways of doing it, actually the choice is not so large. There are just so many things—and no more—that at a given moment one can ask of the pupil—unless, of course, you do not mind calling an ambulance. The following Table IV includes all those movements one can ask a beginner to execute in the course of the first twenty hours in the saddle. In addition to listing them, the table points out how they benefit an average pupil, providing that he is mentally relaxed, in other words, has confidence. The latter is gained through a tactful teacher, a good method, suitable horses and a small (for the first lessons), well-organized ring. Only if the pupil is relaxed mentally is he sufficiently relaxed physically, and only then can you expect the following table to work.

Again you may disagree with some of my check marks; but I am almost certain that the difference in opinion will concern details. Let us imagine two of several possible arguments that you and I might have. Shall we discuss, for instance, exercise #5—the posting trot? I have marked in the table that it develops balance, spring and rhythm, and have left blank the columns for correct design, correct distribution of weight, relaxation and grip. I did so because, in my experience, when a beginner is learning the posting trot he is all over the horse, for the first five hours at least, and hence one can hardly say that he is learning the correct design or the correct distribution of weight. But you may object to this, saying that although what I say is true about first lessons, it does not apply to the last ten, when the pupil begins to control his limbs to the point where he can control his position and distribution of weight while posting (especially if holding the mane). I agree with you and will not object to your putting check marks in the two first columns providing that then you add the words "very much" in the columns for balance, spring and rhythm.

Or you may question my statement in the table that exercise #3, sitting trot with stirrups, develops the design of the position and the correct distribution of weight. I believe it does, providing, of course, that the horse has an easy gait and will trot slowly. But if you don't have such horses then probably your experience with this exercise has led you to different conclusions. But, if you will see the important connection between this exercise and suitable horses, then you naturally will not argue that the efforts to keep a correct design and a correct distribution of weight will simultaneously develop balance and rhythm. By making your pupils increase the speed, you can make this exercise more difficult (when the time arrives), thus keeping it as a fundamental exercise throughout the course. Obviously, it develops neither spring nor relaxation, while the use of grip, if you should make the mistake of asking for it, will

TABLE IV

WHAT THE LESSON DEVELOPS

SUBJECT	Correct design	Correct weight distribution	Balance	Spring	Rhythm	Relaxation	Grip
1. Halt	X chiefly	X				X	
2. Walk	X chiefly	X				X	
3. Sitting trot (slow) on a smooth horse.	X chiefly	X very much	X		X		
4. Sitting trot without stirrups (slow) on a smooth horse.						X if done with legs hanging naturally	
5. Posting trot, from the stirrups.			X	X chiefly	X		
6. Posting trot without stirrups, with correct leg and feet position.					X		X chiefly
7. Canter.			X		X		
8. Canter without stirrups.						X if done with legs hanging naturally	
9. Gallop (galloping position at a canter).	X	X very much	X	X	X		X very

WHAT THE LESSON DEVELOPS

SUBJECT	Correct design	Correct weight distribution	Balance	Spring	Rhythm	Relaxation	Grip
10. Galloping position at a walk and trot.	X very much	X very much	X very much	X very much	X very much		
11. Circles and turns at all gaits.			X		X		
12. Low jumping, up to 2 feet.			X very much	X very much	X very much		
13. Higher jumping, 2 to 3 feet.			X very much	X very much	X very much		X
14. Change of gaits.			X		X		
15. Change of speeds at a trot.			X		X		
16. Hacking on the paths (quiet horses, escort).			X	X	X	X if the ride is well-conducted	X
17. Hacking cross-country (quiet horses, escort).			X	X	X	X if the ride is well-conducted	X
18. Going up and down hills.			X		X		X
19. Gymnastics in the saddle.						X	
20. Theory.	X	X	X	X	X	X	X
21. Making pupil observe and criticize others.	X	X	X	X	X	X	X
22. Change of horses.		X chiefly	X		X		

merely squeeze the pupil up and hence push him toward the cantle. But if you should argue that the sitting trot develops spring, not directly but by teaching the pupil to remain in an angular position with the angles in the hips, knees and ankles I would agree with you. This was, for years, my main exercise from the first lesson on, until comparatively recently I replaced it, but not entirely, by exercise #10—the galloping position at a walk and trot.

I suspect that at this point some of my readers would like to ask me why I haven't mentioned such movements as backing, turn on the forehand, etc.? As you see, I didn't forget them, but I did not give them space in the table because I believe that they pertain to the teaching of control and that they have no value in teaching position. And, in general, I do not think that a pupil should be taught control while struggling with the fundamentals of the Seat. During the first twenty hours the pupil has enough troubles without trying to control his horse. I teach beginners merely how to move the horse forward, how to keep him moving straight, how to turn him, increase and decrease the speed and how to stop; later, how to start a canter in the simplest way, disregarding the lead and with the help of the instructor's command, which I hope most of your horses know. All this I teach in a most primitive manner, just enough to keep the class moving and to have my pupils safe during their homework. I always insist that the reins can be picked up only while giving orders, remaining loose the rest of the time. In this way an easily established habit of hanging on the horse's mouth is prevented. Of course, all the above is possible only if you know how to make horses for beginners and have some horses assigned exclusively for this work. Only toward the end of the position course do I gradually replace loose reins with contact, thus making my pupil ready to start studying control.

Now let us return to the examination of the table. Any one of the exercises, once introduced, should be repeated every lesson until practiced to the point where it is no longer necessary; but the actual introduction of them should be gradual and discriminating for reasons of safety and efficiency.

For the First Five Lessons One Can Use:

		To Develop
#1	Halt	correct design, correct distribution of weight, relaxation
#2	Walk	correct design, correct distribution of weight, relaxation
#3	Sitting trot	correct design, correct distribution of weight, balance, rhythm
#5	Posting trot	balance, spring, rhythm
#10	Galloping position at walk and trot	correct design, correct weight distribution, balance, spring, rhythm
#11	Circles and half circles	balance and rhythm
#12	Low jumping	balance, spring, rhythm

#19 Gymnastics in the sad-
       dle   relaxation
#20 Theory   all elements
#21 Making pupils observe
       and criticize others   all elements

For the Next Five Lessons One Can Add:

                                         To Develop
#22 Change of horses   correct weight distribution, balance, rhythm
#15 Change of speeds at a
       trot   balance and rhythm
#7 Canter   balance, rhythm
#4 Sitting trot without
       stirrups   relaxation for the canter (if necessary and safe)

For the Next Five Lessons One Can Add:

                                         To Develop
#9 Galloping position at correct design, correct weight distribution, balance,
       canter   spring, rhythm, grip
#6 Posting trot without
       stirrups   grip for gallop (if necessary and safe)
#16 Hacking on the paths   balance, rhythm, spring, grip and general confidence
                              and hence relaxation.

For the Next Five Lessons One Can Add:

                                         To Develop
#8 Canter without stirrups relaxation for canter (use only if necessary and safe)
#14 Change of gaits   balance, rhythm
#13 Higher jumping (up to
       three feet)   balance, spring, rhythm, grip
#17 &
#18 Hacking cross country balance, spring, rhythm, grip and general confidence
       and going up and   and hence relaxation.
       down hill

Remarks On The Exercises Of The First Five Lessons.

Analyzing the exercises chosen for the first five lessons we see that the design of the position and the correct distribution of weight can be developed through the use of a halt, walk, sitting trot and through "galloping position at a walk and trot"; the last two are, to a large extent, substitutes for each other. I, personally, prefer the latter to the sitting trot, while you may use the former. But both of us will certainly use the halt, during which the teacher has a chance to adjust the pupil's position; and the walk, during which it is easy to keep the position fixed by the hands of the teacher. It is only recently that I began to use "the galloping position at a walk and trot" as my fundamental exercise, so I would like to give my reasons for doing so. While executing this exercise the pupil must be clear out of the saddle, and low above it, holding the mane (reins loose), balancing himself (without gripping) in the stirrups (for a while with the help of his hands). In order to obtain the equilibrium, the pupil has to bend his legs in the knees sufficiently to bring the stirrups under the body and bend his torso in the hips enough to be able to stand in the stirrups in balance. Thus the correct bending of the legs and the correct inclination of the torso are developed naturally while the pupil merely tries to remain standing in the stirrups without touching the saddle, and without too much help of the hands. Rhythm and balance are being developed from the very beginning, and, with the gradual removal of the hands from the horse's neck (reins still loose), the balance is developed rapidly. Besides which the galloping position with the weight in the stirrups makes pulling the heels down comparatively easy. In the course of the thirteen years since this book was written, this exercise has become the cornerstone of my teaching of the forward seat.

When, in former days, my fundamental exercise was the sitting trot, I had difficulties in teaching the "posting trot," for the pupils, never having enough weight in the stirrups, just couldn't rise in rhythm with the horse's movement. Since I adopted the "galloping position" as my initial subject I usually start posting during the first lesson and am successful in many cases in obtaining it within ten minutes. The same experience applies to jumping. But there is nothing black and white in riding or teaching it, and now I have created a problem for later on when pupils begin to study the canter; not being used to having much contact with the saddle, so many of them bang it. This is why I maintained the sitting trot as an exercise second in importance. All in all, my mathematics tell me that I gain a few hours by introducing "the galloping position at a walk and trot." I would suggest your giving it a trial; you may also find that it works.

An important point to consider when examining all the possible exercises is the fact that some of them are efficient, while others are comparatively ineffective. For instance, low jumping is an extremely efficient exercise for the development of balance, spring and rhythm, while the use of circles and turns is a much slower way to develop balance and rhythm. But one has to use the latter also; first because it develops a specific part of general balance—the balance on a horse not perpendicular to the ground—and then just because it breaks the monotony of the lessons.

Exercise #19 (gymnastics in the saddle) I personally don't use at all; long ago I found out that it was a waste of time. The most that I make my pupils do is to pat their horses on the shoulder and on the croup at all gaits. But perhaps you know how to use gymnastics better than I do, so I left them in the table.

Subject #21, which calls upon the pupil to observe and criticize others, I like very much, and prefer it to merely explaining the theory (which is also important). At first glance there would seem to be a considerable loss of time, for a part of the class is standing in the center of the ring playing teacher, but actually time is gained, for the theory is thus assimilated much faster than in any other way; furthermore, in correcting others, pupils learn to correct their own faults.

Remarks On The Exercises Of The Second Group Of Five Lessons.

Depending on the abilities of the pupil, one may start the canter (exercise #7) anywhere from the sixth to the tenth lesson, and I would try to begin it by merely letting the horse continue the canter upon landing after jumping a low fence. To some it may seem that jumping even one-foot fences is more advanced than a canter. But in reality this is not so. For a jump has just one rough moment, while the canter has a constant repetition of them; it is a succession of unfamiliar shocks of locomotion which stiffen the pupil, make him bang the saddle and even unseat him. As I have already mentioned, the normal difficulty in teaching position at the canter is the inability of the average pupil to be softly in contact with the saddle, while having very little weight in it. To overcome "banging" I use the sitting trot without stirrups (exercise #4), legs hanging naturally and completely loose, with toes hanging down. This exercise does the trick in most cases, but in some of them, the canter without stirrups has to be added and, if such is the case, it hardly can be accomplished even on the tenth lesson, the sixteenth is more likely, if safety is to be considered.

Change of speeds at a trot (exercise #15) is one of the mild exercises and it develops balance and rhythm through making the pupil slightly change his distribution of weight with the horse's extension when increasing speed and his slight gathering when decreasing it. I think it is a very valuable exercise; horses, of course, must decrease and increase the speed mostly from the commands of the teacher.

Change of horses (exercise #22) could be started during the first five lessons. I think it is advisable to postpone it and to give the pupil a chance to gain confidence by riding the same horse several hours. The value of this lesson, of course, lies in the fact that all horses have somewhat different conformations and ways of going and hence the change of them calls for adaptability on the part of the rider.

Remarks On The Exercises Of The Third Group Of Five Lessons.

It may seem strange to you that so far I have not mentioned the "galloping position at a canter" (exercise #9), for since I start my lessons teaching this position at a walk and trot my pupils naturally make their first strides of canter in a galloping position. My reasons for putting it in the third group of lessons are two: 1) if you use sitting trot with stirrups to develop design and distribution of weight, then the galloping position at a canter can hardly be taught earlier; 2) in my own case when teaching this position at a canter I try to develop a *correct* galloping position, low over the saddle and with gripping, which could hardly be asked earlier.

If a pupil has weak muscles and you are anxious to develop them, the efficient way of doing so is through ground exercises. Personally, not knowing a thing about them, I refer my pupil to teachers of gymnastics. Myself —I have only one means—posting trot without stirrups (exercise #6).

As soon as the confidence and ability of a particular pupil permit and, depending on my facilities and horses, I insist on his practicing by himself; sometimes I ask this "homework" after the fifth lesson. For this, of course, you must have a small ring, very quiet horses and an advanced pupil who will be willing to be present, not to teach, but merely to prevent possible abuse of the horse and, in general, to stop reckless procedures. I firmly believe that the average pupil learns a point better by himself, if he knows what to aim at and how to avoid or correct his mistakes. Later on "homework" should be done outside on the bridle paths (exercise #16), with a clear- and fast-thinking escort. There is no reason why any of the points of position cannot be practiced in the fields, besides which, riding in the open, no matter how slow, encourages pupils to work harder.

Remarks On The Exercises Of The Last Group Of Five Lessons.

The strong exercises in this group are hacking cross-country (#17 and #18) and jumping over 2½' fences (#13); in some cases of very able pupils on very smooth horses the height may be raised to 3'.

The change of gaits is similar (although more advanced) to change of speeds at a trot, and is important for it teaches quick readjustments of position during the transitions. This exercise (#14) gives polishing touches to balance and rhythm.

I have already pointed out that the canter without stirrups (exercise #8) is very efficient in eliminating "banging the saddle" at the canter. But since it requires from the pupil a certain amount of security, it is as well not to hurry with it. This is the only reason why you find it in this last group of exercises.

Now, on the basis of what has been said in this chapter, you and I are ready to make a definite program for the first twenty lessons, specifying exactly which exercises are to be used during each hour. Of course it is understood that we reserve the right to change it somewhat when we face the actual problems of particular pupils, horses and facilities. I would suggest that you stop reading at this point, and make a program of your own and then compare it with mine; you may think of some constructive changes.

One Of The Possible Programs For The First Twenty Hours.

1st hour   Halt,
            walk,

sitting trot,
galloping position at walk (and trot where able),
low jumping (at first merely crossing poles on the ground),
theory, while resting.

2d hour The same, plus
posting trot,
more theory.

3d hour The same plus
circles and half circles at a walk,
more theory.

4th hour The same plus
observing and criticizing others,
more theory.

5th hour homework.

6th hour The same exercises as above plus
change of horses,
change of speeds at a trot,
more theory and observing and criticizing others.

7th hour homework.

8th hour The same exercises as above plus
canter,
more theory and observing and criticizing others.

9th hour homework.

10th hour The same exercises as above plus
sitting trot without stirrups (only if necessary),
more theory and observing and criticizing others.

11th hour homework.

12th hour The same exercises as above plus
galloping position at a canter,
more theory and observing and criticizing others.

13th hour homework.

14th hour The same exercises as above plus
posting trot without stirrups (only if necessary),
more theory and observing and criticizing others.

15th hour Homework, on the bridle path (returning to the ring for cantering).

16th hour The same exercises as above plus
change of gaits,
more theory and observing and criticizing others.

17th hour Homework on the bridle path (returning to the ring for cantering).

18th hour The same exercises as above plus
fences being gradually raised throughout the course now reach the
height of 2½′,
canter without stirrups (only if necessary),
more theory and observing and criticizing others.

19th hour Homework cross-country (returning to the ring for cantering).

20th hour An informal competition. Pupils to ride individually for about three
minutes, being judged by the rest of the class.

Glancing through the above program I have become apprehensive lest
you may think that I devote too much time to pure theory and to pupils'

criticisms of each other; the fact that I have put theory into every lesson may seem to indicate this. But what I really meant is that theory should not be presented all at once, in a lump, but should be spread through the whole course, new points being discussed with the introduction of new movements; while observing and criticizing others goes, of course, hand in hand with the unfolding of theory.

In ending this part of the chapter, I should like to stress once more that the above—or a similar—method will work only if you have suitable horses. Such horses can rarely be bought; they are made. Making horses is one of the very important activities of a riding teacher. I purposely avoid the word "schooling" in connection with horses used for teaching position; it isn't exactly schooling, it is a sort of "fixing" of them for a certain work. Of course, when buying horses for this purpose you will be careful to choose those which are not too big, which are absolutely quiet and with easy gaits; but after that it is up to you to teach them to work in a class on loose reins at all gaits, including low jumping. This is not hard to achieve and it has to be done before beginning to think how to increase the efficiency of lessons.

A pupil of mine (a riding teacher) after reading the first draft of this chapter rightly pointed out to me that in the table I omitted one exercise: "change of diagonals at posting trot." This was my oversight and possibly it is not the only one; perhaps you will find others and if so correct them in your own use of the method. I am not doing it here myself for I am choosing the incident as an example of how much constructive thinking you can do in creating a method of teaching position.

Remarks On How To Teach The Forward Seat For Jumping.

As you know, jumping over low fences is one of the exercises for developing a good seat for gaits; while, on the other hand, a good position at gaits is the basis for an efficient seat for jumping high fences. All the different manifestations of a good position are inter-related. Appreciating this fact, the riding teacher must particularly bear in mind that the exercise "galloping position at a walk and trot," and posting *from the stirrups* in rhythm with the horse, as well as the galloping position at a canter are all particularly closely related to jumping. For example, the fault of being left behind is more efficiently corrected by practicing these three things than by anything else.

A good forward seat over obstacles, the kind that is adaptable to the various types of jumping which one will meet in actuality, cannot be taught by always jumping the same ordinary fence at the same gait and speed. The efforts of the rider over a low jump taken at a canter differ somewhat from his efforts over the same jump taken at a trot, and differ again when the same obstacle is taken from a fast gallop. Broad jumps, in-and-outs, jumps with a drop, etc., all somewhat change the problem of remaining with the horse securely and without abusing him. Consequently, in your teaching of jumping, you should use the following groups of obstacles all taken at a trot, canter and gallop:

1) Vertical fences (adaptability to short and steep trajectories)
2) Broad obstacles (adaptability to long and flat trajectories)
3) In-and-outs (adaptability to jumps in rapid succession)
4) Alternating broad and vertical fences (quick adaptability to varying trajectories)
5) Alternating gaits and speeds on successive obstacles (quick adaptability to varying differences between the speed of the approach and the speed of the take-off).

In teaching the jumping seat your first two requirements from the pupil are:

1) The rider must not abuse the horse's back by banging it or by returning to the saddle too early.
2) The rider (even a beginner) should not abuse the horse's mouth by jerking it or by not giving enough reins to enable the horse to extend his neck.

These two points are inter-related and the ability of a beginner to stay out of the saddle throughout the jump largely depends on the additional support, which he should establish by putting his hands on the crest of the neck and by transferring enough weight to his hands so that they will not jump up and throw his body back into the saddle. Obviously, when fixing hands this way on the crest of the neck, the reins must be loose enough to give room for the gestures of the horse's neck and head. Thus a rank beginner should approach the jump on completely loose reins; later on, when approaching an obstacle on contact, the pupil must have his reins rather long and move his hands well forward to the middle of the neck before fixing them.

With the improvement of the pupil's position, he must be required to fix his hands not on the crest of the neck, but on its sides, so that there will be a straight line of action from the elbows to the horse's mouth; this is a step toward the future following of the horse's head and neck by the rider's arms through the air.

The success of the rider's behavior during the jump will be largely the result of how he has prepared himself during the approach. What a pupil should be told during the approach will depend, of course, on his individual strong and weak points. But in the average case this recommendation may be given:

In the course of approximately the last eight strides have your pupil do the following five things:

1) Whether your pupil approaches an obstacle at a trot or a slow

canter, about eight strides away from the jump he must assume a galloping position (at a trot, stop posting).

2) About six strides away from the jump he must make sure that his
weight is really in the stirrups and make an additional effort to depress
his heels.

3) About four strides from the fence he must close in his lower thighs,
knees and upper calves. (Grip. Never let your pupil grip before he has
put his weight in the stirrups.)

4) About two strides from the jump the beginner must either grab the
mane or put his hands on the crest of the neck, immobilizing them with
sufficient weight on them.

5) At the moment of the take-off most beginners will have to make a
little extra movement forward with the torso (onto their hands) in rhythm
with the horse's accelerated speed which accompanies the release of the
spring accumulated in the hindquarters. Failure to do this often causes
being left behind. On the other hand, if this movement exceeds the
horse's effort, the rider will over-balance himself to the front.

It is particularly during this stage that the pupil must look straight
ahead between the horse's ears. Failure to do the latter will result in an
uneven distribution of weight in the stirrups and in the rider's inability to
move straight ahead with the horse.

In teaching, at first, I give commands myself for the execution of these
five things. The commands are given in the following abbreviated form:
"galloping," "weight," "grip," "hands," "forward." Later I have my pupil
say these five words aloud when performing the corresponding actions.

It is needless to say that efficient teaching of the seat over fences can be
accomplished only on horses which jump mechanically without requiring
any controlling efforts on the part of the rider.

Remarks On How To Teach Elementary Control.

Previously in this chapter I have mentioned how simple the control re-
quired of a pupil learning position should be, and in the chapters on
Bringing Control Down To Earth And Forward, and on Elementary
Control, elementary control has been precisely defined.

While teaching position, elementary control should be considered by
the teacher from three points of view:

1) As a means of making the class move in an orderly fashion while
changing gaits and speeds and making turns and whatever else may be
necessary to accustom the pupil to changes of balance and rhythm.

2) As a means of safety while the pupil is doing his "homework" or
hacking on a quiet, obedient horse.

3) As a first step in the education of how to handle horses.

Elementary control is so simple that teaching it does not require much
theoretical knowledge, while merely common sense and a certain knack
are all-important. Therefore, I believe that it would be foolish on my

part to present the study of it in some sort of elaborately organized form; and hence I merely wish to list its basic points:

1) Elementary control can be taught only on suitably prepared horses which work calmly on loose reins. I shall not dwell on this point for it has already been discussed many times in this book.

2) There are no special lessons in elementary control; it is taught together with position, and new points of control are added as new exercises are required for the improvement of the seat.

3) You should include no theory in your instructions as to why certain aids are required in certain cases. The method of elementary control must be extremely simple, so that the reasons for different aids are evident. For example: You tell the pupil that in order to stop the horse he should give the voice command "whoa," then pull on the reins; you should insist that the horse be stopped by the time you have counted three after ordering the pupil to halt. And that is all for a time.

At this stage the fact that your class can halt immediately after receiving the command is a step toward safety in hacking. However, the precise manner in which each pupil has stopped his horse is not all-important. Of course you will correct flagrant mistakes, such as pulling with the hands held too high or being unnecessarily rough; but if you are wise, you will overlook details.

4) This is the time to begin to acquaint a pupil with the psychology of the horse. While the pupil's seat is still unstable and his body uncoordinated in the saddle, you cannot require from him a precise use of hands and legs for control; but there is no reason why he can't be introduced to the mentality and character of the horse. The first step in this direction, riding on loose reins assisting control with voice commands, is an illustration of the fact that the horse is capable of learning and cooperating. Teaching your pupils to talk soothingly to the horse when he has been obedient, to scold him when he has disobeyed, to pat him and to give him an occasional carrot or sugar lump when he deserves it, is, I believe, at this stage, a most important practice in forming a future horseman. If, while teaching position, you succeed in introducing the horse to your pupils as a living being, you will have achieved something very essential. Activities such as grooming, saddling, feeding or caring for the horse in any way, are as important in teaching this necessary understanding between mount and rider. But besides all this you should frequently discuss the horse's character. Telling a pupil at this stage such things as that he must maintain a soft contact with the horse's mouth is useless; he would be unable to do it no matter how hard he tried. On the other hand, there is no reason at all why he should not already be learning to understand and consider the horse.

Toward the end of the course in position, when pupils have already considerable practice in changing gaits, speeds, making circles, etc., I usually devote ten or fifteen minutes of the lesson (divided into two or three periods) to a special exercise in elementary control. It consists of giving different orders in rather rapid succession (one, or even sometimes two orders each round of the ring). For example, the commands can be given in the following order: "walk," "trot," "circle after the leader," "canter," "circle after the leader," "trot," "walk," "change directions," "halt," etc.

It is for a quick execution of my commands without undue roughness and for the general orderliness of the class that I am looking during this exercise.

The first half of this chapter was printed as an article in THE OFFICIAL INDIVIDUAL SPORTS GUIDE *(1950-52), published for The National Section on Women's Athletics by The American Association For Health, Physical Education, And Recreation.*

CHAPTER XVIII

How to Teach Control (Intermediate and Advanced)

The chapter on How To Teach Position, while addressed to teachers, can be used as a practical guide by those who are endeavoring to learn by themselves. The same cannot be said of this chapter; for I don't believe that any refinement of control can be learned unless someone is present to tell the student when he is right and when he is wrong. Therefore, the content of this chapter is meant for teachers who ride well and know the theory of riding, but have not as yet developed a method of teaching. However, a student of riding, while unable to make practical use of the program, may glean some further knowledge of general theory from glancing through it.

The following schedule for teaching control is not new in my practice. I have used it for over ten years, working always to improve it. An essentially similar program was published in *The Rider and Driver,* in a series of my articles which came out during the winter of 1942-43. My own experience, as well as the experience of some of my friends who teach riding, has since altered it for the better.

After experimenting with many different methods in teaching riding, I have come to the conclusion that the only efficient way is to divide pupils rigidly into three main groups. The subjects taught to the first group are position and elementary control; that taught to the second group is intermediate control; and the third group is instructed in advanced control and complete schooling, or merely schooling on an intermediate level. I usually call these three groups "Position," "Control" and "Schooling" groups; some other teachers prefer to call them "Beginners," "Intermediate" and "Advanced." The title after all makes little difference; but I rigidly observe the rules of each group; no pupil is promoted until he is fully prepared to enter the next group. However, while a beginner will remain in the position class perhaps twenty hours or more, a pupil with past experience and needing only some correction of position, may find it necessary to stay in it only two or three hours. This division enables me in the control group, for instance, to talk and teach control, and control only; this system greatly increases the rate of progress.

The teacher must always bear in mind that it is difficult for a pupil to work on several points at once. Therefore not only should lessons on control be concentrated exclusively on control; but each new point in it should be presented by itself. Consequently, the hour, or part of it, assigned to learning the execution of a new movement should be devoted to it and it alone. Furthermore, new movements should not be introduced in a haphazard fashion, but in a logical sequence, one movement leading to another. With this in mind, I have worked out a program for teaching control. In order to keep the logic of the schedule perfectly clear, I am listing only the fundamental lessons; the teacher will find that it is necessary to teach, between the principal lessons, minor points, such as going deep into the corners of the ring, or the use of the "rein of indirect opposition to the rear of the withers" in combatting the horse's resistance.

Before you begin to study the program of teaching control, I should like you to consider the following points:

1) For this course, you cannot use the same horses which you use in teaching position. Horses for teaching control must be at least decently schooled. They must know all the movements required by the program and they must respond correctly to the rider's legs and hands.

2) The word "lesson" is not used in the sense of a single hour's work; here it means a subject which has to be learned. It may take a pupil a few minutes, or it may take him several hours to learn a certain lesson.

3) The order in which the lessons are listed should not be rigidly accepted by teachers. It is subject to change, depending on the particular circumstances encountered when teaching a certain pupil or a certain class.

4) The teacher does not have to wait for one lesson to be perfectly executed before beginning the next one. But since each lesson prepares the pupil for the following one, the degree of efficiency at a given moment is indicative of whether the time has come to go ahead.

5) It is obvious that only in the case of a pupil who does not know control at all will the teacher need to start with lesson #1.

6) Each working hour should begin by reviewing the preceding lesson (pupil's homework) and, in general, the study of the new subject should proceed hand in hand with the work toward perfecting the previous lessons.

7) The theory of control is both longer and more complicated than the theory of position. It might even be said with some justice that position and elementary control could be taught almost without any theory. This is utterly impossible in teaching control. Hence some of the lessons listed are devoted purely to theory, illustrated by the teacher's riding. At the moment a pupil may have the erroneous impression that he is wasting time, not doing anything himself. This is an illusion, for he will save a great many hours of struggle and much money by devoting the necessary time to theory.

THE PROGRAM FOR TEACHING INTERMEDIATE CONTROL

LESSON #1

Subject—The aims of intermediate control. What is a good, efficient movement.

This lesson must make clear to the pupil the aims of intermediate control and outline (very generally) the plan of the course. This lesson is a preface to the detailed description of the theory of control.

Theory—The discussion and demonstration of the following points constitute this lesson:

1) The ordinary and the stimulated movements of a free horse.
2) What constitutes the efficiency of gaits. Why collected gaits should not be used in field riding and jumping.
3) The differences between the principles of the old-fashioned and the modern ways of controlling hacks, hunters and jumpers. Forward Riding is more natural, more efficient and less disturbing to the horse than the Classical 19th century method. It is also much easier to learn.
4) The outline of the plan of the study of Control. Different movements, besides their practical values, *are exercises for the development of cooperation of the rider's legs and hands with the efforts of the horse.*

Practice—The pupil does not mount at all during this lesson. All the riding is done by the teacher, or advanced pupils, on well-schooled horses, and is intended to illustrate the above points.

General Remarks—One hour is just about enough to cover this subject and the pupil must follow it by extensive reading on the subject in different texts suggested by the teacher. No matter how able the pupil and how experienced the teacher, it will take many weeks of riding, observation and thinking before this lesson will become really clear.

The number of topics which could be considered as belonging to this lesson is much larger than the above list. I, personally, prefer to scatter them throughout the course; there is danger in telling too much at one time.

LESSON #2

Subject—Riding on soft contact, with the horse's neck stretched forward.

Theory—The following points should be discussed and demonstrated by the teacher:

1) The difference between riding on soft contact and riding "on the bit."
2) The part which the rider's legs play in establishing contact.
3) The importance of the extended neck.
4) The advantages of riding on soft contact. How light it should be.
5) "Give and take" during riding on contact.
6) How green horses and horses with ruined mouths react to attempts of the rider to establish contact.

Practice—At first practice riding on contact at a trot, because at this gait there are no balancing gestures. It will take a couple of hours before the pupil will be able to follow these gestures harmoniously with his arms at a walk.

Postpone the practice at a canter until the pupil knows more about starting and maintaining this gait (Lesson #6).

General Remarks—As a rule, after several hours of endeavoring to ride on contact, the pupil believes that he has achieved the correct lightness. You may be almost certain that as yet he really does not feel it, and that it will take him many weeks of homework before he will really get it.

LESSON #3

Subject—"On the legs." This lesson is really a part of the preceding one.

Theory—The following points should be discussed and demonstrated by the teacher:

1) The difference between the horse obedient to the legs, lagging behind them and going ahead of them.

2) The importance of harmony between the action of the hindquarters and of the forehand.

3) The expression: "Good Hands" refers actually to a combined use of legs and hands.

4) Control over a well-schooled horse is executed mainly by variations of pressure of the calves. The use of spurs, whip and of the voice as a help to the legs.

5) How green horses and horses with dulled sides react to the rider's legs.

Practice—The pupil must get the feel of what is the minimum leg pressure required by an average, decently schooled horse. To give pupils this feeling, teach walk and trot departure, as well as keeping an even speed at these gaits. Riding different horses is essential for this lesson. This feeling will not come at once; the pupil will be under the impression that he has it long before he actually acquires it.

General Remarks—Probably after half an hour or so this lesson can be combined with the preceding one. It is obvious that both of them make sense only if executed simultaneously and toward the same aim.

LESSON #4

Subject—The basic principles of leg and hand signals.

Theory—The following point should be discussed and demonstrated by the teacher: Efficient riding cannot be done by formula; sometimes, depending on the horse's reactions, it requires a constant change of combinations of leg and hand signals. Many combinations of leg and hand efforts can be produced out of the three fundamental leg actions and the five hand actions.

Describe the natural reactions of the horse to these fundamental signals at a stand-still and while in motion.

Practice—Practice the basic leg and hand signals to develop a correct technique of the use of the aids.

General Remarks—One hour is just about enough to cover the theory of this lesson. At least one more hour with the instructor is necessary to practice these signals and some combinations of them. After this the pupil may practice by himself. It is, of course, obvious that not until the pupil has gone through the whole course will he really know this lesson. In a way, the entire study of control is a development of this lesson.

LESSON #5

Subject—The mechanics of the gaits. An efficient, soft control of the horse is possible only if the rider knows how the horse's body works in different movements. The efforts of the rider's legs and hands depend on the efforts of the horse.

Theory—The following points should be discussed and demonstrated by the teacher:

1) The mechanics of the walk, trot, canter and of the gallop; what are the good and bad points of these gaits. Also departures, transitions and terminations of gaits. The efforts of the hindquarters, forehand, back and neck and head should be considered in the description of each of the above movements. This knowledge must be presented in a simple, practical way.

2) The horse's balance (at different gaits).

3) What the rider can do with his legs and hands to better or to spoil any of the above movements.

Practice—The pupil does not ride during this lesson. All the riding is done by the teacher, or by an advanced pupil, on a well-schooled horse and aims to illustrate the above points. However, this lesson must be followed by the pupil's practicing transitions from one gait to another (including halting).

General Remarks—This lesson is nothing but a lecture illustrated by riding. One hour is just about enough to cover the subject superficially; pupils must follow it up by reading and observing horses' movements.

LESSON #6

Subject—Canter departure on a specific lead. Maintaining the canter is a part of this lesson.

Theory—The following points should be discussed and demonstrated by the teacher:

1) What is the attitude of the horse's body which is conducive to the canter departure on a certain lead (an elaboration of a part of the preceding lesson).

2) What are the aids for the canter departure on a certain lead.

3) What are the aids for maintaining an even, soft canter.

Practice—First teach canter departure disregarding the lead but with neck and head extended and straight. This should be done along the walls of the ring. After this has been learned ask the inside lead; later require either of the leads while the pupil rides through the center of the arena.

General Remarks—As soon as the pupil has learned this lesson (and long before he has reached perfection), begin to teach him to canter on soft contact with following arms (this is the continuation of Lesson #2).

<h3 style="text-align:center">LESSON #7</h3>

Subject—Conformation and mentality of the horse as most influential factors in shaping the character of the horse's performance.

Theory—This lesson, building up the foundation for future efficient control, is a direct continuation of Lesson #5.

It points out how the conformation and the mentality of the horse affect the mechanics of the gaits, their departures, transitions and terminations. The following points should be discussed:

1) Which qualities of the conformation of the hindquarters, forehand, back, neck, etc, the horse should possess to be a "good mover" and which ones result in poor gaits.
2) The different characters of horses and how different mental characteristics affect horses' performances.
3) A rider must realize that no matter how well he rides and how much time he has spent in schooling his horse, the results of his work are either enhanced or limited by his horse's conformation and character. One should learn to expect from a horse just as much as his nature is able to give.

Practice—The most efficient way to conduct this lesson is to have several pupils riding horses of varied conformation and character. Then, after a discussion of a certain point, the pupils may ride, one by one, demonstrating the difference in action and general behavior due to the difference in conformation or character. One of the horses used for this lesson should be a really "good mover" so that the action of other horses can be compared to his.

General Remarks—One hour might be ample to give your pupils enough knowledge for the moment, but the study of this subject continues throughout the course.

<h3 style="text-align:center">LESSON #8</h3>

Subject—"Impulse forward" and "coming back." This is the beginning of actual control. All the previous lessons formed an introduction.

Theory—The following points should be discussed and demonstrated by the teacher:

1) The energy (of the horse), combined with softness and obedience, in starting gaits or increasing speed (impulse forward).
2) The change of balance (of the horse), combined with softness and obedience when slowing down or halting (coming back).
3) The use of legs and hands when starting a gait or increasing its speed (at all gaits).

4) The use of legs and hands when slowing down or halting (at all gaits).

5) "Give and take" with the hands and with the legs. The use of the voice, spurs or a whip as a help to the legs and hands.

Practice—It will take just half an hour to cover the theory of this lesson, because the previous ones have prepared the pupil for it; but the practice will take considerable time. One hour with the instructor is ample in most cases; but many hours of homework will be necessary to develop in the pupil sufficient feelings to have *active softness*. The trot is the gait at which to practice this lesson at first, by decreasing and increasing the speed of it.

General Remarks—This is a very important lesson, for it is the foundation for all other movements. In every movement either the impulse forward or the coming back, or an alternation of both, is present.

LESSON #9

Subject—The three speeds of a trot. This lesson is a direct continuation of the previous one.

Theory—The following points should be discussed and demonstrated by the teacher:

1) Why in cross-country riding the three speeds are called: slow, ordinary and fast; and not collected, ordinary and extended.

2) Smooth, quick transitions from one speed to another are as important a part of the performance as the quality of the gait itself.

3) The changes in the attitude of the horse (balance) when slowing down and when increasing the speed (in the hindquarters, the back, the forehand, the neck and head). What the longitudinal flexibility of the horse is.

4) The rider's use of legs and hands (don't forget "give and take") when slowing down and when increasing the speed.

Practice—The three standard speeds at a trot. Riders must always slow down to the ordinary trot when nearing a corner of the ring. It is advisable (unless your ring is very large) to practice the slow and the ordinary trot along the wall of the arena and do the fast trot while changing directions diagonally across the ring.

General Remarks—This is a very good exercise for the development of soft, active hands and legs, providing that the teacher is not satisfied by mere changes of speeds and insists upon good changes. Half an hour is ample for this lesson; homework will perfect it.

LESSON #10

Subject—Backing. This is a direct continuation of lesson #8—the "coming back" part of it.

Theory—The following points should be discussed and demonstrated by the teacher:

1) The mechanics of backing.

2) The softness, evenness and straightness of backing (in two beats).

3) "Give and take" every step.

Practice—Practice at first along a wall, after a halt from a walk. Later in the center of the ring, and still later after halts from a trot and from a canter, resuming the original gait after backing.

At first back just four steps (using give and take) and halt the horse immobile for a few seconds before and after backing. Later make the halts before and after backing as short as possible, so that transitions from movement forward to backing and from backing to movement forward are very quick, remaining soft, even and straight.

General Remarks—When backing follows a very short halt and in its turn is followed by a quick resumption of the gait, then it is an advanced exercise for both "impulse forward" and "coming back."

Lesson #11

Subject—Turns with movement forward (circles, half-circles, etc.).

Theory—The following points should be discussed and demonstrated by the teacher:

1) Of what the lateral flexibility and lateral agility of the horse consist.

2) What the rider can do with his legs and hands to obtain and to maintain a free, even, relaxed, obedient way of going while making a turn. "Give and take" with legs and hands.

Practice—Practice making circles, half-circles and half-circles in reverse at all gaits; later do serpentine and zig-zag at a trot, still later serpentine and zig-zag at a canter (after the pupil knows the counter gallop, Lesson #13).

General Remarks—One hour is ample time to cover this subject; for the pupil has been prepared for it by a few simple rules given him while he was learning elementary control. Require only turns large enough to be easy for the horse and then ask for softness and precision of turns.

Lesson #12

Subject—Half-turn on the forehand.

Theory—The following points should be discussed and demonstrated by the teacher:

1) The mechanics of the half-turn on the forehand.

2) The aids.

3) Why it is taught; the value of the exercise in developing cooperation between the rider's legs and hands; also its place in actual riding.

Practice—At first practice at the wall, rotating the quarters away from it; later make the turn in the middle of the arena.

General Remarks—About half an hour is all that is necessary to give to your pupil sufficient knowledge of this movement (on a horse which knows this turn), so that he can practice by himself.

Lesson #13

Subject—Counter gallop.

Theory—The following points should be discussed and demonstrated by the teacher:

1) What is a good counter gallop and what are the characteristics of a poor one.
2) The importance of the counter gallop in actual riding, in schooling horses and in teaching pupils the cooperation of legs and hands.
3) The aids for maintaining a counter gallop.

Practice—Begin by making your pupils hold the horse on a counter gallop while cantering around the ring. Later make very large circles and still later serpentines and zigzags holding the same lead.

General Remarks—The counter gallop should be somewhat slower than an ordinary canter. Only a well-balanced horse will keep it even and remain soft.

Lesson #14

Subject—Half-turn on the haunches.

Theory—The following points should be discussed and demonstrated by the teacher:

1) The mechanics of the half-turn on the haunches. The good and the bad points of the turn.
2) The aids.
3) The value of this turn in actual riding, in schooling horses and in developing in the pupil the use of the aids.

Practice—At first practice at the wall of the ring, rotating the forehand away from it. Later make the turn without the help of the wall. Teach the turn from a halt and from a walk.

General Remarks—It will probably take a full hour to give your pupils enough knowledge so that they can practice it by themselves. It is considerably more difficult than the turn on the forehand.

Lesson #15

Subject—Change of leads at a canter with interruption of the gait.

Theory—The following points should be discussed and demonstrated by the teacher:

1) Why, depending on the horse, an interruption should be either a trot or a walk or a halt (it doesn't matter which on a well-schooled horse).
2) The aids.
3) In many cases the mechanics of the canter (already studied) will have to be reviewed.

Practice—Begin by changing leads at the end of the change of direction (diagonally across the arena); later in the center of the ring. The change must take place while the horse is moving along a straight line.

Gradually decrease the length of the interruption, and eventually insist upon it being a trot.

General Remarks—This is a difficult lesson, for the changes in combinations of aids succeed each other too rapidly for an average pupil at this stage of learning. One hour is enough to give your pupils an idea of what to do, but they will have to be corrected during at least two more hours before they are ready to practice by themselves.

LESSON #16

Subject—Short programs consisting of all movements learned so far. Smooth, quick transitions must be required.

Practice—About ten letters should be painted on the walls of the ring and the pupil must start or end every movement upon reaching a specified letter (precision). Programs should be about five minutes long, and executed individually. The pattern for such programs is the training test of the Three-Day Event of the Olympic Games.

General Remarks—The greatest benefit can be derived from this lesson if the class consists of three or four pupils, and while one performs the others judge. The four horses and their four riders will exhibit quite a variety of good and bad points. It is very important to develop an "eye" in your pupils. The ability to see faults in others helps one to see one's own.

Stress the point that a well-executed but isolated movement has not much value, and that smooth, precise transitions are as important as the movements themselves.

LESSON #17

Subject—The three speeds of the gallop.

Theory—The following points should be discussed and demonstrated by the teacher:

1) Why in cross-country riding the three speeds are called—*slow, ordinary* and *fast,* and not *collected, ordinary* and *extended* (this, concerning the trot, has been already discussed during lesson #9).

2) The importance of smooth, precise transitions, from one speed to another.

3) The changes in the attitude of the horse when slowing down and when increasing the speed of the gallop; discuss the quarters, the back, the neck and head (these points, concerning the trot have been already studied in lesson #9).

Don't forget to discuss the change in the strength of the gestures of the horse's neck and head, as well as the changes in the amplitude of the oscillation of the horse's body with the change of speeds. As you know, these elements are not present at a trot.

4) The aids.

Practice—Only the slow and ordinary gallops are possible in a ring, and the latter only providing that the arena is really large; for the fast gallop you must take your pupils to a field.

General Remarks—This lesson is a good exercise for the development of soft, active hands and legs, providing that the teacher is not satisfied with merely obtaining changes of speeds but insists upon quality in them. It is a more difficult lesson than changes of speed at a trot and require really well-schooled, obedient horses.

LESSON #18

Subject—Two tracks at a walk and at a trot.

Theory—The following points should be discussed and demonstrated by the teacher:
1) The characteristics of a good oblique movement.
2) The difference between "two tracks" and "shoulder-in."
3) The aids.

Practice—Begin this exercise in the following manner: while your pupil rides at a walk straight along the middle line of the ring ask him to move his horse very slightly to the side while still progressing forward and while keeping the horse almost perpendicular to the short wall of the ring toward which his horse moves. Impress upon the pupil that the side-movement should be very slight while the progress forward should be very free; always emphasize the importance of forward movement. By no means teach the oblique movement along the wall; such a practice will give your pupils a wrong feeling of a horse moving with short strides.

Once the two tracks at a walk is decently executed, begin the same at a slow, sitting trot.

General Remarks—Practice in making the turns on the forehand and on the haunches has prepared your pupils for two tracks.

LESSON #19

Subject—The mechanics of the horse's jump determine the principles of control in jumping.

Theory—This is a purely theoretical lesson and it consists of a thorough study of the horse's efforts during the approach, take-off, flight and landing, and during the first couple of strides after landing.

The efforts of the horse's legs, back, neck and head should be discussed and pointed out by means of demonstration. The demonstration must make clear how the rider's bad control interferes with the natural efforts of the horse. Evidently, the aim of good riding is to interfere the least with the horse's natural way of jumping while sitting and controlling him.

Follow this lesson by a more detailed criticism of your pupils' control during their regular jumping.

General Remarks—One hour is not enough to cover such a complicated subject as the mechanics of the jump; you probably will need two full hours. Besides this the pupils must do some reading and study pictures. The efficient way to conduct this lesson is by having a group of about six riders mounted on good, bad and indifferent jumpers. Thus a variety of good as well as incorrect efforts can be demonstrated.

This lesson is tremendously important, as are all lessons on the mechanics of the horse's movements, and neither finished jumping nor intelligent criticism of it is possible without the knowledge which this lesson gives.

LESSON #20

Subject—Cross-country riding. Teaching the pupil how to guide a horse across-country, with the maximum of safety, efficiency and consideration of the horse.

Theory—There is no special theory to this lesson. The horse and the rider merely put into practice under natural conditions what they have learned in the ring. Hence the theory merely consists of common sense advice. For instance: "Don't attempt to take fences which are too high for your horse; don't gallop your horse for longer than he is fit; don't forget to rest your horse"; rules of fox hunting, etc. Most of these points the pupil would eventually pick up by himself, so this lesson merely aims to present to a pupil, in one or two hours, knowledge which would take a much longer time to acquire through experience.

Make a strong point of the fact that, fundamentally, the method of controlling a horse when riding cross-country does not differ from the way the horse is controlled in the ring. The possible little differences may result from changes in the horse's attitude when ridden fast and in a large company. He may be sleepy in the ring and alert in the field. But this does not call for a different method of riding but merely for a more skilful execution of the principles learned and practiced in the ring.

Practice—While the theory of this lesson is short and simple, the lesson requires much practice. It will take many hours before the pupil acquires sufficient confidence and will be as certain of himself and as calm at a gallop cross-country as he was when cantering in the ring. Only upon reaching this emotional calm will the pupil feel and control the horse when riding at a fast speed over varying terrain. During the practice of this lesson pupils should ride in small or large groups (depending on their abilities and the horses' characters), changing their places from the leading one to the tail one.

Of course, the speed of the rides and the difficulty of the terrain should be increased gradually.

General Remarks—The next lesson (#21) will greatly improve the jumping part of cross-country riding.

Lesson #21

Subject—Riding over courses.

Theory—The following points should be discussed (elaborating on lesson #19) and demonstrated:

1) Successful jumping of courses depends primarily on schooling and much less on the last-minute dexterity of the rider's control. The rider should be as passive as practical (over a course as well as over a single obstacle).

2) The difference between rating and placing; why the latter should be avoided.

3) How to maintain the necessary impulse while keeping the horse calm.

Obviously the above points of the theory could be as well covered during lesson #19, but practically they are now applied to outside courses while previously they referred to either single obstacles or small groupings in a riding ring.

Practice—This lesson should be given in a large "jumping field" where different groupings of a dozen or so fences (placed far apart) is possible. The obstacles should be of the type which one meets in cross-country riding or in hunter or horsemanship classes. Obstacles should be rearranged the moment pupils learn to negotiate a certain combination well (riding different horses over it). At least one horse should be a lazy jumper, while another should be an over-ambitious one. The essence of this exercise lies not in the height of fences, but rather in different approaches and in various combinations of vertical and broad obstacles. A smooth negotiation of such courses, with the obstacles not over $3\frac{1}{2}'$, is better evidence of the pupil's ability to control his horse than daily jumping over, let's say, four identical post-and-rail fences $4\frac{1}{2}'$ high, but permanently set in a certain position in the arena. The latter may be adequate when developing jumping position or the confidence of the pupil on a high jump, but that is all.

General Remarks—Horses which consistently refuse, rush, or run out should not be used for this lesson, because it does not concern itself with schooling.

The study of the above lessons should result in your pupils' being able to do the following:

1) Maintain the horse calm and relaxed when riding him at all gaits on loose reins or soft contact (with following arms in the latter case); the horse moving forward with long, flat, efficient strides, neck and head stretched.

2) Execute all the departures and terminations of the gaits, as well as transitions from one gait and speed to another efficiently and softly.

3) Turn with movement forward or turn in place, back, change leads at the canter, two track, and maintain a counter gallop, executing all these with precision and softness.

4) Ride cross-country and over courses of the hunter class type.

In other words, your pupil must be ready to *begin* to hunt, to show, or to learn the schooling of horses on the intermediate level.

As a reminder, I am listing below the lessons which we have discussed.

The List of Lessons for Teaching Intermediate Control

1) The aims of intermediate control.
2) Riding on soft contact.
3) "On the leg."
4) The basic leg and hand signals.
5) The mechanics of the gait.
6) Canter departure.
7) Conformation and mentality of the horse as most influential factors in shaping the character of the horse's performance.
8) "Impulse forward" and "coming back."
9) Three speeds at a trot.
10) Backing.
11) Turns with movement forward.
12) Half-turn on the forehand.
13) Counter gallop.
14) Half-turn on the haunches.
15) Changes of lead (at a canter) with an interruption of the gait.
16) Riding short programs from letter to letter.
17) Three speeds of the gallop.
18) Two tracks at a walk and at a trot.
19) The mechanics of the horse's jump determine the principles of control in jumping.
20) Cross-country riding.
21) Riding over courses.

How to Teach Advanced Control

The majority of those who start to learn to ride remain forever in the elementary stage. Not more than one-third of the beginners eventually undertake the study of intermediate control, and of these not over half pursue it to the end. Furthermore, most of those who learn to ride well on the intermediate level feel that as they now can hunt and show successfully, their ambitions are achieved and there is no reason for further study. All this means that only a few will ever be interested in advanced riding and the majority of these will be interested in it for the purpose of being able to school their green horses well.

The normal desire of a young person who owns a horse is to do all the work on him himself. Consequently, I personally (particularly since I have been working as a free lance) have acquired the knack of teaching advanced riding while teaching schooling and while actually schooling a horse. Of course it is not as efficient as teaching advanced riding on well-schooled horses, but life often presents one with no choice. But whether you adopt the one or the other method, the lessons which have to be studied remain the same and only their sequence needs to be changed. Here is the list of lessons arranged in the order to teach advanced control on already well-schooled horses.

THE PROGRAM FOR TEACHING ADVANCED CONTROL

LESSON #1

Subject—The aims of advanced control and how they differ from the aims of intermediate control.

Theory—The following points should be discussed and demonstrated by the teacher:

1) The difference between excellent and merely efficient movements. What the practical values of excellent movements are.
2) The importance of schooling in bettering the quality of the horse's performance.
3) What the rider should know to get the best out of a horse schooled on an advanced level.
4) The outline of the program of the course.

Practice—The pupil does not mount at all during this lesson. All the riding is done either by the teacher or by advanced pupils, on well-schooled horses, and is intended to illustrate the above points.

General Remarks—One hour is just about enough to cover this subject and the pupil must follow it by extensive reading, mostly on the quality of horses' gaits and movements. He must also study still and slow-motion pictures, and make a point of observing different horses in action. Jumping is a part of this study.

LESSON #2

Subject—"On the bit."

Theory—The following points should be discussed and demonstrated by the teacher:

1) What is the difference between riding "on soft contact" and "on the bit."
2) What are the advantages of *occasionally* riding on the bit. Why it improves the horse's gaits and other movements. Why it may be important in jumping complicated, high courses. The connection between "on the bit" and "impulse forward."
3) The aids. Why it is inadvisable to attempt to ride the horse on the bit unless he is well schooled and the rider has well-developed co-

operation of legs and hands (feeling of the horse is imperative). "Give and take" in riding on the bit. The importance of a stretched neck.

Practice—Practice riding on the bit at all gaits and speeds. It will take a few hours before your pupil will be able to connect the action of the hindquarters with the action of the forehand softly, maintaining just the correct amount of impulse and preserving the calmness of the horse. Starting and ending the gaits while having the horse on the bit from the first to the last stride of the gait is also a part of this lesson.

General Remarks—Don't forget that only a part of advanced riding is done on the bit, while most of it is practiced on soft contact, and about one-third of it on loose reins.

Lesson #3

Subject—Direct and lateral flexions.

Theory—The following points should be discussed and demonstrated by the teacher:

1) What direct and lateral flexions are, and how to obtain them (on a schooled horse).
2) The use of direct flexions in slowing down, halting and backing.
3) The use of direct flexions in semi-collected gaits.
4) The use of lateral flexions in small circles (schooling only).
5) Why riding "on the bit" when moving forward should be accompanied by the use of flexions when "coming back."
6) Why some horses are easy and others hard to flex, and why some horses should not be asked to flex at all.

Practice—First practice dismounted (both direct and lateral flexions) at a standstill. Follow this with halts with flexions (mounted) from a walk. Later, ask flexions when slowing down or halting from a trot. Still later practice flexions when slowing down the canter or making a gradual halt from it.

As usual, change horses to give your pupils a variety of possible responses and resistances; this is the only way to develop "feeling."

Make certain that after a halt with flexions, the pupil stretches the horse's neck with the first steps forward. Also look for this extension of the neck and head with the resumption of the speed after the horse has been slowed down for a few strides.

General Remarks—It is understood that even previous to this lesson many of your well-schooled horses have flexed by themselves at the proper time, when their riders softly "gave and took" with their hands. These flexions, however, were produced by the horses without conscious efforts on the part of their riders. A plain hunting snaffle should be used for this lesson, as well as for the entire course in advanced riding, except the last lesson.

Lesson #4

Subject—Semi-collection.

Theory—The following points should be discussed and demonstrated by the teacher:

1) The characteristics of collected gaits (central balance) and why you teach merely semi-collection. The importance of semi-collected gaits in schooling hunters and jumpers.
2) The aids. Don't forget repeated flexions.
3) Why collection is easy for some horses and is difficult for others; in some cases it shouldn't be used at all.

Practice—When practicing collected gaits bear in mind that they are strenuous for the horses, and so don't overdo them. Stress the collection for a few steps only, and make certain that the pupil considers a good resumption of the ordinary gait after a short period of collection as being as important as the semi-collected steps themselves. It is needless to say that many hours will elapse before your pupils will be able to obtain a soft semi-collection at all gaits. Begin, of course, at a walk. The semi-collected canter is much more difficult than a semi-collected trot.

General Remarks—It is much more efficient to give this lesson on well-schooled horses than to teach both horses and riders simultaneously. For this lesson the pupil should use the schooling form of the forward seat.

Lesson #5

Subject—Semi-extension at a trot.

Theory—The following points should be discussed and demonstrated by the teacher:

1) Why a semi-extended trot belongs to the group of emotional movements, while a merely fast walk, trot and gallop do not. What the difference is between the extended and the semi-extended trot.
2) The aids.
3) The value of the semi-extended trot in schooling. Discuss the development of the swing of the shoulders and the use of semi-extended trot for bettering longitudinal flexibility.

Practice—The semi-extended trot is a very strenuous movement (particularly for a young horse), and should be used with discrimination and for short periods only.

Use it only in combination with the ordinary and the semi-collected trots.

Notice that in the case of many pupils, checking with the reins will deteriorate into mere jerks; when this occurs stop it immediately.

General Remarks—It is better to be satisfied with a mediocre semi-extension than to excite a horse by attempting to produce a still stronger push with the hindquarters and a still stronger extension of the forehand.

Lesson #6

Subject—Backing from a trot and canter after a very brief halt and immediately resuming the gait. Also backing a specified number of steps.

Theory—There is no special theory to this lesson.

Practice—A knowledge of flexion and semi-collection now enables your pupils to make rather abrupt halts softly, and to begin backing immediately after achieving a halt. Furthermore, their ability to develop impulse forward quickly will enable them to resume the movement forward without any perceptible halt after the last step of backing. You should give your particular attention to backing from a canter with immediate resumption of the gait, because it is a very important exercise in making jumpers. With most horses insist upon the pupil making a couple of steps forward at a walk as a transition to starting the new canter (to prevent the horse from sprawling). Backing a specified number of steps has no practical value in actual riding; it is used in schooling horses in order to develop obedience to aids and in teaching pupils in order to develop the precision of their use of the aids.

Lesson #7

Subject—Half-turn on the haunches from a halt or walk interrupting a trot or canter.

Theory—Nothing new needs to be added to what the pupil already knows about the turn on the haunches.

Practice—Due to a knowledge of flexion and semi-collection the pupil can effect a very quick transition from a trot or canter to a walk or halt, turn immediately and resume the gait without any waste of time.

General Remarks—This is a very good exercise for the development of quick cooperation of legs and hands.

The turn must consist of four, clearly-defined, well-united steps, one fore leg crossing well ahead of the other. It should not be a pivot.

Lesson #8

Subject—Good movement during two tracks.

Theory—The theory of two tracks, as well as the theory of good movement in general, has been covered previously.

Practice—Practice two tracks at a trot and at a walk, stressing the quality of the movement.

General Remarks—If you think it necessary you can add the zigzag at two tracks to this lesson (the counter changes of hands at two tracks).

Lesson #9

Subject—Flying changes of lead.

Theory—The theory of changes of lead has been covered previously.

Practice—By gradual shortening of the period of interruption (trot) between the two canters on different leads, your pupils should arrive to a flying change. Insist upon your pupils beginning by making changes with interruption, even on horses who can do it flying—this will insure softness.

General Remarks—Only one change is required, but in some cases of extremely able horses and pupils you may call (just for fun) for a series of changes about four strides apart.

LESSON #10

Subject—Good movement during the execution of short programs.

Theory—All the theory necessary for this lesson has been studied previously.

Practice—Practice programs (more complicated than on the intermediate level) and stress good gaits, good transitions, softness through flexions and precision. Include semi-collected gaits and the semi-extended trot.

General Remarks—The program of the training test of the Three-Day Event of the Olympic Games (modified and shortened) can be taken as a pattern.

LESSON #11

Subject—Having the horse on the bit when approaching an obstacle.

Theory—The theory which was presented in lesson #2 applies to this lesson also.

Practice—When asking your pupils to push their horses forward beyond a soft contact, make certain that they don't overdo it and don't develop the impulse forward to the point where the horses are "over the bit" hanging on their hands.

General Remarks—I would suggest your practicing the lesson only on really big obstacles where riding on the bit may be necessary.

LESSON #12

Subject—Riding over complicated jumping courses.

Theory—There is no special theory to this lesson. Riding over complicated courses should be done, in ideal at least, on the same principle as riding hunter class courses. But, of course, in the former case a better schooled horse (or a very talented one) is required, as well as a rider with better judgment and greater dexterity with the aids.

Practice—Courses with constantly alternating broad and high obstacles should be used, as well as triple in-and-outs, two or three changes of directions to every course and some obstacles placed shortly after turns.

General Remarks—The Prix des Nations course of the Olympic Games, modified to suit your facilities and needs, can serve as a pattern.

LESSON #13

Subject—The use of the curb bit.

Theory—The following points should be discussed and demonstrated by the teacher:

1) The difference between the action of the snaffle and the action of the curb.

2) For what different purposes the snaffle and curb are used when riding on a full bridle.
Also discuss the use of a full bridle merely as a stronger brake, and when to use it as such.

3) The difference between the full bridle and the Pelham and when and how to use the latter.

4) When and why a trainer of hunters and jumpers may occasionally use the curb.

Practice—Have your pupil practice flexions and semi-collected gaits in a full bridle. Since it is only for these two purposes that a trainer of hunters and jumpers may find it necessary to use a curb, I would suggest confining your practice to these two actions (don't practice any other movement in a full bridle).

In recapitulation, here is a list of the major lessons for teaching advanced control:

1) The aims of advanced control.
2) On the bit.
3) Direct and lateral flexions.
4) Semi-collection.
5) Semi-extension at a trot.
6) Backing, interrupting a trot and canter.
7) Half-turn on the haunches, interrupting a trot and canter.
8) Good movement during two tracks.
9) Flying changes of lead.
10) Good movement during the execution of short programs.
11) On the bit in jumping.
12) Riding over complicated jumping courses.
13) The use of the curb.

CHAPTER XIX

How to Teach Schooling

There is only one way to learn schooling; it is by actual attempts to school a green horse under the guidance of a teacher.

It has seldom happened in my experience that the teaching of schooling has proceeded "by the book." I can count on my fingers the cases when an accomplished, advanced rider has come to me bringing a four-year-old horse untouched by human hands and said "teach me how to school him. I don't care how long it takes and I have time to ride as much as you want me to."

Normally the situation which I have had to face was quite different. The rider would be an intermediate one at best, his horse either a three-year-old which had already been jumped and upset, or a five- or six-year-old with which the pupil had already had difficulties for two or three years and the owner was coming to me because the difficulties were increasing. Furthermore, only girls usually would have the time to ride every day, and everyone would be in a hurry to complete the schooling.

Practically every one of these combinations of horses and riders was an individual case and what applied to one did not apply to another; it would be very impractical to attempt to classify them and to advise you how to handle this or that category. This is where the teacher's ability to analyze the situation and to use his ingenuity for solving the current problem comes in; I cannot help anyone in this respect.

However, as a general rule, to which I adhere in my own practice, I would like to list the following points:

1) If the rider's seat is really bad I insist upon him taking lessons in position on a school horse before attempting to train his own.

2) If the seat is good but some important points of intermediate control are poor—for instance, if instead of having a soft contact the rider hangs on the horse's mouth, I make him correct these faults before attempting to school his horse.

3) If the rider's position has flaws, but is not disturbing to the horse, and the rider is united with his mount, then I usually attempt to correct the minor position faults while teaching schooling. I do the same if the fundamentals of control are sound and are imperfect only in details. For instance, I would require, as I said, soft contact before attempting to teach schooling, but would not mind developing "give and take" during the schooling itself. And as to advanced riding—I think it can be taught in the course of schooling.

There are three basic points in teaching schooling as I and some of my pupils—riding teachers—very successfully teach it:

1) All the actual riding in schooling should be done by the pupil himself. Only by achieving results himself does the pupil learn schooling. The teacher should mount the horse once in a while to feel him and to give suggestions based on this experience, but he should not ride to improve the horse. But what he must be able to do is to *direct from the ground the pupil's efforts* in bettering the horse. This requires both talent and experience, and this is probably why most teachers mount themselves when a difficulty arises and consequently deprive the pupil of an opportunity to learn a point and take away from him the satisfaction of feeling that "I have done it all." The aim of all teaching should be to make a pupil independent of the teacher.

2) Teaching schooling requires a great deal of talking; many lessons, as a matter of fact, are nothing else than lectures. Just the fact that the pupil under your direction has taught the horse to turn on the haunches, let us say, is of course a great deal in itself, but it is far from everything that the student has to learn about this movement. He must understand how this movement is connected with other schooling movements, and how all of them may influence the actual performance of the horse in the future. For instance, it must be very clear in his mind that the turn on the haunches, being an exercise for the mobility of the shoulders, is primarily a preparatory one for the short turn at the gallop or for two tracks. In its turn, two tracks is a movement which develops the engagement of the hindquarters on one hand and the extension of the forehand on the other; in jumping, the horse needs the first for the take-off and the second for the landing. This simple example is much more complex in practice when one considers that there are other exercises to develop the same leg actions. For instance, soft but abrupt halts will develop the engagement of the hindquarters; while a semi-extended trot or fast gallop will develop the mobility of the shoulders as well as engagement of the hindquarters. For some horses certain exercises are easier and result in a quicker improvement than for others. To solve such problems one must learn how to analyze the good and the bad qualities of the horse, including their peculiar individual characteristics, and to understand how different movements affect the physique of the horse. Nobody is born with this knowledge, and nobody acquired it by mere riding; the theory of it has to be explained by the teacher. This cannot be done in few words; the subject is very complicated and this is why there exists such a confusion of ideas on the subject of schooling.

I know from experience that this knowledge doesn't come easy; a normal pupil fails for a long time to see how the turn on the haunches is connected with jumping. And one of the main aims in teaching schooling is to make the pupil understand the interrelated points of the physical education of the horse.

3) In my experience schooling always went forward in a very efficient

way if I gave an approximately two-hour lesson once a week, while the pupil worked the other four or five days by himself—that is, barring emergencies. Each lesson would start with the pupil demonstrating to me what he had accomplished in the course of the days on which I hadn't seen him. On the strength of his success or failure I would give him a working plan for the next week.

I always begin the course of teaching schooling by analyzing the horse. If he is really an inexperienced colt—then only his conformation and mentality; if the horse already has some experience in carrying a rider, then his present performance as well (whatever that may be). In analyzing the conformation and the mentality of the horse I am particularly interested to see, and to point out to my pupil, the limitations of the horse which he will have to consider in his schooling in order to avoid crippling the horse physically or mentally. For example:

1) In the case of a high-strung horse stabilization will probably require more than normal attention, and throughout schooling every moment that the horse is upset should be a danger signal. Any horse may become upset, but in the case of a placid animal it may merely mean a momentary disturbance, while with a nervous horse any such flaring up of emotions, if not treated rightly, may be the beginning of a permanent and growing excitability.

Your pupil simply must understand the mentality of his horse and learn to consider it throughout his work with him.

2) Suppose the horse in question has weak hocks. In pointing out this defect to his pupil, the teacher must explain why it would be undesirable to emphasize all the exercises where the engagement of the hindquarters is involved, and why, with such a horse, progress in jumping should be particularly slow.

3) If the horse has a full throat and it is therefore difficult for him to bend the head at the poll, the trainer cannot expect that the horse will ever be able to acquire a *soft* collected attitude of the neck and head. He cannot even expect that the flexions will be very distinct, and that the flexions in the jaw will be accompanied by flexions in the poll. With such horses semi-collected gaits are out, and the trainer must be satisfied with merely slow gaits with extended neck and head.

4) If the horse has light bone the student must be advised by his teacher that such bone is easily damaged, and therefore such exercises as fast galloping over varied or rough terrain should be postponed, not only till the ninth month, as the schooling program suggests, but perhaps for a couple of years—until the horse is six years old and his bones are fully formed. In the cases of light-boned horses, progress in jumping should be ultra slow and cautious.

5) If the horse is of excellent conformation and mentality there is the great danger of being tempted to push him too fast. It has happened in my own experience that I have worked with many such horses, and it

was always very difficult to restrain myself, and in some cases *impossible* to restrain the owners. It really takes a great deal of cool logic and sympathy for the animal to keep him at 3' obstacles when one knows the horse can as easily jump 4'6". It requires vision not to do it. These were the cases where I lost some of my pupils who didn't have the patience to wait and who were willing to take a chance on the health of the animal for the sake of winning ribbons. I think all, or almost all of their beautiful horses were buried young.

Success in persuasion in such cases does not depend only on the ability of the teacher, but also on the emotional and mental qualities of the student.

Cases similar to those listed above are innumerable. Where physical defects, like bad hocks or light bone are concerned, I am always reluctant to take full responsibility and insist upon having a veterinary examine the horse at regular intervals of about six weeks; the doctor may spot the beginning of a bone growth, for instance, before actual lameness occurs. I strongly believe that any rider should get in the habit of seeking veterinary advice before things really go bad. In the long run it costs less; but the main point of my suggestion is to teach the pupil to consider the health of his horse. This is one way of making him conscious of the fact that foolish things which he may do in the saddle are capable of crippling his horse.

Starting a course of schooling with this analytical approach, it should be maintained throughout. I have mentioned already that every lesson begins with my pupil demonstrating what he has accomplished during the preceding four or five days. After I have had a visual impression of his successes and failures I pose a question: "Now tell me what you yourself like or don't like in this performance?" I expect my pupil to answer, for example, that he feels there is an improvement in the ordinary trot and in the approach to an obstacle, but that the halts are awkward and the canter too nervous. If there is no controversy over his statements I pose the next question: "Why do you think the halts are awkward and the canter nervous, and how would you attempt to overcome these faults?" I would expect the pupil to have thought over such matters between my lessons and to have opinions. I also would expect that, being a novice trainer and not in the habit of analyzing reasons for the defects in the horse's performance, half of his answers would be wrong. To explain where his pupil is wrong is the main job of the teacher in teaching schooling.

Any performance can be somewhat improved by skilful riding; hence if I were to mount the horse myself, the chances are I would be able get rid of the nervousness at a canter and the awkwardness of the halts. But this will not prove anything; it is teaching neither the horse nor the pupil; it is merely demonstrating my own dexterity; and that is not what I am being paid for. Instead, the teacher must be able to analyze the situation and give suggestions which will basically improve the horse's performance.

Naturally, in all such cases work on improving the technique of the rider may be necessary, but teaching a rider how to sit or how to improve his use of aids is not the main part of this course.

The suggestions which teach the pupil how to school a horse all pertain to the means of: a) further improving the horse in a certain movement or b) of overcoming difficulties met with in some parts of schooling.

As an example of the suggestions which a teacher may make in the first category (further improvement of some movement that is developing well) the following may serve: Let us suppose that the horse is very quiet and clever and in one week has learned to go on a longe (to which the first month of schooling is devoted) quite calmly. Besides this, he obviously wishes to obey voice-commands and makes mistakes here only because he has not yet learned the commands properly. In such a case I always suggest skipping the next three weeks of longeing and proceeding with stabilization while mounted, expecting the horse to continue to learn voice commands while being ridden. As a general rule, schooling should proceed slowly, but whenever there is a chance of speeding it up without risking anything it should be taken.

Here are examples of suggestions of the second category (overcoming difficulties):

1) *The horse is stiff in the poll.* It is very possible in this case that I would suggest teaching flexions earlier than the program calls for, even before the horse is on the bit.

2) *Stabilization at a trot over a single fence doesn't proceed in a satisfactory manner.* In such a case I may suggest the use of Cavaletti earlier than the program calls for this exercise.

3) *The horse becomes upset at the extended trot and although controllable hangs on the hands for a few minutes after.* Here I may suggest either skipping this exercise altogether for a while or increasing the speed at a trot only to the point where it does not upset the horse. This is a case when a further physical development of the horse along a certain direction has to be sacrificed to calmness. If the latter is lost, the physical improvement may be jeopardized in *all* directions.

4) *The horse does not use his hocks in jumping (the hocks are good).* Here I would suggest increasing the frequency and duration of all exercies for the development of the action of the hindquarters: soft but abrupt stops, two tracks, semi-extended trot, galloping, changes of speeds, etc.

If you are a good teacher your pupil will have suggestions of his own, and his opinions, at first beside the point, should become more and more frequently correct. Toward the end of the course in schooling he must, here and there, even have a better suggestion than your own. After all, he rides the horse and, if you have taught him how to think logically, he should be right more often than you who devote to his horse only a couple of hours a week.

The hope of every real teacher should be that eventually his pupil will be better than himself.

If the analysis of the pupil's performance with a discussion of the reasons for its good and bad points were to take half an hour, let us say, then experimentation with different methods of achieving better results in various movements will take twice as much time. As an example of such various methods I want to remind you of what you read in Chapter XIV on The Program of Forward Schooling—on how to teach the horse the change of leads with an interruption. There I presented this change of leads during the diagonal change of direction as a standard method. But, with some horses, better and quicker results can be obtained when using a half-circle to teach the changes. With still other horses, starting a wide circle on the counter gallop, then interrupting and changing to the inside lead may be an easier way to teach the required signal. Or it may happen that merely cantering around the ring with an occasional change (with an interruption of course) from a true gallop to a counter gallop and then back again to the inside lead, and so on, may be the easiest for your horse.

Changes of lead are no exception; teaching every movement can be approached from many different mental and physical angles. Experimenting with different methods and choosing the best one on the strength of practice and logical discussion is the main part of every lesson. I would like to bring this word *discussion* to your attention. A certain part of the conversation between teacher and pupil is bound to take the form of a lecture, here and there interrupted by the pupil's questions. But the teacher must do everything in his power to turn the lesson into an exchange of opinions. If, of necessity at the beginning of the course, most of the questions are posed by the pupil, then in two or three months more and more questions should be asked by the teacher. This is the only way to force the pupil into logical thinking. Little by little the lesson should take a form where most of the talking—the analysis of the performance, the suggestions for bettering it, the plan for the work of the next few days —all this must come from the pupil, the teacher merely correcting and adding new factual knowledge. This constitutes the main part of every lesson.

The end of the lesson should be devoted to planning the work for the next four or five days. Obviously such a plan is conceived on the strength of the experiences of the present lesson.

Very recently I experimented with a new means of teaching pupils to think logically about their work. This method consists in asking the pupil to keep a journal of his schooling (about half a type-written page per day) writing down actual happenings and his ideas about them. So far I have tried it with two pupils only and in these cases it worked very well.

This is about all that can be said on how to teach schooling, and now I would like to sum up the main points of the chapter:

1) The only way to teach schooling is by making the pupil school a green horse under the teacher's supervision.

2) The pupil must have an easy, non-disturbing seat (to the horse) and a knowledge of control at least on the intermediate level. Minor defects of seat and of intermediate control can be corrected during actual schooling; advanced control can be taught at the same time.

3) Before beginning actual work the physique and mentality of the horse must be analyzed by the teacher. The latter must indicate to the pupil which points of the horse will be advantageous and which detrimental in schooling.

4) All the actual riding should be done by the pupil, the teacher mounting from time to time merely to feel the horse.

5) The pupil must work four or five days by himself between successive lessons.

6) Each lesson should begin with the pupil demonstrating his horse and telling what he thinks of his performance.

7) The main part of the lesson should consist in experimenting with different methods of teaching various movements.

8) At the end of the lesson the teacher and the pupil together conceive a plan for the next four or five days.

9) Sound progress in learning how to school a horse can be expected only if the teacher has the ability to promote in his pupil logical thinking about the physical education of a horse.

Index

galloping away, 205
serpentine and zigzag, 188, 189
transitions, 89, 104, 174, 184, 348
trot, 103, 182, 183
turns in place, 191-193, 346, 347
turns while going ahead, 104, 186
two tracks, 105, 193, 194, 349
up and down hill, 197
walk, 103, 182
ADVANCED, 44, 102-105, 110, 111, 184,
    203, 204, 352
backing, 105, 214, 356
canter, 104
circular movements, 104
counter gallop, 105
flying change of leads, 104, 216,
    356, 357
halts, 104, 206, 207
jumping difficult courses, 105,
    219, 220, 224, 225, 357
approaching fences, 216, 357
semi-collected canter, 104, 355
semi-collected gaits, 208, 209
semi-collected trot, 103, 208, 355
semi-extended trot, 103, 210, 355
transitions, 104, 212, 213, 347
trot, 103
turns in place, 104, 105, 214, 215,
    356
two tracks, 105, 216, 356
walk, 103
Forward riding, 5, 58
FORWARD SCHOOLING, 7, 10, 16,
    20, 28, 38, 47, 48, 65, 71, 119,
    127, 170, 171, 184, 185, 203,
    204, 242-247, 255, 256, 306-309
intermediate and advanced school-
    ing, 247
1st month of schooling begins on
    page 261
2nd month of schooling begins on
    page 263
3rd month of schooling begins on
    page 268
4th month of schooling begins on
    page 272
5th month of schooling begins on
    page 276
6th month of schooling begins on
    page 286

7th month of schooling begins on
    page 292
8th month of schooling begins on
    page 303
9th month of schooling begins on
    page 305
SCHOOLING PROGRAM, 261, 262
backing, 287, 296
canter departure, 272, 279-281
Cavaletti, 283-285
change of leads with interruption,
    281, 289
change of leads (flying), 297
circular movements, 273, 295
coming back, 271
contact, 268
cross-country, 305
counter canter, 282
counter gallop, 281
distribution of work, 308, 309
entering corners, 271
fast gallop, 294, 304, 305
field-work, 303
flexions, 277
hacking, 263, 268, 272, 276, 285,
    291, 303
half-turn on the forehand, 274,
    296
half-turn on the haunches, 286,
    287, 296
halts, 267, 294
impulse forward, 268, 269
increase and decrease of speeds,
    273
jumping, 251-253, 289
acrobatics, 282-285
approach, 264, 266, 267
boldness, 272
courses (simple), 297
courses (difficult), 304, 306
defects and their correction,
    298-302
figuring of the take off, 290, 291
flight, 275
longeing, 263
leading, 263
longeing, 261-263, 268
mounting, 263
on the bit, 269, 270
ordinary gaits, 294